PRIESTS AND CULTS IN THE BOOK OF THE TWELVE

ANCIENT NEAR EASTERN MONOGRAPHS

General Editors
Alan Lenzi
Juan Manuel Tebes

Editorial Board:
Reinhard Achenbach
C. L. Crouch
Esther J. Hamori
René Krüger
Martti Nissinen
Graciela Gestoso Singer

Number 14

PRIESTS AND CULTS IN THE BOOK OF THE TWELVE

Edited by
Lena-Sofia Tiemeyer

SBL PRESS

Atlanta

Copyright © 2016 by SBL Press

All rights reserved. No part of this work may be reproduced or transmitted in any form or by any means, electronic or mechanical, including photocopying and recording, or by means of any information storage or retrieval system, except as may be expressly permitted by the 1976 Copyright Act or in writing from the publisher. Requests for permission should be addressed in writing to the Rights and Permissions Office, SBL Press, 825 Houston Mill Road, Atlanta, GA 30329 USA.

Library of Congress Cataloging-in-Publication Data

Names: Tiemeyer, Lena-Sofia, 1969- editor. | Krispenz, Jutta. Idolatry, apostasy, prostitution : Hosea's struggle against the cult. Container of (work):
Title: Priests and cults in the Book of the Twelve / edited by Lena-Sofia Tiemeyer.
Description: Atlanta : SBL Press, [2016] | ©2016 | Series: Ancient Near East monographs ; number 14 | Includes bibliographical references and index.
Identifiers: LCCN 2016005375 (print) | LCCN 2016005863 (ebook) | ISBN 9781628371345 (pbk. : alk. paper) | ISBN 9780884141549 (hardcover : alk. paper) | ISBN 9780884141532 (ebook)
Subjects: LCSH: Priests, Jewish. | Semitic cults--Biblical teaching. | Bible. Minor Prophets--Criticism, interpretation, etc. | Semites--Religion.
Classification: LCC BS1199.P7 P758 2016 (print) | LCC BS1199.P7 (ebook) | DDC 224/.906--dc23
LC record available at http://lccn.loc.gov/2016005375

Printed on acid-free paper.

Table of Contents

Abbreviations		vii
Introduction *Lena-Sofia Tiemeyer*		1
1.	Idolatry, Apostasy, Prostitution: Hosea's Struggle against the Cult *Jutta Krispenz*	9
2.	Hosea's Exodus Mythology and the Book of the Twelve *Mark Leuchter*	31
3.	Penitential Priests in the Twelve *Mark J. Boda*	51
4.	Joel, the Cult, and the Book of the Twelve *Jason T. LeCureux*	65
5.	Priests and Profits: Joel and Malachi *Deborah W. Rooke*	81
6.	A Farewell to the Anticultic Prophet: Attitudes towards the Cult in the Book of Amos *Göran Eidevall*	99
7.	Attitudes to the Cult in Jonah: In the Book of Jonah, the Book of the Twelve, and Beyond *Lena-Sofia Tiemeyer*	115
8.	The "Idolatrous Priests" in the Book of Zephaniah *Jason Radine*	131
9.	The Priesthood in the Persian Period: Haggai, Zechariah, and Malachi *Lester L. Grabbe*	149

10. King, Priest, and Temple in Haggai-Zechariah-Malachi and   157
    Ezra-Nehemiah
    Paul L. Redditt

11. On the Way to Hierocracy: Secular and Priestly Rule in the   173
    Books of Haggai and Zechariah
    Jakob Wöhrle

12. How Does Malachi's "Book of Remembrance" Function for the   191
    Cultic Elite?
    James Nogalski

13. Cult and Priests in Malachi 1:6–2:9   213
    Aaron Schart

Author Index   235

Scripture Index   241

Contributors   257

ABBREVIATIONS

AB	Anchor Bible
ABD	*The Anchor Bible Dictionary* (ed. David Noel Freedman *et al*; 6 vols: New York: Doubleday, 1992).
ABGe	Arbeiten zur Bibel und ihrer Geschichte
ABRL	Anchor Yale Bible Reference Library
ACCS	*Ancient Christian Commentary Series*
AcBib	Academia Biblica
AIL	Ancient Israel and Its Literature
ALBO	Analecta Lovaniensia biblica et orientalia
ANEM	Ancient Near Eastern Monographs
AOAT	Alter Orient und Altes Testament
AOTC	Abingdon Old Testament Commentaries
ASOR	American Schools of Oriental Research
ASV	*American Standard Version*
ATD	Das Alte Testament Deutsch
AzTh	Aufsätze und Vorträge zur Theologie und Religionswissenschaft
BBET	Beiträge zur biblischen Exegese und Theologie
BBR	*Bulletin of Biblical Research*
BDB	*A Hebrew and English Lexicon of the Old Testament* (ed. Francis Brown, S. R. Driver, and Charles A. Briggs; Oxford: Clarendon Press, 1907/1953).
BEATAJ	Beiträge zur Erforschung des Alten Testaments und des antiken Judentums
BHS	Biblia Hebraica Stuttgartensia
Bib	*Biblica*
BibS(N)	Biblische Studien
BIS	Biblical Interpretation Series
BJS	Brown Judaic Studies
BKAT	Biblischer Kommentar Altes Testament
BN	*Biblische Notizen*
BT	Book of the Twelve
BThSt	Biblisch Theologische Studien
BZAW	Beiheft zur Zeitschrift für die alttestamentliche Wissenschaft
CAT	Commentaire de l'Ancien Testament
CBC	Cambridge Bible Commentary
CBQ	*Catholic Biblical Quarterly*

CBR	*Currents in Biblical Research*
CCS	Continental Commentary Series
DDD	*Dictionary of Deities and Demons in the Bible* (ed. Karel van der Toorn, Bob Becking, and Pieter Willem. van der Horst; 2nd extensively rev. ed.; Leiden: Brill, 1999).
DOTP	*Dictionary of the Old Testament Prophets* (ed. Mark J. Boda and J. Gordon McConville; Downers Grove, IL: InterVarsity Press, 2012).
EBib	Etudes Bibliques
ESV	*English Standard Version*
FAT	Forschungen zum Alten Testament
FOTL	Forms of Old Testament Literature
FRLANT	Forschungen zur Religion und Literatur des Alten und Neuen Testaments
HBM	Hebrew Bible Monographs
HBS	Herders Biblische Studien
HBT	*Horizons in Biblical Theology*
HCOT	Historical Commentary on the Old Testament
HCSB	*Holman Christian Standard Bible*
HeBAI	*Hebrew Bible and Ancient Israel*
HSM	Harvard Semitic Monographs
HThKAT	Herders theologischer Kommentar zum Alten Testament
ICC	International Critical Commentary
ITC	International Theological Commentary
JBL	*Journal of Biblical Literature*
JETS	*Journal of the Evangelical Theological Society*
JHS	*Journal of Hebrew Scriptures*
JNES	*Journal of Near Eastern Studies*
JNSL	*Journal of Northwest Semitic Languages*
JPS	Jewish Publication Society
JQR	*Jewish Quarterly Review*
JSJSup	Supplements to the Journal for the Study of Judaism
JSOT	*Journal for the Study of the Old Testament*
JSOTS	Journal for the Study of the Old Testament: Supplement Series
JTS	*Journal of Theological Studies*
KAT	Kommentar zum Alten Testament
KHAT	Kurzer Hand-Commentar zum Alten Testament
KJV	King James Version
KTU	Keilalphabetische Texte aus *Ugarit*
LD	Lectio divina
LHBOTS	Library of Hebrew Bible/Old Testament Studies
LSTS	Library of Second Temple Studies

MT	Masoretic Text
NASB	*New American Standard Bible*
NCBC	New Century Bible Commentary
NIBCOT	New International Biblical Commentary Old Testament series
NICOT	New International Commentary on the Old Testament
NIV	New International Version
NKJV	New King James Version
NOSTER	Nederlandse Onderzoekschool voor Theologie en Religiewetenschap
NRSV	New Revised Standard Version
NSBT	New Studies in Biblical Theology
OBO	Orbis biblicus et orientalis
OG	Old Greek
OLA	Orientalia Lovaniensia Analecta
OTE	*Old Testament Essays*
OTL	Old Testament Library
OTM	Old Testament Monographs
OTS	*Oudtestamentische Studiën*
Pesah.	Pesahim
SBL	Society of Biblical Literature
SBLDS	Society of Biblical Literature: Dissertation Series
SBS	Stuttgarter Bibelstudien
SEÅ	Svensk exegetisk årsbok
SFSHJ	South Florida Studies in the History of Judaism
SHANE	Studies in the History of the Ancient Near East
SHBC	Smyth & Helwys Bible Commentary
SJSJ	Supplements to the Journal for the Study of Judaism
SOTSMS	Society for the Old Testament Study Monograph Series
STDJ	Studies on the Texts of the Desert of Judah
SymS	Symposium Series
ThStKr	*Theologische Studien und Kritiken*
TOTC	Tyndale Old Testament Commentaries
TUAT	Otto Kaiser, Bernd Janowski, Gernot Wilhelm and Daniel Schwemer (ed.), *Texte aus der Umwelt des Alten Testaments* (Gütersloh: Gütersloher Verlagshaus, 1982–2001).
VT	*Vetus Testamentum*
VTSup	Vetus Testamentum Supplements
VWGTh	Veröffentlichungen Der Wissenschaftlichen Gesellschaft Für Theologie
WAW	Writings from the Ancient World
WBC	Word Biblical Commentary
WEB	*World English Bible*

WUNT	Wissenschaftliche Untersuchungen zum Neuen Testament
ZAW	*Zeitschrift für die alttestamentliche Wissenschaft*
ZBK	Zürcher Bibelkommentare
ZSTh	*Zeitschrift für systematische Theologie*
ZThK	*Zeitschrift für Theologie und Kirche*

INTRODUCTION

The current volume focuses, as the title suggests, on the depictions of the cult and its personnel—primarily but not limited to priests and Levites—in the Book of the Twelve. The contributing authors do not share one methodological approach and they do not always reach conclusions that are mutually compatible. This variety is intentional insofar as it reflects contemporary scholarship. The current volume further seeks to showcase different scholarly traditions. In this volume, scholarship from continental Europe, Scandinavia, the United Kingdom, North America, and Australia is represented. What holds these scholars together is their interest in the so-called Book of the Twelve. Most of the individual contributions focus on a single prophetic book, but they also all place their research and their findings in the wider context of the Book of the Twelve. Due to their content, the books of Hosea and Joel, as well as the Haggai-Malachi corpus, have received the most attention. Other books, where the cult is at most a peripheral topic, have accordingly received less. While there has been no conscious effort to cover all the twelve books in the Twelve, this volume has sought to discuss all the key cultic texts in the Book of the Twelve.

The articles are organized in accordance with the order of the Book of the Twelve. Jutta Krispenz's article on idolatry, apostasy and prostitution in the book of Hosea opens the volume. She surveys the uses of cultic vocabulary (i.e., nouns associated with cultic personnel and places of cultic performances and verbs associated with cultic acts) throughout the text. She begins by noting that cultic vocabulary is unevenly distributed throughout the book, with a higher frequency in chapters 4–11 than in the surrounding material. Based on her survey and accompanying discussion, she notes, among other things, that the priests (כהנים) are not connected with actual cultic actions; instead this is the realm of the people, as well as of the כמרים and the קדשות. Krispenz further observes that cultic acts take place in a multitude of cultic places. While this might suggest a "thriving religious life which permeated the people's daily life," the prophetic voice in Hosea regards all of this as merely idolatry and apostasy.

Mark Leuchter's article explores the exodus mythology employed in the book of Hosea within its wider context of the Book of the Twelve and argues that Hosea has a pivotal role in the overall Levitical redaction of this collection of texts. Leuchter begins by highlighting the differences between the two northern Exodus traditions that are preserved in the Hebrew Bible: one state-supported myth which saw the establishment of the Northern kingdom as a mythic rehearsal of the exodus, and another, Levitical, counter-tradition that emphasized the earlier, prestate mythical exodus traditions. Turning to Hosea, Leuchter demonstrates that the prophet not only adhered to the latter Levitical tradition but also added mythical motifs to it. Adhering to the Levitical critique of the official cult of the Northern Kingdom, Hosea sought to distinguish between the actual tradition of the exodus and those traditions which related to ancestral worship that had come to be embedded in the state-version of the exodus. Finally, Leuchter suggests that the editing of the Book of the Twelve—with Hosea's Exodus mythology at its opening statement—served as a Levitical challenge to the Aaronide interests of combining prophetic texts with imperial ideology (as seen, for example, in Ezra-Nehemiah).

Mark Boda looks wider afield and investigates the concept of "penitential priests" in the book of the Twelve, with focus on Joel and the Haggai-Malachi corpus. He begins by noting their shared structural diversity: they all begin with a description of a local crisis / matter and they all end on a cosmological / international note. They further all combine the prophetic message with a concern for priestly figures. Boda proceeds by surveying the portrayal of priests in Joel and Zechariah and how they can fruitfully be read together. Joel 1–2 presents the priests as the key players within the community at the time of crisis, calling the people to repentance. In contrast, Zech 7–8 shows their failure to take that call to repentance on board. The same emphasis on the priestly leadership in penitential response is also attested in Haggai and Malachi. In their pivotal positions at the beginning and at the end of the Book of the Twelve, Joel and the Haggai-Malachi corpus together highlight the importance in the Twelve to challenge the priests to take up their role as "penitential catalysts" within the postmonarchic community.

Jason LeCureux, continuing with the book of Joel, challenges the common view that its portrayal of the cult is wholly positive. He begins with an overview of scholarship on Joel's relationship with the cult, before turning to a discussion of all references to the cult in the book. He argues that nothing in the text demands the view that the author was part of the cultic elite or that he was a so-called cultic prophet. This (negative) impression is strengthened when approaching the book of Joel as part of the Book of the Twelve. Read on its own, the command in Joel 2:12–14 is ambiguous: is the notion of שוב a call to repentance or a more general call to turn back to God in supplication? Read within the wider context of the Twelve, however, situated in between the two "cult-critical" books of Hosea and Amos, Joel 2:12–14 suggests the former sense. Furthermore, when Joel is being read together with Jonah, the non-cultic overtones of the envisioned repentance become even clearer: the king of Nineveh enacts Joel's call to repentance apart from a functioning temple setting. Thus, when understood as an integral part of the Book of the Twelve, Joel challenges rather than supports the priestly and sacrificial system.

Deborah Rooke offers yet another comparative study—this time between Joel and Malachi—with focus on the close relationship between sacrifices and food. Beginning with Joel, Rooke highlights the interplay between the natural disaster which has caused famine and the dual roles of the priests not only to give what little food there is to God as a sacrifice but also to call the community to a fast. These actions will, in turn, serve as a plea to God to restore fertility in the land. A similar connection between priests, sacrifices, and food exist in Malachi. Yet, while Joel portrays the priests as an exemplary model of faithful servants, Malachi presents the opposite scenario where the priests, by their lack of proper teaching and by their acts of defiling the altar through faulty sacrifices, have actually caused the current crisis. Rooke further explores the notion of sacrifices as a meal which is prepared for the deity in his honor and which serves as a means of communication between the community and the divine. If God receives his due at his "table," then the people will also receive their due in the form of a good harvest. Rooke concludes that Joel and Malachi agree on the priests' vital role in the community: "faithful priests mean reliable food supplies."

Göran Eidevall's article asks whether the book of Amos has a consistent attitude towards the cult. Eidevall opens with a survey of past scholarship on both sides of the Amos-debate: was Amos an antiritualistic prophet or was he rather a cultic prophet? Eidevall, however, argues that this quest is methodologically unsound insofar as the book of Amos does not yield data about a historical prophet named Amos. Rather, our aim should be to investigate the attitudes towards the cult in the *book* of Amos. Eidevall proceeds by examining all passages in the book which refer to the cult. In each instance, he seeks to determine whether or not a given passage expresses a general attitude towards the cult (and, if so, whether negative or positive), or whether it articulates a view on a specific (geographic) place of worship or a particular group of worshippers. Eidevall concludes that it is "time to say farewell to Amos, the anti-cultic prophet." Rather, the book of Amos claims that YHWH has abandoned all northern cultic sites (as part of its theological explanation of the fall of the Northern Kingdom in 722 BCE). Furthermore, its silence about the Jerusalem temple can be interpreted as a tacit approval of its temple cult, in line with the general positive approach in the postmonarchic era.

Lena-Sofia Tiemeyer explores the (sparse) references to the cult in the book of Jonah. Her investigation takes place on three levels. She begins by discussing the extant cultic behavior (praying, casting lots, sacrificing, vow-taking, and fasting) in the book of Jonah as carried out by three set of actors (the sailors, Jonah, and the Ninevites), and highlights that all key characters are involved in activities that can be categorized as belonging within the cultic sphere. Turning to the Book of the Twelve, Tiemeyer argues that when read together with Joel and Malachi especially, its existing references to the cult are strengthened and new connections are being forged (cf. LeCureux). The same tendency reaches its peak in the writings of the Sages and the mediaeval Jewish commentators. Looking at material including Pirqe de-Rabbi Eliezer, the Jewish-hellenistic sermon *On Jonah*, Mekilta de-Rabbi Ishmael, and Pesiqta de-Rab Kahana, Tiemeyer concludes that they all, each in different ways, bring the biblical text of Jonah closer to Jerusalem, the temple, and its cult.

Jason Radine's article seeks to uncover the identity of the so-called "idolatrous priests" (כמרים) in Zeph 1:4. First, Radine argues that, given that (1) it is an Aramaic word, (2) in Aramaic this word has no specific "idolatrous" connotations, and (3) the normal Hebrew word כהן is often used in idolatrous contexts, the term in Zeph 1:4 refers to priests of Aramaic background and/or priests involved in Aramaic rites. Radine's analysis of the contexts of the three biblical occurrences of the term (Zeph 1:4; Hos 10:5; 2 Kgs 23:5) suggests the latter, as there is no evidence to suggest that the כמרים were foreigners. Further, it appears that they were a special group of royally appointed religious practitioners and formed part of Judah's state policy towards Assyria. Radine then explores the relations between the content of Zechariah and Josiah's reform (with focus on the relative chronology of Zeph 1:4–6 and 2 Kgs 23), as well as the character, historicity, and extent of that reform. Turning to matters of dating, Radine dates the book of Zephaniah to the time shortly after the fall of Jerusalem. Its message, however, is to be read as given to a prophetic character at the time of Josiah who, like Huldah, foresaw and announced Jerusalem's imminent fall, a fall which was in part due to Judah's false leadership which included the כמרים.

Lester Grabbe's article opens a series of studies which investigate the cult and the priesthood in the final three books in the Book of the Twelve. Grabbe surveys the material in Haggai, Zechariah, and Malachi which deal with the priesthood, and he highlights the high probability that all three men were associated with the cult, possibly being both prophets and priests. Grabbe further compares the depictions of the priesthood in the Haggai-Malachi corpus with the rest of the Book of the Twelve (as well as with Kings and Ezra-Nehemiah) and notes several shared points of contact. First, the priests are described as men invested with political power. Secondly, a division between altar clergy and lower clergy is presupposed in many texts. Thirdly, priests possess a body of legal material (torah), and they were held responsible for giving rulings which related to cult and temple and their associated practices. Grabbe concludes by listing how the Haggai-Malachi corpus can help us to reconstruct the priesthood in Yehud in the Persian period.

Paul Redditt's study is also devoted to the Haggai-Malachi corpus, with the aim of elucidating the depicted relationship between priestly and royal power. Redditt proceeds systematically through the corpus and notes a roughly linear development. The material from the early postmonarchic period in Yehud (especially Haggai but also, albeit in a different way, Zech 1–8) attests to a close connection between temple, priest, and king. The authors expressed the hope for a Davidide who could make Yehud into an independent kingdom again. In the later Zech 9–14, however, these hopes appear to have disappeared and given rise to a new view point. While chapter 9 speaks of a king, this humble new king is markedly different from the royal prophecies in the earlier Haggai-Zech 1–8. The subsequent chapters 10–14 make no mention of earthly kings and in parallel condemn the priestly leaders. The concluding chapter 14 envisions an eschatological scenario when God has become king. Likewise, Malachi criticizes the current priesthood and further speaks only of divine kingship (Mal 1:14). These depictions stand in sharp contrast to the approach to clergy and kingship in Ezra and Nehemiah. Both books differentiate between royal power (which belongs to the Persian authorities) and clerical leadership (which belongs strictly to the returnees).

Jakob Wöhrle's contribution continues on the same topic and offers a more detailed study of the material in Haggai and Zech 1–8. It explores the attitudes towards the political power of the high priest as expressed in the various textual layers. Beginning with Haggai, Wöhrle highlights that Hag 2:23 anticipates the reestablishment of the Davidic kingdom under Zerubbabel. Turning to the material in Zech 1–8, Wöhrle detects a three-stage development. The earliest material envisions a royal-priestly diarchy where the high priest and the Davidic king share equal power. This view is found in, among other places, Zech 4:14 where the image of the two "sons of oil" symbolizes Joshua and Zerubbabel, and in an early version of Zech 6:9–14* which, like Zech 4:14, depicts a royal-priestly diarchy consisting of the Davidic king and the high priest. In contrast, the final form of Zech 6:9–14 is a later version, written at the time where Zerubbabel was no longer a political persona. In this version, all references to Zerubbabel have been erased and all political power is instead assigned to Joshua. The material in Zech 3:1–7 stems, according to Wöhrle, from the same time and likewise portrays the crowning of the high priest and, as such, the establishment of a hierocracy. Yet an even later textual layer exists which anew seeks to correct Zechariah's political vision. In Zech 3:8, the political power of the high priest is diminished and the expectation of a Davidic king, present in concrete form in the first layer, resurfaces in the expectation of the future coming of the "branch."

The final two articles investigate matters in the book of Malachi. James Nogalski's article deals with the so-called "Book of Remembrance" in Mal 3:16–18. Nogalski begins by challenging the common Christian interpretation which equates this book with a "book of life" which contains the names of those who have survived the (coming) "Day of YHWH." Rather, the book, written in the presence of YHWH, is given to the survivors and contains information for their benefit: teaching them to differentiate anew between the righteous and the wicked. The "remembrance" thus refers to the consequences of YHWH's actions and serves to remind the *people*. This book may contain the book of Malachi but it does not need to be limited to it. In fact, it is possible to regard it as some form of the Book of the Twelve. Nogalski continues by exploring scribal culture, with the aim of determining the specific background to the formation of this "Book of Remembrance" / Book of the Twelve. Who became a scribe? Where were they trained? What texts were available to them during their training and in what form (oral or written)? What did they do once they were trained? Who employed them? How did their situation change in the postmonarchic period? Furthermore, what is the connection between the work of these scribes and the creation and formation of what later became the Canon? Also, what role did the Levites have in this scribal enterprise (cf. Leuchter)? Nogalski concludes that Mal 3:16–18 offers a snapshot into the world of scribes and into the scribal processes that ultimately culminated in the publication of an authoritative and didactic book.

Aaron Schart's source-critical study of Mal 1:6–2:9 concludes the collection. Schart proceeds systematically through the pericope and detects, by noting its changing terminology, four different textual layers: the "lay people-layer," the "priest-layer," the "Levi-layer," and the "nation-layer." In addition, he argues that Mal 1:9a, 2:7, and 2:9b are later individual interpolations. Schart subsequently defines the key message of each textual layer, as well as the historical setting of its composition. He concludes by analyzing the different layers within the context of the Book of the Twelve. The primary lay people-layer alludes to Mic 2:1–2 and Amos 5:22. These allusions show that the author of this layer wished to display continuity with earlier prophetic texts, yet they do not constitute sufficient grounds for postulating that this layer was part of a wider Book of the Twelve. Turning to the priest-layer, the situation is similar. There is clear affinity between Mal 1:6–2:9 and Hos 4, yet this affinity cannot prove that the priest-layer was part of a wider multi prophets-corpus. The Levi-layer provides no information on this issue. In contrast, the dependency of Mal 1:11 upon the book of Jonah, as well as its allusion to Zech 14:9, 16, suggests that by the time of the composition of the nation-layer, the formerly independent text of Malachi had become incorporated into the final version of the Book of the Twelve that included the book of Jonah and Zech 9–14.

Several people have helped to make this volume a better volume. In particular, I am grateful to the SBL group "The Book of the Twelve" for their insight and support throughout the process of creating this book. An earlier version of five of the articles in the present volume were presented in a session devoted expecially to "Priests and Cult in the Book of the Twelve" at the Annual Meeting of the SBL in San Diego in 2014. My heartfelt thanks also go to Ms. Amy Erickson, a graduate student at the University of Aberdeen, who proof-read all the articles in this volume. Last but not least I would like to thank the series editors for accepting this volume into the Ancient Near Eastern Monograph series of the Society of Biblical Literature. I am also very grateful to Prof. Alan Lenzi for the excellent and prompt help and support on the way towards producing a camera-ready copy. In producing this book, I have become convinced in the benefits associated with Open-Access Publication. It is my hope that this series will go from strength to strength and that its scholarship will reach a wide audience.

Lena-Sofia Tiemeyer
Aberdeen, December 2015

1
IDOLATRY, APOSTASY, PROSTITUTION: HOSEA'S STRUGGLE AGAINST THE CULT

Jutta Krispenz

1. THE TOPIC AND THE TEXT

Beyond the Pentateuch, readers of the Hebrew Bible will not find many books dealing as intensely with cultic issues as the writing in the Book of the Twelve that is attributed to "Hosea Ben Beeri." The statements to be found there are all negative. Hosea[1] renders a smashing verdict over the people of Israel of his time and has hardly anything positive to report about his contemporaries.

The attempt to reconstruct Hosea's views nonetheless has its limits. Besides the well-known difficulties which the readers face in Hosea's writing,[2] it be-

---

[1] The name "Hosea" is used to denote the fictional speaker of the texts and, with that, to summarize the human being(s) who produced the text of "Hosea." It is not used to state a historical person "Hosea" beyond the statement of a human origin of the writing, although in the history of the text of "Hosea" such a person may have existed. Yet, the text we have does not give us historically reliable information at that point.

[2] In the first range we have to mention the text itself, which at some points seems to be badly preserved and is sometimes not understandable without conjectures. Quite often the text—which is obviously not written for the readers in a distant future—seems to presuppose knowledge which was at hand for the reader in antiquity but is not so for us. The peculiar way of sequential argumentation invited modern exegetes to source-critical differentiations in the text. See on this the redaction-critical publications on Hosea, e.g., Susanne Rudnig-Zelt, *Hoseastudien redaktionskritische Untersuchungen zur Genese des Hoseabuches* (FRLANT 213; Göttingen: Vandenhoeck & Ruprecht, 2006); Roman Viel-

comes clear that the "cult"-topic is not easily extracted from the texts, since it is interwoven with many other issues and themes, which in our perception appear clearly distinct from one another. There is no clear separation between politics and religion,[3] between cult and the personal conduct of life. The tendency of Hosea to use wordplay[4] for his reasoning does not make it easy for us modern readers to perceive his thoughts accurately, nor does his addiction to the use of metaphors.[5] Those metaphors are always open to different interpretations: the imagery of prostitution (זנה) and adultery (נאף)[6] opens for cultic as well as political connotations—which line of understanding did the text want us to follow? Moreover it is not easy to pinpoint the addressee exactly and in a reproducible manner; quite often a section starts with referring to a clearly defined addressee only later to widen and change, step by step, the circle of people it is talking to: in Hos 5:1 the text starts with addressing the priest, then the "house of Israel" is added, and finally the "house of the king"—who is this text actually addressing? Is this section about cultic issues or is it rather embracing the field of politics? Or does the distinction between these two fields miss the reality of ancient Israel? And even the always critical evaluation of the cult does not make it easier to depict Hosea's opinion on this topic, since we do not know very much about the cultic reality in preexilic times. Besides Hosea's writing itself only a few biblical texts can be used as historical sources.[7] In the first range, extra-biblical texts allow the reconstruction of cultic customs in the culture of Canaanite societies.[8] It is hard to say for sure that the practice in Hosea's Israel was the same as in

---

hauer, *Das Werden des Buches Hosea: Eine redaktionsgeschichtliche Untersuchung* (BZAW 349; Berlin: de Gruyter, 2007; James M. Bos, *Reconsidering the Date and Provenance of the Book of Hosea: The Case for Persian-period* (LHBOTS 580; London: T&T Clark, 2013).

[3] Concerning politics and religion, see Izabela Jaruzelska, "State and Religion in the Light of the Books of Amos and Hosea," in *Basel und Bibel* (ed. Matthias Augustin and Hermann Michael Niemann; Beiträge zur Erforschung des Alten Testaments und des antiken Judentums 51; Frankfurt am Main/New York: Peter Lang, 2004), 161–67.

[4] Francis Landy notes numerous wordplays in Hosea. See Francis Landy, *Hosea* (Readings; Sheffield: Sheffield Academic Press, 1995).

[5] On metaphors in Hosea, compare Brigitte Seifert, *Metaphorisches Reden von Gott im Hoseabuch* (FRLANT 166; Göttingen: Vandenhoeck & Ruprecht, 1996); John Andrew Dearman, "Yhwh's House: Gender Roles and Metaphors for Israel in Hosea," *JNSL* 25,1 (1999): 97–108, and Ehud Ben Zvi, "Reading Hosea and Imagining Yhwh," *HBT* 30,1 (2008): 43–57.

[6] The two terms are actually used in Hosea as if they were synonymous.

[7] It is a matter of ongoing discussion to what extent biblical texts can be used as historical sources at all.

[8] See, e.g., those of Ugarit.

those societies.⁹ The texts in Hosea only criticize existing practices without ever referring to a positive alternative. The addressees seem to act in every respect against the religion of YHWH. They are, as already Hos 1:9 states, not the people of God.

In this article, I will try to find out where in the writing of Hosea the text broaches the issue of the cult and its protagonist: the priests. This should help to clarify what exactly is being criticized in Hosea and what positive ideas the criticism might imply. I will start by examining the vocabulary on the cult and its distribution in the writing. This will lead to some central texts on the topic and at the same time it will provide us with a rough overview and should keep the examination of the text from becoming biased by (unconscious) presuppositions. I will nonetheless include sections of the text of Hosea beside those found with the help of the vocabulary where it is appropriate.

I will, due to the limits of space given to an article, not discuss the specific definition of "cult." The majority of the words in the vocabulary under consideration should be significant for the topic beyond doubt.

The literary history of the texts will likewise not be discussed in this article in detail. The only distinction inside the writing of Hosea that will be presupposed is that of chapters 4–11 as some sort of literary core of the book, with chapters 1–3, 12, 13, and 14 representing another type of voice in the writing. These different voices might represent later reactions on the "core" in chapters 4–11. In any case, the texts in these chapters differ in many ways from that in chapters 4–11, making a distinction reasonable. This study will start with considering chapters 4–11 and it will within those chapters differentiate between the bulk of texts writing from the perspective of Hosea or God and the four citations of the people in Hos 6:1–3; 8:2; 9:7, and 10:3.

As to the chronology of the book of Hosea, some recent publications tend to give it a rather late date compared with the testimony of the book itself.¹⁰ This seems to follow a trend in the exegetical discussion on the Hebrew Bible, which wants to decline the existence of literature in preexilic times and its conservation through the tribulations of the exile. There are, however, good arguments in favor of an early (preexilic) date for the writing of Hosea.¹¹ The chronology is, in any case, not decisive for a presentation of the thematic field of the cult.

---

⁹ For some critical considerations, see Jörg Jeremias, "Der Begriff 'Baal' im Hoseabuch und seine Wirkungsgeschichte," in *Hosea und Amos Studien zu den Anfängen des Dodekapropheton* (ed. Jörg Jeremias; FAT 13; Tübingen: Mohr Siebeck, 1996), 86–103.

¹⁰ E.g., Bos, *Reconsidering*.

¹¹ Hans M. Barstad, "Hosea and the Assyrians," in *"Thus Speaks Ishtar of Arbela": Prophecy in Israel, Assyria, and Egypt in the Neo-Assyrian period* (ed. Robert P. Gordon and Hans M. Barstad; Winona Lake, IN: Eisenbrauns, 2013), 91–110.

2. Cultic Vocabulary and Its Distribution in Hosea

There is no methodology which would allow us to proceed from a topic to a complete vocabulary; nonetheless, some words are clearly connected with the cult. We will leave the names of God and of gods aside[12] as well as the names of cities that might have been or even have been places connected with a cult. Within the vocabulary we may distinguish between nouns and verbs. Verbs are, as we will see, often less specific for a single topic compared to nouns. Particles, of course, do not come into consideration, since they are not confined to specific issues.

As to the verbs which pertain to our topic, we find some roots which usually refer to cultic acts: "to burn incense, to fumigate" (קטר), "to hold an offering-meal" (זבח), "to burn an offering" (עלה, *hiphil*),[13] and "to be a priest" (כהן). Other roots denote the approach to God: "to search" (בקש) and "to ask" (דרש)[14] are included in the vocabulary as well as verbs denoting that the relation to God through the cult is successful (רצה) or broken due to the quality of a part of the cultic setting (טמא) or the quality of a relevant action (חטא). The root שוב is often used to denote the attempt to heal actively the relation to God after human misconduct. This use of the root cannot be taken for granted in all its occurrences in Hosea, however.

The list of relevant nouns is more extensive. We need to take a look at the words that possibly denote the cultic place: "house of YHWH" (בית ה') or "house of God" (בית אלהים) as well as "high place" (במה). These should be included together with words which usually denote the inventory and the tools of a cultic place: "altar" (מזבח), "stela" (מצבה), "image" (עגל; פסל; עצב), "shophar" (שופר), "ephod" (אפוד) and "teraphim" (תרפים), as well as with words which denote cultic actions such as "sacrificing" (זבח; עולה). Nouns that are used to point to cultic (dis)qualification such as "sin" (חטא), "iniquity" (עון) or "impurity" (טמא) are introduced and, of course, all the different terms denoting those who act as

---

[12] Using the divine name as a marker for texts on cultic issues would widen the range of texts in a way that would rather distract from the theme. As to the use of the names of other gods, the text of Hosea does not always use the name in its known form and in some instances there is no consensus among exegetes whether a word is the name of a god or not.

[13] The verb itself has a much wider semantic range and may therefore not always mark a section as dealing with cult.

[14] The root שאל occurs only once in Hosea in Hos 4:12.

officials in a cultic setting: "priest" (כהן), "priest of idols" (כמר) and "priestess" (קדשה).[15]

An overall look at the distribution of the vocabulary listed above shows that it is not distributed evenly across the whole writing, but more of the words appear more often in chs. 4–11. Only four verses mention cultic terms in the three opening chapters (2:9, 15; 3:4, 5), using six words of the listed vocabulary. Within the final chapters 12–14, six verses use eight terms (12:9, 12; 13:2, 12; 14:2, 9). Only chapter 7 has a comparable low frequency of the relevant words with two terms in two verses. The distribution helps to locate those sections in the writing of Hosea that can somehow be expected to tell us about Hosea's specific attitude towards the cult. It is a tool that should prevent the omission of statements that might not seem to add information to the topic. The procedure should not keep us from including more sections that might give us further insight.

The following table gives an overview of the distribution:

Chapter	1	2	3	4	5	6	7	8	9	10	11	12	13	14
Amount of verses containing cultic vocabulary	0	2	2	9	6	3	2	5	4	7	1	2	2	2
Amount of cultic terms	0	2	5	9	5	4	2	11	6	9	3	4	6	2

Table 1: Distribution of the relevant vocabulary within the chapters of the writing of Hosea according to quantity (amount of verses) and diversity (amount of terms)

---

[15] The role of the *qedeshot* is still not absolutely clear although there seems to be a consensus that the women denoted as *qedeshot* were employees of a temple with more or less cultic duties rather than prostitutes who acted as the sexual partners of a priest in a fertility cult. For literature, see n. 18 below.

3. Persons, Places, and Actions Connected with the Cult in Hosea 4–11

3.1. persons

The aim of this paragraph is to take a look at those persons who in that piece of literature called the book of Hosea are connected with the cult, to find out what roles the different characters play, how they are positioned against one another, and how their roles and actions are evaluated in the text.

The officials of a cult, those who are in charge of performing cultic actions, are the "priests." We find three words in Hosea which can be used to denote persons with priestly characteristics: כהן, כמר, and קדשה. While the first mentioned term is the usual one for a priest all over the Hebrew Bible, the two latter ones are quite rare words, the כמר with only three occurrences in the Hebrew Bible.[16] The קדשות are mentioned more frequently, especially if one takes into consideration both the feminine and the masculine form.[17] Notwithstanding the question whether the *qedeshot* were or were not engaged in some sort of ιερος γαμος-rites,[18] they are depicted in Hos 4:14 as acting in a cultic performance, the זבח, which is a cultic meal. The section Hos 4:13, 14 is saturated with terms from the semantic field of adultery and prostitution. This could be due to the aim of the text to discredit a cultic practice, which the attending people would not have assessed in the same way as does the prophetic text. The text tries to scandalize a behavior, which we do not know well enough. The example in Hos 4:13b is obviously made to shock the generation of grandfathers (who have "daughters" of the age of being married and "daughters-in-law"), to whom the prospect of the family's losing control over the women's sexuality will have

---

[16] 2 Kgs 23:5; Hos 10:5; Zeph 1:4.

[17] Gen 38:21, 22; Deut 23:18; 1 Kgs 14:24; 15:15; 22:47; 2 Kgs 23:7; Hos 4:14; Job 36:14.

[18] This assumption from the history of religion has been taken for granted for a long time. It seemed to explain much of Hosea's rage against the cult in Israel. Recent publications are more critical about the depiction of the *qedeshot* derived from Herodotus and Lucian. For a discussion of the arguments, see Christine Stark, *"Kultprostitution" im Alten Testament? Die Qedeschen der Hebräischen Bibel und das Motiv der Hurerei* (OBO 221; Fribourg: Academic Press; Göttingen: Vandenhoeck & Ruprecht, 2006); Kristel Nyberg, "Sacred Prostitution in the Biblical World," in *Sacred Marriages: The Divine-human Sexual Metaphor from Sumer to Early Christianity* (ed. Martti Nissinen and Risto Uro; Winona Lake, IN: Eisenbrauns, 2008), 305–20; Hennie J. Marsman, *Women in Ugarit and Israel: Their Social and Religious Position in the Context of the Ancient Near East* (OTS 49; Leiden: Brill 2003), 548–72, on cultic prostitution and the "Holy Marriage" in the third millennium Mesopotamia.

been a serious threat. That might also be the reason why Hos 4:14 puts the *qedeshot* in parallel with "the prostitutes" (זנות). What remains, if we disregard the allusions to illicit sexuality, is the fact that the *qedeshot* join the people in a sacrifice in an open place. Moreover, this sacrifice is condemned by the prophetic voice, which in this case comes under the veil of the divine voice.

The *komerim* in Hos 10:5 are discredited in a similar way. The three occurrences of the word are all very negative, connecting these cultic functionaries with the high places (2 Kgs 23:5; Hos 10:8) and the cult for Baal (Zeph 1:4). Naming the priests of Beth-El *komerim* thus turns them into priests of a different religion which the prophet will not tolerate. This religion is signified in Hosea by the cultic veneration of the image of a calf in Beth-El. Both terms *qedeshot* and *komerim* are connected with cultic actions in the strict sense, both are connected with special places (the hills and mountains in chapter 4, the high place in chapter 10), and both refer to a religion different from the religion of Israel whenever the term is used in the Hebrew Bible.

The priests (כהנים), on the other hand, are mentioned in chapters 4, 5, and 6 and the connection to cultic action seems to be quite weak. Hos 4:4 addresses the priest directly: "Yet let no one contend, and let none accuse, for *with you is my contention*, O priest."[19] The priest is criticized for not having conveyed the necessary knowledge to the people.[20] This misbehavior is the reason for dismissing him as a priest of YHWH and threatening him with death and elimination of his family.[21] Hos 4:7, 8 accuse the priests for (1) having multiplied and (2) having a strong economic interest in the people's sin. Both charges are, of course connected with one another: since those offerings which were not burnt completely belonged to the priests, they could be interested in the people's "sin" in the same particular way that is described in Mic 3:11. The more the people would "sin," the more income they would have. An increase in numbers among the priests would also aggravate the economic needs of the priestly class. The accusation in chapter 4 is in any case not so much that of cultic misbehavior, but of a neglect of an educational mission furthered by economic interests on the

---

[19] The translation of biblical texts follows the ESV with some adjustments by the author. In Hos 4:4, the text is not intelligible as it stands. The emendation, marked by asterisks, eliminates *kaph* and *mem* from כמריבי as an ancient correction of the text (substituting the plural for the singular but leaving both possibilities in the text). See the commentaries on this, e.g., Jörg Jeremias, *Der Prophet Hosea* (ATD 24.1; Göttingen: Vandenhoeck & Ruprecht, 1983), 63.

[20] This will be true even if v. 4bβ is secondary, as some exegetes assume.

[21] Reading אָם "kin" instead of אֵם "mother."

priest's side in an ignorant and therefore erring people.[22] The two shorter occurrences of the "priest" in Hos 5:1 and 6:9 confirm that view of the priests: in 5:1 the priests are accused together with the "house of Israel" and the "house of the king" for committing crimes—not for cultic misbehavior. Even more explicit is Hos 6:9, which accuses the priests for engaging in violent crimes (רצח).

In sum, Hosea accounts for the possibility of someone being a priest to YHWH, but this possibility is not what the priests of his time embraced. Instead of instructing the people and providing them with a role model of a righteous person, they primarily care for their own economic well-being. If Hosea's accusation is not a terrible exaggeration, they are even ready to commit severe crimes. However, in comparison to the *qedeshot* and the *komerim* in Hos 4:14 and 10:5, they are not explicitly accused of engaging in illicit cultic actions!

This is the case with the group that in most cases in Hosea's writing is intimately connected with cultic actions: the people. Almost all the cultic actions in the writing are enacted by "them," as they are mostly called. "They" are the people, or the people of Israel, of Ephraim, of Samaria; they are in any case "like the priest" (and vice versa Hos 4:9). They are those who care for the different types of offerings, they burn incense, bring cattle and sheep, and so on. Yet, the prophet and YHWH do not appreciate all that cultic enthusiasm. The people, however, seem to be very much at ease with all the cultic functionaries who keep them doing rituals, which again please the people. This is, as far as I can see, the first accusation against the people's engagement with rites: they do it for their own pleasure. "They sacrifice on the tops of the mountains and burn offerings on the hills, under oak, poplar, and terebinth, because their shade is good" (Hos 4:13a). And they follow their own agenda without asking for the will of God. All that comes to a climax in God's woe on Ephraim: "Woe to them, for they have strayed from me! Destruction to them, for they have rebelled against me! I would redeem them, but they speak lies against me" (Hos 7:13). The people are, in Hosea's perspective, the main character in the cult.

There is one important minor character in the constellation of Hosea's depiction of cult: the prophet. He turns up in Hos 4:5; 6:5; and 9:7, 8. The mentioning of the prophet in Hos 4:5 is probably a later insertion: not only because it is the only one that is negative about the prophet, but rather because it disturbs the literary form in 4:5.[23] The picture is very clear in Hos 6:5 and 9:7, 8. There

---

[22] For a slightly different view, see Lena-Sofia Tiemeyer, *Priestly Rites and Prophetic Rage: Post-exilic Prophetic Critique of the Priesthood* (FAT 2/19; Tübingen: Mohr Siebeck, 2006), 209.

[23] The form is built up on the repetition of equal words in different contexts, relating the reaction of God exactly to the accusation. Moreover the verse on the prophet misinterprets the phrase היום, "today" (indicating an immediate punishment), when it uses

the prophet is the instrument of God, who because of his call is prosecuted and ridiculed.

3.2. PLACES AND CULTIC INSTALLATIONS

Among the numerous places referred to by their names only Samaria and Beth-El (Beth-Aven) in the writing itself are clearly pointed out as relevant for a cult. The other references to places by their names remain more or less cryptic to us. This is why I will disregard the place names.

A manifest place for the cult would be the temple. In fact, the writing of Hosea mentions the terms בית יהוה and בית אלוהים. Both phrases are in the Hebrew Bible used to denote a temple. In Hosea, however, the word "house" (בית) is used mostly as a social or socio-political term in the phrases "house of Judah," "house of Israel," or "house of the king." These usages form the meaning of "house" in Hosea in such a way that a social understanding is more probable than that of a building. Only in Hos 9:4 can we grasp the thought of a temple with a sacrificial cult. But Hos 9:4 turns out to be a bit strange in its context: while the section Hos 9:3–6 stresses that a relationship with YHWH is not possible outside of the land (called ארץ ה'!), because there the people cannot be pure enough. Verse 4 relates the impossibility of a sacrifice to the people's need: they only have enough for their life (נפש) and cannot bring anything to the temple. Those two arguments stand side by side without being related to one another. The "temple" in Hos 9:4 thus looks very much like a later addition.

The threatened "house of God" in Hos 8:1 is surely not a temple but the land, as is clear from Hos 9:15, where the people will be expulsed "from my house" because of their bad deeds.[24] This is a clear allusion to the exile or the destruction of Samaria and not just a threat of closing the temples. And even in Hos 9:8—dealing with the threat against the prophet on the way and in the house of his God—"house" will refer to a social item rather than to an architectonical one, making a translation like "in the congregation of God" possible. So a "temple" is possibly not even mentioned in the writing of Hosea. Yet the land, which is called the "house of God," is the place where Israel had the possibility to stay in touch with its God. This land will be taken away from them: in Egypt (Hos 8:13; 9:6) they will not be able to sacrifice. God is withdrawing from them (Hos

---

הלילה, "in the night," as a complementary time specification in the parallel phrase on the prophet. The text as it stands suggests that the priest will stumble during the daytime (while the prophet does the same during the night).

[24] The situation described in Hos 8:1 is moreover parallel to that in 5:8. In both cases, the *shophar* is not used as a ritual instrument but for giving a signal of military alert. The threat would be not only against the temple, but against the whole land.

5:6) because they have abandoned God (Hos 5:4). Wherever they try to meet their God, they will not succeed. The only place in Hosea that is positively connected with God is the one which in the divine speech is called "my place" (5:15, מקומי). It is the place where God is unavailable for the defeated people, until they will have atoned for their guilt. Although God in Hosea (5:6) stresses the claim that Israel should seek him, it becomes obvious that they will not find him, because God prevents them from doing so.

But obviously there are some more places mentioned with clearly cultic reference and associated with cultic installations: an altar, a high place, stelae, and cultic images. The writing clearly puts down all these installations in chapters 4–11.

First of all the places in chapter 4 have to be mentioned here, the "tops of the mountains ... and ... the hills, under oak, poplar and terebinth" (Hos 4:13). The negative connotations connected with these places become obvious only from the fact that Hosea uses the vocabulary of prostitution and adultery when he talks about those cultic places. The only negative point mentioned about the places themselves is the fact that their "shade is good"; and so there are the actions performed on the mountains and hills, which might be condemnable. Maybe chapter 10 will provide more information about the mountains and hills: there the mountains and hills become part of the destruction of Israel and its highplaces, and the hills and mountains will finally fall upon the people / the altars. That apocalyptic picture not only ends the high-place of Beth-El, the "sin of Israel," but it also refers to the depiction of the cultic practice in Hos 4:13, 14. The references are interesting: Hos 10:1 complains about the multiplication of altars and stelae, and Hos 4:13 uses the plural for mountains and hills and had already in connection with the priests made a point of their multiplicity (4:7; also 8:11). Beside the plurality of the cultic places, Hosea complains in 10:1, 2 about the altars and stelae which seem to be obviously unacceptable.

But worst among all those things is the image of a calf. It is twice called "the calf of Samaria" (8:5, 6) but seems to have been venerated at Beth-El, the cultic centre of the Northern Kingdom (10:5)[25] and a place that in Hosea is not often called by its name "Beth-El" but by a name of shame "Bet-Aven," that is "house of iniquity."[26] All the references to the picture of the calf (8:4b–6; 10:5, 6) have that image in mind. It forms the centre of one field of cultic items, which

---

[25] In Hos 13:2 the calf reoccurs in the framing chapters.

[26] The parallel between Hos 4:15 and Amos 5:4, 5 makes a distinction between Beth-El and Beth-Aven rather unlikely. The name "Beth-Aven" is thus not just a normal name of a town different from Beth El but a specific form invented by the authors of the writing of Hosea in order to express their disgust and contempt for the cultic tradition of Beth El and the Northern Kingdom.

fall under the verdict of Hosea: in chapters 4–11 all the cultic installations from the altar (10:1, 8; 8:11, מזבח) to the cultic image (8:4; 4:17, עצב; 11:2, פסל) and the stela (10:1, 2, מצבה) are condemned. None of them can be thought of in the context of the religion of YHWH; they are in the view of Hosea illegitimate and the reason for the destruction of Samaria and the downfall of the Northern Kingdom.

Whether the "threshing floor and the wine vat" had any cultic function is hardly determinable from the text in Hos 9. The words *tirosh* (wine) and *dagan* (corn) echo the names of the Canaanite deities Dagon (or Dagan) and Tirash.[27] The texts do not reveal enough about the places to certify that they are of cultic significance.

3.3. CULTIC ACTS

The view of the persons and the places connected with the cult in Hosea has provided us with information that should make it easier to understand the proper cultic activities. In the following paragraph, I will examine the relevant texts (in 4; 5; 6; 8; 9; 10) chapter by chapter, following the lines of their presentations as close as possible.

The priests (כהנים) are not much connected with cultic acts; cult is predominantly the preserve of the people. Wherever cultic officials are dealing with cultic issues, they will be designated with pejorative words (כמרים; קדשות). The priests (כהנים) are blamed to disdain knowledge; it is their theological competence which the texts doubt, not their competence to fulfill a certain ritual. Hos 4:8 additionally accuses them of "feeding from the sin of the people," an accusation which, as we have seen, is similar to Mic 3:5. There is a material interest, which affects the way they deal with their priestly duties. For the priests this means that they are interested in the people's offerings given as a compensation for their guilt. Nowhere in the writing of Hosea do the priests (כהנים) come closer to being involved in real cultic acts.

As mentioned earlier, the cultic acts in Hos 4 are connected with the people, which in Hos 4:9 is equalized with the priests in acting wrong. Hos 4:11, 12 give a tripartite description of their actions, which again in 4:12b are traced back to the "spirit of prostitution" as their cause: "*wine*, and new wine take away the heart *of my people*. They inquire of a piece of wood/a tree, and their walking

---

[27] See Udo Rütersworden, "Vom Numen zum Nomen," in *Gott—Götter—Götzenbilder. XIV. Europäischer Kongress für Theologie (11.–15. September 2011 in Zürich)* (ed. Christoph Schwöbel; VWGTh 38; Leipzig: Evangelische Verlagsanstalt, 2012), 282–91; John F. Healy, "Dagon," *DDD*, 216–18, and John F. Healy, "Tirash," *DDD*, 871–72.

staff gives them oracles. For a spirit of prostitution has led them astray, and they have prostituted themselves away from their God."²⁸

While Hos 4:12b interprets the people's action with the catchword "prostitution," the three preceding phrases inform us about the objected action: wine makes them lose their mind (לב) and they perform oracles (שאל) with the help of some wooden objects. The second statement is expressed in two parallel phrases; the first one seems to be a bit vague: since "wine and new wine" is the subject of the action, the result—loss of mind—seems to be beyond the people's responsibility. But if we need to hear the name of the goddess "Tirash" behind the word תירוש, it becomes clear that the oracle in Hos 4:12 is not just wrong because it uses the wrong technique; the verse does not only tell us that some mantic practices are disallowed, but that the people are accused of having venerated a deity different from YHWH.

A second accusation is to be found in Hos 4:13, 14 and is complex. It starts with the statement that the people at some places perform sacrifices and offerings. Both זבח (sacrifice) and קטר (burn incense) are terms of a legitimate cult and do not necessarily denote a cultic action for other deities than the God of Israel. But it is immediately qualified as inadequate by the last phrase in Hos 4:13: "because their shade is good," which implies that the place is chosen by those who do the sacrifice only according to their comfort. The following section explains what turns the sacrifices on the hilltops into an abomination. The responsible men "go aside with prostitutes and with the *qedeshot* they sacrifice" (Hos 4:14aβ). The phrase is connected to Hos 4:13 through the catchword זבח. This type of sacrifice under the open sky together with the *qedeshot* is wrong in Hosea's view. The statement "with the prostitutes they go aside" is parallel to the second part of Hos 4:14bβ and has no independent meaning; it does not necessarily point to sexual excesses.²⁹ The "prostitutes" are in the same way set in parallel to the *qedeshot* as the "daughters" are parallel to the "daughters-in-law" and as "to prostitute oneself" is parallel to "to commit adultery." The section aims at the last phrase in the series of phrases: "with the *qedeshot* they sacrifice."

When Hos 4:13a, 14aα confronts its listeners with the harsh declaration that the (real) women are going to prostitute themselves—or that they will need to prostitute themselves—without being made responsible for this by God, this

---

[28] The text of the two verses has to be changed according to the Septuagint: in both v. 11 and v. 12 the first word has to be connected with the foregoing verse. The respective parts of the text are marked with asterisks.

[29] Nyberg, "Sacred Prostitution," 305–20, discusses the questions of the historical reliability of Herodotus's account about the rite of the Holy Marriage and cultic prostitution and turns both down. See also Marsman, *Women*, 548–72.

proposition is due to the fact that the addressees are the men of the grandfather's generation. These men are being criticized for their false cult, which is (in Hosea's view) probably directed towards gods different from YHWH. The shocking reference to the daughters and daughters-in-law may well include a threat of military destruction.[30] The main concern of the section is, yet, on the cultic actions of the men, who are made responsible for those actions. The final judgment points with לא יבין back to Hos 4:11 לקח לב.[31]

Both chapters 5 and 6 are dealing with questions which we would connect with politics and not with religion. In ancient thought, this differentiation does not work in the same way as it does for us. Already the beginning of Hos 5 demonstrates this when it addresses the priest alongside the king's house and the house of Israel. The text of Hos 5:6 intertwines political with theological reasoning in a long speech which starts by referring to YHWH in the third person and then changes abruptly in verse 10 to the first person divine speech. This long prophetic/divine speech is interrupted to give room to a citation of the people's voice only in Hos 6:1–3. The text of the two chapters refers to cultic practices only in two verses, in Hos 5:6 and in Hos 6:6. However, the two verses were placed in what can be regarded as being a demonstratively final position. Since they may represent the most fundamental statements on the cult in Hosea's writing, and since the two chapters show an unusually strong literary structure, it might be in order to summarize main points of that structure briefly in table form:

---

[30] Melanie Köhlmoos, "Töchter meines Volkes: Israel und das Problem der Prostitution in exilischer und nachexilischer Zeit," in *"Sieben Augen auf einem Stein" (Sach 3,9): Studien zur Literatur des zweiten Tempels FS Ina Willi-Plein* (ed. Friedhelm Hartenstein and Michael Pietsch; Neukirchen-Vluyn: Neukirchener, 2007), 213–28 (213), points to the possibility that the image of prostitution might be used to denote a military threat.

[31] Hosea 4:15 has been identified as a later commentary. For the argumentation for this qualification, see Jeremias, *Hosea*, 71. Since the verse does not bring in further information on our topic, it is left aside here.

5:1aα	Address: the priests; the house of Israel; the house of the king
5:1aβ, 2	Accusation
5:3, 4[32]	Judgment in concentric form: 3a: ידע 3b: זנה 4a: imposibility of reversion 4bα: זנונים 4bβ: ידע
5:5	Consequences for Israel/Ephraim/Judah
5:6	*Reaction of the people: approach with animals for sacrifice—God has withdrawn*
5:7	Reason and consequences
5:8	Military alarm
5:9	Announcement of destruction
5:10–15	Accusation with change to divine speech: 5:10, 11: first set of accusations 5:12: first divine punishment (nominal clause) 5:13: reaction on the punishment 5:14, 15: second announcement of divine punishment: destruction; God withdraws from Israel
6:1, 2	Voice of the people Connected to 5:10–15 through: לכו נשובה/אלך אשובה (6:1; 5:15aα) and טרף (6:1aβ; 5:14b)
6:4–6	God's reaction: 6:4a: Two rhetoric questions 6:4b: Diagnosis of the people's fallibility 6:5: Gods former reaction (6:5a) and its aim (6:5b) *6:6: God refuses all sacrifice:* חסד חפצתי ולא זבח ודעת אלהים מעלות

Table 2: Overview of Hosea 5:6

Besides this structure, which follows macro-syntactic signs and the logical development of the argument on its different levels (prophetic/divine speech; voice of the people), the section shows a great number of internal links through both

---

[32] See Jeremias, *Hosea*, 75.

catchwords and paronomasia. It would take too long to unfold this here,[33] but it shows that this section has a distinctive literary form, which again underscores the weight that is put on its content.

The offering, brought by the people in Hos 5:6, does not achieve its purpose, since God has withdrawn from them. The underlying reason for this is given in Hos 5:3, 4, a speech which is built in a concentric manner[34] around its central statement: "their deeds do not permit them to return to their God." An acoustic thread connects the explanation "the spirit of prostitution is within (5:4aα, בקרבם) them" with the animal planned for sacrifice (5:6, בבקרם) and the punishment for Judah (5:12b, כרקב); this thread puts the offering between an expression of the inner motivation of the people and the divine punishment. The people still do not understand that returning (שוב) to YHWH is not an option for them. YHWH has withdrawn from them and returns (שוב) to his place, where he is not available to them.

The words of the people in Hos 6:1–3 are full of confidence in the reliability of YHWH's help; they seem to be completely unaware of the situation. The answer of YHWH mirrors this. Starting with almost helpless rhetorical questions, they finally respond to the speech of the people with ironic references.[35] According to Hosea, the people pretend to trust in God but they themselves are not trustworthy in the eyes of God. YHWH's justice (משפט), which in Hos 5:1 had been stressed as referring to priests, king and the people, will only be operative when God castigates the people with the help of the prophets. The verb חצבתי from Hos 6:5aα resounds in the final sentence in Hos 6:6: "For I desire (חפצתי) solidarity (חסד) and not sacrifice, the knowledge of God rather than burnt offerings."

This sentence closes the long and complicated pericope in Hos 5:1–6:6, which deals with the pending catastrophe. Questions on politics turn out to be of religious relevance. The citation of the voice of the people and the people's futile attempt to save the day by sacrificing animals are replete with a network of assonances, which show the people's attitude to be completely inadequate. The consequence is a refutation of any sort of cultic offering in favor of an ethical attitude and theological consciousness. The priests are unable to stimulate this, as Hos 6:9 shows: they even engage in violent criminal acts.

Very similar to chapters 5 and 6, chapter 8 combines socio-political issues with cultic and theological topics; and as in Hos 5:8 the shophar is calling to

---

[33] See Landy, *Hosea*, 66–83.

[34] See Jeremias, *Hosea*, 75.

[35] Hosea 6:4b mirrors the meteorological pictures used by the people in Hos 6:3b. But while the people expect God to be as reliable as the seasonal rain, God attests the people that their most requested attitudes are as fugitive as a cloud or as dew.

arms. Now it is not Ephraim who is under attack but "the house of YHWH." This term, however, does not denote a temple or even the temple of Jerusalem, but rather the land belonging to YHWH[36] and endangered by something "like a vulture."[37] The following text traces the danger back to unauthorized elections of kings and rulers and to the fact that Israel uses its fortune to the fabrication of cult images. Especially the "calf of Samaria" (Hos 8:5) is identified by the text as being the work of a craftsman and not a god (Hos 8:6). From the latter note it may be assumed that some people indeed considered the calf as a god. The announcement of punishment (Hos 8:6b–8) is followed by another accusation: the multiplication of altars which is paralleled by the multiplication of priests in chapter 4 and again the multiplication of altars in chapter 10. In Hos 8:11, the altars are said to "have become to [Ephraim] altars for sinning."[38] And Hos 8:13 explicates "*they love*[39] sacrifices, they sacrifice meat and eat it, but the Lord does not accept them." The sacrifices seem to serve the wellbeing of the participant in the cult, a hedonistic attitude, which already Hos 4:7–8 and 4:13 indicated. A possible gloss adds that even the decisive disqualification of the sacrifice (ה' לא רצם) does not impress those participating in the sacrifice very much. But this reminds (זכר) YHWH of Israel's sin and thus brings his punishment upon it, while Israel forgets (שכח) its creator and has to return to Egypt.

In Hos 9:1–5, the section 9:3–5 stresses the impossibility of performing cultic offerings for those who had to leave the land, thus continuing the thought from Hos 8:13:

> [3]They shall not remain in the land of the Lord, but Ephraim shall return to Egypt, and they shall eat unclean food by[40] Assyria. [4]They shall not pour drink offerings of wine to the Lord, and their sacrifices shall not please him. It shall be like mourners' bread to them; all who eat of it shall be defiled; [for their bread shall be for their hunger only; it shall not come to the house of the Lord]. (Hos 9:3–4)

---

[36] See Hos 9:15.

[37] The reputation of the vulture in the Ancient near East and in pharaonic Egypt was much better than in the later European tradition. See Othmar Keel, Max Küchler, and Christoph Uehlinger, *Orte und Landschaften der Bibel: Ein Handbuch und Studienreiseführer zum Heiligen Land (Bd. 1)* (Zürich: Benziger, 1984), 154–57.

[38] Compare on this also Tiemeyer, *Priestly Rites*, 210.

[39] Following BHS, read אהבו instead of הבהבי which is not clearly understandable. Jeremias, *Hosea*, 103, translates "voller Gier."

[40] Reading the *beth* as a *beth constitutionis* avoids the contradicting places for the exile.

The sacrifices made impossible to Israel correspond exactly to the accusation, which Hos 9:1aβ–2 puts forward, when it localizes the guilt on the "threshing floor" and the "wine vat." The words דגן and תירוש are ambiguous; they do not only denote "corn" and "wine" but resound the names of the deities Dagon and Tirash.[41] What looks like mere agricultural work is at the same time cultic veneration of deities different from YHWH, so that the accusation in 9:1aβ, 1bα makes sense: "you have played the whore, forsaking your God. You have loved a prostitute's wages." The punishment corresponds to the guilt. The ambiguity of the people in relation to Dagon and Tirash makes it impossible to sacrifice the gifts (grain and wine) it had expected from these forces to the God of Israel.[42] The sequence on the cult ends in Hos 9:5 with a double question, which is, of course, a rhetorical question, since the answers to it have already been given in the negative imperatives of Hos 9:1: there will not be any festival of YHWH.

The cultic acts in Hos 10 seem to be comparably clear but not very differentiated. The opening section in Hos 10:1, 2 points to the altars and the stelae as the cultic evil. Meant as installations which should promote the proximity of God, they only excite God's wrath. Again the multiplication of altars is being criticized. It does not become clear to whom the installations are related from the perspective of the people. Either way they will be destroyed, which is unfolded in Hos 10:8. This verse again concludes the paragraph on the "calf of Beth-Aven" (Hos 10:5–8), which we shall look at now. It starts with a depiction of the different reactions on the possible loss of the image of a calf:

> ⁵The inhabitants of Samaria tremble for the calf of Beth-Aven.
> Its people mourn for it, but its idolatrous priests will rejoice over it, over its glory, although it has departed from them.
> ⁶The thing itself shall be carried to Assyria as tribute of king Yareb.[43] (Hos 10:5, 6a)

Reading ירב as the name of king Jeroboam, the text tells us that the image of the calf was sent to Ashur by that king. While the people are mourning over the loss, the priests seem to forget the loss and to put the glory (כבוד) in the place of the image. The tribute paid by the king does not yet hinder the downfall, the

---

[41] See above, n. 27, for literature on the topic.
[42] See John Andrew Dearman, *The Book of Hosea* (NICOT; Grand Rapids, MI: Eerdmans, 2010), 213, for a similar interpretation of this text.
[43] For this interpretation of the difficult "ירב," see Barstad, *Hosea*, 108–9, who argues that "Yareb" is a short form of the name of king Jeroboam, in this case referring to Jeroboam II.

king is flushed away,[44] the sanctuaries are destroyed (Hos 10:7, 8). Whether in the end the wish to be buried by mountains and hills is expressed by the people or by the high places and altars remains open.

This section may well reflect actual knowledge of an incidence of giving away a cult image to Assyria. An interpretation precludes this in Hos 10:1, 2. Between the interpretation and the description of events mediates a citation of the peoples voice in Hos 10:3, which makes sure that the people are aware of their guilt: "we have no king, for we do not fear the Lord; and a king—what could he do for us?"

The people consider their lack of "fear of the Lord" as the cause of the loss of their king, not without immediately adding that the king is not needed anyway. Under such a presupposition the cult, too, may be adjusted to opportunity—cultic veneration to the one who gives best effect. Hos 10:4 might be read as part of the voice of the people or as a prophetic commentary. Taken as part of the voice of the people the verse would express a fathomless disrespect of the king. If it is a prophetic comment it would rather give expression to the prophet's concern about a people, which is drifting into complete arbitrariness. Hos 10:3, 4 do in any case depict an attitude, which again sharpens the understanding of Hos 10:1, 2: in the time of prosperity and safety the people and the officials of state and cult did not care for their relation to the God of Israel. They had been in this relation right from the beginning but followed their own will to do what they considered as opportune: to multiply altars and stelae. But this had been to no avail. And even the abandonment of the cult image of Beth El, the central cultic place of the Northern Kingdom, was not successful. Assyria's striving for power flushed it all away. Neither the king nor the image turned out to be forces of historical impact.

The section stating that the cult had become impossible introduced the notion that "wine" and "corn" might refer to the names of the deities Tirash and Dagon. Considering this as a possibility, Hos 7:13–16 sheds additional light on the prophet's perception of the cultic practice of his contemporaries. In a word of woe (אוי, Hos 7:13), the main accusation contrasts the people's attitude towards God ("They speak lies against me. They do not cry (זעק) to me from the heart" (Hos 7:13bβ, 14aα) with its attitude towards grain and wine—or perhaps also towards Dagon and Tirash: "But they wail upon their beds; for grain (דגן)

---

[44] On the iconographic connection of Assur with "water," see Friedhelm Hartenstein, "Tempelgründung als 'fremdes Werk': Beobachtungen zum 'Ecksteinwort' Jesaja 28,16–17," in *Das Archiv des verborgenen Gottes: Studien zur Unheilsprophetie in Jesajas und zur Zionstheologie der Psalmen in assyrischer Zeit* (ed. Friedhelm Hartenstein; BThSt 74; Neukirchen-Vluyn: Neukirchener, 2011), 31–61 (39–41).

and wine (תירוש) they *gash*[45] themselves" (Hos 7:14aβ.bα). The section seems to mirror distinct rites of mourning performed in order to secure the income gained through agriculture. And the text even seems to have referred to Baal where it summarizes the sin committed by the people. Although the text is defective in the beginning of Hos 7:16, it is still possible to guess behind "they return not upward (לא על)" the mentioning of Baal (בעל).[46]

SUMMARY AND COMPARISONS

So far, the texts sorted by vocabulary have shown us a cultic reality performed at a multitude of cultic places with altars, stelae and even a cultic image; we would perhaps call it a thriving religious life which permeated the people's daily life. To the prophet it was idolatry and apostasy. His claim was for a religion that focused on a certain theology and ethics instead of cultic actions. But did the people share his view that it was involved in a non-Israelite, non YHWH-istic religion? The citations of the people's voice do not give us a clear picture. But they may at least provide us with some information.

The first of the four citations is the longest. Hos 6:1–3 shows a people who explicitly want to "return" to YHWH and even seem to accept the prophet's central point, when it explains: "…let us press on to know the Lord" (Hos 6:3aα). The next quotation in Hos 8:2 also indicates that the people basically agreed with Hosea: "To me they cry, My God, we—Israel—know you." Not only do the people "know" God, which in Hosea's perspective means that they are aware of how important it is to have the correct theology and attitude. They also do what they should do, they "cry" (זעק) to YHWH. Yet, here the context shows that the prophet is not convinced: only some verses before Hos 8:2 the divine speech tells us that "They do not cry to me from the heart" (Hos 7:14aα). The people, which the text shows us through its citations, are aware of how they should be, and they pretend to conform to the norms. However, in the perspective of the prophetic voice, the truth is different, as becomes evident from the next citation in Hos 9:7 which does not relate to cultic issues at all but shows clearly how prophet and people are set over against one another: "The prophet is a fool; the man of the spirit is mad." Those who talk in such a way

---

[45] Reading יתגדדו instead of יתגררו.

[46] Jeremias, "Baal," 89, has shown that Baal in Hosea refers to a category rather than the name of a specific god. In Hos 7:13–16, the concept of "Baal" would then be explicated as "Dagon and Tirash." On this subject, see also John Andrew Dearman, "Interpreting the Religious Polemics against Baal and the Baalim in the Book of Hosea," *OTE* 14.1 (2001): 9–25.

about the prophet will hardly follow the prophet's call to refrain from all those rites, which give the feeling of not having missed out on anything. The people are by this citation depicted as mean and unreliable. The last citation adds to the picture a stubborn reluctance to act according to its knowledge: "We have no king, for we did not fear the Lord; and a king—what could he do for us?"

The prophet in Hos 4–11 is in conflict mainly with a people who stick to performing cultic rites and is supported by cultic officials who either support the ritualistic tendencies within the people (קדשות and כמרים) or who do not contradict the people's desire, notwithstanding their knowledge, which they (the כהנים) keep to themselves. The prophet, on the other hand, holds that the only adequate answer to the problems of his time is a religion strictly confined to the veneration of the one and only God of Israel, veneration strictly without any sort of cult.

A look at the framing chapters of the writing shows that this central concern of the prophet was generally also pursued there. Hosea 12:10–15, which unfolds the prophet's role in the history of salvation, points in verse 12 to the sacrifice as the exemplary guilt of the people. Hosea 13:2 draws from chapters 8 and 10 for a summarizing verdict of the "calf" and any other cult image. All that is the continuation of: "[Ephraim] incurred guilt through Baal" (Hos 13:1). And in Hos 14:9, Ephraim finally finds out that the idols are of no use. All these statements are in line with the intentions brought forward in Hos 4–11. They only seem to be more condensed and straightforward.

The opening chapter of the writing does not refer to the cult at all. The second chapter unfolds the image of Israel as a disloyal wife and frankly calls the woman's lovers "the Baalim." Moreover, the woman is said to have loved the festivals, especially the New Moon and the Sabbath, and to have burnt incense as offerings. As in Hos 13, "Baal" has at this point become the codeword for all false forms of encounter with the divine. It remains astonishing that the Sabbath is among the condemned festivals. The short chapter Hos 3 is the one with the richest representation of cultic vocabulary in Hos 1–3. Absolutely in line with the rest of the writing, Hos 3:4 announces that the woman/Israel as a punishment for her/its misconduct will lose not only its political leaders, but also its cult, represented by sacrifice, stela, ephod, and teraphim. While sacrifice and stela obviously refer to the proper cult, the two remaining items (ephod and teraphim) point to an oracular technique. The oracle had not been an important topic in the rest of Hosea, only Hos 4:12 had mentioned a practice of prospection. Besides that, Hos 3:4 seems to account for the possibility of a renovation of the cult, since it states that the Israelites will have to live without the institutions of their history just "for a long time." Hos 6:6 would decline the cult for all times, because it blurs the perception of God's will. The composition of the writing in its final form may have followed a strategic line when it positioned the softer assertions in the first chapters and the clearer and conclusive ones towards the end.

Hosea's message about the cult will hardly have been welcome at any time in the history of Israel. This writing with that specific message now opens the Book of the Twelve Prophets, which ends with the rebuilding of the temple (Hag 1), the re-establishment of the cult (Mal 1) and the end of prophecy (Zech 13). But the Book of the Twelve Prophets also ends with stressing the Torah as the signpost for a life in righteousness and with the announcement of the return of the prophet Elijah.

2
HOSEA'S EXODUS MYTHOLOGY AND THE BOOK OF THE TWELVE

Mark Leuchter

The Book of the Twelve ("the Twelve") is several things at once—a collection of independent books, a composite work redacted from distinct sources, and a single literary edifice embodying a stream of prophetic discourse presented as coherent by its redactors.[1] This is an important point because it speaks to one feature of literary diachronics, namely, that coherence does not demand uniformity, and this extends to the concept of the cult as preserved in the book. The diverse prophetic materials within the book carrying different views on matters of the cult are presented as consistent with a specific type of priestly

---

[1] On the redactional intertwining of the once-independent prophetic works, see James D. Nogalski, *Redactional Processes in the Book of the Twelve* (BZAW 218; Berlin: de Gruyter, 1993); idem, *Literary Precursors to the Book of the Twelve* (BZAW 217; Berlin: de Gruyter, 1993), and Aaron Schart, *Die Entstehung des Zwölf-prophetenbuchs: Neubearbeitungen von Amos im Rahmen schriftenübergreifender Redaktionsprozesse* (BZAW 260; Berlin: de Gruyter, 1998). See further the recent collection of essays in *Reading and Hearing the Book of the Twelve* (ed. Marvin A. Sweeney and James D. Nogalski; SymS 15; Atlanta: SBL, 2000), and *Perspectives on the Formation of the Book of the Twelve* (ed. Rainer Albertz, Jakob Wöhrle, and James D. Nogalski; BZAW 433; Berlin: de Gruyter, 2011). For the view that The Twelve were not redacted to function as a unity, see Ehud Ben Zvi, "Is the Twelve Hypothesis Likely from an Ancient Reader's Perspective?" in *Two Sides of a Coin: Juxtaposing Views on Interpreting the Book of the Twelve/Twelve Prophetic Books* (ed. Thomas Romer; Analecta Georgian 201; Piscataway, NJ: Gorgias, 2009), 47–96.

worldview—namely, a Levite worldview—that long mediated between different traditions, cultic or otherwise. As James Nogalski and I have each argued in different ways, the primary redactors of The Twelve were probably Levite scribes in the late Persian period, who created the work as an intellectual and sacral testament to how prophecy might look, sound, and function in the context of an Aaronide-dominated temple cult.[2]

Pursuant to this is the fact that the opening and closing units in the Twelve are Hosea and Malachi, both of which are saturated with Levite ideology and language, subsuming the intervening contents.[3] Even if Amos, Micah, Nahum, etc. were not Levite works in and of themselves, their contents are presented as components of Levite intellectual heritage. This rhetorical strategy, wherein diachronic difference is highlighted but hermeneutically transformed into a cohesive prophetic discourse, appears in antecedent works that carry a Levitical imprimatur; the book of Jeremiah is a case in point. The diverse traditions in the book represent disparate social and theological perspectives, the primary redactors of the book (the Deuteronomistic-Shaphanide scribal circle) subsumed them all within a hermeneutical framework demarcated by the "words of Jeremiah" (Jer 1:1/51:64b) qualifying them as consistent despite their apparent differences.[4] One might also look to Deuteronomy, whose opening and closing frames differ markedly from the legal collection in the middle of the work, yet the entirety of the work is presented as the single and coherent transmission of Moses by virtue of its embedding within a scribal report (Deut 1:1–5; 34); the implication is that the author of this report is a Levite scribe entrusted with Moses' teachings.[5] The Twelve follows in this regard through its Hosea/Malachi frame-

---

[2] James D. Nogalski, "One Book and Twelve Books: The Nature of the Redactional Work and Implications of the Cultic Source Material in the Book of the Twelve," in *Two Sides of a Coin*, 40–46; Mark Leuchter, "Another Look at the Hosea/Malachi Framework in the Twelve," *VT* 64 (2014): 249–65 (260–62).

[3] Leuchter, "Hosea/Malachi Framework," 257–58.

[4] I have elsewhere highlighted the Levitical character of the Shaphanide circle (*The Polemics of Exile in Jeremiah 26–45* [Cambridge/New York: Cambridge University Press, 2008], 160–76). The late preexilic and exilic Deuteronomists themselves appear to have had strong Levitical sympathies as well; see the note immediately below.

[5] On the embedding of Moses' discourses within a scribal report, see Mark Leuchter, "The Medium and the Message, or, What is 'Deuteronomistic' about the Book of Jeremiah?" *ZAW* 126 (2014): 208–27 (221–23). For a recent discussion regarding the Levite character of the Deuteronomistic tradition, see Jeffrey C. Geoghegan "'Until This Day' and the Preexilic Redaction of the Deuteronomistic History," *JBL* 122 (2003): 201–27; idem, *The Time, Place and Purpose of the Deuteronomistic History: The Evidence of "Until This Day"* (Brown Judaic Studies 347; Providence, RI: Brown University, 2006), 149–51; Jack R. Lundbom, "The Inclusio and Other Framing Devices in Deuteronomy i–

work, which claims all of the intervening materials as part of a comprehensive Levitical theology of history, revelation, and mediation. In what follows, we shall focus on how Hosea in particular contributes to this process, and I wish to draw attention to a major feature of Hosea's oracles, namely, the mythology of the Exodus.[6]

1. NORTHERN EXODUS TRADITIONS IN MONARCHIC ISRAEL

Several years ago, Yair Hoffman compared the references to the Exodus in the books of Amos and Hosea.[7] Hoffman concluded that the references in Amos conceived of the Exodus as an important event in the past, but that for Hosea, the Exodus constituted a myth of identity formation. Karel van der Toorn continued this line of inquiry in his monograph on family religion, noting that Hosea's use of the Exodus motif was connected to its role as a "charter myth" for northern Israelite identity.[8] And indeed, many scholars have drawn attention to the fact that the earliest layers of the Exodus tale (in the canonical book of Exo-

---

xxviii," *VT* 46 (1996): 296–315 (314–15), and Mark Leuchter, *Samuel and the Shaping of Tradition* (Biblical Refigurations; Oxford: Oxford University Press, 2013), 19–22.

[6] I shall not delve too deeply into the thorny matter of how much within the book of Hosea should be credited to the prophet himself. There is certainly room for views such as that of Martti Nissinen, *Prophetie, Redaktion, und Fortschreibung im Hoseabuch* (AOAT 231; Neukirchen-Vluyn: Neukirchener, 1991), that the book shows signs of heavy scribal orchestration, or that of Roman Vielhauer, *Das Werden des Buches Hosea: Eine redaktionsgeschichtliche Untersuchung* (BZAW 349; Berlin: de Gruyter, 2007), 178–79, that a good deal of exilic-era redaction may be found in the book. But the arguments of Nissinen and Vielhauer need to be moderated or qualified, as they do not account for sociological features in Hosea's oracles that are consistent with the prophet's own (ostensible) northern and Levitical background that a purely scribal origin for the material would not have possessed. On this, see Stephen L. Cook's study *The Social Roots of Biblical Yahwism* (Atlanta: SBL, 2004), especially pages 231–66. Finally, as Marvin Sweeney notes, the book of Hosea does not address the calamity of the Babylonian exile, making unlikely the substantial exilic or postexilic origin of its primary blocks of discourse ("A Form Critical Re-Reading of Hosea," *JHS* 2 [1998] 1.3.8—1.3.9; online at www.jhsonline.org). It thus seems entirely feasible that many of the oracles in the book derive from an eighth century BCE setting, or that they were associated with the eighth century prophet from a relatively early point. In any case, his oracles function rhetorically as relics from that era within the Twelve.

[7] Yair Hoffman, "A North Israelite Typological Myth and a Judean Historical Tradition: The Exodus in Hosea and Amos," *VT* 39 (1989): 169–82.

[8] Karel van der Toorn, *Family Religion in Babylonia, Syria and Israel* (Leiden: Brill, 1996), 287–315.

dus) should be traced to the formation of the northern state under Jeroboam I in the late tenth century BCE.⁹ It is in the foundation of the northern state that the Exodus was fused with the religion of the family: Jeroboam fortified various ancestral sanctuaries (1 Kgs 12:25, 28), adopted iconography long associated with lineage-based devotion to El and incorporated clan ancestors into the national "pantheon" (1 Kgs 12:28), and appointed priests from those leading clans rather than Levites (1 Kgs 12:31).¹⁰ The northern state's Exodus myth harmonized the religion of the clan or family with that of the state—perhaps as a

---

⁹ Rainer Albertz, *A History of Israelite Religion in the Old Testament Period* (2 vols.; Louisville, KY: Westminster John Knox, 1994), 1:141–43; van der Toorn, *Family Religion*, 300–301; John J. Collins, "The Development of the Exodus Tradition," in *Religious Identity and the Invention of Tradition. Papers read at a NOSTER Conference in Soesterberg, January 4–6, 1999* (ed. Jan Willem van Henten and Anton Houtenpen; Assen: Van Gorcum, 2001), 145–55; Michael Oblath, "Of Pharaohs and Kings: Whence the Exodus?" *JSOT* 87 (2000): 23–42.

¹⁰ The famous liturgical mantra הנה אלהיך ישראל in 1 Kgs 12:28 is a deliberate double entendre; אלהיך can be read both as "your god/gods" or "your deified ancestors", as אלהים) is a common expression relating to the ancestral cult; see van der Toorn, *Family Religion*, 219, 221, 233–34; Francesca Stavrakopoulou, *The Land of Our Fathers: The Roles of Ancestor Veneration in Biblical Land Claims* (LHBOTS 473; London: T&T Clark, 2011), 17, 19, 103; Baruch Halpern, "Late Israelite Astronomies and the Early Greeks," in *Symbiosis, Symbolism and the Power of the Past* (ed. Seymour Gittin and William G. Dever; Winona Lake, IN: Eisenbrauns, 2003), 323–52 (334–35, 341, 343). Additional evidence surfaces in Amos 2:8, where the audience at Bethel is criticized for practices involving a "house" to their "[deified] ancestors" (בית אלהיהם). For a fuller treatment defending this reading, see Jeremy Schipper and Mark Leuchter, "A Proposed Reading of the בית אלהיהם in Amos 2:8," *CBQ* 77 (2015): 441–48.

Some scholars view the notice in 1 Kgs 12:31 regarding non-Levite priestly appointment as a Deuteronomistic criticism. See, e.g., Albertz, *History of Israelite Religion*, 308, fn. 34, and Frank M. Cross, *Canaanite Myth and Hebrew Epic* (Cambridge, MA: Harvard University Press, 1973), 199. Juha Pakkala, "Jeroboam Without Bulls," *ZAW* 120 (2008): 501–25 (508–9), has more recently suggested that the passage was secondarily interpolated. However, Jeremy M. Hutton's analysis points to its authenticity within the pre-Deuteronomistic source and its pertinence to reconstructing genuine events. See further Jeremy M. Hutton, "Southern, Northern and Transjordanian Perspectives," in *Religious Diversity in Ancient Israel and Judah* (ed. John Barton and Francesca Stavrakopoulou; London/New York: T&T Clark, 2010), 149–74 (160–61).

measure against the patrimonial hierarchy that had taken root in Jerusalem under Solomon.[11]

This northern Exodus myth, however, draws from extant antecedents that pre-dated the rise of the monarchy. I have elsewhere termed this "Eisodus as Exodus," where the flourishing of agrarian society is not a result of YHWH's defeat of Egypt, it *was* YHWH's defeat of Egypt.[12] In this conception, the hinterland is transformed from an unsewn steppe—the מדבר—into a sacred landscape wherein YHWH's people exist far beyond the reaches of Egyptian Pharaohs or subservient Canaanite rulers. It is YHWH's sweeping away of these Egypto-Canaanite forces which allowed for him to claim the landscape as his own, and to plant his people therein to cultivate it.[13] Of course, the motif of the cultivation/settlement of the land eventually took shape as a mythotype distinct from the Exodus in the growth of later narrative traditions in the Pentateuch and the Deuteronomistic History. But even so, wisps of the early, pre-textual tradition can be found within these literary works. Identifying these archaic concepts points to an Exodus myth deeply connected to the flourishing of the people in YHWH's sacred landscape over against the encroachment of foreign threats beyond the Israelite hinterland.

Jeroboam's propagandists transmuted this tradition into a political concept that made the northern state itself an Exodus Redivivus: participation in the state and the support of its cultic institutions was a sort of mythic rehearsal of the Exodus, a renewed experience of the deity's liberation from Egypt. But as has long been noted, major Levitical factions were disenfranchised from the cultic infrastructure of the northern state, and developed powerful traditions of protest.[14] The critique of the bull cult at Dan/Bethel with its caustic demythologization of this cult iconography would have formed at this time;[15] we may also

---

[11] Lawrence E. Stager, "The Patrimonial Kingdom of Solomon," in *Symbioses, Symbolism, and the Power of the Past: Canaan, Ancient Israel, and Their Neighbors from the Late Bronze Age Through Roman Palaestina* (ed. William G. Dever and Seymour Gitin: Winona Lake, IN: Eisenbrauns, 2003), 63–74.

[12] Mark Leuchter, "Eisodus as Exodus: The Song of the Sea (Exod 15) Reconsidered," *Bib* 93 (2011): 333–46.

[13] Leuchter, "Eisodus as Exodus," 337–43.

[14] Baruch Halpern, "Levitic Participation in the Reform Cult of Jeroboam I," *JBL* 95 (1976): 31–42 (33–38). Halpern identifies some Levitical groups that Jeroboam seemed to have recruited to the cause, but notes that the influential Shiloh priesthood was marginalized from the cultic infrastructure of the state.

[15] While the Golden Calf narrative in literary form probably has its origins in the late monarchic era, Hosea already relies upon it as an ancient and authoritative tradition; see Cook, *Social Roots of Biblical Yahwism*, 252–54. Hosea may be drawing from an old and

trace the anti-monarchic posture of the Song of Moses in Deuteronomy 32 to this era and circle of authorship. The former tradition expressly condemns the northern state Exodus myth; the latter invokes the pre-state Exodus tradition in the context of a liturgical work that was regularly reheased among northern Levite circles over a span of many generations.[16] Thus two types of Exodus myths circulated in the north, each claiming to be fundamental to Israelite identity, and each standing in effective opposition to the other—one state-bound, one Levitical.

2. Hosea's Reliance on the Levitical Exodus Myth

Hosea's references to the Exodus fall into the latter category, and emphasize an additional mythic motif: that of the cosmic foe, Mot or Death, as a threat to Israel's ability to flourish in the land. This motif draws heavily from Late Bronze Age Canaanite mythological tradition attested at Ugarit; it is suggestive of the role these myths continued to play in the cultural lexicon of Israel throughout the Iron Age. Hosea's reliance upon this mythology indicates that it was a firmly entrenched part of Levite discourse pre-dating Hosea's activity. If this is so, then we may view it as arising as part of a Levite response to the formation of the northern state as a perceived threat to their theological traditions.[17] We will consider three examples demonstrating how Hosea's oracles apply this mythological motif to the Exodus over against the status quo of the northern state, especially insofar as it relates to what he perceived as illegitimate concepts and prac-

---

well-formed critique that circulated on the oral level even down to his own day. A parallel is found in Hosea's use of the Jacob narrative, which departs from what we find in the book of Genesis and which likely draws from oral traditions regarding the patriarch circulating at Bethel. See William D. Whitt, "The Jacob Traditions in Hosea and their Relation to Genesis," *ZAW* 103 (1991): 18–43 (41), and Steven L. McKenzie, "The Jacob Tradition in Hos xii 4–5," *VT* 36 (1986): 311–22 (321).

[16] On the function of Deuteronomy 32 as a liturgy, see Matthew Thiessen, "The Form and Function of the Song of Moses (Deuteronomy 32:1–43)," *JBL* 123 (2004): 401–424. On the poem's origination as a Levitical anti-monarchic protest, see Mark Leuchter, "Why is the Song of Moses in the Book of Deuteronomy?" *VT* 57 (2007): 295–317 (314–16). Though Egypt is not mentioned in Deuteronomy 32, the highland agrarian imagery in the poem invokes a component of the pre-state Exodus tradition akin to what we encounter in Exod 15:13, 17.

[17] On Hosea's deep enculturation in this myth, see Adina Levin, "Hosea and North Israelite Tradition: The Distinctive Use of Myth and Language in the Book of Hosea" (Ph.D. Dissertation, University of Toronto, 2009), 225–32.

tices regarding the ancestral cult. The first of these examples is found in a textual unit in Hosea 2:

> ¹Yet the number of the children of Israel shall be as the sand of the sea, which cannot be measured nor numbered; and it shall come to pass that, instead of that which was said to them: 'You are not My people,' it shall be said to them: 'You are the children of the living God.' ²And the children of Judah and the children of Israel shall be gathered [נקבצו] together, and they shall appoint themselves one head, and shall go up out of the land [עלו מן הארץ]; for great shall be the day of divine fructification [ביום יזרעאל]. (Hos 2:1–2 [Eng. 1:10–11])

> ¹⁶Therefore, behold, I will allure her, and bring her into the wilderness [מדבר], and speak tenderly unto her. ¹⁷And I will there give her vineyards to her, and the valley of Achor for a door of hope; and she shall respond there, as in the days of her youth, and as in the day when she came up out of the land of Egypt (Hos 2:16–17 [Eng. 2:14–15])

Theodore Lewis has noted that the term קבץ relates to the gathering together of the dead with departed ancestors;[18] this is set alongside the term ארץ, often identified with the underworld—both the residence of the departed ancestors and, notably, the residence of Mot in earlier Canaanite myth.[19] Hosea's rhetoric is suggestive of an association that runs counter to the state liturgy which aligned the departed ancestors with the state deity; in the prophet's rhetoric, these ancestors (as appropriated by the state) are actually companions of the cosmic foe Mot and reside in his realm. Yet the rhetoric also suggests that Israel will be gathered away from these ancestors and will be released from the underworld (עלו מן הארץ). With a return to YHWH, the Exodus will occur anew—the people will again be brought into the wilderness (מדבר), and YHWH will transform this space into a flourishing land in a day of divine fructification (ביום וזרעאל).[20]

This line of thought is further developed in Hosea 11:1–4, which redefines what constitutes "ancestral" tradition:

> ¹When Israel was a child, then I loved him, and out of Egypt I called My son [ממצרים קראתי לבני]. ²The more they called them, the more they went from them;

---

[18] Theodore J. Lewis, *Cults of the Dead in Ancient Israel and Ugarit* (HSM 39; Atlanta: Scholars Press, 1989), 16.

[19] Mark S. Smith, "The Baal Cycle," in *Ugaritic Narrative Poetry* (ed. Simon B. Parker; SBLWAW 9; Atlanta: Scholars Press, 1997), 81–180 (165, fn. 10).

[20] See the similar discussion of Francis I. Anderson and David Noel Freedman, *Hosea* (AB 24; Garden City, NJ: Doubleday, 1980), 209.

they sacrificed to the Baals [הבעלים], and offered to graven images. ³And I, I taught Ephraim to walk, taking them by their arms; but they knew not that I healed them. ⁴I drew them with cords of a man, with bands of love; and I was to them as they that take off the yoke on their jaws, and I fed them gently. (Hos 11:1–4)

Hosea 11:1–4 invokes the Exodus as the basis for Israel's covenant with YHWH, but juxtaposes it against the role of ancestral devotion within state religion.²¹ Some scholars see here a polemic against Baalism and assume the prophet's critique of devotion to a Canaanite deity,²² but it is significant that Hosea utilizes the term הבעלים, rather than the singular בעל. The latter typically refers to Baal worship, but the term הבעלים carries a different connotation. As Baruch Halpern has discussed, הבעלים (or הבעל as a collective singular) refers to the deities of the Israelite ancestral cult.²³ Both Jeremiah and the author of 2 Kgs 23, for example, use these terms in depicting the dimensions of ancestral devotion fit for criticism or demolition (respectively), juxtaposing clan-based atomism against the national covenant delineated in Deuteronomy.²⁴ This is, no doubt, a function of the Deuteronomistic interest in leveling clan religion following Josiah's centralization efforts. But given the Deuteronomists' debt to northern Levitical tradition, Hosea is likely utilizing the term הבעלים in the same manner, that is, as a critique of ancestral devotion, with the בעלים signifying the deified ancestors themselves now embedded in the state cult.²⁵

---

²¹ The remainder of Hosea 11 is difficult to address due to its composite nature, much of which obtains as redactional expansions of Hosea's oracles as Nissinen has argued (*Prophetie, Redaktion und Fortschreibung*, 298, 339–40). Yet Hos 11:1–4 does appear consistent with the prophet's rhetorical and mythological predilections. See further Nissinen, *Prophetie, Redaktion und Fortschreibung*, 338–39, who allows for this as well to a certain degree.

²² John Day, "Hosea and the Baal Cult," in *Prophecy and Prophets in Ancient Israel: Proceedings of the Oxford Old Testament Seminar* (ed. J. Day; LHBOTS 531; New York/London: T&T Clark, 2010), 202–24 (205–7).

²³ Baruch Halpern, "The Baal (and the Asherah) in Seventh-Century Judah: YHWH's Retainers Retired," in *Konsequente Traditionsgeschichte: Festschrift für Klaus Baltzer zum 65. Geburtstag* (OBO 126; ed. Rüdiger Barthelmus, Thomas Krüger, and Helmut Utzschneider; Freiburg: Freiburger Universitätsverlag; Göttingen: Vandenhoeck & Ruprecht, 1993), 115–54 (130).

²⁴ Halpern, "Late Israelite Astronomies," 333–43.

²⁵ Further evidence is found in Jeremiah's usage of the locution from both Deut 32:17 (לא אלה) and Hosea (הבעלים) in his critique of the ancestral cult (Jer 2:11; 5:7; 7:9 [לא אלהים]; 11:12–13, 17; 12:16; 23:13[הבעל]; see Halpern, "The Baal," 128–29). Jeremiah's rhetoric presupposes the conceptual continuity of his sources; by the late seventh

If this is so, then Hosea's critique follows the older Levitical protests against the state's assimilation of the deified ancestors into the national "pantheon" (Exod 32:7; Deut 32:17). Hos 11:1–4 de-legitimizes this aspect of the state theology/mythology as distinctively non-Israelite; devotion to the בעלים is now a foreign abomination that stands in polar opposition to Israelite religion. It is significant that Hosea elsewhere qualifies the בעלים as foreign deities competing for Israel's devotion (Hos 2:15–19). Hosea claims that devotion to the ancestors connected to the state cult was equivalent to worshipping the cosmic enemies of YHWH. Here, another dimension of the pre-monarchic Exodus mythology is invoked by Hosea, namely, that of YHWH as the divine kinsman.[26] With the reframing of the בעלים from deified ancestors to the status of foreign, cosmic foes, Hosea repositions YHWH's kinship status in more clearly defined terms: in Hos 11:1 it is YHWH who is now the deified ancestor that liberated his child from Egypt (וממצרים קראתי לבני).[27] Just as Hos 2:1–2 decouples Israel from the clutches of Mot and the underworld, Hos 11:1–4 decouples Israel's northern population from the state's Exodus mythology and its claim on the ancestors.

The emphasis in Hos 11:1–4 on the inefficacy of state-bound ancestral tradition is an effective prelude to the drama that unfurls in Hosea 12–14. A pivotal passage is found in Hosea 12, which encapsulates the essence of the conflict:

> [13]And Jacob fled into the field of Aram, and Israel served for a wife, and for a wife he kept sheep. [14]But by a prophet [נביא] YHWH brought Israel up out of Egypt, and by a prophet was he kept [ובנביא נשמר]. (Hos 12:13–14 [Eng. 12:12–13)

Hosea's reference to Moses (the "prophet" of 12:14) is cast against the Jacob tradition cultivated at Bethel, the major state sanctuary. Van der Toorn correctly noted the opposition constructed here between the Exodus and Jacob traditions

---

century, then, Hosea's critique of the בעלים was understood as consistent with the Levitical protest of the Song of Moses.

[26] Leuchter, "Eisodus as Exodus," 342–43, and Frank M. Cross, *From Epic to Canon: History and Literature in Ancient Israel* (Baltimore, MD: Johns Hopkins University Press, 1998), 5–8.

[27] Here Nissinen's view that much of Hosea 11 is secondary/redactional holds considerable appeal (*Prophetie, Redaktion und Fortschreibung*, 339–40). If Hos 11:5ff. are largely redactional, then the assertion in vv. 1–4 that YHWH is now the deified ancestor receives significant reification from what ensures almost immediately thereafter in Hos 12:5–6, where the Bethel liturgy cited by Hosea (v. 5) is boldly reversed by the declaration that YHWH—not El (or YHWH-as-El) or any of the associated deified ancestors—commands devotion (v.6). See R. Scott Chalmers, "Who is the Real El? A Reconstruction of the Prophet's Polemic in Hos 12:5a," *CBQ* 68 (2006): 611–30 (629).

in Hosea's rhetoric.[28] Yet van der Toorn did not consider the degree to which the northern state cult had earlier *fused* these traditions, or the degree to which Hosea seeks to divorce them as a Levite opposed to the religion of the state.[29] Hosea continues to separate state-based ancestor devotion from the Exodus by pitting Jacob, the archetypal northern ancestor, *against* the memory of Moses. By referring to Moses not by name but by typology (נביא), Hosea suggests that his own prophetic oracles, replete as they are with Levite teaching, are precisely how the nation had been "kept" by similar figures in the past.[30]

It is thus with the Levitical bearers of Moses' teachings and responsibilities that the defining pre-monarchic myth of the nation is properly understood, despite the long claims to the contrary by the northern state officialdom. Indeed, Hos 13:4–11 reiterates this concept:

> ⁴Yet I am Yhwh your god since the land of Egypt; and you know no god but me, and beside me there is no savior. ⁵I knew you in the wilderness [מדבר], in the land of great drought. ⁶When they were fed, they became full, they were filled, and their heart was exalted; therefore have they forgotten me.
>
> ⁹It is your destruction, O Israel, that you are against me, against thy help. ¹⁰Ho, now, your king, that he may save you in all your cities, and your judges, of whom you said: "Give me a king and princes!" ¹¹I give you a king in my anger, and take him away in my wrath. (Hos 13:4–6, 9–11)

The claim that Israel should know only Yhwh presupposes devotion to competing constructs such as those created by the northern state.[31] Most forcefully, the criticism of northern royalty at the end of the unit is conditioned by Hosea's appeal to the Exodus mythology at its outset: the emergence from Egypt is invoked in the same breath as the remembrance of the unsown highlands (the מדבר in Hos 13:5), a realm that has been contested and claimed by Mot (Death)

---

[28] Van der Toorn, *Family Religion*, 301.

[29] Ibid., 298–99.

[30] See here van der Toorn's discussion of the overlap between Levitical and prophetic tradition in Hosea (*Family Religion*, 313–14).

[31] With Karel van der Toorn, "The Exodus as Charter Myth," in *Religious Identity and the Invention of Tradition*, 113–27 (118), this is not a monotheistic claim at home in an exilic or postexilic temporal environment as Nissinen argues (*Prophetie, Redaktion und Fortschreibung*, 157–66). The theology of the verse is not substantially different from that of Deut 32:16, and speaks to an exclusive relationship between Yhwh and Israel over against alignment with a cosmic foe.

through the apparatus of the northern state.³² But this territory belongs to YHWH, and he will once again claim it—by removing the regime that governs it. It is all the more striking, then, that the oracle continues with reference to the cosmic conflict with Mot (Death):

> ¹⁴Shall I ransom them from the power of the underworld? Shall I redeem them from Death [ממות]? Ho, your plagues, O Death [מות]! . . . ¹⁵ . . . and his (Death's) spring shall become dry, and his fountain shall be dried up; he shall spoil the treasure of all precious vessels. ¹Samaria shall bear her guilt, for she has rebelled against her God [תאשם שמרון כי מרתה באלהיה]; they shall fall by the sword; their infants shall be dashed in pieces, and their women with child shall be ripped up. (Hos 13:14–14:1 [Eng. Hos 13:14–16])

Hosea subverts and re-assigns the roles of the characters in the older myth: whereas Baal takes his mythic waters down with him into the underworld (KTU 1.5: vv. 4, 6–17), here it is Death who must do so.³³ And yet in the very next verse, Hosea is emphatic that it is not Israel itself that is identified with Death but, rather, the royal administration in Samaria that rules it (תאשם שמרון כי מרתה באלהיה). The conflict between Levites like Hosea and the state administration is no less than the conflict between YHWH and Death; the "dashing" and "ripping" of Samaria's inhabitants recalls the fate of Death at the hands of Anat (KTU 1.6: I 33–35). With the decoupling of Israel from the state cult in Hos 2:1–2 and 11:1–4, Israel is presented as a pawn led astray by the true enemy (Samaria), but fit for redemption at the enemy's destruction. This, too, recalls Baal's rising from the realm of Death (KTU 1.6: III 6–7), and the closing oracle in Hosea 14 thus takes on new significance:

> ⁵I will heal their backsliding, I will love them freely; for my anger is turned away from him. ⁶I will be as the dew unto Israel; he shall blossom as the lily, and cast forth his roots as Lebanon. ⁷His branches shall spread, and his beauty shall be as the olive-tree, and his fragrance as Lebanon. ⁸They that dwell under his shadow shall again make corn to grow, and shall blossom as the vine; the scent thereof shall be as the wine of Lebanon. ⁹Ephraim [shall say]: "What have I to do any more with idols?" As for me, I respond and look on him; I am like a leafy cypress-tree; from me your fruit is found. (Hos 14:5–9 [Eng. 14:4–8])

---

³² Mark S. Smith, *The Origins of Biblical Monotheism* (Oxford: Oxford University Press, 2001), 27–29; idem, *Ugaritic Narrative Poetry*, 165, fn. 10.

³³ See also Day, *Prophets and Prophecy*, 218–19, who notes the similarities between Hosea's oracles and the Mot mythology. On Hosea's reassignment of roles from Canaanite mythology, see Levin, "Hosea and North Israelite Tradition," 123–25.

While the resonances with the Baal/Death cycle are unmistakable here,[34] the position of this oracle also follows the same pattern as the pre-monarchic Exodus mythology. There, the conflict with the foe (Exod 15:3–12) is followed by the deity's leading of the people into the sacred landscape and planting them therein (Exod 15:13–17). The same concept informs the use of agrarian imagery in Hos 14:2–9, following as it does upon YHWH's conflict with the northern state as a manifestation of Death (Hos 13:14–14:1). The former is not simply a deployment of general fertility motifs. Rather, the prophet lays out what he considers to be the true and legitimate Exodus Redivivus: after confronting his cosmic enemies, YHWH will once again plant his people in a fertile land. But most significant is the fact that this only occurs after the enactment of the following terms:

> ²Return, O Israel, to YHWH your god; for you have stumbled in your iniquity. ³Take with you words, and return to YHWH; say to him: "forgive all iniquity [עון תשא], and accept that which is good so will we render for bullocks the offering of our lips ונשלמה פרים שפתינו]. ⁴Ashur shall not save us; we will not ride upon horses; neither will we call any more the work of our hands [מעשה ידינו] our gods; for in you the fatherless [יתום] find mercy." (Hos 14:2–4 [Eng. 14:1–3])

In these verses, Hosea's Levitical function is perhaps most strongly felt, for he offers his audience a form of *torah*-instruction (as an alternative to the teachings of the corrupt state priests). In these verses, we find a counter-liturgy (vv. 3–4) that associates political fortunes with the rejection of the state cult.[35] The people are instructed to declare that the state's religious icons are no more than man-made objects (מעשה ידינו), and rejecting them will constitute an offering (ונשלמה פרים שפתינו) that will bring about divine forgiveness (תשא עון). That this also constitutes a rejection of the ancestral dimensions of the state cult is implied in the finale of the liturgy, where it is the "fatherless" (יתום) who find mercy in turning to YHWH and away from a corrupted veneration of the ancestors. It is only then that the Exodus can be experienced anew, where the people no longer venerate ancestors from the pioneering past, but will in effect become those ancestors themselves, emerging from Egypt and communing with YHWH in the hinterland as in days of old (Exod 15:17; Deut 32:10, 13; 33:29).

---

[34] Levin, "Hosea and North Israelite Traditions," 135–36.

[35] Compare this to what Chalmers, "The Real El," 629, has identified as a quotation of the official Bethel liturgy in Hos 12:5 criticized by the prophet.

3. Hosea's Place in the Twelve

For Hosea, the Exodus is the vehicle whereby Israel can escape the clutches of Death, and arise anew from the underworld. But this is not a matter of metaphor; the northern state cult is evidence of Death's presence, which turns the northern state itself into the underworld. If the people are able to reject the clutches of the elite forces controlling the state, they shall once again be liberated from "Egypt," and YHWH will again settle them in the sanctified land. Placing this type of discourse at the outset of the Twelve is a powerful rhetorical maneuver, as it affirms the existence of cosmic threats that create the adversarial forces that YHWH will dissolve or destroy. The ensuing discourses in the Twelve flesh this out, even in those prophetic books that do not seem to have much to do with Egypt or the Exodus. The implication is that diverse forms of subsequent threats all share the same cosmic profile *vis á vis* the Exodus: the rise of Assyria, the conquest of Babylon, the duplicity of Edom, and even the apathy of the *golah* repatriates to rebuild YHWH's house in Jerusalem—all of these are iterations or expressions of cosmic forces that threaten YHWH's intentions for Israel in the land, which we have seen is a major component of Hosea's Exodus mythology.[36]

The redactors have set up the Twelve in such a way that prophetic books subsequent to Hosea provide evidence for these various iterations of the larger cosmic concern, even those books deriving from prophets who predated Hosea temporally (such as Amos) or who addressed decidedly Judahite geo-political issues (like Micah) or spoke of the eschaton (like Joel). The later rabbinical statement that "there is no early or late in the Torah" (*Pesakhim* 6b) may be applied here—the Exodus, as a myth of identity, is *always* happening to Israel, and the prophetic word testifies to this irrespective of when or where it was uttered and transcribed. What licenses the hermeneutical equation of these discourses with Hosea's Exodus mythology is another feature of Hosea's oracles, namely, that of wisdom. The verse that immediately comes to mind, of course, is the wisdom colophon in Hos 14:10—"he who is wise, let him consider these things," etc.[37] In its current position, this colophon not only closes the book of

---

[36] Here the Exodus notice in Hag 2:5 (את הדבר אשר כרתי אתכם בצאתכם ממצרים), which is often identified as a redactional addition to its surroundings, provides a nice case in point for how the redactors of The Twelve look back to Hosea's mythology to qualify the contents of other books. I am indebted to Professor John Kessler for directing me to this passage.

[37] Positions vary on the provenance of this verse. Choon Lee Seow, "Hosea 14:10 and the Foolish People Motif," *CBQ* 44 (1982): 212–24, argues that it was consistent with the repeated appeals to wisdom within the book of Hosea, and thus should be

Hosea but points to what follows it. "These things" are both Hosea's oracles and the oracles in the ensuing prophetic books. But "these things" are also the relationships *between* these various books—something that does not exist on the material page but is cultivated in the intellect and imagination of the reader who studies Hosea and the prophetic texts that follow. The essence of the textual discourse is thus meta-textual, as the reader's response and intellectual awareness is subsumed within "these things."[38]

The wise person is being asked to consider how a northern prophet so deeply engaged in a particular mythological worldview serves as a lens through which the subsequent prophets may be viewed, or how these subsequent prophetic discourses may expand the scope of Hosea's words and maintain their vitality long after the kingdom of Israel had vanished from history. It is, in essence, a call to consider an alternative sacred history than what one encountered in narrative works such as the Pentateuch or the Deuteronomistic History, both of which had been commandeered at some point by the Aaronides (a point to which we shall return below).[39] But this also had been a recurring motif within the book of Hosea; the prophet promotes the Levitical traditions regarding the Exodus as an alternative to that of the northern state, and beckons his audience to recognize the difference between them and the illegitimacy of the latter. Cognition, evaluation, consideration, deliberation—all of these are part of Hosea's message, required by the prophet of his audience. As Choon Lee Seow noted over 30 years ago, Hos 14:10 is only part of a larger strategy of wisdom running throughout the book of Hosea.[40] At virtually every turn, Hosea punctuates his oracles with appeals to the wisdom tradition. The people—his ostensible audi-

---

viewed as part of the original collection of oracles rather than stemming from a redactional hand. Vielhauer, *Das Werden des Buches Hosea*, 201–3, also recognizes that the verse looks back to the totality of the book but not the remainder of the Twelve. The opposite view, however, is common, i.e., that it is part of a late wisdom redaction of the book (see, *inter alia*, van der Toorn, *Scribal Culture*, 257–58). The origin of the verse is not important to the present study, only its current function in relation to Hosea's place in The Twelve.

[38] See further my discussion in Leuchter, "Hosea/Malachi Framework," 264–65.

[39] Gabriele Boccaccinni, *Roots of Rabbinic Judaism: An Intellectual History, from Ezekiel to Daniel* (Grand Rapids, MI: Eerdmans, 2002), 52–57, refers to these works as part of the "Zadokite Historiography," (or "Priestly Historiography") i.e., authoritative works that reified the place of the Zadokite clan at the top of the sacral pecking order. For these texts as the eventual "property" of Aaronides in general, see James W. Watts, *Ritual and Rhetoric in Leviticus: From Sacrifice to Scripture* (Cambridge: Cambridge University Press, 2007), and David M. Carr, *The Formation of the Hebrew Bible: A New Reconstruction* (Oxford: Oxford University Press, 2011), 195–201, 213–14.

[40] Seow, "Foolish People."

ence—are a "foolish" nation that does not recognize the folly of supporting corrupt institutions, and prophetic and priestly functionaries operating within these institutions are complicit in laying the trap that ensnares this foolish nation.[41]

The true prophet, by contrast, is a watchman for YHWH (צופה in Hos 9:8), one who can evaluate the faults in a corrupt system (including misguided cultic prophets) and chart a better course for the nation's restoration.[42] Perhaps it is no surprise that it is this same prophetic type that is instrumental in Israel's liberation from Egypt in Hos 12:14. While we have seen that this is very likely a reference to Moses, we have also seen that it is a typology first *embodied* by Moses but not limited to him. Like the Exodus itself, the prophet who sustains the nation is a mythic construct that delineates and defines the identity of subsequent prophets (Hosea or otherwise). Here, we find an antecedent to Deuteronomy's similar view that a "prophet like Moses" will arise in every successive generation (Deut 18:15–18).[43] Anticipating the ongoing prophetic word that will affirm Deuteronomy's covenantal terms, the Exodus in Hosea can be re-experienced when the wise pay heed to the prophets like Moses who affirm the traditions of the Levites on behalf of YHWH, thereby identifying the forces that stand between Israel and their liberation from the clutches of cosmic enemies.

This is important for our understanding of the Twelve for two reasons. First, it sheds light on why Hosea is positioned as the opening canto of a redactional work that was constructed not simply to be read but, as I have suggested else-

---

[41] Seow, "Foolish People," 223–24.

[42] See Lena-Sofia Tiemeyer, "The Watchman Metaphor in Isaiah lvi–lxvi," *VT* 55 (2005): 378–400 (379–81).

[43] Some steps were taken in this direction already by Wolff (*Hosea*, 216) and Joseph Blenkinsopp, *A History of Prophecy in Israel* (Louisville, KY: Westminster John Knox, 1983), 50. James D. Atkins, "Reassessing the Origins of Deuteronomic Prophecy: Early Moses Traditions in Deut 18:15–22," *BBR* (2013): 323–41(326), argues that the Deuteronomy's association of this motif with the Sinai event rather than the Exodus renders the Mosaic prophet tradition independent from what obtains in Hosea, but this is too precipitous a position. Given the Deuteronomists' great interest in abstracting lemmas from older sources and transforming them into new iterations and contexts (as discussed thoroughly by Bernard Levinson, *Deuteronomy and the Hermeneutics of Legal Innovation* [New York/Oxford: Oxford University Press, 1997]), there is no reason to doubt that the Deuteronomists drew from Hosea's oracles in this regard, developing the Mosaic prophet motif in relation to the teaching of Sinaitic law. See also Christophe Nihan, "'Moses and the Prophets': Deuteronomy 18 and the Emergence of the Pentateuch as Torah," *SEÅ* 75 (2010): 21–55 (33–34). Nihan's dating of this Deuteronomic text to the Persian period may be debated but his observations on the scribal exegesis and fusion of earlier material are sound.

where, to be taught.[44] If the typology of a persistent Mosaic prophet originates in Hosea, then one of the teachings emerging from the Twelve is that the prophets who follow Hosea are also prophets like Moses.[45] We may sense here, perhaps, a corollary or even a challenge to the closing of the Pentateuch, which tells us that after Moses' death, none like him would ever arise again (Deut 34:10–12). Hosea's inaugural place in the Twelve creates a counter-point to this position, and a perceptive reader would no doubt have sensed the intertextual argument.[46] But the placement of Hosea also establishes a model for how wise readers should engage their literary curriculum. The redactional seams that place the various books within the Twelve in conversation with each other provides instructive examples for how learned, inspired writers were supposed to speak, teach, and transmit their revelations to each other.

This perhaps offers us a window into how Levites actually engaged in scribal teaching duties, because other texts of the late Persian period seem to present Levites of the era in similar terms. Chronicles and Ezra-Nehemiah certainly characterize Levites as teachers, exegetes and sages (Ezra 8:15–19; Nehemiah 8; 2 Chr 15:3; 17:7–9; 35:3), and the redactional shape of the Psalter implies the same.[47] If Levites stand behind the late-Persian redaction of the Twelve, the placement of Hosea's wisdom-oriented discourse at the outset of the work falls in line with this spectrum of literature. It makes Levites the trustees of a wisdom tradition that is more than just a matter of elite enculturation: it is the key to actualizing divine blessing and sustaining identity.[48] As a sapiential curriculum, the Twelve becomes an extended meditation on what one encounters in the inaugural book of Hosea, and presents itself as a rehearsal of Israel's foundational ideologies that Hosea invoked. It creates a plan for Jewish life in late Persian Yehud to transcend the limits of imperial structures, as those structures be-

---

[44] Leuchter, "Hosea/Malachi Framework," 264–65.

[45] Van der Toorn comments that the final redactors of the work have Deut 18:15–18 in mind when invoking Elijah in the book's colophon (*Scribal Culture*, 254), but this is also suggestive of the titular prophets within the book as well.

[46] Aaron Schart's observation that the opening books of the Twelve all invoke the Torah from Sinai (in Exodus 19–Numbers 10) provides some sense of how the redactors of the Twelve may have attempted to counter the rhetorical impact of Deut 34:10–12. See his essay "The First Section of the Book of the Twelve Prophets: Hosea–Joel–Amos," *Interpretation* 61 (2007): 138–52 (146–47).

[47] Mark S. Smith, "The Levitical Compilation of the Psalter," *ZAW* 103 (1991): 258–63.

[48] See further Smith, *Origins of Biblical Monotheism*, 147, for a discussion of the Levites as the trustees of wisdom.

come international expansions of the state system against which Hosea originally railed.

But another reason as to why the placement of Hosea at the start of the Twelve is important pertains to a paradigm shift that had been building since the Babylonian exile. During that time, the loss of the Jerusalem temple left different populations without an anchor for identity formation. This led to a variety of responses, one of which was a shift in the role and perception of texts. Texts became surrogate sanctuaries, occupying conceptual spaces where ancestral tradition could be embedded, legal traditions could be studied, rituals could be encountered and prophecy could be conveyed and developed.[49] This may explain why, as David Carr has argued, ancestral narratives appear to be extensively developed during the exilic period: separated from their ancestral estates and institutions, texts provided the only means for Judahites to engage in any form of communion with their ancestors.[50] Even with the restoration to Jerusalem and the rebuilding of the temple, this understanding of text provided a potential challenge to the Aaronide status quo. If the redactors of the Twelve constructed their work to function as a literary sanctuary, it is fitting that it opens with Hosea's wisdom oracles. Sigmund Mowinckel's classic suggestion that preexilic wisdom functioned within the cult in creating entry rites into sanctuary spaces may be worth reconsidering here: if the Twelve is a sort of textual sanctuary, then Hosea's wisdom oracles function as an "entry text" into the material that follows.[51]

Some support for this is found in the fact that Hosea's companion text, Malachi, closes the Twelve with an appeal to wisdom as well:

> [16]Then the YHWH fearers [יראי ה'] spoke one with another; and YHWH hearkened, and heard, and a book of remembrance was written before him, for the YHWH fearers [יראי ה'] who meditated upon his name... (Mal 3:16)

---

[49] For a fuller discussion of this phenomenon, see my essay "Sacred Space and Communal Legitimacy in Exile: The Contribution of Seraiah's Colophon (Jer 51:59–64a)," in *The Prophets Speak on Exile/Forced Migration* (ed. Mark J. Boda, Frank Ames, Mark A. Leuchter, and John Ahn; SBLAIL; Atlanta: SBL, 2015), 77–99.

[50] Carr, *Formation of the Hebrew Bible*, 286–89. This textual/rhetorical ancestral communion, however, must have been rather different from the funerary rites and rituals associated with family religion in the homeland. Engagement seems to be limited to typological/symbolic discourses especially regarding Abraham; see Lena-Sofia Tiemeyer, "Abraham: A Judahite Prerogative," *ZAW* 120 (2008): 49–66.

[51] Katharine Dell, "'I Will Solve My Riddle to the Music of the Lyre' (Psalm xlix 4 [5]): A Cultic Setting for Wisdom Psalms?" *VT* 54 (2004): 445–58 (455).

David Petersen has proposed that the closing utterances in Mal 3:22–24 provide an "answer" to Hosea 14:10 (insofar as both serve as epilogues in each book), but it is in the verses above that the better connection may be found by virtue of their specific concerns with wisdom.[52] Malachi 3:16 identifies the entirety of the Twelve as the product of the יראי ה',[53] and lest we forget, it is the יראת ה' that Proverbs specifies as the fountainhead of wisdom (Prov 1:7; 9:10; cf. Ps 111:10). Additional support is found in the same structural logic in the Psalter, for Psalm 1 serves as an "entry text" that makes wisdom the hermeneutical prism through which the meaning of the subsequent psalms is refracted. What Psalm 1 is to the Psalter, Hosea is to the Twelve in this regard, and Malachi's sapiential notice functions as a refrain for Hosea's opening discourses regarding the discernment of the Exodus in relation to northern politics. It is the יראי ה' who have discerned, and who will continue to discern, "these things" as they pertain to subsequent eras and institutions.

Conclusion

The foregoing suggests that a major stream of wisdom within the Twelve placed Hosea's Exodus mythology at its heart. The Exodus, as an event in the distant past, is replayed again and again in history, and the wise will sense how the prophets in the Twelve affirm this. This sheds light on some currents of thought circulating among the priestly circles of late Persian Yehud. The careful redaction into a *single* scroll of once-independent prophetic works reveals a desire to reframe how those works were to be understood,[54] which in turn suggests a response to an extant set of circumstances. More to the point, it suggests that prophetic texts had earlier been used to buttress a different mythology—that constructed within the Aaronide temple cult which, in turn, supported Persian political mythology. The various inscriptions sponsored by Darius and Artaxerxes promote an imperial ethos where the physical geography of the empire was a testament to the driving out of cosmic chaos.[55] The cultic systems of the cultures

---

[52] David L. Petersen, *Zechariah 9–14 and Malachi* (OTL; Louisville, KY: Westminster John Knox, 1995), 233, though his observations regarding the resonances between the epilogues in Hosea/Malachi and other portions of the canon remain possible.

[53] Nogalski (among others) notes that the "book of remembrance" looks back to the entirety of the Twelve (*Redactional Processes*, 207–10).

[54] See further van der Toorn, *Scribal Culture*, 251–52.

[55] For a concise summary of this mythology, see Christine Mitchell, "Achaemenid Persian Concepts Pertaining to Covenant and Haggai, Zechariah and Malachi," in *Cove-

within that empire supported this larger mythological construct, and were subsumed by it.

Even if the Aaronides stopped short of overtly affirming the imperial myth, there can be little doubt that the Aaronide priests utilized earlier prophetic texts to support their position at the apex of Yehudite society under Persian authority. The evidence from the redaction history of Ezra-Nehemiah points to the prominent role of prophetic texts in supporting Aaronide interests, aligning priestly power with imperial decrees.[56] Furthermore, if the account of Ezra's mission to Yehud was conceived as a sort of Second Exodus as some scholars have argued,[57] then Israel's Exodus tradition was fused to Persian imperial ideology, and we may surmise that prophetic traditions were deployed to support this view. The redaction of the Twelve challenged this by re-deploying the very same prophetic texts in a way that reminded audiences that YHWH had, in the past, voiced disapproval of foreign imperialism, and had done so since the beginning, with Egypt. By placing Hosea at the outset of the Twelve, the redactors show that its prophetic contents worked in the service of an older mythology that was far more fundamental to Israelite identity, and that "the wise" would understand and promote "these things" as such. Hosea's Exodus mythology therefore carried a much greater significance than simply testifying to northern Israelite mythotypes from the preexilic period. It declared that the priests charged with preserving prophetic texts were obligated to prioritize their mythological allegiances. It spells out how cultural negotiations must reinforce rather than sideline the hallmarks of identity that connected Israel to their history, their land, and their deity.

---

nant in the Persian Period (ed. Gary N. Knoppers and Richard Bautsch; Winona Lake, IN: Eisenbrauns, in press).

[56] See the concluding comments in Mark Leuchter, "The Exegesis of Jeremiah in and beyond Ezra 9–10," *VT* 65 (2015) 62–80.

[57] Klaus Koch, "Ezra and the Origins of Judaism," *JSS* 19 (1974): 173–97 (184–89).

3
PENITENTIAL PRIESTS IN THE TWELVE

Mark J. Boda

Considerable debate has revolved around the structure and integrity of the book of Joel. Many have noted the contrast between the first part of the book which is dominated by language concerning a contemporary agricultural crisis (1:2–2:27) and the second half of the book which is dominated by language concerning a future cosmic and international crisis (3:1–4:21 [Eng. 2:28–3:21]).[1] However, literary integrity can be discerned at least in the references to "the day" and employment of agricultural and cosmic/international language in both halves of the book.[2]

Other books among the Twelve share the structural diversity evidenced in the book of Joel, in particular, those books which bring the collection to a close.[3]

---

[1] See Duane A. Garrett, "The Structure of Joel," *JETS* 28 (1985): 289–97, for a possible dual role for 2:18–27. For structural approaches to Joel (Wolff, Prinsloo, Garrett, Barton, Sweeney, Bauer and Traina, and Nogalski) see the superb review by Thomas Lyons, "Interpretation and Structure in Joel," *The Journal of Inductive Biblical Studies* 1 (2014): 80–104 (who also provides his own approach), but also note the more recent works of Eliyahu Assis, *The Book of Joel: A Prophet between Calamity and Hope* (LHBOTS 581; New York: Bloomsbury, 2013) and Joel Barker, *From the Depths of Despair to the Promise of Presence: A Rhetorical Reading of the Book of Joel* (Siphrut 11; Winona Lake, IN: Eisenbrauns, 2014).

[2] See further connectivity in Assis, *Book of Joel*, 24–54.

[3] On the intertwining of penitential and eschatological in the Twelve and the key role played by Joel, see Jason LeCureux, *The Thematic Unity of the Book of the Twelve:*

Haggai begins with a focus on an agricultural crisis much like Joel and provides promises in terms of historically rooted prosperity (Hag 2:19) in the Persian period before shifting to more cosmic/international language in "that day" (Hag 2:20–23). Malachi is also initially focused on issues within the Persian period community (Mal 1–2; 3:7–15), but in the end shifts into cosmic/international language with reference to the coming "Day" (Mal 3:1–6, 16–24 [Eng. Mal 3:16–4:6]). Zechariah is also similar to Joel, emphasizing repentance at the outset within the Persian period community, but in its second half then shifting to cosmic/international language with an emphasis on the coming "Day," especially in chapters 12–14.[4]

These similarities between Joel and Haggai-Malachi prompt further reflection on the relationship between the two sections of the Twelve. Another element that they share in common is that both Joel and Haggai-Malachi relate the prophetic message to priestly figures, the focus of the present volume. In this contribution we will investigate penitential messages addressed to priestly figures with particular focus on striking similarities yet contrasts between Joel 1–2 and Zech 7–8. In Joel the priests are afforded a leading role in the call to repentance and while there is some question over the relationship between the penitential cry of the prophet and the priestly response which it prompts, it is clear that YHWH responds in the section following the call for priestly led repentance and prayer. Zechariah also contains a call to penitential liturgy, but highlights the failure of priests among the people of the land to truly repent. These contrasting portraits of priests in relation to repentance in the Book of the Twelve is key to the overall shape of the Twelve, setting a penitential agenda for the collection which is addressed not only to the community as a whole but especially to temple leadership.

The Call to Return and the Nature of the Minor Prophets (HBM 41; Sheffield: Sheffield Phoenix, 2012), 111, 236.

[4] But there are also striking similarities between Joel and Zech 9–10 in the reference to the Phoenicians and Greeks. Zephaniah, which is closely related to the Haggai-Malachi collection in the redaction which saw Haggai-Malachi incorporated into the Twelve (Mark J. Boda, "Babylon in the Book of the Twelve," *HeBAI* 3 [2014]: 225–48), is more integrated than these books, intertwining the cosmic/international with the historically rooted language throughout (see especially ch. 1).

1. Joel 1–2, Fasting, Penitence, and Priests

Joel 1:2–2:27 is punctuated by a series of imperatives addressed to a variety of audiences: 1:2, 8, 11, 13–14; 2:1, 15–17, 21–23 as well as a series of interrogatives that prompt reflection by the literary audience (1:2b; 2:11b, 14, 17).[5]

Ref	Imptv	Aud	Ref	Imptv	Aud	Ref	Imptv	Aud
						2:17b	איה אלהיהם	
1:2a	שמעו	הזקנים	2:1	תקעו		2:18a		ויקנא
	והאזינו	יושבי הארץ		והריעו		2:18b	Waw / Relative Transition	ויחמל
1:2b	ההיתה זאת		2:11	ומי יכילנו		2:19a		ויען
1:5	הקיצו	שכורים	2:12	שבו		2:19b		ויאמר
	ובכו	כל־שתי יין	2:13	וקרעו		2:21	אל־תיראי	אדמה
	והילילו			ושובו		2:21	גילי	
1:8	אלי		2:14	מי יודע		2:21	ושמחי	
1:11	הבישו	אכרים	2:15	תקעו		2:22	אל־תיראו	בהמות
	הילילו	כרמים		קדשו		2:23	גילו	בני ציון
	חגרו	הכהנים		קראו		2:23	וְשִׂמְחוּ	
1:13	וספדו	משרתי מזבח	2:16	אספו				
	הילילו			קדשו				
	באו			קבצו				
	לינו	משרתי אלהי		אספו				
1:14	קדשו		2:17a	חתן ... וכלה	יצא			
	קראו			הכהנים משרתי יהוה	יבכו			
	אספו				ויאמרו			

Imperatives, Interrogatives, and Waw-Relative Transition as Structural Markers in Joel 1:2–2:27

The opening imperatives in Joel 1:2–3 address the community as a whole with references to the leadership (הזקנים) and the general populace (יושבי הארץ), calling them to attend to the prophetic words and then relay a report of the severity

---

[5] See Marvin A. Sweeney, "The Place and Function of Joel in the Book of the Twelve," in *Thematic Threads in the Book of the Twelve* (ed. Aaron Schart and Paul Redditt; BZAW 325; Berlin: de Gruyter, 2003), 139–43. For the overall structure of Joel, see Assis, *Book of Joel*. I follow Assis's identification of 1:2–2:17 as the first major unit, even though I differ on the breakdown of the sub units.

of the present agricultural crisis to future generations. At the outset an interrogative (1:2b) is used to prompt reflection by the audience. Two other imperative sections (1:5, 11) address this same community in terms of those who consume (כל־שׁתי יין, שׁכורים; 1:5) and produce agricultural products (כרמים, אכרים; 1:11).[6] Between these two imperative sections, however, we find a distinct imperatival address to a feminine singular audience who is likened to "a virgin girded with sackcloth for the bridegroom of her youth" (1:8). While some have suggested that this feminine singular audience is Zion,[7] more likely it is אדמה ("land") the only other feminine singular addressee in the book (2:21).[8] Interestingly, while the motivation for the imperatives directed to those who produce and consume agricultural harvest is restricted to the devastation caused by the natural disaster (locusts, drought), the motivation for the imperative directed to the land is not only the natural disaster (1:10), but its impact on the offerings destined for the temple and the priests who facilitate these offerings (1:9). Thus, while this first subsection of 1:2–2:27 (1:2–12) is dominated by exhortations to the general populace, here at its centre lies address to the entity most directly affected (אדמה) and here we find emphasis on priestly activity at the temple.[9] Joel 1:8–9 foreshadows the emphasis on address to priests in the second sub-section of 1:2–2:27 (1:13–2:17).

At the outset of 1:13–2:17 we find echoes of the vocabulary already encountered in 1:8–9 with the repetition of the words: priests (הכהנים), ministers (משׁרתי), grain offering (מנחה), drink offering (נסך), and house (בית, as temple). The priests who were described as mourning in the address to the land in 1:8–9 are now the addressees of the prophet. They are called first to mourn due to the agricultural crisis (1:13), but then they are exhorted to arrange a day of fasting at the temple (1:14) with specific reference to the designations for the populace

---

[6] See Assis, *Book of Joel*, 96, for a superb comparison between 1:5 and 1:11.

[7] Cf. Barker, *From the Depths of Despair*, 84.

[8] Note how אדמה is identified as mourning (אבלה) in 1:10. For options, see the short review by Assis, *Book of Joel*, 83–84, who concludes that it is addressed to the people personified as a woman longing for the husband of her youth.

[9] On the cultic orientation of the first section of Joel, see Barker, *From the Depths of Despair*, 70–73. See Assis, *Book of Joel*, 90–91, for how reference to grain and drink offerings suggests an exilic setting (cf. Jer 41:5); *contra* John Barton, *Joel and Obadiah: A Commentary* (OTL; Louisville, KY: Westminster John Knox Press, 2001), 53, who notes that elsewhere the combination of מנחה and נסך only appears in what he considers postexilic texts (Exod 29:38–42; Lev 23:13, 18; Num 6:15; 15:24; 28:3–9; 29:11, 16–39) and always in connection with animal offerings. The fact that no animal offerings are mentioned in Joel highlights the uniqueness of Joel and possibility of exilic origins.

which opened the book in 1:2 (זקנים, כל ישבי הארץ).[10] Similar exhortations are repeated in 2:1 and 2:15–17. This evidence, along with that already noted in 1:8–9, bolsters our contention that the rhetorical force of 1:2–2:27 is directed towards this priestly audience who are being commissioned to lead the community in a day of fasting. What begins as a call to the general populace subtly shifts into a commissioning of the priestly caste. For this reason Joel is a key resource for studying priests in the Book of the Twelve.

This creative subtlety is not limited to the shift in addressees in the first half of the book. The motif of the "day" is introduced in 1:15 (אהה ליום כי קרוב יום יהוה) and along with it allusion to an intensity of destruction that appears to transcend a more limited agricultural crisis (וכשד משדי יבוא). This only increases as the reader continues into chapter 2 and the day is referred to as גדול ... ונורא מאד ("great and very awesome") which prompts the question: מי יכילנו ("who may endure it?" 2:11b). The impact on creation is far more cosmological ("day of darkness and gloom ... clouds and thick darkness ... the earth quakes, the heavens tremble, the sun and the moon grow dark and the stars lose their brightness" 2:2a, 10) and the imagery increasingly martial (2:4–9). This shift from agricultural crisis to cosmological and military crisis foreshadows the second half of the book, suggesting that the overall rhetoric of the book is designed to move the reader to treat a present agricultural crisis as a sign of something much bigger, possibly an approaching punishment not unlike the destruction of Jerusalem and Judah in the early sixth century BCE.[11]

But there is one further subtle rhetorical shift in the first half of the book of Joel and this shift is found in the exhortations to the priests in 1:13–2:17. The first exhortations in 1:13–14 end with the provision of the words which the priests are to "cry out" to YHWH. These words, expressed in first person in 1:15–20, focus attention on the agricultural crisis as would be typical of the lament tradition of ancient Israel.[12] Such laments, as Gunkel noted long ago, were ex-

---

[10] Barker, *From the Depths of Despair*, 68, identifies Joel 1:14 as the "emotive peak" of 1:1–14.

[11] See further Assis, *Book of Joel*, 39–50, 122–123, and Barker, *From the Depths of Despair*, 116–7, on these two levels. Note a similar intertwining of agricultural and martial levels in Jer 14:1–15:4; see Mark J. Boda, "From Complaint to Contrition: Peering Through the Liturgical Window of Jer 14,1–15,4," *ZAW* 113 (2001): 186–97.

[12] See Mark J. Boda, "A Deafening Call to Silence: The Rhetorical 'End' of Human Address to the Deity in the Book of the Twelve," in *The Book of the Twelve New and the New Form Criticism* (ed. Mark J. Boda, Michael H. Floyd, and Colin Toffelmire; ANEM 10; Atlanta: Society of Biblical Literature, 2015), 164–85. Barker, *From the Depths of Despair*, 93–106, distinguishes 1:15–20 from 1:1–14, but I see the speech in 1:15–20 as

pressed on days of fasting.¹³ But as the reader enters into chapter 2 there is a subtle shift in language. The exhortation is to blow a trumpet and to sound an alarm, language associated with both religious assembly as well as military muster.¹⁴ The shift to more severe cosmological and martial imagery in chapter 2 then follows ending with the desperate question regarding the great and very awesome day of Yhwh: "who can endure it?" in 2:11b. It is then that the prophetic voice reveals that the solemn assembly to which the priests are to gather the people is to be one that transcends the language of lament first voiced in 1:15–20 and instead is to feature the actions, attitudes, and words of penitence according to 1:12–13. Balancing the question "who can endure it?" in 2:11b is now the question "Who knows whether He will not turn and relent and leave a blessing behind him, even a grain offering and a drink offering for the LORD your God?" in 2:14, alluding by reference to the grain and drink offerings to the focus on the temple service and personnel at the heart of chapter 1 (1:8–9). The first question (2:11b) focuses on the possibility of the survival of members of the community, the second (2:14) on the possibility that Yhwh will allow their survival. What lies between the two questions is a series of exhortations related to repentance based on the gracious character of Yhwh; clearly the only hopeful path is linked to a penitential community (2:12–13a) and the sovereign grace of Yhwh (2:13b).¹⁵

---

embedded within the final call to the priests; cf. Assis, *Book of Joel*, 99 (even though Assis refers to 1:13–15 as a "call to the people").

¹³ Hermann Gunkel and Joachim Begrich, *Einleitung in die Psalmen: Die Gattungen der religiösen Lyrik Israels* (2nd ed.; Göttingen: Vandenhoeck & Ruprecht, 1933), 117–21; cf. Édouard Lipiński, *La liturgie pénitentielle dans la Bible* (LD 52; Paris: Les éditions du Cerf, 1969), 27–35.

¹⁴ רוע: religious assembly—e.g., 1 Sam 4:5; Ezra 3:11, 13; martial—e.g., Num 10:9; Josh 6:5, 10, 16, 20; Judg 7:21; 15:14; 1 Sam 10:24; 17:52; Isa 42:13; Hos 5:8; see Num 10:1–10 for the close relationship between these two uses. שופר (תקע): religious assembly—e.g., Exod 20:18; Lev 25:9; Ps 81:4 (Eng. 3); 2 Sam 6:15; martial—e.g., Judg 3:27; 6:34; 7:18, 20; Neh 4:12; Jer 6:1; see Josh 6:4–20 for the close relationship between these two uses.

¹⁵ There has been considerable debate over the meaning of שוב in Joel 2:12–13, whether it refers to repentance from sin or a return to God in faith or prayer; see Mark J. Boda, *A Severe Mercy: Sin and Its Remedy in the Old Testament* (Siphrut: Literature and Theology of the Hebrew Scriptures 1; Winona Lake, IN: Eisenbrauns, 2009), 304–9, for the former, and Assis, *Book of Joel*, and Ronald A. Simkins, "'Return to Yahweh': Honor and Shame in Joel," *Semeia* 68 (1994): 41–54. While it is true that no reference is made to sin in Joel, the placement of Joel within the Book of the Twelve, especially after Hos 14:1–3, and before Amos 4, shapes the reader's (and rereader's) understanding of שוב; see Aaron Schart, *Die Entstehung des Zwölfprophetenbuchs* (BZAW 260; Berlin: de

As the earlier exhortations in 1:13–14 ended with the provision of words for the priests to cry in lament (1:15–20), so the final exhortations to the priests in 2:15–16 provide a priestly prayer in 2:17, a prayer that cries for God's mercy and motivates this request by appeal not to the severe predicament of the people but to the honor of YHWH's name among the nations. The use of a question in the prayer echoes the earlier questions in 2:11b and 2:14 (cf. 1:2b).[16] The prayer for mercy, however, is uttered now in light of the call for repentance in 1:12–13. We see then a shift between 1:13–20 and 2:1–17, the first section calling the priests to organize a day of fasting to lament the deplorable situation and the second section calling the priests to organize a day of fasting to return to God.[17]

What follows in 2:18–27 is YHWH's response or expected response to the penitential liturgy outlined in 2:1–17. YHWH's zeal is aroused to show pity upon his people and his answer entails the promise of agricultural renewal in 1:19–20, 23b–27. At the centre of this divine answer to the people are three exhortations, reminiscent of the exhortations which punctuate 1:2–2:17, replacing the negative language of weeping, wailing, mourning, shaming, lamenting and calls to days of national emergency with the positive language of rejoicing and not fearing in 2:21–23a. In verses 21–23a the land (1:10; cf. 1:8), the beasts of the field (1:20; cf. 1:18), and the community (1:12) are all exhorted to respond to YHWH's gracious act. Interestingly, the people are described as בני ציון ("children of Zion"),

---

Gruyter, 1998), 176, 266; James D. Nogalski, *Redactional Processes in the Book of the Twelve* (BZAW 218; Berlin: de Gruyter, 1993), 19–22; James D. Nogalski, "Joel as 'Literary Anchor' for the Book of the Twelve," in *Reading and Hearing the Book of the Twelve* (ed. James D. Nogalski and Marvin A. Sweeney; SymS 15; Atlanta: Society of Biblical Literature, 2000), 92–99; Jörg Jeremias, "The Function of the Book of Joel for Reading the Twelve," in *Perspectives on the Formation of the Book of the Twelve: Methodological Foundations, Redactional Processes, Historical Insights* (ed. Rainer Albertz, James Nogalski, and Jakob Wöhrle; BZAW 433; Berlin: de Gruyter, 2012), 84; Paul R. House, *The Unity of the Twelve* (Bible and Literature Series 27; Sheffield, England: Almond, 1990), 130, and LeCureux, *Thematic Unity*, 120–28. Connections to Haggai-Malachi in the present article provide further evidence for this understanding of Joel's use of שוב.

[16] See especially Lyons, "Interpretation and Structure," 101, who notes how the three questions in 2:11, 14, 17 signal the climax of the rhetorical unit. Assis, *Book of Joel*, 65, sees a progression in the rhetoric of 1:2–2:17, climaxing for him in his fourth oracle in 2:15–17. Assis focuses on the prayer dimension of 2:17. The present article, while not losing sight of the prayer, seeks to highlight the role of the priests and demand of repentance.

[17] As Assis, *Book of Joel*, 17, has noted, 2:16–17 is not a prayer but a command to pray and so 2:18ff. simulates how God would respond to this kind of prayer (and I would add repentance).

focusing their identity on Zion, the place of YHWH's temple and worship of his name facilitated by the priests.

The evidence above highlights the key role that the priests play in the rhetoric of the book of Joel. While the agricultural disaster does prompt the lament of both producer and consumer alike, the land's concern is for its inability to supply the temple cult (1:8–10). This is why the priests are the dominant recipients of the exhortative text and why their leadership, not in a liturgy of lament but in a liturgy of repentance, is what leads to the resolution of the predicament. If this is true for an agricultural crisis, it is certainly true for the military crisis veiled here through imagery and probably bringing into view the importance of repentance to the restoration of the community after the destruction of Zion. Certainly, the concern for God's name endangered by severe disaster of his nation is reminiscent of passages like Ps 79 (cf. v. 19; cf. Deut 29:24–26; 1 Kgs 9:6–9; Jer 22:8–9).

The book of Joel then calls priests to play a key role within the community when they faced national crises.[18] Allusions to a "day" far more significant than an agricultural disaster, suggests a role that the priests could play during the exilic period and the passage which immediately follows 1:2–2:27, that is, 3:1–5 (Eng. 2:28–32), shows that beyond agricultural restoration is a vision for national restoration as "those who escape" and "the survivors" are delivered safely to Mount Zion/Jerusalem (3:5 [Eng. 2:32]). Allusions to exile and restoration can also be discerned in chapter 4 (4:1, 2 [Eng. 3:1, 2]).[19]

2. ZECHARIAH 7–8, FASTING, PENITENCE, AND PRIESTS

With this overview of the rhetorical structure of Joel in mind we now turn to the book of Zechariah in order to highlight similarities and differences.

Even on a cursory reading of the book of Zechariah one discerns significant contrasts between sections of the book. Most have noted the contrast between chapters 1–8 and chapters 9–14, but there are distinctions also within these sections with 1:1–6 and 7:1–8:23 standing apart from 1:7–6:15 within chapters 1–8 and chapters 9–10 standing apart from chapters 12–14 as well as chapter 11

---

[18] Thus, slightly different from Stephen L. Cook, *Prophecy and Apocalypticism: The Postexilic Social Setting* (Minneapolis, MN: Fortress, 1995), 167–209, who sees Joel as prompting support for the Zadokite priestly programs. See Sweeney, "Place and Function of Joel," 138, who considers Joel as "designed to have an impact on the perspective of its audience that will prompt it to some sort of decision or action." For a rhetorical approach to Joel, see Barker, *From the Depths of Despair*.

[19] For the exilic context for the genesis of the Joel tradition, see Assis, *Book of Joel*.

within chapters 9–14.[20] At the same time there are rhetorical connections which integrate the materials found in chapters 1–8 (e.g. "the word of YHWH came to me," 4:8; 7:4; 8:18) on the one side and chapters 9–14 on the other (e.g. the shepherd units). The greatest disjunction within the book lies in the transition between chapters 8 and 9. This disjunction has been played down in the recent work of Marvin Sweeney.[21] Taking the historical introductions at 1:1, 7; and 7:1 as discourse markers for the literary structure of the book, he identifies 7:1–14:21 as a single literary unit. While most scholars have focused on 7:1–8:23 as the concluding unit of chapters 1–8, Sweeney identifies it as the introductory unit to chapters 7–14. In the past I have identified chapters 7–8 as a rhetorical transition within the book, moving the reader from restoration realized to restoration frustrated.[22] It may be better to reframe this as two visions of restoration: one realized through repentance and the other through refinement.[23]

Zechariah 7:1–8:23 surprises the reader who has progressed from Zech 1–6. The opening scene depicts the community embracing the penitential message of the prophet, repenting and confessing YHWH's justice and their culpability in line with the penitential prayer tradition.[24] Zechariah 1:8–17, the opening unit of the next major section of Zechariah (1:7–6:15), echoes the call to repentance in 1:1–6 employing similar vocabulary (e.g. קרא, קצף, שוב) to show YHWH's fulfillment of his promise to return to the people when they had returned to him.[25] The visions and oracles throughout Zech 1:7–6:15 emphasize the implications of YHWH's return to the people including the reconstruction of city and temple, renewal of prosperity to the land, vengeance upon past enemies, return of a vibrant community, restoration of human leadership, and removal of sin from the

---

[20] For more detail on these issues, see Mark J. Boda, *Zechariah* (NICOT; Grand Rapids, MI: Eerdmans, 2015).

[21] Marvin A. Sweeney, *The Twelve Prophets* (2 vols.; Berit Olam; Collegeville, MN: Liturgical, 2000), 2:634–36.

[22] See Mark J. Boda, "From Fasts to Feasts: The Literary Function of Zechariah 7–8," *CBQ* 65 (2003): 390–407.

[23] One finds the same two agendas for renewal for Zion at the outset of the book of Isaiah with repentance the focus of Isa 1:1–20 (esp. 1:19) and refinement the focus of 1:21–31 (foreshadowed in 1:20), see Boda, *Severe Mercy*, 191–93.

[24] See Mark J. Boda, "Zechariah: Master Mason or Penitential Prophet?" in *Yahwism after the Exile: Perspectives on Israelite Religion in the Persian Era* (ed. Bob Becking and Rainer Albertz; Studies in Theology and Religion 5; Assen: Royal Van Gorcum, 2003), 49–69.

[25] Jakob Wöhrle, *Die frühen Sammlungen des Zwölfprophetenbuches: Entstehung und Komposition* (BZAW 360; Berlin: de Gruyter, 2006), 375–80, and Mike Butterworth, *Structure and the Book of Zechariah* (JSOTS 130; Sheffield: Sheffield Academic, 1992), 80–94, 241.

land. This final element is the focus of the two vision-oracle reports in chapter 5 and calls into question the authenticity or comprehensiveness of the initial penitential response of the community in 1:6b.[26] Concern over the penitential response and thus the fulfillment of the divine promises throughout Zech 1:7–6:15 increases in the final clause of this section of Zechariah in 6:15b: והיה אם־שמוע תשמעון בקול יהוה אלהיכם ("and it will take place if you completely obey YHWH your God").[27] In the immediate context of the report of a prophetic sign-act in 6:9–15, this calls into question whether the temple of YHWH will be rebuilt which in 1:16 is the first sign that YHWH had reciprocated by returning to Jerusalem.[28] The condition placed on fulfillment of the hopes of Zech 1–6 in 6:15b is then made clearer in what follows in chapters 7–8. The vague obedience in 6:15b now is linked to social justice in chapters 7–8. Thus, chapters 7–8 do represent an important juncture in the book of Zechariah. What was thought to be resolved at the outset of the book is now called into question, linked to a lack of repentance by the people in relation to social justice. Interestingly the priests at the temple of YHWH are implicated in the prophetic speech in 7:5 as the people are called to move from commemorative to penitential fasts.[29] Thus, the rhetorical focus of the first half of the book of Zechariah is placed on the anticipated response articulated in 6:15b–8:23.

---

[26] See Lena-Sofia Tiemeyer, *Priestly Rites and Prophetic Rage: Post-exilic Prophetic Critique of the Priesthood* (FAT 2/19; Tübingen: Mohr Siebeck, 2006), 143–46, for the possible connection between Zech 5:1–4 and priests. See Tiemeyer, *Priestly Rites*, 248–55, and Mark J. Boda, "Perspectives on Priests in Haggai-Malachi," in *Prayer and Poetry in the Dead Sea Scrolls and Related Literature: Essays in Honor of Eileen Schuller on the Occasion of Her 65th Birthday* (ed. Jeremy S. Penner, Ken Penner, and Cecilia Wassen; STDJ 98; Leiden: Brill, 2011), 13–33, on Zech 3 and critique of priestly justice.

[27] That 6:15b was probably added at a later point can be seen in the fact that it follows the phrase: "then you will know that YHWH of hosts has sent me to you." While the phrase "those coming from far off to build the temple" is first linked to the authenticity of the prophet, lack of fulfillment is secondly linked to inactivity of the people.

[28] I make a distinction between YHWH returning and YHWH taking up residence in a rebuilt temple/Jerusalem. The first is a covenantal response in line with the people's return to YHWH in 1:6b and is considered completed according to 1:16 (שבתי, suffix conjugation), while the second is still future according to 1:16 (יבנה, ינטה, prefix conjugation) and 2:14–15 [Eng. 10–11] (ושכנתי, *waw*/relative suffix conjugation). See further Boda, *Zechariah*, 142–43.

[29] Cf. Tiemeyer, *Priestly Rites*, 94–97.

3. JOEL AND ZECHARIAH

Zechariah 7–8 bears striking similarities to Joel 1–2. Both texts begin with a focus on the entire community before drawing in priestly leadership. Both express concern over the devastation of the land. Both consider the role that mourning, fasting, and penitential rituals play in reversing this devastation. There are, of course, differences. In Joel the rhetoric is directed by the prophet towards the people and priests, calling them to mourn and fast over their predicament, while in Zech 7 the people of the land approach the prophet and priests with an enquiry related to their practice of mourning and fasting over their predicament. While in Joel the priests are given a key role to play in organizing the mourning, fasting, and penitential rituals, in Zech 7 the people have been eagerly pursuing mourning and fasting, apparently under the supervision of the priests (since they are seeking advice from them), but have not been embracing the penitential dimension that is so key to Joel 1–2. Not surprisingly, then, Zech 7–8 emphasizes a lack of response from the deity to the community's cries (7:13) although maintaining hope for future resolution of the predicament once penitence was expressed (8:16–19). Thus, while the priests play a key role in promoting the prophetic penitential message in Joel 1–2, the priests are accused along with the people of inappropriate fasting (unaccompanied by repentance) in Zech 7–8 (e.g. 7:5–6).

In both Joel and Zechariah the address to the priests related to fasting and repentance lies at a key juncture in the book, showing the potential for a significant transformation if the penitential cry is heeded.[30] This transformation will entail a transformation of the land and city in both cases as well as a return of the community and YHWH, and judgment of and hegemony over the nations.

Thus, in the overall flow of the Book of the Twelve, Joel provides a template for repentance, along with Jonah inserting a vision of hope for repentance into the first half of the book of the Twelve where there is little optimism expressed by the prophets over human ability to repent.[31] Joel focuses particularly on the role that priests should play in promoting penitence, but it is clear from Zech 7–8 that while the priests seem to be in charge of promoting lament, they

---

[30] If one places Joel in the exilic period with Assis, *Book of Joel*, then this brings Joel and Zechariah together with the Babylonian/early Persian period Penitential Prayer tradition. Cf. Mark J. Boda, *Praying the Tradition: The Origin and Use of Tradition in Nehemiah 9* (BZAW 277; Berlin: de Gruyter, 1999), 189–95, and Boda, "Penitential Prophet."

[31] See Mark J. Boda, "Penitential Innovations in the Book of the Twelve," in *On Stone and Scroll: A Festschrift for Graham Davies* (ed. Brian A. Mastin, Katharine J. Dell, and James K. Aitken; BZAW 420; Berlin: de Gruyter, 2011), 291–308.

are not promoting repentance, so that God will not answer them and they will not move from fasts to feasts. Thus, we see in Joel the agenda for repentance and in Zech 7–8 a confrontation of the priests over their lack of fulfillment of this agenda.[32]

4. JOEL AND THE HAGGAI-MALACHI CORPUS

This similarity between the books of Joel and Zechariah is also apparent in the other two books of Haggai-Malachi corpus.[33] Haggai also emphasizes the need for repentance, related to a major agricultural crisis and to priests who are sacrificing for a people who are not penitent.[34] As with Joel there is an expansion from an initial transformation on the historical level (Hag 2:19b) to a more cosmic and eschatological level (2:20–23). Similarly, Malachi emphasizes the theme of repentance related to priests and community, with some connections to Joel in terms of inappropriate sacrifices and weeping/mourning over the altar with a lack of repentance and priestly involvement. As with the other books there is a shift to the eschatological and cosmic level in Mal 3 (Eng. chapters 3–4).

Joel and the Haggai-Malachi corpus are closely related in emphasizing priestly leadership in penitential response[35] and placing this penitential response

---

[32] Cf. LeCureux, *Thematic Unity*, 126, who sees Joel 2:12–14 as "a kind of intermediate step" between the call to return in Hos 14 and the calls in Zech 1:3; Mal 3:7. LeCureux does not focus on the call to repentance in Zech 7–8 because his study is limited to the root שוב rather than the concept of repentance. Cf. Mark J. Boda, *"Return to Me": A Biblical Theology of Repentance* (NSBT 35; Leicester: Apollos, 2015), 24–32.

[33] For the Haggai-Malachi corpus, see Mark J. Boda, "Messengers of Hope in Haggai-Malachi," *JSOT* 32 (2007): 113–31. Another point of connection is one observed by Lyons based on Barton's assertion that besides Joel 2:18–19a, "the only other parallel of narrative breaking into prophetic material" is Mal 3:16–17. See Lyons, "Interpretation and Structure," 101; cf. Barton, *Joel and Obadiah*, 87. This feature of narratival description of response within the Twelve is also evident in Hag 1:12–15 and Zech 1:1–6. This may also explain the connections between Joel, Haggai-Malachi and the book of Jonah which is dominated by narrative description. Cf. Boda, "Penitential Innovations."

[34] See Boda, "Perspectives on Priests."

[35] By this I am not suggesting "anticultic" prophecy, since the rhetorical hope is for priestly leadership. See especially Barton, *Joel and Obadiah*, 80. There appears to be hope throughout the collection for transformation of the priestly caste.

at the transition between curse and blessing, a blessing with historical and local as well as eschatological and cosmic implications.³⁶

5. JOEL, THE HAGGAI-MALACHI CORPUS, AND THE BOOK OF THE TWELVE

Nogalski has highlighted the role that Joel played in the development of the Book of the Twelve. For him Joel was key to bringing together the older Deuteronomistic Corpus (original Hosea, Amos, Micah, Zephaniah) with an original Haggai-Zech 1–8 corpus.³⁷ Wöhrle also emphasizes the role of Joel in the redaction of the Twelve. For him the book of Joel replaced Hosea at the head of the growing corpus which became the Book of the Twelve and so was influential on "all further redactional levels of the Book of the Twelve."³⁸ Not surprisingly then several have noted the key role that Joel plays in reading the Book of the Twelve. For example, Sweeney argues that Joel establishes "the paradigm for Jerusalem's punishment and restoration."³⁹ For Nogalski Joel is the "literary anchor" which unifies major literary threads in the Twelve.⁴⁰ Nogalski focuses

---

³⁶ See LeCureux, *Thematic Unity*, 118, on the interlinking of the Day of YHWH and return motifs in the Twelve and Joel's role in this development.

³⁷ E.g., Nogalski, *Redactional Processes*, 275–78. Of course, Nogalski's "Joel layer" included also Nahum, Habakkuk, Obadiah, and Malachi. Nogalski, "Joel as 'Literary Anchor,'" 92, notes three ways Joel unifies major literary threads in the Twelve: "dovetailing genres, recurring vocabulary, and the presumption of a 'historical paradigm' that 'transcends' the chronological framework of the dated superscriptions."

³⁸ Schart, *Entstehung*, 316–17, sees Joel (along with Obadiah and Zech 9–14) as a later addition after the Haggai-Zech 1–8 Corpus had been combined with an earlier collection that included the Deuteronomistic Corpus and Nahum and Habakkuk.

³⁹ Sweeney, *Twelve*, 149; cf. Sweeney, "Place and Function of Joel." Note, however, that Sweeney, "Place and Function of Joel," 152, thinks that Joel's placement in the OG sequence (Hosea, Amos, Micah, Joel...) "provides for a far more logically consistent progression among the individual books" than the MT sequence. The OG order focuses on the use of the experience of northern Israel (Hosea, Amos, Micah) as "a model or paradigm for that of Jerusalem" (Joel), while the MT focuses on Jerusalem throughout and "provides a typological portrayal of Jerusalem's experience in relation to the nations." The OG order was relevant to the Babylonian and early Persian periods, while the MT to the late-Persian, Hellenistic, Hasmonean or Roman periods. Cf. LeCureux, *Thematic Unity*, 117.

⁴⁰ Nogalski, "Joel as 'Literary Anchor'," 105. This has been affirmed by Paul L. Redditt, "The Production and Reading of the Book of the Twelve," in *Reading and Hearing the Book of the Twelve* (ed. James D. Nogalski and Marvin A. Sweeney; SymS 15; Atlanta: Society of Biblical Literature, 2000), 17, who thinks that Joel is either the

on the way Joel relates to the call to repentance at the end of the book of Hosea. Jeremias calls Joel "a kind of hermeneutical key to the Twelve" which, due to its literary placement among the Twelve, shapes the reader's view of the material which follows in the collection.[41]

The works of Nogalski, Sweeney, and Jeremias focus most attention on the placement of Joel among the earlier books in the twelve.[42] In the present work we have noted striking similarities between Joel and the Haggai-Malachi corpus suggesting a connection between Joel and the literary efforts of those responsible for the Haggai-Malachi corpus. More importantly, these similarities highlight a key rhetorical purpose of this literary activity and as a result of the Book of the Twelve as a whole. This prophetic collection is designed at least in part to prompt a penitential response from the priestly caste, both in terms of turning from sinful patterns which were probably linked to injustice in the temple courts, but also in terms of taking up their role as penitential catalysts within the community that had survived the catastrophes of the sixth century BCE.

---

work of a key redactor of the Twelve (with Nogalski) or "the book exerted strong influence on the redactors of the Twelve."

[41] Jeremias, "Function of the Book of Joel," 21–34.

[42] See also Jason LeCureux's article in the present collection.

4

JOEL, THE CULT, AND THE BOOK OF THE TWELVE

Jason T. LeCureux

Attempting to study the book of Joel is always a challenging endeavour. The lack of scholarly consensus on almost all aspects of the book, most significantly its date, shows that it is one of the more difficult prophetic books to interpret. This difficulty is especially noticeable in regard to Joel's relationship to the cult. Scholars have variously found Joel a prophet directly connected with the central Jerusalem sanctuary to a collected composition from outsiders who preached against the central authorities' abuses. As discussed below, many believe the book functions as temple liturgy. Such diverse readings lay out significantly different relationships between the book of Joel, the role of the prophet, the sacrificial system, and especially the priesthood. These issues are further complicated by the second half of the book, which leaves the temple setting behind and envisions an age of restoration for Israel when the nations are judged, and YHWH's spirit is poured out on all flesh. This paper will argue that because Joel is an exilic text, but was incorporated into the Book of the Twelve (BT), the writing takes on anticultic overtones, particularly in chapters 1–2 and the call to return in 2:12–14. The prophet's diminished view of the cult and priesthood ultimately envisions a relationship with YHWH apart from the cultic setting, a reading which may not exist independently of Joel's location in the Twelve.

1. Joel's Relationship with the Cult in Scholarship

As mentioned above, scholars have long associated Joel with the Jerusalem cult in varying and complicated capacities. Kapelrud identifies Joel as a "temple-prophet" whose sayings were "preserved in certain circles which were associated with the temple."[1] He claims that the outpouring of the Spirit in Joel 3:1–5[2] is a type of ecstatic ritual, in which Joel as a temple prophet participated in some way in the cultic ritual.[3] Ahlström contends that while Joel is a postexilic prophet, his rebuke, much like the preexilic prophets, is against a corrupt temple and sacrificial system that has fallen into a preexilic type of syncretism.[4] He argues, however, that despite the cultic critique, the book is nonetheless filled with cultic language and closely associated with a liturgical lament, though the book itself is a literary work rather than a liturgical one.[5] The argument that Joel contains cultic liturgy, but is not actual liturgy, is also reflected notably in Wolff, Ogden, Allen, and Barton.[6]

---

[1] Arvid S. Kapelrud, *Joel Studies* (Uppsala: A. B. Lundequistska Bokhandeln, 1948), 176.

[2] All versification will follow the MT. There is a discrepancy between the MT and the English versions as Joel 3:1–5 (MT) aligns with Joel 2:28–32 (Eng.); and Joel 3:1–21 (MT) corresponds to Joel 4:1–21 (Eng.).

[3] Kapelrud, *Joel Studies*, 133. Kapelrud argues this based on a connection between Joel 3:1–5 and Zech 12:10 (126–40). It is important to note, however, that while Kapelrud believes that Joel played a part in cultic ritual, he was a temple prophet, associated with the priesthood, but was not a priest himself (182–87).

[4] Gösta W. Ahlström, *Joel and the Temple Cult of Jerusalem* (VTSup 21; Leiden: Brill, 1971), 28.

[5] Ahlström, *Joel and the Temple Cult*, 130–31. While Ahlström makes it clear that he draws a distinction between the literary book of Joel and actual temple liturgy, when reading his work the influence of the cult is so strong that finding this distinction is difficult, or at least in some cases, impractical.

[6] Hans Walter Wolff, *Joel and Amos* (trans. Waldemar Janzen, S. Dean McBride Jr., Charles A. Muenchow; Hermeneia; Philadelphia: Fortress, 1977), 9; Graham S. Ogden, "Joel 4 and Prophetic Responses to National Laments," *JSOT* 26 (1983): 97–106 (97); Leslie C. Allen, *The Books of Joel, Obadiah, Jonah, and Micah* (NICOT; Grand Rapids, MI: Eerdmans, 1976), 31, and John Barton, *Joel and Obadiah* (OTL; Louisville, KY: Westminster John Knox, 2001), 21. Allen believes Joel to be a member of the cultic prophets, associated with the temple, who produced psalms. However, he maintains that the eschatological nature of the book precludes it from being used as cultic liturgy.

Engnell differs slightly from those above by identifying Joel and Habakkuk as cultic liturgy.[7] Carroll and Coggins[8] reflect a similar position by identifying Joel as a cult prophet. Cook, however, goes a step further and incorporates Joel fully into the cult by arguing that the book is the product of a priestly, postexilic, proto-apocalyptic group that was centred at the temple. According to him, this group "pictures Joel as an official of the central cult" and that "the end-time language of Joel is the product of a group of the priests in control at Jerusalem."[9] Sweeney seems to agree with Cook's position, and similar to Allen, proposes the possibility that Joel was a "prophetic Temple singer."[10]

From the above, it would appear that the connection between Joel, the cult, and liturgy at least in some form, is well established. However, the details of that connection remain in dispute, best illustrated by Garrett and Dillard, who question the very existence of "cult prophets."[11] The issue is indeed a complex one. Even Wolff, who finds liturgical influence in the composition of the book, ultimately places Joel in an outside, literary eschatological "opposition party" similar to those who composed Jonah.[12]

---

[7] Ivan Engnell, *Critical Essays on the Old Testament* (trans. John T. Willis; London: SPCK, 1970), 167.

[8] Robert P. Carroll, "Eschatological Delay in the Prophetic Tradition?" *ZAW* 94 (1982): 47–58, and Richard Coggins, "An Alternative Prophetic Tradition?" in *Israel's Prophetic Tradition: Essays in Honour of Peter R. Ackroyd* (ed. Richard Coggins, Anthony Phillips, and Michael Knibb; Cambridge: Cambridge University Press, 1982), 77–94.

[9] Stephen L. Cook, *Prophecy and Apocalypticism* (Minneapolis, MN: Fortress Press, 1995), 194.

[10] Marvin Sweeney, *The Twelve Prophets* (2 vols.; Berit Olam; Collegeville, Minnesota: Liturgical Press, 2000), 1:151.

[11] Duane A. Garrett, *Hosea, Joel* (New American Commentary 19A; Nashville, TN: Broadman & Holman, 1997), 297; Raymond Dillard, "Joel," in *The Minor Prophets*. Vol. 1 *Hosea, Joel, and Amos* (ed. Thomas Edward McComiskey; Grand Rapids, MI: Baker, 1992), 239–313 (239). Despite his objections to Joel as cult prophet, Garrett still believes that Joel envisions repentance as taking place within the confines of the temple and the cult (298). He repeats a similar argument against Kapelrud, Ahlström, and Ogden in idem, "Joel, Book of," *DOTP* 4:449–455 (449).

[12] Wolff, *Joel and Amos*, 12. Theodore Hiebert, "Joel," in *ABD* 3:872–79 (874, 877–78), likewise denies Joel the position of cult prophet, and places him within a society that was distinct from the cult, though he believes Joel also uses temple liturgical language.

2. Priestly Function in Joel

So what has led to such diverse views on Joel's role, his relationship to the cult, and the overall function of the book itself? Much of the conflict is centred on the restoration sections found in chapters 3–4, as well as the understanding of the role that the Day of YHWH plays within the book. But perhaps the more foundational issue is the uncertain nature of Joel's call to return (2:12–14) and the prophet's view of the cult laid out in the first two chapters.

The amount of literature devoted to Joel's cultic connections is indeed disproportional to the references to priests and sacrifices found in the book itself. Priests (כהן) are mentioned only three times in the book, all within the first two chapters (1:9, 13; 2:17), and all with some connection to mourning (1:9 אבל, 1:13 ספד, ילל, 2:17 בכה). In all three instances, the priests are additionally described as "ministers" (שרת, four times total) either of YHWH (1:9, 2:17) or of the altar and "my God" (1:13). In each instance, the priests are among a group of societal representatives (elders/people [1:2; 2:16],[13] children [1:3; 2:16], drunkards [שכור 1:5], and farmers [1:11]) who are being addressed by the prophet.

The lists of priestly actions in 1:13–14, and 2:15–17 are similar, focused mainly on mourning[14] and calling the people to assembly. In chapter 1, however, the mourning/lamenting is tied specifically to the lack of grain/drink offerings (1:9, 13), a categorical parallel similar to the drunkards being called to wail because of a lack of wine (1:5). The call to wear sackcloth (1:13; cf. 1:8) is not only a priestly responsibility, but ideally that of the whole nation as it mourns the destructive invasion. Admittedly, chapter 2 offers a few more specific actions for the priests, such as blowing the shophar (2:15) and a detailed reference to a location in the temple (2:17).[15] The latter is perhaps the strongest evidence for Joel's knowledge of the temple's interworking, but as will be discussed below, this knowledge is not exclusive, or perhaps as telling as it may first appear.

From the first two chapters, Joel knows where the priests work ("between the vestibule and the altar," 2:17), that they sound the shophar and gather the people together for holy assemblies before the temple (1:14; 2:15); and that they weep and cry out to YHWH (1:9; 2:17). Leaving aside for a moment the actions

---

[13] In fact, "elders" occur as frequently as "priests" in the first two chapters (though 4x in the entire book 1:2, 14; 2:16; 3:1).

[14] Along with the drunkards (1:5), the priests (1:13) and the farmers (1:11) are also told to "wail" (ילל).

[15] The term "temple" (היכל) does not appear in Joel in reference to the Jerusalem Temple. However, the terms "house" (בית, 1:9, 13, 14, 16; 4:18) and Zion (ציון, 2:1, 15, 23; 4:16, 17, 21) appear frequently.

of 2:12–14, the above knowledge of the priesthood is far from extensive, and does not demonstrate a knowledge of priestly temple function surpassing that of anyone living in Jerusalem or who visited the temple, as many prophets did. It definitely does not demand that Joel become a member of the temple elite, a cultic prophet, or a temple singer.[16]

Along with this, the absence of any kind of detailed discussion concerning sacrifice is noticeable. The only cult offerings specifically mentioned are drink-offerings and grain offerings in chapters 1–2 (1:9, 13; 2:14; cf. Amos 2:8; 3:14; 4:4–5; 5:21–26). This issue is particularly important in the famous verses of Joel 2:12–14, which lacks specific mention of cultic sacrifice.

In Joel 2, the locust invasion of chapter 1 has morphed into a full scale invasion of enemy armies,[17] more locusts,[18] or more metaphors[19] depending on the commentator. In the face of this invasion, the prophet calls out:

> [12]"But even now," declares YHWH "return to me with all your heart, with fasting, weeping, and mourning." [13]Rend your hearts and not your garments. Return to YHWH your God, for gracious and compassionate is he, slow to anger and abounding in covenant kindness, and he relents from evil. [14]Who knows? He may turn and relent and leave a blessing after him—a gift and drink offering for YHWH your God. (Joel 2:12–14)

The appeal, and problems, of these verses are fairly obvious. The call to return (שוב), apart from any mention of sin and cultic specifics is so open as to allow commentators to find support for every personal position. At the heart of the issue is the debate surrounding the nature of Joel's statements in 2:12 (i.e. whether or not repentance is in the mind of the prophet) and whether or not the people have committed covenant violations. It is indeed a unique situation,[20] and both sides are well represented by commentators. Ahlström, Wolff, Allen,

---

[16] In fact, Joel demonstrates a far greater knowledge of wine (יין, 1:5; 4:3 / עסיס, 1:5; 4:18 / תירוש, 1:10; 2:19, 24) than of "priests," yet no one argues that Joel should take his place among the drunkards.

[17] E.g., Sweeney, *Twelve Prophets*, 161; Wolff, *Joel-Amos*, 42, though slightly nuanced as an "apocalyptic enemy army"; Gordon McConville, *Exploring the Old Testament: A Guide to the Prophets*, vol. 4 (Downers Grove, IL: InterVarsity Press, 2002), 160, and Garrett, "Joel, Book of," 452–53.

[18] Barton, *Joel and Obadiah*, 44, and Hiebert, "Joel, Book of," 875.

[19] Ogden, "Prophetic Responses," 104–5.

[20] Douglas Stuart, *Hosea-Jonah* (WBC 31; Waco, TX: Word, 1987), 231, claims that Habakkuk and Nahum also deliver prophecies of judgment without specific mention of sin. However, Hab 1:1–5, as well as the mention of "city of blood" in Nah 3:1, at least offers some indication of human violations.

Sweeney, Stuart, Hayes, and Redditt all find some kind of fault, even if it is unmentioned in the text;[21] while Barton, Crenshaw, Ogden, Simkins, Linville, Watson, and Assis do not.[22] In general, those arguing that Joel finds no fault with the people believe that שוב is not a call to repentance, but rather a call for the people to turn back to God in supplication.[23] Overall, however, it seems that those holding this position have not taken seriously enough Joel's canonical position; the role of YHWH at the head of the destroying army in 2:11;[24] as well as the punishing roles that the Day of YHWH (cf. Amos 5:18–20; Zeph 1) and

---

[21] Ahlström, *Joel and the Temple Cult*, 26 (Baalism); Wolff, *Joel-Amos*, 49 (prideful cult practices that diminish the prophetic word); Allen, *Joel, Obadiah, Jonah, and Micah*, 78–79 (unspecified covenant violation); Sweeney, *Twelve Prophets*, 164 (unspecified); Stuart, *Hosea-Jonah*, 231 (unspecified covenant violation); Katherine Hayes, '*The Earth Mourns*': *Prophetic Metaphor and Oral Aesthetic* (AcBib 8; Leiden: Brill, 2002), 196–99 (unspecified), and Paul Redditt, "The Book of Joel and Peripheral Prophecy," *CBQ* 48 (1986): 225–40 (priests relegated their duties during the crisis).

[22] Barton, *Joel-Obadiah*, 77–80; James L. Crenshaw, "Who Knows What YHWH Will Do? The Character of God in the Book of Joel," in *Fortunate the Eyes that See* (ed. Astrid B. Beck, Andrew H. Bartelt, Paul R. Raabe, and Chris A. Franke; Grand Rapids, MI: Eerdmans, 1995), 185–96; Ogden, "Joel 4," 105; Ronald Simkins, "'Return to Yahweh': Honor and Shame in Joel," *Semeia* 68 (1994): 41–54; James R. Linville, "The Day of Yahweh and the Mourning of the Priests in Joel," in *The Priests in the Prophets: The Portrayal of Priests, Prophets and Other Religious Specialists in the Latter Prophets* (ed. Lester L. Grabbe and Alice Ogden Bellis; JSOTS 408; London: T&T Clark, 2004), 98–114 (100–101); Douglas Watson, "Divine Attributes in the Book of Joel," *JSOT* 37 (2012): 109–29 (121), and Elie Assis, *The Book of Joel: A Prophet Between Calamity and Hope* (LHBOTS 581; New York: T&T Clark, 2013), 139–40.

[23] See Watson "Divine Attributes," 121, f. 42. Such a reading pushes Joel into the realm of theodicy (see James L. Crenshaw, "Who Knows What YHWH will Do?" 186–88). In a previous work, I have offered a detailed examination of every occurrence of שוב within the Twelve, and I would agree that שוב calls the people back into a relationship with YHWH, and YHWH back into a relationship with his people. However, the word does at times carry connotations of repentance, most notably Hos 14:2–3, 5 (Eng. 14:1–2, 4); Zech 1–6. See Jason T. LeCureux, *The Thematic Unity of the Book of the Twelve* (HBM 41; Sheffield: Sheffield Phoenix Press, 2012), 99–107, 180–192. William L. Holladay, *The Root ŠÛBH in the Old Testament* (Leiden: Brill, 1958), 78–79, notes the use of שוב in Joel 2:12 as meaning "repent!"

[24] This is further emphasized by the broader prophetic understanding of YHWH leading foreign ("northern," cf. Joel 2.20) nations against his own people for reasons of covenant violations (e.g. Isa 10:1–11; Jer 1:13–16; 6:22–23; Hos 8:10, 13:15–14:1 [Eng. 13:16]; Amos 6:14; Hab 1:1–11).

locusts (e.g. Amos 4:9; 7:1–2; Nah 3:17)[25] play in the Book of the Twelve. These aspects are especially important in light of Joel's well-documented intertextuality.[26]

The existence of covenant violations, however, is only part of the issue in regards to cultic matters. Joel 2 is a masterpiece of literary composition, beginning by carrying over the locust metaphor of chapter 1, then slowly bringing the march of that army from the far away hills (2:2) to the city, the walls, and then into the houses themselves (2:9). All of this builds to the slow reveal that it is YHWH himself at the head of this irresistible, destructive force and the threatening Day of YHWH (2:11). The prophet then calls the people to return with "fasting, and with weeping, and with mourning" (2:12), three minor ritual elements that have been a part of the prophet's call to the people since chapter 1 (1:13–14).[27] What is noticeably absent from the prophet's challenge in 2:12–14 is the lack of specific temple cultic ritual, or for that matter, a specific role for the priests. Instead, in its place, is a call that sounds very antiritualistic, "rend your hearts and not your garments" (2:13). Within this section, the only mention of sacrifice is the hope that YHWH's turning will leave behind enough of a blessing to offer grain and drink offerings (2:14).

In terms of cultic discussion, it is admittedly difficult to determine exactly what Joel envisions when he calls the people to return. While Wolff argues that Joel is calling the people away from priestly ritual toward eschatological prophecy,[28] most commentators disagree, and Linville's summary of the various commentaries is apt. "Typically, commentators say that, for Joel, the liturgical rites are an acceptable and important vehicle to express an inner-felt spirituality, even if the rites are not an end in themselves."[29] However, in light of the lack of specifics surrounding the cult laid out in the book, is such a conclusion obvious or mandated? Moreover, the choice to read Joel as part of the BT, along with Hosea and Amos, changes the context of this passage and offers a different lens

---

[25] LeCureux, *Thematic Unity,* 122–23; Stuart, *Hosea-Jonah,* 232. Cf. Linville, "Day of Yahweh," 100–101.

[26] See James D. Nogalski, "Joel as 'Literary Anchor' for the Book of the Twelve," in *Reading and Hearing the Book of the Twelve* (ed. James D. Nogalski and Marvin A. Sweeney; SymS 15; Atlanta: Society of Biblical Literature, 2000), 91–109. This is especially true given YHWH's characteristics displayed in Joel 2:13. See Christopher R. Seitz, *Prophecy and Hermeneutics* (Studies in Theological Interpretation; Grand Rapids, MI: Baker Academic, 2007), 216.

[27] Assis, *Book of Joel,* 143, and Sweeney, *Twelve Prophets,* 164.

[28] Wolff, *Joel-Amos,* 12–13.

[29] "The Day of Yahweh," 98. I also took a similar position in LeCureux, *Thematic Unity,* 124.

of interpretation in regards to Joel's use of cult, one I believe argues against a temple-centric and priest-centric background to this passage.[30]

3. Joel in the Book of the Twelve

Hosea's influence on Joel, particularly Hos 14, is important. As Sweeney has noted, Joel plays an important role in the development of the overall theology of the BT, and the emphasis in the BT differs between the LXX and the MT canonical orders dependent in large part on the position of the book.[31] In the MT, Joel introduces the concepts of the Day of YHWH, and the theological concerns about the future of Jerusalem, the latter of which, without Joel, would not be presented in detail until Micah (e.g. Mic 3:12–4:5). Thus, if one assumes that Joel's position within the Twelve is intentional, the surrounding books, particularly Hosea and Amos, take on special significance. Many of the problems discussed above, most significantly Joel failing to mention a specific fault, are relieved if Joel is read in light of Hosea. As Nogalski notes, "Hosea ends with an extended call to repentance to the northern kingdom, a call whose response is never narrated. Joel begins by doing the same for Jerusalem and Judah. Joel takes up the images of Hos 2 and its threat to the land while calling Judah and Jerusalem to re-

---

[30] Some scholars have been reluctant to adopt a Book of the Twelve approach to Joel, notably Linville, "Day of Yahweh," 100; Assis, *Book of Joel*, 4; cf. Ehud Ben Zvi, "Twelve Prophetic Books of 'The Twelve': Some Preliminary Considerations," in *Forming Prophetic Literature: Essays on Isaiah and the Twelve in Honor of John D. W. Watts* (ed. James W. Watts and Paul R. House; JSOTS 235; Sheffield: Sheffield Academic, 1995), 125–56. However, the practice has strong scholarly support, notably Jörg Jeremias, "The Function of the Book of Joel for Reading the Twelve," in *Perspectives on the Formation of the Book of the Twelve* (ed. Rainer Albertz, James D. Nogalski, and Jakob Wöhrle; BZAW 433; Berlin: de Gruyter; 2012), 77–88; Marvin A. Sweeney, "The Place and Function of Joel in the Book of the Twelve," in *Thematic Threads in the Book of the Twelve* (ed. Paul L. Redditt and Aaron Schart; BZAW 325; Berlin: de Gruyter, 2003), 133–54; James D. Nogalski, "Joel as 'Literary Anchor' for the Book of the Twelve," in *Reading and Hearing the Book of the Twelve* (ed. James D. Nogalski and Marvin A. Sweeney; SymS 15; Atlanta: Society of Biblical Literature, 2000), 91–109.

[31] Marvin A. Sweeney, "Sequence and Interpretation in the Book of the Twelve," in *Reading and Hearing the Book of the Twelve* (ed. James D. Nogalski, and Marvin A. Sweeney; SymS 15; Atlanta: Society of Biblical Literature, 2000), 49–64, and idem, "Place and Function," 154.

pent."³² Most significantly, the call to repentance that ends Hosea (Hos 14), and the covenant violations it implies, sets the context for Joel's opening chapter.³³

In Hosea 14:4 (Eng. 14.3), the prophet calls the people to renounce political alliance, military might, and a corrupt sacrificial system. The latter is a recurring theme in Hosea, and in general, the priests and cult are viewed as corrupt (4:6–9; 6:6; 8:11–13). In the closing chapter, the prophet calls the people back into a relationship with YHWH, four times using the word שוב, in language similar to that of Joel 2:12–14.³⁴ What is most important here, besides the imperative connections with שוב in both Hosea and Joel, is that Hosea, like Joel, calls the people back to YHWH with language that seems intentionally to circumvent the cult. "Take words with you and return to YHWH. Say to him: 'Pardon all iniquity and accept what is good, and we will offer our lips as bulls'" (Hos 14:3 [Eng. 14:2]). Like Joel 2:12, sacrifice is potentially replaced with commands to demonstrate inward repentance, in Hosea's case, by intentionally offering words in place of sacrifices. In many ways, the prayer offered by Hosea in chapter 14 is not unlike Joel's and would fit the context of Joel 2:12–14.

Likewise, Amos, the book that follows Joel in the MT order of the Twelve, offers a similar view of a corrupt priesthood (7:10–17) and cult (e.g. 2:4–5, 8, 12; 3:14; 4:4–5; 5:21–26; most notably the use of ילל with שירות היכל "temple songs" in Amos 8:3; cf. Joel 1:5, 11, 13). In fact, a problematic cult is a strong theme among the Twelve's eighth century prophets (e.g. Mic 1:5–7; 6:6–8),³⁵ and Joel's position in the beginning of the BT falls within that distinct eighth

---

³² James D. Nogalski, *The Book of the Twelve: Hosea-Jonah* (SHBC 18.1; Macon, GA: Smyth & Helwys, 2011), 205.

³³ Nogalski, *Hosea-Jonah*, 206: "This call to repentance [Hos 14] concludes with a contingent promise. When the beginning of Joel asks, 'Has this happened?' (1:2), the syntactical awkwardness in the context dissipates considerably if one reads Joel as a continuation of Hosea. The missing antecedent to 'this' suddenly has a clear referent, namely the promise of Hosea 14:4–8. Additionally, the expected answer to this question of Joel 1:2 ('No') makes sense if the reader assumes Joel continues Hosea. The people have not repented, and thus the promises have not been fulfilled." I have also argued that the imperative use of שוב in Joel 2:12–14 intentionally builds on the imperative uses of שוב found in Hos 14:2–5 (Eng. 14:1–4). See LeCureux, *Thematic Unity*, 126–28.

³⁴ For more on the use of שוב in Hosea 14, see LeCureux, *Thematic Unity*, 99–107.

³⁵ I am referring to the traditional settings for Hosea-Amos-Micah (Hos 1:1; Am 1:1; Mic 1:1), a canonical grouping which begins the Book of the Twelve in the LXX. For more on how the writings were edited together, see James D. Nogalski, *Literary Precursors to the Book of the Twelve* (BZAW 217; Berlin: de Gruyter, 1993), and Aaron Schart, "Reconstructing the Redaction History of the Twelve Prophets: Problems and Models," in *Reading and Hearing the Book of the Twelve* (ed. James D. Nogalski and Marvin A. Sweeney; SymS 15; Atlanta: Society of Biblical Literature, 2000), 34–48.

century block (Hosea-Micah),[36] and can be read in light of these issues. By doing so many of the tensions from Joel, most notably the problem of unidentifiable sin and a call to return apart from the cult are explained and clarified. Therefore, while Hosea and Amos are critical of the northern cult, within the BT Joel allows for that same criticism to be introduced against the southern cult, which ultimately leads to later prophetic calls for its destruction and renewal (Mic 3:12–4:5). This seems especially significant given that Israel never seems to solve its cultic problems within the flow of the BT (cf. Mal 1:6–2:9).

But does Joel 2:12–14 leave room for this reading that finds fault with the cult? As mentioned, most commentators still place Joel's words within the confines of a functioning cult. The tension that is found in this and other prophetic texts that seem to ignore or even disparage the cult (i.e. Hos 6:6) is often dismissed in the belief that the idea of the cult was too pervasive. As Barton notes, "Probably the easiest way to reconcile such a defence of ritual in religion with what the prophets appear to be saying is to argue that they were not speaking against cultic ritual in principle, but rather wanted to introduce an order of priorities. Sacrifice is not unacceptable in itself, but is simply of a lower order of importance than social justice or heartfelt repentance."[37] Thus, "'Rend your hearts and not your clothing' means 'Rend your hearts as well as your clothing,' 'Let your torn clothing represent true inward contrition—but tear them all the same.'"[38] However, in light of Joel's surrounding context in the BT, in between two cult-critical books, it is important to reconsider this view of the cult in this passage, particularly in light of the date of the book.

4. Exilic Date of Joel

As briefly mentioned above, Sweeney has made a good argument for a chronological ordering to the MT, which still allows for flexibility within the ordered eighth-seventh-sixth century blocks. His conclusion that Joel is a chronologically flexible (undated) book that allows it to speak to all periods of Israelite history is important. However, a general consensus has been reached which dates

---

[36] Sweeney, "Sequence and Interpretation," 53, n. 10, argues that Joel is an undated book that can speak to all periods of Israelite history. He likewise dismisses the argument that a late date for Obadiah disproves MT chronological concerns, since the writing was traditionally read as a ninth century text (53, n. 9).

[37] John Barton, "The Prophets and the Cult," in *Temple and Worship in Biblical Israel* (ed. John Day; LHBOTS 422; London: T&T Clark, 2007), 111–22 (114).

[38] Barton, "Prophets and Cult," 114.

Joel to sometime in the postexilic period.[39] Recently, Assis has challenged this consensus and offered a strong argument that the book is actually an exilic composition,[40] which significantly alters the view of cult in the book. While most scholars assume that Joel's frequent mention of the temple implies that it is standing, Assis argues, "Even though Joel refers to the Temple and even to specific places in the Temple precinct ('between the vestibule and the altar' [2:17]), this does not necessarily preclude the period before the Temple has been rebuilt. The habit of calling a place by a certain name is not easily changed, even when there are substantial changes in the character of the place, so it is unlikely that the people ceased calling the Temple area 'the house of YHWH' after its destruction."[41] Assis similarly allows for the continued practice of cultic ritual apart from a rebuilt temple, "This does not mean that a regular cult existed in Jerusalem throughout the exilic period, only that some cultic activities took place there when possible."[42] In terms of the specific grain and drink offerings mentioned in Joel, Assis draws the helpful parallel to Jer 41:5, where similar offerings were made after the destruction of the temple, then concludes, "Perhaps this source speaks of grain-offerings because this was a simple sacrifice which was possible to offer even without an institutionalized and organized cultic system."[43]

An exilic setting explains why Joel calls the people to assemble at the site of the temple, but specifically avoids the call for sacrifice, mentioning only grain and drink offerings along with the minor rituals of fasting, weeping, and mourning—rituals that can take place apart from a fully functioning temple. It would also explain why the priests' most important role in the book is to assemble the people and lament. If the temple is not standing, the role of the cult, and by connection the priests, is diminished. Such a setting would by natural implication cast serious doubts on the ability of Joel, especially in chapters 1–2, to function as a so called "cultic-prophet."

---

[39] Richard Coggins, "Joel," *CBR* 2 (2003): 85–103 (89).

[40] Assis, *Joel*, 3–23.

[41] Ibid., 9.

[42] Ibid., 10. He continues, "Indeed, the cult referred to in the book of Joel speaks of grain and drink offerings (1:13; 2:14), just as Jeremiah describes in 41:5. Joel speaks of the Temple as a place of gathering for public fasting and mass prayer (1:13; 2:1, 15–17), which reinforces the view that it was not possible to bring animal sacrifices. It must be noted that Joel makes no mention whatsoever of sacrificing burnt-offerings, peace-offerings or sin offerings, another indication that Joel was active in the period after the destruction of the Temple in 587 BCE but before its rebuilding in 515."

[43] Assis, *Joel*, 10.

5. Joel and Jonah

So what is envisioned by a setting that portrays repentant acts apart from a fully functional cultic system? Here the context of the BT again becomes helpful when Joel is read in relation to the book of Jonah. Scholars have long noted the strong connections between Jonah 3:9 and Joel 2:13–14.[44] Much of that discussion has focused on the use of the confession from Exod 34:6–7, and deals primarily with matters of authorial influence which will not be entered into here.[45] In terms of the MT order of the BT, Jonah intentionally actualizes the call for repentance first envisioned in Joel. In other words, what Joel calls for in 2:12–14 is acted out, in an eighth century historical narrative, by the people of Nineveh.

In Jonah, as in Joel, the people face destruction from YHWH (Jonah 3:4; Joel 2:11), and just like Joel, the prophet Jonah does not mention any sin, preaching only that destruction is imminent: "Forty days more and Nineveh will be overturned" (3:4). In an interesting twist, it is the King of Nineveh who infers guilt from Jonah's prophecy of destruction, calling the people to turn from the generic "evil ways" and more specific "violence that is in their hand" (3:8). The King announces a fast (3:7); then commands that both humans and animals put on sackcloth, that everyone should cry out to YHWH, and that they should all turn (שוב, 3:8)—all of which are acts of lamentation prescribed in Joel.[46] YHWH then notices this act of repentance (שוב, 3:10) and, as Joel hopes (2:14, 18–27) but to

---

[44] See, e.g., Mark J. Boda, "Penitential Innovations within the Twelve," in *On Stone and Scroll: Essays in Honour of Graham Ivor Davies* (ed. James K. Aitken, Katharine J. Dell, and Brian A. Mastin; BZAW 420; Berlin: de Gruyter, 2011), 391–407, and Jack M. Sasson, *Jonah* (AB 24C; New York: Doubleday, 1990), 137–41.

[45] See Joseph Ryan Kelly, "Joel, Jonah, and the YHWH Creed: Determining the Trajectory of the Literary Influence," *JBL* 132.4 (2013): 805–26; John Strazicich, *Joel's Use of Scripture and the Scripture's Use of Joel: Appropriation and Resignification in Second Temple Judaism and Early Christianity* (BIS 82; Leiden: Brill, 2007), 147–51; Hyun Chul Paul Kim, "Jonah Read Intertextually," *JBL* 126 (2007): 497–528; Alan Cooper, "In Praise of Divine Caprice: The Significance of the Book of Jonah," in *Among the Prophets: Language, Image and Structure in the Prophetic Writings* (ed. Philip R. Davies and David J.A. Clines; JSOTS 144; Sheffield: JSOT Press, 1993), 144–63. Both Strazicich and Kelly ("Joel, Jonah," 811) argue that Joel is dependent on Jonah, and Kelly notes that this is the less popular opinion. While most scholars deal with this issue, it is nonetheless important to note that Joel precedes Jonah in both the MT and LXX orders, thus implying that, despite any critical arguments of dependence, once it was incorporated into the BT Jonah was intended to be read in light of Joel.

[46] For more on the discussion of Jonah's use of שוב in comparison with Joel, see LeCureux, *Thematic Unity*, 133–45.

Jonah's despair (Jonah 4), relents (נחם) and does not destroy the city of Nineveh (Jonah 3:10). Therefore, in Jonah the people of Nineveh, facing a message of destruction by an Israelite prophet that does not contain a mention of wrong doing, return to YHWH with fasting, weeping, and mourning, and they do so apart from any priestly or temple intervention. Furthermore, such activities are deemed appropriate when YHWH notes their repentance and relents—thus historically answering the question "who knows?" posed by both texts. In this way, Jonah reiterates and historically enacts Joel's call to repentance apart from a functioning temple setting, albeit with one of Israel's most hated enemies.

6. Joel as Anticult?

But could Joel (and Jonah, Amos, Hosea, and Micah) really envision a call to return that took place apart from a sacrificial system? Barton, based on work by Mary Douglas, believes so, particularly in light of Psalm 50:9–12 and other preexilic writings.[47] This, coupled with the absence of any "real concrete evidence" for the existence of cultic prophets, as well as few other nuances to the term "prophet" and "cult" leads Barton to conclude:

> The nineteenth-century scholars who first saw clearly that the prophets had been revolutionary in their turning away from the sacrificial cultus thus seem to me in essence to have been right; and I do not think the fact that they were liberal Protestants, who were therefore very happy to find their own ideas about the character of true religion endorsed by the prophets, vitiates the essential truth of their perception. It is a condition of seeking the truth about other cultures that we do not predetermine what we are going to find there, and if what we think we find is congenial to us, we should be suspicious. But our suspicion should not be absolutized to the point where we come to think we are bound to be wrong wherever we feel we have recognized a kindred spirit in a past cult. If Douglas is right, Protestantism and the kind of anti-ritualism that can be found in the prophets genuinely do share certain features in common.[48]

---

[47] Barton, "Prophets and Cult," 116–17.

[48] Ibid., 121. So while Barton is open to the probability that ancient prophets could envision a call to return that took place outside of a cultic setting, it is important to mention that he spends much of his article arguing that Joel is not one of them. Many of the issues Barton identified have been discussed above in relation to reading Joel within the context of the Twelve. Most importantly, he argues that it is the preexilic texts that demonstrate an anti-cultic message, a setting for Joel implied by the MT editors of the Twelve.

In light of this, and within the broader context of the Book of the Twelve, Joel can be read within a framework that challenges the priestly and sacrificial system, rather than supports it.

7. Implications

Issues in Joel studies are indeed complex, no less so, once one begins examining the role of the cult in the book. What I have tried to argue above is that when Joel is read within the context of the Twelve, many of these difficulties are resolved, but by doing so de-emphasize the cult—an implication that is not immediately clear when Joel is read independently of the Twelve. What I have argued against is the strong support in scholarly literature that places the prophet Joel, or the book that was produced under his name, squarely in support of the priests and temple establishment. The problem, as I see is it, is asked by Linville, "Why does everything have to be turned into ritual?" While Linville and many others would argue that Joel reflects a community lament ritual, or even engages in questions of theodicy like Job, the importance of the priestly role and sacrifice is almost always assumed as a background setting for such actions.[49] This has especially been true for Joel 2:12–14.

However, by examining the cult as described in the first two chapters, a robust argument for the overall cultic setting for the book is difficult to find. The priests are present, but so are many others. The prophet calls for them to lead the people in minor lament rituals, avoiding mention of temple-exclusive activities, and even goes so far as to offer a probable critique (2:13). The second half of the book (chapters 3–4) presents a separate challenge and the limits of space only allow for a few reflections. In these chapters Linville, Cook, and others argue for a cultic setting for Joel's visions of restoration. However, the cultic world of chapters 1–2 weighs against this, and I would continue to argue that though the temple is always present in chapters 3–4, and is even viewed as a source of life (4:18), it is difficult to know exactly what activities Joel envisions taking place in this apocalyptic setting. This is especially true in light of similar restoration images found in the Twelve (cf. Torah-centric Mic 4:1–5). In chapters 3–4 YHWH dwells in Zion, and it is the seat of his power (4:16, 17, 21). But does this mean that priests and sacrifices are envisioned? Here, I think caution is needed. This matter is further complicated because the mention of priests ceases at 2:17, and Joel in fact envisions the demarcation of YHWH's Spirit to all people, empowering them with prophetic gifts and opening salvation to all (3:1–3:5a). This, at least in some way, seems to imply a type of levelling of societal structure. A

---

[49] Linville, "Day of YHWH," 99.

natural question should be, "since everything is overturned at the end of the book, is it possible that Joel envisions an overturning of cultic processes as well?"

Linville correctly notes that while many scholars believe that priests and cult play an important role in Joel, they often fail to highlight that importance in their studies.[50] I believe the reason for this is a natural one. If Assis is correct and Joel is an exilic text, commentators have failed to argue for the importance of priest/cult because it is simply not a major concern displayed in the writing. In an exilic Joel, the cult functions within the confines of a destroyed temple and decimated priesthood, attempting to minister to a dispirited people. This would then give reason for the prophet to call the people to the cultic-ambivalent return of 2:12–14. Furthermore, the call to "rend your hearts and not your garments" detracts from the argument that the cult has a central role to play in the book.

Much of what I have offered above turns on my understanding of how the book of Joel functions within a completed BT. I believe the textual dependence between the surrounding books makes for a strong argument. Most significantly, the use of the שוב language and the antiritualistic call to return in Joel 2:12–14 picks up right where the anticult language of Hos 14 leaves off. The fact that Jonah 3 seems intentionally to relate to Joel 2:12–14, and offers in a similar setting—a return to Yhwh apart from the priests and sacrifices—is difficult to dismiss.

Much of this is based on Joel's position, and perhaps here it is possible to imagine some debate among the editors of the Twelve, who were unclear on the historical setting of Joel as evidenced by its two locations in the MT and LXX. The exilic message of Joel, with the diminished priest and cult, the antiritualistic sounding 2:12–13, as well as a restoration section that included a renewed Jerusalem but no mention of priests, would align nicely with the similar visions of the surrounding eighth century prophets, even if this was not Joel's original intention. Once incorporated into the BT, Joel's exilic view of a diminished priesthood took on an accompanying eighth century anticultic setting. Perhaps this is part of the reason for its position within MT Twelve. While in the MT, Joel introduces the reader to the Day of Yhwh and concerns about Jerusalem, it also carries on the trouble with the priesthood and cult first introduced by Hosea.

---

[50] Linville, "Day of Yhwh," 99.

5
PRIESTS AND PROFITS: JOEL AND MALACHI

Deborah W. Rooke

As compared with other parts of the Hebrew Bible, priests are not much in evidence in the Book of the Twelve; nor do they always get a very good press. In four of the Twelve (Obadiah, Jonah, Nahum, Habakkuk), priests do not occur at all, and in two others (Micah, Zephaniah) they are mentioned only in passing to be condemned for their immorality (Mic 3:11; Zeph 1:4, 3:4). In Amos the one mention of a priest is of Amaziah, the priest of Bethel (7:10), who tries to silence Amos and is condemned for so doing; and in Hosea there are several passing condemnations of priests (5:1; 6:9; 10:5), together with a longer passage in which priests are condemned for rejecting God's law and misleading the people (4:4–10). Some of the Twelve, however, take a less wholly condemnatory view of the priesthood and a more positive view of the temple cult. Haggai and Zechariah, for example, in their efforts to get the cult reinstated after the exile, speak of the high priest Joshua in positive terms and of the ordinary priests with equanimity. But it is the remaining two of the Twelve, Joel and Malachi, that will be the focus of this paper, because they share not only with Haggai and Zechariah a more marked focus than some of the others on priests and cult, but also with each other a distinctive perspective on these institutions.

The two books' shared perspective begins with their dating. Joel and Malachi are generally both dated to the postexilic period, Malachi somewhat more definitively than Joel on the basis of a number of features. First, it uses the term פחה, "governor" (1:8), which indicates the presence of an imperial official as a figure of authority in Judah, and makes no mention of a monarch or a system of elders. Such an arrangement is most readily understandable in the postexilic period. In addition, the opening verses of the book (1:2–5) imply the destruction of Edom, which is not generally thought to have occurred prior to the Babylonian conquest of Judah; and some of the issues addressed in Malachi have affinities with those addressed in Ezra and Nehemiah, particularly the questions of mixed marriages (2:10–16) and full payment of tithes (3:8–10). Together with other linguistic and literary features, these elements lead many scholars to locate the book's composition in Persian-period Judah, dating it to somewhere in the fifth century BCE.[1] The arguments for a postexilic dating of Joel are rather more nebulous, and rely on the observation that the book contains no mention of a monarch or elders, while giving a certain prominence to the cult and priesthood in its first two chapters. Although the lack of definitive dating evidence means that Joel has been dated to periods ranging from the ninth to the second centuries BCE,[2] the book's cultic perspective is certainly compatible with a postexilic dating, on the assumption that the cult and priesthood gained in significance in the absence of other indigenous forms of societal structuring such as a monarchy or a tribal eldership.[3] Indeed, the fact that Malachi gives similar prominence to the cult and priesthood tends to support a postexilic dating for Joel inasmuch as it is compatible with the postexilic Malachi in this respect. In both books, too, the prominence given to the cult is a sign of the regard in which it is held. Joel for his part bemoans the fact that famine and drought have caused the cessation of sacrifices from the temple, and urges a cultic response (an assembly, fasting, and prayers) in order to restore the food supplies whereby the sacrifices can be reinstated. Malachi by contrast criticizes cultic abuses, but unlike the prophecies of Amos or Micah with their more social focus (e.g. Amos 5:21–24; Mic 6:6–8), Malachi's complaints do not lend themselves to being interpreted as a call for the abolition of cultic worship and its replacement with something more "spir-

---

[1] Julia O'Brien, *Priest and Levite in Malachi* (SBLDS 121; Atlanta: Scholars Press, 1990), 113–33, reviews all these arguments and concludes in favor of a somewhat earlier date, i.e. somewhere in the sixth century BCE.

[2] See Raymond B. Dillard, "Joel," in *The Minor Prophets. Vol. 1. Hosea, Joel, Amos* (ed. Thomas Edward McComiskey; Grand Rapids: Baker Book House, 1992), 239–313 (240–43), for a summary of the dating positions. Most recently, Elie Assis has argued that Joel should be dated to exilic-era Judah; for details, see Assis, "The Date and Meaning of the Book of Joel," *VT* 61 (2011): 163–83, and idem, *The Book of Joel: A Prophet Between Calamity and Hope* (LHBOTS 581; London: Bloomsbury T&T Clark, 2014), 3–23. I do not find Assis's arguments convincing, either for the exilic dating of the book, or for the idea that Joel is actually attempting to foster a less cultic approach to worship.

[3] This is to some extent an argument from silence; nevertheless, Joel is not incompatible with a postexilic situation, and the second part of the book (3:1–4:21 [Eng. 2:28–3:21]) is undeniably apocalyptic in tone which indicates that it at least is postexilic.

itual." Rather, they advocate regularizing of cultic practice to bring it into conformity with YHWH's requirements, in order to assure the community's wellbeing. For the purposes of this paper, therefore, I shall assume that both books find their most appropriate social setting in the postexilic period.

A second perspective shared between Joel and Malachi, and the main focus of this paper, is that both books picture priests primarily in terms of their sacrificial duties, that is, as those who are concerned with the correct manipulation of food and drink when it is offered to God in the temple. This means, as I shall demonstrate, that in these two books there is a significant and close relationship between the priests and food, and moreover that the community's wellbeing both depends on and is reflected by that relationship. Each book presents the priest-food relationship from a different perspective, but both presentations fit within the same paradigm, and this gives a distinctive view of the priesthood's significance for the community's prosperity. Each book will be examined in turn for its particular understanding of how priests and food fit together, and then conclusions will be drawn. Since Joel is both the shorter of the two and comes before Malachi in the Book of the Twelve, I shall begin with Joel.

1. PRIESTS AND FOOD IN JOEL

Although (as noted above) the precise context of the book of Joel cannot be determined, its first two chapters present a picture of natural disaster in which the people's food supply is decimated. Initially the disaster looks to be a plague of locusts (1:4), although later on there are hints of a drought that has caused crop failure, as the text speaks of the seed shrivelling under the earth and the drying up of vegetation and water courses (1:12, 17–20). There are also hints of an inferno of some kind (1:19; 2:3), which may be connected with the drought.[4] The

---

[4] Interpretations of the disasters presented in Joel have ranged from the literal to the metaphorical to the cosmic and the stereotypes of liturgical lament. Graham S. Ogden, "Restoring the Years: A Commentary on the Book of Joel," in *Joel and Malachi: A Promise of Hope, A Call to Obedience* (ed. Graham S. Ogden and Richard R. Deutsch; ITC; Grand Rapids, MI: Eerdmans / Edinburgh: The Handsel Press, 1987), 3–60 (10–12), regards the book of Joel as a community lament that like many of the psalms of lament has no specific historical referent; this means that the pictures of locust devastation and drought are stereotyped liturgical images of crisis rather than descriptions of actual events. John Barton, *Joel and Obadiah* (OTL; Louisville, KY: Westminster John Knox, 2001), comments that the text may well envisage a literal locust plague, but as a cultic call to lament it may include stereotyped disaster elements (e.g. drought, animal suffering) that do not quite fit with the main topos, something which is also the case in psalms of lament (46–47). The reading offered here understands the text literally as describing

scenario is presented largely but not exclusively from the perspective of those who are affected by it, describing the events as the prophet sees them taking place. What is significant for present purposes, though, is that regardless of the famine's cause, one of the first negative effects mentioned is the cessation of grain and wine offerings for the temple, and the priests' concomitant distress (1:9). Mentioning this so early on, even before the distress of the agricultural workers (1:11) and the farm and wild animals (1:18, 20), to say nothing of the populace at large, demonstrates the enormous significance that the prophet attributes here to the sacrificial cult, and indicates that maintaining the cult is a matter of life and death. Sweeney's comment that "the Temple and its service symbolize the stability of creation"[5] offers a light in which to understand this anxiety over the cult, and indicates that disruption of the cult is a serious matter in that it presages cosmic meltdown. That being the case, it is no wonder that the priests should mourn the lack of sacrifices (1:9), because as the ones who perform the offerings on the altar in the temple they are the ones responsible for maintaining the sacrificial cult with its reciprocal relationship to the created order. By their manipulation of food on the altar, the priests help to ensure the stability of creation, which will in turn mean stable food supplies for the community—a heavy responsibility indeed. But this is a responsibility that through no fault of their own they are currently unable to fulfil, and the consequences must inevitably be bad.[6]

Nor is it just the potential cosmic consequences of a failed cult that cause the priests to mourn the lack of sacrifices: assuming that the priests depended on the offerings for their own sustenance,[7] as is indicated in the Pentateuchal legal codes,[8] they themselves would be among the first to suffer if a general lack of provisions led to the cessation of sacrificial worship because worshippers needed all their food to keep themselves alive. Indeed, this may be why the priests' distress is mentioned so early on as one of the effects of the famine: because the

---

natural disasters resulting in famine rather than as a symbol or metaphor for some other type of crisis.

[5] Marvin A. Sweeney, *The Twelve Prophets* (Berit Olam; 2 vols.; Collegeville, MN: Michael Glazier, 2000), 1:160. Compare Hans Walter Wolff, *Joel and Amos* (trans. W. Janzen et al.; Hermeneia; Philadelphia: Fortress, 1977), 31: "The incipient events . . . endanger precisely that which goes on in the Temple and in which one finds assurance of salvation."

[6] James L. Crenshaw, *Joel* (AB 24C; New York: Doubleday, 1995), 99, comments of the priests, "[I]n their eyes the failure of the cult was a serious event, one that affected the way YHWH related to the people of Judah."

[7] Wolff, *Joel and Amos*, 31; Crenshaw, *Joel*, 99, and Barton, *Joel and Obadiah*, 53.

[8] See particularly Num 18:8–32 and Deut 18:1–5.

priests depend on food provided by others, they are vulnerable to shortages which decrease the amount of spare food capacity in the community. Because of this dependence, too, their fortunes are a barometer for those of the community at large: what the priests experience, the entire community is also at risk of suffering. Where priests are deprived of foodstuffs by which to maintain the cult and themselves there is the threat of starvation for the people, unless order can be restored.

According to the picture given in Joel, then, the priests in their capacity as sacrificial agents are closely connected with the nation's food supply, and their relationship with that supply reflects the status of the entire nation's relationship with food, so that the priests' lack of sacrificial materials indicates an impending crisis in the food supply. Equally, in such circumstances Joel indicates that it is the priests who have the duty of taking action to address the situation.[9] Noteworthy is the call to the priests in the absence of food (that is, of offerings) not only themselves to mourn but to summon the rest of the community for a fast (1:14). Fasting as such is not addressed in the legal material of the Hebrew Bible, and so there are no specific guidelines for how or under what circumstances a communal fast is to be initiated.[10] It seems clear, however, that in this instance the priests are those who are to implement the action: the prophet gives the order to "sanctify a fast" (קדשו צום) (1:14), by contrast with the terminology of "proclaiming a fast" (קרא צום) that is used elsewhere in the Hebrew Bible,[11] and the instruction to "sanctify" suggests that it is a sacral action, most naturally undertaken by the priests. In addition, priests are the logical addressees throughout 1:13–14, the passage of which the command to sanctify a fast is part.[12] Fasting

---

[9] So also Leslie C. Allen, *The Books of Joel, Obadiah, Jonah and Micah* (NICOT; Grand Rapids, MI: Eerdmans, 1976 / London: Hodder and Stoughton, 1978), 58.

[10] A point made by Barton, *Joel and Obadiah*, 79. H.A. Brongers, "Fasting in Israel in Biblical and Post-Biblical Times," in *Instruction and Interpretation: Studies in Hebrew Language, Palestinian Archaeology and Biblical Exegesis. Papers Read at the Joint British-Dutch Old Testament Conference held at Louvain, 1976, from 30 August to 2 September* (ed. Adam Simon van der Woude; OTS 21; Leiden: Brill, 1977), 1–21, investigates the question in detail. Brongers comments that fasting is not generally the subject of legal prescriptions because it "ranks among customs and manners" (2), presumably rather than being a requirement in particular circumstances.

[11] Joel is the only book in which the terminology of "sanctifying" is used of arranging a fast, an observation also made by G.W. Ahlström, *Joel and the Temple Cult of Jerusalem* (VTSup 21; Leiden: Brill, 1971), 55.

[12] The 2m.pl. command in 1:14 to institute a fast follows commands addressed explicitly to the priests in 1:13 to don sackcloth and lament, and there is no indication of a change of addressee between the two verses. Also, 1:13 which is addressed to the priests speaks of grain and wine offerings being withheld from "the house of *your* God," while

and mourning are of course established communal responses to various kinds of disaster, including military defeat, death, and the threat of persecution (Judg 20:26; 2 Sam 1:12; Esth 4:3), but abstaining from food has a particular poignancy, indeed, an irony, when it is undertaken in the face of limited food supplies. It is an unexpected action to require of a famine-ridden populace; perhaps the command to fast implies that the community still has some food, but not enough to spare for offerings. The main point is, though, that in the absence of (sufficient) food the appropriate course of action is seen to be to abstain from even the little that there is in an appeal to God—it is as if neither God nor people are to eat, or if God cannot eat then neither are the people entitled to do so; and it is the priests who initiate this course of action. This is another example of how Joel presents the relationship between priests and food: not only do the priests manipulate food in the sacrificial cult as part of the service that symbolizes the stability of creation and is itself linked with the diet and produce of the general populace,[13] the priests have the right (or responsibility) to curtail general consumption entirely, again presumably as a means of rebalancing the cosmic equilibrium when it threatens to fail.

The command to fast, together with weeping and mourning, is verbalized again by the prophet a little further on, this time framed as a direct instruction from God (2:12) rather than simply the prophet's own advice as in 1:14, and the positive result that might accrue from fasting is said to be that God might relent and leave behind a blessing in the shape of a grain offering and a drink offering (2:14). Here there is no specific mention of priests, but the continued description of the famine issue in cultic terms is striking, as is the description of the grain

---

1:14 again urges that for the fast all the elders and inhabitants of the land be gathered to "the house of the Lord *your* God." This makes most sense as being addressed to the priests like 1:13. Wolff, *Joel and Amos*, 33, comments, "The instructions of v 14 still pertain to the priests."

[13] As Alfred Marx observes, all of the items offered in the sacrificial cult are those that form part of the diet of the ordinary people ("Familiarité et transcendance: La fonction du sacrifice d'après l'Ancien Testament," in *Studien zu Opfer und Kult im Alten Testament* [ed. Adrian Schenker; FAT 3; Tübingen: Mohr Siebeck, 1992], 1–14 [6]). It is true that there are some items that can be eaten that are not offered on the altar, but equally nothing that is forbidden to humans as food can be offered on the altar. It is also true that there are certain parts of sacrificial animals (blood and fat) that are forbidden for human consumption because they are reserved for the deity; nevertheless, the only blood and fat that can be offered to YHWH is that from animals that are permissible to humans for consumption. See further on this below in the discussion of Malachi.

and drink offering as a "blessing."[14] It is as if return to normal cultic service is what is craved above all as the guarantee of cosmic stability, and thus of food for the people at large. The term "blessing" that is used here of the grain and drink offerings implies that if there is enough for offerings then there will certainly be enough to feed the people. The offerings thus stand for the general food supply by metonymy.[15]

Note, too, that the priests are those who have the job of verbalizing to God the communal pain and imploring that some kind of merciful action should be taken by the deity (2:17). Their pleas appeal to YHWH's honor: a people who are unable to worship appropriately—indeed, unable to survive—because of lack of sustenance will inevitably bring disgrace both upon themselves and upon the God who has failed to maintain them.[16] The priests' location as they plead, between the vestibule and the altar (2:17), again highlights the nature of the lack that the people are suffering: there is nothing being brought to the altar except the priests' tears. As 1:16 proclaims, "Is not the food cut off before our eyes, joy and gladness from the house of our God?" If these are construed as the words of the priests, summoned by the prophet in 1:13–14 to initiate a fast and mourn and cry out,[17] then 2:17 functions as an actualization of their lament in 1:16: they have no food on the altar, and so all that there is in the temple is mourning.

As a result of this cultic action that is initiated and headed up by the priests, YHWH does indeed take action, restoring the land to fertility and ensuring an abundance of food so that the people can eat and be satisfied (2:18–27). The priests' manipulation of the general food supply has thus contributed towards restoring the cosmic balance so that YHWH, priests and people all have the food

---

[14] Sweeney, *Twelve Prophets*, 1:166, seems to think that the grain offering and libation are to be offered to YHWH along with repentance in order to secure a blessing, but this is surely a misreading of the text.

[15] So also Crenshaw, *Joel*, 139.

[16] Wolff, *Joel and Amos*, 62, argues that nowhere in ch. 1 is the food crisis said to lead to potential mockery among the nations, but that such mockery is envisaged as the result of the apocalyptic army described in 2:1–11. This assumes that the army is a different threat from the locust plague mentioned in ch. 1, a position also adopted by Sweeney, *Twelve Prophets*, 1:161–64. However, it does not give sufficient weight to the description of the invaders as behaving *like* soldiers, *like* chariots and horses, *like* warriors (Joel 2:4, 5, 7), which implies that they are something other than a recognizable military force, and makes good sense when understood as a metaphorical description of the locust plague. This is the position adopted by Barton, *Joel and Obadiah*, 44, 68–70.

[17] Barton, *Joel and Obadiah*, 62, regards the words as those of the people's lament rather than of the priests, but they make equal if not better sense as the priests' words. Wolff, *Joel and Amos*, 35, regards them as the words of the prophet.

they need to maintain themselves. But the reason for this restoration is not just a mechanical one; here we see the invocation of a relationship between deity and people. YHWH does not simply respond because he is obliged to, but because of an emotional response—he becomes jealous for the land and has pity on the people (2:18).[18] And his spoken response, promising to restore the people's fortunes, is now framed in terms of food rather than of sacrifices (2:19), because what the people need is food for their own sustenance.[19] Just as the earlier laments complained of the cessation of offerings, because the prophet and priests were speaking of the effect of the famine on YHWH and the cult, here the restoration is pictured as an abundance of foodstuffs because YHWH is speaking of the restoration's significance for the people. This is shown also in the declaration that as a consequence of YHWH's intervention his people's reputation rather than (or alongside) his own will be salvaged (2:19). The perspective in these promises of restoration is "top down," with YHWH speaking of how things look to him, rather than the "bottom up" perspective of the earlier material in Joel which took a distinctly human's-eye view of the calamities facing the people.

In Joel, then, the crisis of the famine, whatever its cause, is expressed repeatedly in terms of disruption to the temple service, which means that the priests have a significant responsibility in taking action to avert its worst effects. Despite the efforts of exegetes to interpret the events as punishment for some kind of sin, there is no direct support for that in the text.[20] Indeed, the priests' appeal to the deity not to make the people a byword and a reproach among the nations (2:17) implies that they are conscious of no sin that might have precipitated such a disastrous response from the deity. And since this seems to be what

---

[18] Barton, *Joel and Obadiah*, 88, calls YHWH's jealousy as it appears here his "passionate commitment to his people." See also Crenshaw's comments on YHWH's zeal that arise from this verse (*Joel*, 147–50).

[19] Wolff thinks it "strange" that there is no mention of meal-offerings and libations at this point, despite noting that the text speaks with compassion of the people having enough to eat again (*Joel and Amos*, 61). He has not made the connection between the perspective of the speaker and what is being said.

[20] Barton, *Joel and Obadiah*, 77–80. Dillard, "Joel," 280, assumes that the people have sinned, despite admitting that there is no evidence for what the sin might be other than what he sees as the drunkenness mentioned in 1:5, which is not presented as a condemnation of sin. Allen, *Joel*, 79, comments that Joel's interpretation of the crisis presupposes serious sin in the people's life, and assumes that they are to search their own hearts in order to identify it. Ahlström, *Joel and the Temple Cult*, 25–30, thinks that the famine is the result of the people carrying out a syncretistic cult in breach of the covenant with YHWH, as a result of which some of the covenant curses enumerated in Deut 28 are being inflicted upon them.

the prophet is telling the priests to say in order to avert the crisis, the prophet apparently sees no such sin either. Instead, what Joel portrays is priests who faithfully undertake their duties, expressing their distress at the lack of offerings, calling the people to fast, and pleading with YHWH to be merciful to the people. The result is entirely positive: YHWH hears their cries, and restores the food supply in all its fullness (2:18–27). Joel thus offers a model for how to deal with such a crisis, and indicates that it is up to the priests with their distinctive food-related responsibilities to take the lead in initiating this course of action.

2. Priests and Food in Malachi

As already noted, Malachi as well as Joel presents a picture of a significant relationship between priests and food; in Malachi, however, the relationship is depicted rather differently. Unlike the book of Joel, where the priests are shown as faithful cultic actors deprived of the wherewithal to carry out their food-related responsibilities through no fault of their own, and whose conscientious fulfilment of their responsibilities in a no-food situation is a significant factor in restoring an abundant food supply, in Malachi there is overt and direct criticism of the priests, particularly for the way in which they are carrying out their food-related sacrificial duties, and the prophet urges them to repent and adopt a better attitude. Contrary to Joel, too, the perspective adopted in Malachi is not that of the people and priests, but that of the deity; Joel takes a "bottom-up" view of the troubles facing his community, whereas Malachi takes a "top-down" view of the misdemeanours being committed in his. Malachi shares with Joel, however, the view that the cult is a significant and legitimate element in the community's life and worship. Of the six oracles of which the book of Malachi is composed, and which are structured as dialogues and accusations between YHWH and various groups in the population,[21] four have an explicitly cultic reference: in the second the priesthood is criticized for facilitating inappropriate sacrifices (1:6–2:9); in the third, YHWH rejects the people's offerings because of their illegitimate practices concerning marriage and divorce (2:10–16); in the fourth, YHWH is accused of delighting in wrongdoers, and responds by promising first to purify the priesthood so that they offer righteous offerings, and then to purge the rest of the community (2:17–3:5); and in the fifth YHWH via the prophet stresses the need to bring in the full tithe to the temple storehouse (3:6–12). Thus, the prophet

---

[21] The oracles are 1:2–5; 1:6–2:9; 2:10–16; 2:17–3:5; 3:6–12; 3:13–21 [Hebrew]. O'Brien, *Priest and Levite*, 49–84, argues that the book as a whole is based on the *rîb* or lawsuit form that is used by other prophets to indict the people for violation of the covenant between Israel and YHWH.

clearly views the cult as an important and integral element in the community's life; his complaint is not against the existence of the cult as such, but the improper operation of it, as is indicated by the promise of purification for the priesthood so that offerings may be made in righteousness (3:3).[22]

Within Malachi's critique of flawed cultic practices, the clearest link to the priests comes in the second oracle (1:6–2:9), in which the priests are condemned for offering inferior animals for sacrifice because they have an attitude problem: they despise the "table of the Lord," that is, the altar (1:7). Here there is a reversal of the reputation issues in Joel. Joel's priestly audience was urged to challenge YHWH over his failure to provide appropriate nourishment for his people, a failure which led to suspension of the temple rites and potential dishonor for a deity who abandoned those for whom he was supposed to be able to care (Joel 1:16; 2:17). There in Joel, YHWH's own delinquency in food provision was what threatened to lead to his dishonor. Here in Malachi, however, it is the priests who are castigated for bringing dishonor to their God by the poor quality of the sacrifices and their negative attitudes towards the rituals of worship (1:7–8, 12–13), together with their failure to fulfil their duty to educate the people correctly in what YHWH requires of them (2:7–9). Indeed, the situation here is presented as more dishonoring to YHWH than that in Joel; suspension of offerings altogether as envisaged in Joel is apparently preferable to the second-rate offerings that Malachi's addressees are currently making (cf. Mal 1:10).

The contrasting perspectives of complaint in the two books are mirrored by contrasting modes of expression. Whereas Joel symbolizes the lack of food for the people by speaking mostly in terms of offerings, thereby viewing human comestibles primarily as the material of divine service, Malachi highlights the failures in sacrificial practice by speaking in terms of food, thereby viewing the

---

[22] A number of scholars have argued that this material about the priests in ch. 3 is a secondary insertion. In the BHS edition of Malachi (Karl Elliger, 1970), Mal 3:3–4 are marked as a probable addition. Among more recent commentators David L. Petersen, *Zechariah 9–14 and Malachi* (OTL; Louisville, KY: Westminster John Knox, 1995), 211–12, regards 3:1b–4 as a second author's commentary on the identity of the messenger, and Paul Redditt, *Haggai, Zechariah, Malachi* (NCBC; London: Marshall Pickering / Grand Rapids, MI: Eerdmans, 1995), 175, similarly regards them as a redactional addition. Beth Glazier-McDonald, *Malachi: The Divine Messenger* (SBLDS 98; Atlanta: Scholars Press, 1987), 149, however, supports the literary unity of this passage with the rest of the fourth oracle, as do Pieter A. Verhoef, *The Books of Haggai and Malachi* (NICOT; Grand Rapids, MI: Eerdmans, 1987), 283, and Andrew E. Hill, *Malachi* (AB 25D; New York: Doubleday, 1998), 260. As will be evident from the following discussion, the verses make a good deal of sense in their present context, and for present purposes they are treated as an integral part of the message of Malachi.

material of divine service primarily as comestibles. These differences reflect the parties to whom the prophets' complaints are addressed. Joel verbalizes his complaints from the human perspective in terms that resonate with the deity. Malachi, however, is verbalizing his from the deity's perspective in terms that will resonate with humans. By speaking of the altar as a "table"[23] and the offerings on it as "bread," "fruit," and "food" (Mal 1:7, 12), the prophet characterizes the priests' enactment of sacrificial rituals as officiating at a meal for YHWH. The differences between the two perspectives are set out in table 1 below:

JOEL	MALACHI
"Bottom up" perspective—prophet addresses priests on behalf of the people	"Top down" perspective—prophet addresses priests on behalf of YHWH
Priests are not failing—need to continue doing their duty	Priests are failing—need to amend their ways
Food spoken of as offerings for YHWH	Offerings spoken of as YHWH's food
No food results in no sacrifices	Poor sacrifices results in poor food supplies
YHWH's food failure is bad for his reputation	Priests' food failure is bad for YHWH's reputation
Priests should address YHWH on behalf of the people—plead for mercy	Priests should address people on behalf of YHWH—teach them the law

Table 1: Comparison between Joel and Malachi in their presentations of priests and food

Malachi's use of the terminology of food to speak of sacrifices is a particularly clear example of a conception that Alfred Marx argues is fundamental to the Old Testament, namely, that sacrifice is a meal which is prepared for the deity.[24] As Marx observes, all of the materials offered on the altar are prepared foodstuffs—the meat is prepared ready for cooking, and grain, olives, and grapes are offered as flour, oil, and wine, respectively; the quantities offered to YHWH are those that would be offered to an honored guest; and the types of sacrifice reflect the two types of hospitality evidenced in the Old Testament, one where food is offered to the guest but not shared by the host (corresponding to whole offerings, and those shared only between YHWH and priests), and one where the guest has

---

[23] This occurs elsewhere in the Hebrew Bible only in Ezek 41:22 and 44:16.

[24] Marx, "Familiarité et transcendence," 5–6, excludes from the category of sacrifice proper the חטאת and אשם rituals in Lev 4–5, which are distinguished from other types of sacrificial rituals by the vocabulary used to speak of them; he regards them rather as rites of passage or penalty that are obligatory in certain circumstances and have as their intention some kind of purification, of which YHWH is never the object.

the place of honor at the table along with the host and other diners (corresponding to communion offerings).[25] However, while it is true that such a meal serves the human need for physical nourishment, in the context of a sacrifice and conceived of as an opportunity for hospitality with the deity it is much more than that. YHWH may not need the food offered to him by humans in order for him physically to survive, but his commensality with his people enables links to be forged between deity and humans.[26] Just as they would when serving a meal for an illustrious guest, the people honor the deity with appropriate portions of food, and he honors them with his presence. But there are limits to the communion; worshippers and deity never share the sacrificial meat, which goes to either one party or the other depending on the type of sacrifice, and the deity always gets the blood (and in P, the fat), of which humans are forbidden to partake.[27] Additionally, YHWH eats his portion in a different realm from that in which humans eat theirs, and it has to be delivered to him via the fire on the altar. And with the growing consciousness of the deity's sanctity, priests become the necessary intermediaries to enact this delivery.[28] As such, concludes Marx, sacrifice, which by its rituals expresses both the similarity and the otherness of the deity in relation to humans, "is the place where Israel learns to know its God, not in an intellectual manner, in the form of factual knowledge, but in a concrete fashion, through the hospitality of the sacrifices which it offers to him."[29]

And this is the point of the "table" imagery used in Malachi of the altar. For all the social and cultural complexities of food-related customs, consumption of food is nevertheless a necessity for humans, and not to eat is not to live.[30] The people's survival depends on the food that they can produce from the land on which they live. But there are many factors affecting food production that they cannot control, and so if they are to survive and prosper they need the assistance of a higher power, namely, the deity who as owner of the land is seen as the provider of their food. Having foodstuffs—that is, the produce of the land—as an essential element in the system of cultic worship for the deity highlights the

---

[25] Marx, "Familiarité et transcendence," 6–7.
[26] Ibid., 11.
[27] Ibid., 11–12.
[28] Ibid., 12.
[29] "Il est le lieu où Israël apprend à connaître son Dieu, non pas d'une manière intellectuelle, sous la forme d'un savoir, mais de façon concrète, par l'hospitalité sacrificielle qu'il lui offre" (Marx, "Familiarité et transcendence," 12).
[30] Marx, "Familiarité et transcendence," 9, cautions that reducing the function of a meal to no more than its nutritional purpose is a misunderstanding; however, that is not to deny that nutrition and the maintenance of life is a fundamental purpose of eating.

people's connection with and dependence upon him,[31] a state of dependence that makes the maintenance of the relationship between people and deity via the cult a primary survival strategy that can no more be ignored than can production of the food that the people consume. However, this is not a mechanistic conception of the cult that just requires the people to make the sacrifices in order for everything to be all right, with no further commitment from the human side. The whole point is that there is a *relationship* to maintain, and according to Marx's analysis of sacrifice, the visible expression of that relationship is in communal dining involving deity and people, in which the parties share the comestibles that link them to each other and to the land. At a human level, to eat with another is to acknowledge a shared need for sustenance, to admit to vulnerability, and therefore implies a level of mutual trust that contains the potential for intimacy. In the same way, bringing food to the deity, making an offering and sharing a meal with him, implies a level of mutual trust between offerer and deity and contains the potential for intimacy. Although unlike the human participants God does not need the physical nourishment provided by the food, he does require the nourishment of reputation, the honor, that such actions bring when they are appropriately carried out. The priests who facilitate the offerings are therefore extremely significant in that according to the standards and the attitude which they employ when they manipulate the sacrificial foodstuffs, they either nurture or degrade the relationship between deity and people by nourishing or starving the deity's honor. This in its turn will have consequences for the well-being and prosperity of the people, since the deity, responsible as he is for food provision, may withhold food supplies from those who dishonor him and reject his proffered relationship (cf. Mal 1:9; 2:2).[32] Speaking of the altar as a table enables the prophet to compare what the priests are offering YHWH with the foodstuffs that

---

[31] For the relationship between people, deity and land as expressed in offerings of produce, see Marx, "Familiarité et transcendence," 6, and idem, "Tuer, donner, manger dans le culte sacrificiel de l'Ancien Israël," in *La cuisine et l'autel: Les sacrifices en questions dans les sociétés de la Méditerranée Ancienne* (ed. Stella Georgoudi, Renée Koch Piettre, and Francis Schmidt; Bibliothèque de l'École des Hautes Études Sciences Religieuses 124; Tournhout: Brepols, 2005), 3–13 (8)

[32] Steven L. McKenzie and Howard N. Wallace, "Covenant Themes in Malachi," *CBQ* 45 (1983): 549–63, read the entire book of Malachi in the light of a covenant between YHWH and Israel that is being broken by the people, with the result that they are suffering the hardships—including food shortages—that are threatened in the covenant curses in Deut 28. Although expressed in somewhat different terms, this is compatible with the reading offered here. Likewise, Glazier-McDonald, *Malachi*, 65–66, argues that Mal 2:2, in which YHWH claims to have cursed the priests' blessings, refers to the diminishing of agricultural fertility because of the priests' lack of respect for YHWH.

they might offer to a figure of human authority (Mal 1:8), thereby invoking the etiquette of human dining, including all the social implications that accompany food consumption at an earthly level, in order to make them see just how unacceptable their behavior is.

The critique of the priests' sacrificial practice in Mal 1:8, 12–14 raises the question of whether we should think of the priests' own sacrifices as blemished and inappropriate, or whether they are accepting blemished animals to offer on behalf of ordinary worshippers. Either or both could be the case, although the continuation of the passage fits more readily with the latter situation, namely, that the priests are accepting blemished animals to offer in sacrifice from ordinary worshippers. The castigation goes on to bewail how the priests have violated YHWH's covenant with Levi by not giving the people proper instruction (2:4–9).[33] This invokes the concept of a divine primaeval commission given to Levi the patriarch and his sons,[34] according to which they are entrusted with the job

---

[33] Petersen, *Zechariah 9–14 and Malachi*, 189–93, differentiates here between priests and Levites, arguing that the (Aaronide) priests who are condemned for improper exercise of sacrificial functions are not the same as the sons of Levi who received this covenant and are responsible for teaching the people. According to Petersen, YHWH's threat in 2:2–3 to curse the priests' blessings, remove their seed and spread dung on their faces reverses the covenant of eternal priesthood granted to the Aaronide Phinehas in Num 25, by defiling (i.e. un-ordaining) the priests and thereby cutting off the priestly line (pages 187–89). The Levites by comparison have been faithfully exercising their teaching responsibilities, but have been undermined by the priests' actions (pages 191–92, 193). Petersen thus reads into Malachi's diatribe the priest/Levite (Aaron/Levi) distinction that is evidenced in other postexilic materials such as Chronicles and Ezra-Nehemiah. However, the distinction is hard to maintain convincingly in Malachi, and other exegetes reject it in this context (as do I). See O'Brien, *Priest and Levite*, 47–48, and eadem, *Nahum, Habakkuk, Zephaniah, Haggai, Zechariah, Malachi* (Abingdon Old Testament Commentaries; Nashville: Abingdon Press, 2004), 297.

[34] At least three passages in the Pentateuch present versions of how the Levites gained their calling to divine service, namely, Exod 32:25–29, Num 3:6–13, and Num 8:5–22. None of these traditions, however, specifies any duty of teaching entrusted to the sons of Levi, or speaks of a 'covenant' that YHWH has made with them. The combination of sacrificing and teaching that characterizes Levitical priesthood in Malachi appears rather in Ezek 44:15–16, 23–24 (although with Zadokite overtones) and Deut 33:8–10. Jer 33:18–22 also speaks of a covenant with the Levites, although it does not mention teaching, only offering sacrifice on the altar. Scholars have often argued for associating Malachi's "covenant with Levi" with the sayings in Deuteronomy and/or Jeremiah, although others link it with the covenant with Phinehas in Num 25; so, for example, Glazier-McDonald, *Malachi*, 77–80, and Douglas Stuart, "Malachi," in *The Minor Prophets.* Vol. 3. *Zephaniah, Haggai, Zechariah, Malachi* (ed. Thomas Edward McComiskey;

of instructing the people about what God requires.³⁵ Precisely what instructions, whether oral or written, and if written, which (if any) version or part of the present Pentateuchal law is envisaged, is open to speculation; however, such instruction would certainly have included stipulations about worship and sacrifice, so the inclusion of a complaint about the priests' improper exercise of their duty of instruction immediately after complaints about them offering blemished victims for sacrifice implies that the priests have been insufficiently rigorous in applying the proper standards of perfection for sacrificial animals, and have failed to inform worshippers when a potential victim is unsuitable, thereby giving the impression of acceptability to what is not acceptable.³⁶ The final responsibility for what makes it onto the altar lies with the priests, whether the offerings in question are their own personal offerings or those of the general populace; hence the priests are castigated not only for defiling the altar but also for failing in their duty of instruction.³⁷

The priests appear again in the fourth complaint (2:17–3:5). This concerns an expressed weariness with YHWH's (non-)exercise of justice (2:17), to which the reply is that a figure is coming to purge the community (3:1–5), and the first thing he will do is to "purify the sons of Levi ... until they present offerings to the Lord in righteousness" (3:3), resulting in the offering of Judah and Jerusalem

---

Grand Rapids, MI: Baker Books, 1998), 1245–396 (1316–18). It is probable, however, that the conception in Malachi is the author's own re-reading of tradition for his own purposes, just as different prophets present the wilderness period differently according to their own particular interests—Hosea sees it as a honeymoon period of blissful faithfulness between YHWH and Israel (Hos 2:16–17 [Heb.]), while Ezekiel views it rather as a period of infidelity and sin (Ezek 23:2–4). A similar conclusion about Malachi's "covenant of Levi" is reached by O'Brien, *Priest and Levite*, 111 (she discusses the relationship of Malachi's covenant of Levi to Deut 33 and Num 25 on pages 104–106, and to Jer 33 briefly on pages 135–36).

[35] A similar duty of instruction, and failure to fulfil it, is attributed to the priests in Hos 4:6.

[36] René Vuilleumier, "Malachie," in Samuel Amsler, André Lacocque, and René Vuilleumier, *Aggée, Zacharie, Malachie* (CAT 11c; Neuchâtel/Paris: Delachaux & Niestlé, 1981), 217–56, suggests that the priests have been accepting blemished animals out of compassion for the people at a time of hardship, although this is unacceptable because "Si, dans les temps difficiles, le peuple n'offre plus que des bêtes tarées, son geste perd le sens du témoignage de confiance en la toute-puissance et la providence de Dieu" (page 229).

[37] O'Brien, *Priest and Levite*, 36, 41, argues for a broad interpretation of the term תורה ("instruction") to include both specific and general matters rather than just limiting it to rulings on matters of ritual purity.

being acceptable to YHWH as in former years (3:4).[38] This is certainly the solution to the problems noted in the first and second chapters about unsuitable sacrifices being made—ensuring that the priests once again fulfil their responsibilities for vetting the sacrifices as they ought, so that what is offered is appropriately honorific all round. There are two observations to be made here. First, the clean-up starts with the priests, rather than with the community at large: adulterers, sorcerers and oppressors, who might seem to modern ethical sensibilities to be the greater and more dangerous sinners, are dealt with only after the priesthood has been purified (3:3–5). This points to the immense significance of the priests' role in Malachi's conception of societal structure. Second, priesthood is again conceptualized in terms of making offerings, that is, in terms of its connection with ritual manipulation of food on the altar (3:3–4). This is clearly a very strong and significant element of priesthood for Malachi; indeed, it would be fair to say that for Malachi, to be a priest is by definition to make offerings of food on the altar. Put another way, according to Malachi it is vital to have a properly constituted and functioning priesthood, and for that priesthood to make appropriately performed sacrifices, if the community is to prosper.[39] Such prosperity includes not just ample food supplies but ethical and godly living, as is indicated by the general purging that will follow once the priesthood has been purified (3:5).

The final complaint for our consideration is the fifth one (3:7–12). This is again food-related, namely, that everyone is failing to bring in sufficient tithes to the temple.[40] Here, for the first time, there is a clear hint that the deficits in offerings (and possibly too the other complaints about God's injustice) might be in part the result of the people suffering hardship. The prophet urges the people to bring in the full amounts of food that are specified, promising that God will reward them with plenty for so doing and that agricultural pests and plagues will

---

[38] See n. 22 above on the question of whether or not these verses are secondary to the present text.

[39] Compare O'Brien, *Priest and Levite*, 148: "The priests are corrupt and must be radically purged, but the priesthood remains an ordained channel for the deity's communication with his people." Glazier-McDonald, *Malachi*, 154–55, argues that the correct covenant relationship with YHWH, by which everything functions in righteousness, or right order, can only be maintained via a correct cult, so it is no surprise that the priests should be the first in the order of those to be purified.

[40] Petersen, *Zechariah 9–14 and Malachi*, 215–17, understands the tithing practice referred to here in the light of Neh 10:35–40, where Levites collect the people's tithe into local storehouses and from there take a tenth of the tithe up to the Temple in Jerusalem; this latter "tithe of the tithe" would serve to provision the Temple and its personnel.

be removed (3:10–11).[41] This is reminiscent of the logic found in Haggai, where the people are urged to get on with rebuilding the temple despite their own less-than-ideal circumstances: put devotion to YHWH, as expressed in rebuilding the temple, before your own needs, says the prophet, and YHWH, who has been striking you with famine and hardship for neglecting the temple, will cause you to prosper (Hag 1:5–11; 2:15–19). Both Haggai and Malachi understand the people to have been suffering hardships because of their failed devotion, although it is equally possible in each case to see the failed devotion as stemming from hardship and from the concomitant inability to bring the required offerings without serious self-deprivation. This complaint in Malachi about the shortfall in tithes is less illuminating than some of his other complaints about the priests, but it is significant for its insistence on what is yet another cultic food-related practice—another sharing of food with God—as the remedy for food shortages within the community at large. Assuming that the whole book of Malachi refers to the same general time-period rather than being a compilation of oracles from different periods, the implied food shortages in 3:10–11 provide a background against which to interpret the demands for cultic rigour—specifically, rigour as related to offering comestibles—in the previous complaints. This in turn gives a particular significance to the role of the priests, since it is they who are to be responsible for giving instruction, including how to make appropriate offerings, and for monitoring the quality of sacrificial offerings, both of which (instruction and quality control) are important elements in ensuring that appropriate honor is given to YHWH so that the people's relationship with the deity, and thus their food supply, can be maintained.

CONCLUSION

For both Joel and Malachi, then, priests have an important role as facilitators and enactors of sacrifice in the temple; and, given that sacrifice involves the offering of foodstuffs to God, this gives the priests an intimate connection with the nation's food supply. When they (are able to) carry out their sacrifice-related duties in a manner that is compatible with sacral requirements, provision of food both for themselves and for the community on whose behalf they serve is ensured. When (for whatever reason) those duties are not carried out correctly, there will be food shortages. Each prophet takes a different perspective on the priests' failure to perform sacrifices in an acceptable manner. In the case of Joel,

---

[41] Hill, *Malachi*, 183, suggests that the phrase מידכם היתה זאת addressed to the priests in 1:9 may be an indirect allusion to this agricultural hardship, laying the blame for it on the priests.

the priests' failure is not their own fault, but the result of environmental disaster (famine and locusts) by which they are deprived of the wherewithal to offer sacrifices, and so they need to plead with God to rectify the situation. In the case of Malachi, the priests' failure is more culpable: they are apparently accepting inappropriate animals for sacrifice instead of holding worshippers to the requisite high standards, so they themselves need to be chastised by Y$_{HWH}$ and brought into line. There are implications of agricultural shortages that accompany this impure worship, and it is unclear whether these are viewed as being the cause or the effect of the blemished sacrifices; it is certainly possible to read the shortages as the effect of failure to prioritize the worshipful use of food, possibly at a time of hardship. What is clear, though, is that the priests are being instructed by God to "clean up their act" in order to buttress the community's well-being and prosperity. In each case, then, the priests are responsible for ensuring the proper food supply for the temple and the deity; this will not only bring Y$_{HWH}$ honor commensurate with his deserts, but will also safeguard the food supply for the people at large by nurturing the people's relationship with the one who is the source of the nation's produce. This indicates that in the eyes of both Joel and Malachi, the priests have a vital role in ensuring that the people of God have ample provision of food; and while (as Joel demonstrates) the priests may not be able to prevent fluctuations in the food supply altogether, if they are not doing their duty properly then no-one can expect to enjoy abundant food supplies. The priests are there to facilitate communion between people and deity by their manipulation of the food brought to his table, and to teach the people their liturgical duty of respect and honor for the God who provides the nation with food, as expressed in the way that the people use that food. Faithful priests mean reliable food supplies; and so faithful priests are as fundamental for the community's well-being as are abundant harvests.

6
A FAREWELL TO THE ANTICULTIC PROPHET: ATTITUDES TOWARDS THE CULT IN THE BOOK OF AMOS

Göran Eidevall

Generations of biblical scholars have sought to answer the question: how did Amos from Tekoa view the temple cult? Two rivalling hypotheses have been formulated. Amos has been categorized either as an anticultic dissident or as a cultic functionary. On the basis of a survey of previous research I shall argue that both hypotheses are untenable. What they have in common is the erroneous presupposition that we have access to accurate biographical information about Amos from Tekoa. Clearly, another kind of approach is called for. On the basis of an examination of all passages in the book of Amos containing allusions or references to the temple cult, I will discuss to what extent it is possible to speak of a consistent (editorial) attitude towards the cult in this prophetic book.

1. AMOS AS AN ANTICULTIC PROPHET

Issues relating to the temple cult are only treated in a few passages in the book of Amos. These passages are often called "cult-critical." Hence, it is perhaps not surprising that the image of Amos as an anticultic prophet has been a recurring motif through the entire era of modern biblical research. In the opinion of Julius Wellhausen and other nineteenth century scholars, prophets like Amos, Hosea, Isaiah, and Jeremiah were religious reformers with an anticultic agenda. Allegedly representing a new stage within the history of religion, ethical monotheism, these prophets proclaimed that ethical conduct was more important than sacrifices or other rituals.[1] According to Wellhausen, the zeal of prophets like Amos and Hosea was directed not only against cultic abuses, but against the cult itself, because worship emphasizing the value of sacrificial gifts implied that YHWH might be bribed.[2] The view that prophets (being charismatic) tended to stand in opposition to the established institutional religion of the priests was bolstered by the theories propounded by the sociologist Max Weber.[3]

In commentaries from the early twentieth century, certain passages in the book of Amos (4:4–5; 5:4–5; 5:21–24) are often interpreted as prophetic rejections of sacrificial cult as such. In the words of Harper, commenting on 5:21–24, "[i]t is the cultus which seems to the prophet to be the occasion of all trouble."[4] Discussing the same passage, in conjunction with 5:25, Cripps concluded that "Amos, like the other great prophets, esteemed daily conduct above sanctuary duties, sacrifice in particular," and that "sacrifice cannot really be necessary."[5] This trend reached a peak in the 1930s, with an article written by Paul Volz, where it was argued that both Amos and Jeremiah denounced all sacrificial cult, because such practices were ultimately of Canaanite origin.[6] For Volz, who made an analogy between Jeremiah and Martin Luther, it was almost self-evident that the classical prophets advocated worship centred on YHWH's word.[7] The Protestant bias in such antiritualistic and antisacrificial scholarship is unmistakable.

---

[1] For a sustained critique of the evolutionist tendency in Wellhausens's writings on these issues, see Jonathan Klawans, *Purity, Sacrifice, and the Temple: Symbolism and Supersessionism in the Study of Ancient Judaism* (Oxford: Oxford University Press, 2006), 6–9, 75–76.

[2] Julius Wellhausen, *Prolegomena to the History of Israel* (trans. W. Robertson Smith; Cambridge: Cambridge University Press, 1885), 23, 471–72.

[3] For a critical discussion of the Weberian opposition between priests and prophets, which shows that it is not applicable to the Hebrew Bible, see Ziony Zevit, "The Prophet versus Priest Hypothesis: Its History and Origin," in *The Priests in the Prophets* (ed. Lester L. Grabbe and Alice Ogden Bellis; JSOTS 408; London: T&T Clark, 2004). See also Klawans, *Purity, Sacrifice*, 79–80.

[4] William R. Harper, *A Critical and Exegetical Commentary on Amos and Hosea* (ICC; Edinburgh: T&T Clark, 1905), 133. Cf., in a similar vein, Ernst Sellin, *Das Zwölfprophetenbuch* (KAT XII/1; Leipzig: Deichertsche Verlagsbuchhandlung, 1929), 234–35.

[5] Richard S. Cripps, *A Critical and Exegetical Commentary on the Book of Amos* (London: SPCK, 1929), 198. Cf., similarly, Karl Marti, *Das Dodekapropheton* (KHC XIII; Tübingen: J.C.B. Mohr, 1904), 180–81, on Amos 4:4–5.

[6] Paul Volz, "Die radikale Ablehnung der Kultreligion durch die alttestamentlichen Propheten," *ZSTh* 14 (1937): 63–85 (64–66).

[7] See Volz, "Radikale Ablehnung," 63, 79–84.

In more recent Amos commentaries, the perspective is usually more nuanced and balanced. As a rule, it is stated that Amos' proclamations that YHWH rejected the worship performed in a number of sanctuaries in the eighth century BCE do not entail a condemnation of sacrificial cult *per se*.[8] It is often suggested that the prophetic cult criticism, which may have been closely related to the wisdom tradition, mainly targeted the attitude of the worshipers, not the worship as such.[9] Still, some modern commentaries interpret Amos 5:21–24 in terms of a fundamental opposition between cult and ethics, claiming that the text exhorts the reader to choose between either striving for justice and righteousness or participating in sacrificial worship.[10] According to Shalom Paul, "the prophetic attacks against the cult did introduce a new dimension into the religion of Israel," according to which the "essence of God's demand ... is not to be found in the cult but in the moral and ethical spheres of life."[11] Such statements seem to be based on a questionable contrast between cultic issues, which belonged to the priestly sphere, and moral issues, which were a prophetic concern.

Somewhat updated versions of the anticultic prophet hypothesis have been defended in recent scholarship on the prophets.[12] Drawing on the theories of

---

[8] Thus, e.g., James L. Mays, *Amos* (OTL; London: SCM, 1969), 106–9.

[9] See, e.g., Hans W. Wolff, *Joel and Amos* (trans. W. Janzen, S. Dean McBride, and Charles A. Muenchow; Hermeneia; Philadelphia: Fortress, 1977), 220, and Shalom Paul, *Amos* (Hermeneia; Philadelphia: Fortress, 1991), 141. See also Alexander B. Ernst, *Weisheitliche Kultkritik: Zu Theologie und Ethik des Sprüchebuchs und der Prophetie des 8. Jahrhunderts* (BThSt 23; Neukirchen-Vluyn: Neukirchener, 1994), 97–197, and Otto Kaiser, "Kult und Kultkritik im Alten Testament," in *"Und Mose schrieb dieses Lied auf": Studien zum Alten Testament und zum Alten Orient* (ed. Manfred Dietrich and Ingo Kottsieper; AOAT 250; Münster: Ugarit-Verlag, 1998), 401–26.

[10] Thus Wilhelm Rudolph, *Joel—Amos—Obadja—Jona* (KAT XIII/2; Gütersloh: Gerd Mohn, 1971), 208–12. A sharp critique of the idea that 5:21–24 is about a choice between cult and justice has been delivered by Alberto Soggin, *The Prophet Amos* (trans. John Bowden; London: SCM, 1987), 99: "the alternative ... seems intrinsically absurd, given that in the ancient world ... a society that was not founded on religion and the cult was inconceivable."

[11] Paul, *Amos*, 139.

[12] Ronald S. Hendel, "Prophets, Priests, and the Efficacy of Ritual," in *Pomegranates and Golden Bells: Studies in Biblical, Jewish, and Near Eastern Ritual, Law, and Literature in Honor of Jacob Milgrom* (ed. David P. Wright, David Noel Freedman, and Avi Hurvitz; Winona Lake, IN: Eisenbrauns, 1995), 185–98; Thomas Krüger, "Erwägungen zur prophetischen Kultkritik," in *Die unwiderstehliche Wahrheit: Studien zur alttestamentlichen Prophetie* (ed. Rüdiger Lux and Ernst-Joachim Waschke; ABGe 23; Leipzig: Evangelische Verlagsanstalt, 2006), 37–55; John Barton, "The Prophets and the Cult," in *Temple and Worship in Biblical Israel* (ed. John Day; LHBOTS 422; Lon-

Mary Douglas (rather than Weber), John Barton claims that Amos was an "antiritualist."[13] As pointed out by Barton, the strength of this hypothesis is that it can account for the radical formulations found in some passages, for example, Amos 4:4–5 and 5:21–24, which seemingly express a total rejection of the cult.[14] However, despite Barton's claim to the contrary, the notion of an anticultic prophet remains suspiciously anachronistic.[15] No such prophets surface in the extant extra-biblical sources from the Ancient Near East.[16] With Max Polley, I find it highly unlikely that Amos and other biblical prophets took a position on cultic matters which made them, more or less, "the only persons in the ancient world who believed religion could be properly practiced without sacrifices."[17] Hence, it is necessary to look for alternative explanations of those passages in the book of Amos which seem to imply a total rejection of the sacrificial cult.

2. Amos as a Cultic Prophet

Already in the 1940s some scholars began to question the view that Amos acted as a free-lancer, without any involvement in organized cult. Cross-cultural comparisons, they averred, made it likely that prophets, as a rule, were affiliated to the temple cult, in one way or other—also in Israel and Judah. Sigmund Mowinckel had suggested that some passages in the Psalms were meant to be spoken by prophets active in the cult.[18] Developing such ideas in a radical way, the Swedish scholar Alfred Haldar claimed that all the protagonists of the biblical prophetic literature were members of "associations forming part of the cultic personnel."[19] According to Haldar, Amos thus "belonged to the cult staff."[20]

---

don: T&T Clark, 2005), 111–22; idem, *The Theology of the Book of Amos* (Cambridge: Cambridge University Press, 2012).

[13] Barton, "The Prophets," 116–21, and idem, *Theology*, 84–92.

[14] Barton, *Theology*, 66–67, 84–89.

[15] As regards the classical prophets of Israel, Barton, *Theology*, 90, avers that "it is not necessarily an anachronism to paint them in the colors of Protestant reformers."

[16] For a comprehensive documentation, see Martti Nissinen, *Prophets and Prophecy in the Ancient Near East* (with contributions by Choon Leong Seow and Robert K. Ritner; WAW 12; Atlanta: Society of Biblical Literature, 2003).

[17] Max E. Polley, *Amos and the Davidic Empire: A Socio-Historical Approach* (New York: Oxford University Press, 1989), 87.

[18] Sigmund Mowinckel, *Psalmenstudien III: Kultprophetie und prophetische Psalmen* (Kristiania: Dybwad, 1923), 2–29. See also John Hilber, *Cultic Prophecy in the Psalms* (BZAW 352; Berlin: de Gruyter, 2005).

[19] Alfred Haldar, *Associations of Cult Prophets among the Ancient Semites* (Uppsala: Almqvist & Wiksell, 1945), xi.

This was evident, he claimed, since the term *nōqēd*, employed to describe Amos' profession (in 1:1), was "a designation of the watchers of the temple herds."[21] However, beyond this vague connection to temple administration, Haldar failed to prove that Amos had a function in the cult itself.[22]

Concentrating above all on chapters 1–2, Aage Bentzen made an attempt to connect parts of the book of Amos to concrete rituals.[23] He claimed that the series of oracles against neighbouring nations should be understood in the light of the Egyptian "execration texts," and an accompanying ritual procedure which involved crushing ceramic pots representing the nation's enemies.[24] However, Bentzen could not point to any specific formulations in Amos 1–2 which would imply cultic usage. Expanding this approach, Arvid Kapelrud made a study covering the entire book.[25] He claimed that Amos was "strongly influenced by the cult," and that he had borrowed speech forms from that sphere.[26] However, apart from the well-known cult-critical passages (4:4–5; 5:21–24), and possible references to feasts (5:18–20), he was not able to detect any palpable connections to the cult.

According to Ernst Würthwein's reading of the book, Amos went through two distinct phases in his prophetic career.[27] The former herdsman started out as a cultic prophet. In that capacity, he proclaimed judgment over other nations (1:3–2:3), while acting as an intercessor for his own people (7:1–6).[28] Later, he became a radical prophet of doom, dissociated from the official cult—a development reflected in the series of vision reports, where Amos first ceases to pray for the people (7:7–8) and then proclaims that the judgment is irrevocable (8:1–2).[29] In this way, Würthwein managed to account for the diversity found in the book, where cult-critical oracles are juxtaposed with passages which seem to

---

[20] Haldar, *Associations*, 112.

[21] Ibid., 79, n. 5.

[22] On the term *nqd* in Ugarit and the Hebrew Bible, see Peter C. Craigie, "Amos the *nōqēd* in the Light of Ugaritic," *Studies in Religion* 11 (1982): 29–33. According to Miloš Bič, "Amos: Ein Hepatoskopos," *VT* 1 (1951): 293–96, the term *nōqēd* denoted a cultic functionary, who inspected the livers of animals in order to obtain omens. For an early critique of this idiosyncratic proposal, see A. Murtonen, "Amos: A Hepatoscoper?" *VT* 2 (1952): 170–71.

[23] Aage Bentzen, "The Ritual Background of Amos i 2–ii 16," *OTS* 8 (1950): 85–99.

[24] Bentzen, "Ritual Background," 87.

[25] Arvid Kapelrud, *Central Ideas in Amos* (Oslo: Aschehoug, 1956).

[26] Kapelrud, *Central Ideas*, 69.

[27] Ernst Würthwein, "Amos-Studien," *ZAW* 62 (1950): 10–52 (19–40).

[28] Ibid., 24–28, 35–40.

[29] Ibid., 28–35.

presuppose the validity of certain cultic acts (such as intercession). However, this hypothesis was based on a strained interpretation of 7:14–15 as describing three stages in Amos' career: 1) a herdsman and tender of sycamore trees (v. 14b), 2) a cultic prophet (v. 14aβ, understood in the past tense), and 3) a freelancer called by YHWH to prophesy (v. 15).[30] Antonius Gunneweg modified and simplified Würthwein's theory.[31] Assuming that Amos defined his role as a *nābî'* in a broad an inclusive way, he argued that it was unnecessary to postulate two successive call experiences. The mission of such a cultic prophet, he averred, would encompass messages of judgment as well as of salvation, since both aspects were important in rituals of covenant renewal.[32]

In a similar vein, René Vuilleumier maintained that the covenant cult included both blessings and curses. Therefore, he thought that the entire section 1:3–2:16 could fit such a cultic event.[33] In addition, Vuilleumier called attention to the so-called doxologies (4:13; 5:8; 9:5–6), which he interpreted as admonitions to participate in cultic praise of YHWH.[34] Henning Graf Reventlow went further, integrating also other parts of the book of Amos (such as 4:6–11 and the vision reports in chapters 7–9) in such a reconstruction.[35] Indeed, he proposed that the book in its entirety could be related to "die kultische Situation des Bundesfestes."[36] However, the hypothesis defended by Gunneweg, Vuilleumier, and Reventlow suffers from a fatal weakness. As is now widely recognized, there is no evidence that covenant renewal ceremonies were part of the cult during the eighth century BCE (or at any time during the monarchic era). Thus, whereas these scholars endowed Amos with an active role in a purely hypothetical cult, featuring prophetic diatribes and indictments, the prophet's relation to (or: role within?) the regular temple cult, which involved sacrifices, remained unclear. To sum up this line of research, which has been discontinued after the 1960s, the textual support for the theory that Amos was a functionary within the cult proved to be very meagre.

---

[30] See Ibid., 16–24, 27–28.
[31] Antonius Gunneweg, "Erwägungen zu Amos 7, 14," *ZThK* 57 (1960): 1–16.
[32] Gunneweg, "Erwägungen," 5–16.
[33] René Vuilleumier, *La tradition cultuelle d'Israël dans la prophétie d'Amos et d'Osée* (Cahiers théologiques 45; Neuchâtel: Delachaux & Niestlé, 1960), 81–82.
[34] Vuilleumier, *La tradition*, 88–90.
[35] Henning Graf Reventlow, *Das Amt des Propheten bei Amos* (FRLANT 80; Göttingen: Vandenhoeck & Ruprecht, 1962), 30–90.
[36] Ibid., 111.

3. A Farewell to the Quest for the Historical Amos

It has been shown above that the scholarly efforts to prove that Amos was either an anticultic activist or a cultic functionary have failed to yield any secure results. These lines of research are based upon the presupposition that it is possible to reconstruct the life and career of Amos from Tekoa. However, all we have, in terms of biographical "data" about Amos, is the superscription in 1:1, which belongs to the book's editorial framework, and a short conflict narrative (7:10–17), mostly consisting of dialog, which appears to be a rather late legend without any biographical intent.[37] Hence, I suggest that it is time to call off the quest for the historical Amos: to switch the focus of attention from the elusive *prophet* Amos to the *book* of Amos, which is available to us.

4. A Systematic Study of Attitudes Towards the Cult in the Book of Amos

In order to obtain a reliable picture of the attitude(s) towards the temple cult in the book of Amos it is necessary to conduct a systematic study. Every single reference or allusion to cultic matters should be taken into account. In each case, it is important to assess the function within the literary context. As regards those passages which contain explicit discussions of cultic issues, it is essential to make a rhetorical analysis. In the following, I will present the results of my analysis of the relevant passages rather briefly.[38]

2:6–8. The enumeration of offences in 2:6b–8 is of interest, because it reaches its climax with the following depiction: "They stretch themselves out beside every altar, on garments taken in pledge, and they drink the wine of those who have been fined, in the house of their god" (2:8). In order to increase the reader's indignation, it is emphasized that the corrupt oppressors use expropriated goods in banquets held at sanctuaries. Hence, one may infer that the author was concerned about the holiness of altars and temples dedicated to YHWH.

3:14. The oracle in 3:14 predicts the destruction of the temple in Bethel "When I deal with the misdeeds of Israel, I will deal with the altars of Bethel: the horns of the altar will be cut off, and fall to the ground." Arguably, the pri-

---

[37] See A. Graeme Auld, *Amos* (Old Testament Guides; Sheffield: JSOT Press, 1986), 38–40, and Jürgen Werlitz, "Amos und sein Biograph: Zur Entstehung und Intention der Prophetenerzählung," *BZ* 22 (2000): 233–51.

[38] In the following sections of the book of Amos I could not find any allusions or references to the cult: 1:3–2:5; 2:9–16; 3:1–8; 4:1–3; 4:6–12; 5:1–3; 5:6–7; 5:10–17; 5:26–27; 6:8–14; 7:7–8; 8:1–9; 8:11–12; 9:2–4; 9:7–15.

mary target is Bethel, not altars in general. It is possible that this oracle originated in circles endorsing the idea that sacrificial worship of YHWH should be performed only in the Jerusalem temple.[39] Nothing in 3:14 indicates that the author despised sacrificial cult as such. On the contrary, the rhetorical force of this utterance relies on the notion that altars and sacrifices were extremely important. One may add the observation that the motif of cutting off the horns might allude to the practice of seeking refuge in a sanctuary by grabbing the horns of the altar (1 Kgs 1:50–53; 2:28–29).

4:4–5. The passage 4:4–5 has been characterized as a "sarcastic imitation of the priestly call to worship."[40] However, the biting sarcasm is mainly limited to verse 4a. The invitation to participate in the sacrificial cult at Bethel and Gilgal is, quite unexpectedly, phrased as an exhortation to "multiply transgressions" (v. 4aβ). In light of the following (rather uncontroversial) description of various sacrifices (vv. 4b–5a), this should probably be interpreted as a total rejection of the cult performed at these two sites, Bethel and Gilgal. But on which grounds is the cult being rejected? It has been suggested that this oracle denounces the attitude of the worshipers.[41] Admittedly, their tendency to advertise their acts of piety is ridiculed (v. 5aβ). However, that would hardly be a sufficient reason for wholesale rejection. Another explanation must be sought. According to Hans Barstad, "the cults performed at these ancient places were non-Yahwistic or strongly Yahwistic/syncretistic."[42] However, this hypothesis is not supported by any formulations in the text. Since verse 4a implies a strong link between frequenting these two cultic sites and transgressing, I suggest that the sacrifices were rejected because they were offered in the wrong place: in Bethel or Gilgal, instead of Jerusalem. In an eighth century setting, the idea might be that these two sites were doomed because of the crimes and wrongdoings committed by

---

[39] I find it likely that 3:14 represents a *vaticinium ex eventu* referring to Josiah's desecration of Bethel and its main altar, see 2 Kgs 23:15–16. Thus also Jörg Jeremias, *The Book of Amos* (trans. D. W. Stott; OTL; Louisville, KY: Westminster John Knox, 1998), 62–63.

[40] Francis I. Andersen and David Noel Freedman, *Amos: A New Translation with Introduction and Commentary* (AB 24A; New York: Doubleday, 1989), 433.

[41] Thus, e.g., Mays, *Amos*, 75; Wolff, *Joel and Amos*, 220; Robert Martin-Achard, "The End of the People of God: A Commentary on the Book of Amos," in *God's People in Crisis* (ed. R. Martin-Achard and S. Paul Re'emi; ITC; Edinburgh: Handsel, 1984), 1–74 (35), and Karl Möller, *A Prophet in Debate: The Rhetoric of Persuasion in the Book of Amos* (BZAW 389; Berlin: de Gruyter, 2003), 264. In the words of Paul, *Amos*, 141, "the sacrifices themselves are proper; only the people offering them are acting improperly."

[42] Hans M. Barstad, *The Religious Polemics of Amos* (VTSup 34; Leiden: Brill, 1984), 56.

the people and the leaders of Israel that are described elsewhere in the book. Alternatively, if this passage originated toward the end of the seventh century or later, it can be interpreted in line with Deuteronomistic ideology which regarded the very establishment of YHWH temples in the Northern kingdom as sinful (see 1 Kgs 12:26–30; 13:33–34; 15:30; 16:31; 2 Kgs 23:15; cf. also Deuteronomy 12).

4:13. This is the first in a series of three doxologies which have been inserted by an editor into three different sections within the book: at 4:13; 5:8; 9:5–6. They have several features in common, such as cosmological themes, a particular style (where participles serve as divine epithets) and a shared refrain.[43] For the purpose of this investigation it is not necessary to decide whether these doxologies are cited from a preexisting hymn, or if they were composed for their present positions.[44] The two aspects that I would like to stress are the hymnic character of these passages, and the observation that they (together with 1:2) constitute a framework for the collections of oracles.[45] This arrangement suggests some kind of liturgical setting for the reading of the book of Amos, at some (late) stage of its history of composition and redaction.[46]

5:4–5. This passage can be interpreted along the same lines as 4:4–5 (see above). While two of the three sites mentioned, Bethel and Gilgal, were situated within the borders of the kingdom of Israel, the third, Beer-Sheba, was a pil-

---

[43] See further Klaus Koch, "Die Rolle der hymnischen Abschnitte in der Komposition des Amos-Buches," *ZAW* 86 (1974): 504–37; Fabrizio Foresti, "Funzione semantica dei brani participiali di Amos: 4,13; 5,8s; 9,5s," *Biblica* 62 (1981): 169–84; and Thomas McComiskey, "The Hymnic Elements of the Prophecy of Amos: A Study of Form-Critical Methodology," *JETS* 30 (1987): 139–57. See also Jeremias, *Book of Amos*, 76–79, and Aaron Schart, *Die Entstehung des Zwölfprophetenbuchs: Neubearbeitungen von Amos im Rahmen schriftenübergreifender Redaktionsprozesse* (BZAW 260; Berlin: de Gruyter, 1998), 234–37.

[44] For two different versions of the hypothesis that one hymn has been split up, see Friedrich Horst, "Die Doxologien im Amosbuch," *ZAW* 47 (1929): 45–54; and John D. W. Watts, *Vision and Prophecy in Amos* (Expanded Anniversary Edition; Macon, GA: Mercer University Press, 1997 [1958]), 9–27. Others have stressed the close connections to the literary context. Thus, e.g., McComiskey, "Hymnic Elements," 155–56, and Gerhard Pfeifer, "Jahwe als Schöpfer der Welt und Herr ihrer Mächte in der Verkündigung des Propheten Amos," *VT* 41 (1991): 475–81.

[45] See Koch, "Die Rolle," 534–35.

[46] So already Horst, "Doxologien," 50–54, who even claimed that it was possible to outline a very specific ritual setting, within the sphere of sacral jurisdiction. For a more nuanced position, see Koch, "Die Rolle," 536, who observes that this "Gebrauch geprägter poetischer Stücke legt liturgische Verwendung nahe." Jeremias, *Book of Amos*, 78, speaks of an "exilic/postexilic penitential ritual."

grimage site far to the south which was frequented also by people from the north. According to Amos 5:4–5, all three had apparently been rejected by YHWH. Therefore, it was pointless to participate in worship there. However, this does not imply a rejection of all temple cult whatsoever. On the contrary, the exhortation דרשוני, "seek me!" seems to have cultic connotations (Deut 12:5; Ps 34:5, 11).[47] It is worth noting that offering sacrifices in Jerusalem is not prohibited by this prophecy.

5:8. See the comments on 4:13 above.

5:18–20. It is likely that the term יום ה', "the day of YHWH," once referred to a major temple feast, and that Amos 5:18–20 should be understood against that background.[48] Hence, it is conceivable that the rhetoric of this passage can be described in terms of reversal of cultic expectations. However, despite all scholarly efforts devoted to this topic, it has not been possible to reach any consensus concerning the precise cultic connotations of the phrase יום ה'.[49] As regards the occurrence of "the day of YHWH" and closely related formulations in the book of the Twelve, James Nogalski has shown that the common denominator would seem to be "divine intervention," rather than "cultic feast."[50] Thus, it is uncertain whether 5:18–20 contains any specific references to the cult.

5:21–24. The first part of this oracle, comprising verses 21–22, can be described as an inverted version of a cultic *Gattung*, viz. the priestly declaration that the offerings which had been brought forward had been accepted by the deity.[51] This shocking announcement of divine dislike, which begins with שנאתי ("I hate ..."), contains the phrase לא ארצה, "I do not accept" (v. 22aβ). It is important to note that the verb רצה was used as a technical term for divine acceptance of sacrifices.[52] In verse 22, moreover, all major types of sacrifice are mentioned, and denounced: the burnt offering (עלה), the communion sacrifice (here: שלם), and the grain offering (מנחה). Hence, this passage should probably

---

[47] See further J. Lust, "Remarks on the Redaction of Amos v 4–6, 14–15," *OTS* 21 (1981): 129–54 (138–40), who has shown that the expression "seek YHWH" may carry either a cultic or a moral sense, depending on the context.

[48] For a recent defense of this hypothesis, see Reinhard Müller, "Der finstere Tag Jahwes: Zum kultischen Hintergrund von Am 5,18–20," *ZAW* 122 (2010): 576–92.

[49] For an overview, see Stig Norin, "Der Tag Gottes im Alten Testament: Jenseits der Spekulationen—Was ist übrig?" in *Le Jour de Dieu / Der Tag Gottes* (ed. Anders Hultgård and Stig Norin; WUNT 245; Tübingen: Mohr Siebeck, 2009), 33–42.

[50] See James D. Nogalski, "The Day(s) of YHWH in the Book of the Twelve," in *Thematic Threads in the Book of the Twelve* (ed. Paul L. Redditt and Aaron Schart; BZAW 325; Berlin: de Gruyter. 2003), 192–213.

[51] With, e.g., Jeremias, *Book of Amos*, 101–3.

[52] See Lev 1:3–4; 7:18; 19:7; 22:22, 25, 27; cf. also Jer 14:12 and Ezek 20:40–41.

be interpreted as a rejection of the sacrificial cult *in its entirety*. However, this is *not* the same as a total rejection of *all* sacrificial cult! On a closer examination, the declaration in verses 21–22 is expressly relational. According to this text, YHWH rejects something particular and precise: the worship performed by the addressees. The rejection is total, but *situational*. In the following translation of 5:21–22 (which is my own), I have emphasized the consistent use of the second person plural:

> ²¹I hate, I reject *your* festivals, and I do not delight in *your* assemblies. ²²Even if *you* bring me burnt offerings, and *your* grain offerings, I will not accept (them). I will not even look at the communion sacrifice(s) of *your* fatlings. (Amos 5:21–22)

Arguably, this cannot be interpreted as a general statement concerning YHWH's view of sacrificial cult as such. As far as I know, no one has ever suggested such a generalizing interpretation of verse 23, concerning this deity's attitude towards music! In my opinion, it is reasonable to read 5:21–24 in the light of those preceding passages which denounce major cultic sites in the Northern kingdom: 3:14; 4:4–5; 5:4–5. As a consequence, this declaration of divine rejection should be regarded as limited to sacrifices offered in temples located in Israel. In this way, the Amos text provides a theological explanation for the catastrophe that took place in 722 BCE. Because of their alleged sins and crimes, here summarized in terms of lacking concern for justice (v. 24), YHWH had decided to reject all sacrificial worship performed by the people of the Northern kingdom. This meant a unilateral cancellation of the reciprocal relationship between YHWH and Israel, entailing that divine protection would be withdrawn.[53] Notably, nothing is said concerning Judah, or the temple cult in Jerusalem.

5:25. The topic of the rhetorical question in 5:25 is sacrificial cult during the wilderness wanderings. It is difficult, however, to determine whether this implies a general statement concerning sacrifices.[54] I find it utterly unlikely that verse 25 alludes to a tradition about the desert period as a time without cult.[55]

---

[53] For a more elaborate analysis of Amos 5:21–24 along these lines, see Göran Eidevall, "Rejected Sacrifice in the Prophetic Literature: A Rhetorical Perspective," *SEÅ* 78 (2013): 31–45 (34–41).

[54] As pointed out by Andersen and Freedman, *Amos*, 531, it is possible to construe more than one answer to this rhetorical question. My own suggestions include: a) "No, of course not" (but the idea that the ancestors did not bring any sacrifices during those forty years stands in opposition to some Pentateuch traditions); b) "No, not those sacrifices (that is, זבח and מנחה)—but perhaps others?"; c) "Yes they did, but on a limited scale."

[55] With Soggin, *Prophet Amos*, 100. See also Rudolph, *Joel—Amos*, 212–23.

Rather, a contrast seems to be made between the lavish cult of the monarchic era, on the one hand, and the more limited worship during the wilderness period, on the other hand.[56] I suggest that this utterance makes sense in an exilic or postexilic setting, as a way of relativizing the significance of sacrificial cult, in a situation when large groups of YHWH worshippers had no access to a "legitimate" temple.[57]

6:1–7. Since the term מרזח occurs in verse 7 (in the plural), it is likely that the main ingredients in a banquet of the *marzēaḥ* type are described (and denounced?) in verses 4–6. One word used in verse 6, מזרק ("bowl"), carries cultic connotations.[58] Possibly, then, the text alludes to some kind of ritual. Alternatively, the point made could simply be that the loungers consumed large amounts of wine.[59] The extant evidence from different parts of the Ancient Near East indicates that *marzēaḥ* feasts were held within closed élite groups.[60] Therefore, the passage 6:4–7 is not relevant to a discussion of attitudes toward the public temple cult.

7:1–6. Within these two vision reports, the motif of prophetic intercession is of potential interest for this investigation. Acting like Moses (cf. Exod 32:11–14), the seer/speaker pleas for the sinful people (personified as "Jacob"): "O Lord YHWH, please forgive!" (v. 2), or "please stop!" (v. 5).[61] The author and the first readers may have regarded such intercession as some kind of cultic act.[62] In that case, 7:1–6 would reveal a positive attitude toward at least one aspect of the temple cult. However, in the absence of clear textual evidence this

---

[56] With Paul, *Amos*, 194.

[57] See further Göran Eidevall, *Sacrificial Rhetoric in the Prophetic Literature* (Lewiston: Edwin Mellen, 2012), 163–69.

[58] See Exod 27:3; 38:3; Num 4:14, and the fourteen attestations in Numbers 7. Also in the remaining biblical attestations of מזרק, there is a link to ritual procedures, see, e.g., 1 Kgs 7:40, 45, 50; 2 Kgs 25:15; 1 Chr 28:17; 2 Chr 4:8, 11, 22.

[59] According to Jonathan Greer, "A *Marzeah* and a *Mizraq*: A Prophet's Mêlée with Religious Diversity in Amos 6.4–7," *JSOT* 32 (2007): 243–62, the mention of the bowls implies that Amos 6:4–7 is primarily a critique of syncretistic cult. However, I do not find the argumentation convincing.

[60] For an insightful treatment of all biblical and extra-biblical texts mentioning the *mrzḥ*, see John McLaughlin, *The* Marzēaḥ *in the Prophetic Literature: References and Allusions in Light of the Extra-Biblical Evidence* (VTSup 86; Leiden: Brill, 2001). See especially the helpful summary on page 264.

[61] As regards the Moses analogy, see further Georg Steins, *Gericht und Vergebung: Re-Visionen zum Amosbuch* (SBS 221; Stuttgart: Katholisches Bibelwerk, 2010), 58–59.

[62] The cultic character of intercession has been emphasized by, e.g., Mowinckel and von Rad. For a discussion, see Uwe Becker, "Der Prophet als Fürbitter: zum literarhistorichen Ort der Amos-Visionen," *VT* 51 (2001): 141–65 (141–44).

can be no more than speculation. Still, I find it intriguing that the two motifs of rejected sacrificial cult and prohibited prophetic intercession are juxtaposed in Jer 14:11–12.

7:9. This oracle of disaster presages the destruction of all cultic sites in Israel: temples (מקדשי) as well as open space sanctuaries (במות, "high places"). Although the terminology is different, the perspective of 7:9 is perfectly consistent with that of previous passages like 3:14 and 5:4–5. Nothing is said about Judah or Jerusalem.

7:10–17. The lexeme כהן, "priest," occurs only once in the book of Amos, in the introduction to the narrative section 7:10–17. This story can be characterized as a reported dispute between Amos and Amaziah, "priest of Bethel" (v. 10).[63] Similar stories about confrontations between a prophet and a priest, where the latter appears to have the role of overseer of the local prophets, are found in the book of Jeremiah (see Jer 20:1–6; 29:24–32). It is important to point out that the negative portrayal of Amos' antagonist Amaziah need not indicate a general condemnation of the priesthood in every temple throughout the history of Israel and Judah. In 7:10–17, the focus lies on Amaziah's political loyalties and maneuvers. He reports to Jeroboam, describing Amos as involved in a conspiracy against the king (vv. 10–11), and he refers to the temple in Bethel as "a royal sanctuary, a national temple" (v. 13). Thus, the role assigned to Amaziah in this drama is to represent the royal power, over against the authority of YHWH, represented by Amos.[64] The controversy concerns prophecy, rather than priestly matters. The issue debated is: who has the right to command a prophet like Amos? Hence, whereas this narrative may tell us something about authorial and editorial attitudes towards prophecy, it says very little about perspectives on priests or temple cult. The final words of the debate proclaim that Amaziah, as a punishment for his attempt to silence Amos, is going to "die in an unclean land" (7:17). For a priest who was preoccupied with matters of purity, this would be a horrible fate. Arguably, the rhetoric presupposes a world view where cultic and ritual issues are of great importance.

8:10. The topic of mourning has surfaced before (5:16–17 and 8:3), but without allusions to temple cult. In the opening line of 8:10, the cultic consequences of an impending disaster are described: "I will turn your feasts into

---

[63] Cf. Gene M. Tucker, "Prophetic Authenticity: A Form-Critical Study of Amos 7:10–17," *Interpretation* 27 (1973): 423–34 (428).

[64] See further Meindert Dijkstra, "'I am neither a Prophet nor a Prophet's Pupil': Amos 7:9–17 as the Presentation of a Prophet like Moses," in *The Elusive Prophet: The Prophet as a Historical Person, Literary Character and Anonymous Artist* (ed. Johannes C. de Moor; OTS 45; Leiden: Brill, 2001), 105–28 (118–19), and Patrick D. Miller, "The Prophetic Critique of Kings," *Ex Auditu* 2 (1986): 82–95 (84–86).

mourning, and all your songs into dirges." One may infer that certain aspects of the major feasts, such as the singing of hymns, are regarded as important constituents of a good life.

8:13–14. According to verse 14, all those who swear certain oaths will be put to death. Three cultic sites are mentioned: Samaria, Dan, and Beer-Sheba. Although the trio of toponyms is not the same as in 5:4–5, the underlying logic seems to be similar. Since Amos 8:13–14 most probably was written in Jerusalem, and since Jerusalem is not mentioned, one may reasonably assume that the author regarded these three sanctuaries as illegitimate places of worship. Hence, participating in the cult there could be seen as sinful in itself (cf. Deut 12). Apparently, verse 14a contains more specific accusations, as well. However, for the purpose of this study it is not necessary to discuss the point of reference of the enigmatic expressions involved in the oath formulas cited.[65] It does not matter much whether accusations of idolatry are involved in the condemnations of those who participated in the cult at these three sites. On either account, 8:14 does not express a general attitude toward temple cult.

9:1. The opening of the so-called fifth vision is of interest for this study, since it describes an event taking place inside a temple. Unfortunately, though, 9:1 is extremely difficult to interpret. Even if one resorts to emendations, the language remains terse and obscure. However, it is possible to reconstruct the main outlines of a chain of events.[66] The speaker reports seeing YHWH "standing on/by the altar." Then the deity commands someone to strike against one of the pillars of a temple. As a consequence, the thresholds of the building begin to shake. The unidentified agent is further instructed to cut off something (probably the capitals of the pillars).[67] A major disaster of some kind is implied (an earthquake?).

Apparently, Amos 9:1 depicts the destruction of a temple. But which one? Scholars have often opted for Bethel, because of Bethel's prominent place in several preceding passages. Alternatively, as suggested by some similarities with Isaiah 6, this vision report refers (implicitly) to the Jerusalem temple, as an

---

[65] For detailed discussions, see, e.g., Jeremias, *Book of Amos*, 151–53; Paul, *Amos*, 268–72, and James R. Linville, *Amos and the Cosmic Imagination* (SOTSMS; Aldershot, UK: Ashgate, 2008), 156–58.

[66] Similar reconstructions have been made by several others. See, e.g., Paul, *Amos*, 274–76; Ernst-Joachim Waschke, "Die fünfte Vision des Amosbuches (9,1–4)—Eine Nachinterpretation," *ZAW* 106 (1994): 434–45 (441), and Aaron Schart, "The Fifth Vision of Amos in Context," in *Thematic Threads in the Book of the Twelve* (ed. Paul L. Redditt and Aaron Schart; BZAW 325; Berlin: de Gruyter, 2003), 46–69 (48–51).

[67] This part is extremely obscure. See Schart, "Fifth Vision," 48. Paul, *Amos*, 273, even leaves the words ובצעם בראש untranslated.

attempt to come to terms with the traumatic experience of its destruction in 586 BCE.[68] In either case, I suggest, this vision presupposes a world view where the temple (with a functioning cult) is at the very centre. I thus agree with Aaron Schart, who spells out the theological implications of the oldest layer of 9:1–4 as follows: "Since the temple is the center that gives refuge, stability, and prosperity...to the land, its elimination sets off disorder and death."[69] Somewhat paradoxically, then, this vision of temple destruction would seem to support the hypothesis that the editors of the book of Amos were not critical against temple cult as such.

9:5–6. See the comments on 4:13 above.

CONCLUSIONS

It is time to say farewell to Amos, the anti-cultic prophet. On the basis of the analysis presented above, it is possible to maintain that the book of Amos is permeated by a basically positive attitude to sacrificial cult. In several cases, the rhetorical strategy employed presupposes a world view where the temple cult is of central importance. Moreover, if the analysis above is correct, the cult-critical oracles do not imply a negative view of sacrificial cult in itself.

In a pioneering study, Lena-Sofia Tiemeyer has shown that the book of Jeremiah does not, as is often claimed, contain contradictory points of view on temple cult and priesthood.[70] It is imperative, she explains, to realize that there is a clear chronological division between cult-critical and cult-affirmative prophecies: "texts that betray a critical disposition towards the priests and/or the cult are found in passages that speak about the pre-exilic situation ... texts that view the priests and/or the cult positively are found in passages that speak about the future."[71] On the basis of the analysis presented above, I suggest that the book of Amos constitutes a similar case, although texts explicitly affirming the sacrificial cult are missing in Amos.

---

[68] For interpretations of Amos 9:1 along these lines, see, e.g., Becker, "Der Prophet als Fürbitter," 147; Waschke, "Die fünfte," 444, and Siegfried Bergler, "'Auf der Mauer—auf dem Altar': Noch eimal die Visionen des Amos," *VT* 50 (2000): 445–71 (450–54, 466–71).

[69] Schart, "Fifth Vision," 51. Cf. similarly Jörg Jeremias, *Hosea und Amos: Studien zu den Anfängen des Dodekapropheton* (FAT 13; Tübingen: Mohr Siebeck, 1996), 254–55.

[70] Lena-Sofia Tiemeyer, "The Priests and the Temple Cult in the Book of Jeremiah," in *Prophecy in the Book of Jeremiah* (ed. Hans M. Barstad and Reinhard G. Kratz; BZAW 388; Berlin: de Gruyter, 2009), 233–64.

[71] Ibid., 234.

The interpretative key lies in the geography, and to some extent also in the chronology. In several passages, sanctuaries frequented by the people of the Northern kingdom are condemned: Bethel, Dan, Gilgal, Samaria, and Beer-Sheba (3:14; 4:4–5; 5:4–5; 8:14). It is announced that YHWH does not accept the sacrifices offered *there* (4:4–5; 5:21–24). Apparently, the underlying idea is that YHWH had abandoned those sites. However, this need not imply a rejection of all temple cult whatsoever. On the contrary, the specific rejection of the sacrificial cult performed in Israel before 722 BCE is linked to an unmistakable Judean perspective. The topic of rejected sacrifice serves, I suggest, as an integral part of the theological explanation of the downfall of the Northern kingdom provided by this book.

Whereas rivalling YHWH sanctuaries, such as Bethel, are doomed, the temple in Jerusalem is never condemned in the book of Amos. But which conclusions may be drawn from this silence? As noted in the analysis of 9:1 above, it is possible to find some veiled references to the destruction of the first temple in Jerusalem in 586 BCE. This event was probably interpreted as a punitive act of YHWH, in analogy with the previous destruction of sanctuaries in the kingdom of Israel. Nevertheless, the postexilic editors seem to have taken the central position of Jerusalem for granted. Because the book begins and ends with positive references to Zion and to David's "booth" (1:2; 9:11–15), one may infer that the explicit critique of cult at other sites is linked to an (implicit) affirmation of the temple cult in Jerusalem. In line with Deuteronomistic theology, the temple in Jerusalem was probably seen as the only legitimate place of sacrificial worship.

Finally, widening the scope to the book of the Twelve, the following can be said. The cult-critical passages in Amos 4:4–5 and 5:21–24, with their radical rejection of sacrifices in Israel (and Beer-Sheba) during the monarchic era, are perfectly compatible with a positive attitude towards sacrificial cult in the second temple in Jerusalem. Thus, it is reasonable to assume that the editors of the Book of the Twelve saw the perspective of Amos as roughly consistent with the perspective of such books as Haggai and Zechariah, which openly endorse the cult of the second temple.

7
ATTITUDES TO THE CULT IN JONAH:
IN THE BOOK OF JONAH, THE BOOK OF THE TWELVE, AND BEYOND

Lena-Sofia Tiemeyer

A schematic reading of the book of Jonah reveals very little interaction with the cult. A closer look also fails to uncover any deeper interaction with cultic behavior, beyond the rather general references to praying, fasting, and sacrificing. At the same time, this article aims to show that there are openings in the text that enabled later interpreters to "fill in the blanks." We shall explore how the Rabbis found textual support for reading the cult into the text.

1. CULTIC BEHAVIOR IN THE BOOK OF JONAH

There are three key groups of people in the book of Jonah—the sailors, Jonah, and the citizens of Nineveh—and they are all involved in behavior which can be labelled "cultic." As we shall see, their behavior complements each other, with the sailors coming out as the most accomplished cultic figures.

1.1. THE SAILORS

The sailors are involved in several cultic acts. Not only do they pray but also cast lots, make vows, and, most importantly, sacrifice.

PRAYING The sailors *prayed*, each to their own deity (Jonah 1:5). The verb used is זעק אל = "cry out to," which is a common verb for prayer in the Hebrew Bible.

The captain further encourages Jonah to do likewise instead of lying asleep (Jonah 1:6), albeit using a different verb קרא אל = "call to." Later in chapter 1, the sailors pray to YHWH, asking for his permission to cast Jonah over board lest they be held accountable for his death (v. 14).

CASTING LOTS The sailors further *cast lots* (Jonah 1:7, ויפלו גורלות). Cleromancy is another activity that is often considered to belong in the cultic realm as it is used to obtain an unambiguous answer from a deity to a specific question. Although anyone may cast lots (e.g. Neh 11:1, ושאר העם הפילו גורלות), priests are often reported as being occupied with this kind of divinatory practice. Notably, Lev 16:8–10 speaks of Aaron casting lots as part of the ritual of the Day of Atonement. The lots casting involving Saul and Jonathan in 1 Sam 14:35–42 is also a cultic matter and it seems to have been carried out by a priest (v. 36b, ויאמר הכהן נקרבה הלם אל האלהים). The cultic ritual performed by Joshua in Josh 7:14–18 further appears to contain some form of lots casting although the particular word "lots" is not attested. A few passages are ambiguous. The Levite in Judg 20:9 speaks of lots casting (בגורל) although it is unclear whether the Levite himself was responsible for the act.[1]

We should not read too much into the text, given that lots casting is not an activity that is limited to clerical personnel. Even so, the fact remains that the sailors are showing a cultic awareness in that they (1) assume a single guilty party who is responsible for the calamity and (2) allow the deity to discern the identity of that guilty party.

SACRIFICING The sailors also *sacrificed*. In verse 15, their act of lifting Jonah up and casting him into the sea can be construed as an act of sacrifice. The language is reminiscent of sacrificial vocabulary as they "lift Jonah up" (וישאו את יונה). As Sasson notes, the verb נשא is seldom used for lifting up an individual. Rather, it belongs semantically to the sphere of sin, evil, and guilt.[2] The theology is furthermore cultic in the sense that the sailors' act reveals the notion of appeasement and expiation. The sacrifice of Jonah results in the calming of the sea. Jonah is sacrificed for the salvation of the sailors. Of course, it is entirely possible that what the text seeks to convey is some form of general belief about divine retribution, yet the sailors' insights pertaining to the cause of the storm as well as its remedy remain.

---

[1] For a discussion of lot-casting, see Johannes Lindblom, "Lot-Casting in the Old Testament," *VT* 12 (1962): 164–78.

[2] Jack M. Sasson, *Jonah* (AB 24B; New York: Doubleday, 1990), 124.

In the following verse 16, the sailors sacrifice anew, this time explicitly and to YHWH: they "fear" him (וייראו האנשים יראה גדולה את ה'), they "offer sacrifices" to him (ויזבח זבח לה'), and they "make vows" (וידרו נדרים).

The verb זבח in *Paal*, unless used metaphorically (e.g., Hos 13:2), tends to refer to animal sacrifice.[3] More specifically, it is used in Lev 7:12 to denote a sacrifice of thanksgiving (זבח התודה) and also in Ps 107:22 (ויזבחו זבחי תודה).[4] This raises the obvious question: *what* did the sailors sacrifice? As Sasson has shown, however, the notion that a ship contained animals and that they could be sacrificed while at sea is not to be discarded as impossible. Although it can be argued that the sailors, in their attempt to lighten the ship (v. 5), are likely to have tossed any sacrificial animals over board, it is no to be ruled out that the sailors, at least theoretically, had animals at their disposal.[5] The verb זבח also raises a less obvious question: *where* did they sacrifice? It can be assumed that the intended Jewish audience of the book of Jonah regarded the temple in Jerusalem to be the only acceptable place to offer up sacrifices to YHWH. Furthermore, the only people authorized to perform such sacrifices would have been the priests (and most definitely not Gentile sailors, see further below).

VOW-TAKING Finally, the sailors *made vows* (וידרו נדרים). The Hebrew Bible records two main occasions for making vows.[6] Most commonly, vows are uttered when facing extreme danger. On these occasions, the person making the vow is at the same time also promising to do something in exchange for survival (e.g. Judg 11:30). The other occasion is when a person wishes to make a request from God. Psalm 61:5 falls into this category, as the psalmist states that God has heard his vows and given him the heritage of those who fear God's name. Along similar lines, Hannah makes a vow to God that if he gives her a son, then she will give that son to God as a life-long dedicated servant (1 Sam 1:11). In several instances, the same person who is making the vow is also offering up a sacrifice (e.g. Elkanah and his family in 1 Sam 1:21–22; cf. also Pss 50:14; 66:13; 116:17–18), but such a combination is not inevitable.

---

[3] See BDB, 256–57. Cf. also Sasson, *Jonah*, 138.
[4] Cf. Hans Walter Wolff, *Obadiah and Jonah: A Commentary* (CCS; trans. Margaret Kohl; Minneapolis, MN: Augsburg, 1986), 121.
[5] Sasson, *Jonah*, 138–40.
[6] See further Ibid., 140.

1.2. JONAH

On the whole, the book of Jonah does not portray Jonah as a cultic figure. Even so, a careful reading of the text reveals several minor cultic nuances associated with his behavior and his utterances.

SACRIFICING Jonah does not commit any cultic actions in chapter 1. He does, however, show a rudimentary cultic understanding in verse 12 where he makes a connection between his own death (in the sea) and the calming of the sea. He offers himself up as a willing sacrifice and he expresses his trust in the power of this sacrifice: it will accomplish the desired effect, namely the calming of the sea. At the same time, Jonah demands of the sailors to "lift" him up (שאוני) and "throw" him (והטילני) into the sea. In other words, Jonah is not going to commit suicide; rather the sailors are ultimately the ones who have to perform the sacrifice.[7]

PRAYING In chapter 2, Jonah becomes much more involved in the cult. The text is shaped in the form of a prayer which Jonah prays and this prayer is centred on several cultic matters. The prayer as a whole offers a succinct declaration in the power of prayer: God responds to prayer (v. 3 [Eng. v. 2]) regardless of the whereabouts of the person praying. Outside of Jonah 2, Jonah prays to God also in chapter 4, yet with a very different tone of voice as he complains about God's compassion and asks God to take his life (4:2–3).

In his prayer in Jonah 2, Jonah mentions God's "holy temple" (היכל קדשך) twice. In verse 5 [Eng. v. 4], Jonah expresses his firm belief that he will gaze at the temple again (אך אוסיף להביט אל היכל קדשך). Somewhat differently, verse 8 [Eng. v. 7] has Jonah declare that his prayer came before God in the temple ותבוא תפלתי אל היכל קדשך (אליך). Although the expression "holy temple" is likely to be a reference to the Jerusalem temple (e.g. Ps 79:1), the term has on occasion wider connotations. It is, for example, possible that the poet here refers to the heavenly temple (e.g. Mic 1:2; Hab 2:20; Ps 11:4) and thus laments his separation from God and his power rather than from Jerusalem in particular.[8] Our interpretation depends in part on our view of the relationship between the poem in Jonah 2 and the rest of the book (see further below). Notably, the surrounding chapters

---

[7] Cf. the comment by Sasson, *Jonah*, 124.

[8] Cf. Ibid., 181. This interpretation is advocated by Ibn Ezra, *Rabbinic Bible*, commentary to Jonah 2:2, who rejects the idea that Jonah is speaking about the temple. Rather, he is referring to the sky (on the basis of Ps 11:4).

אך אוסיף להביט אל היכל קדשך שהוא השמים וה' בהיכל קדשו ורבי' ככה

1, 3–4 never mention Jerusalem and are instead associated with the Northern Kingdom (cf. 2 Kgs 14:25).

SACRIFICING AND VOW-TAKING In addition to the references to the temple in Jonah 2, verse 9 [Eng. v. 8] uses cultic vocabulary as it speaks about those who cling to vanity and thus forfeit "their grace" (משמרים הבלי שוא חסדם יעזבו). It is not fully clear to what verse 9 refers exactly, yet we can surmise that it is the opposite of worshipping YHWH. Finally, in verse 10a [Eng. v. 9a] Jonah expresses his intention to "sacrifice" to God with a "vow" ואני בקול תודה אזבחה לך אשלמה (אשר נדרתי), thus mirroring the words of the sailors in Jonah 1:16.

1.3. THE CITIZENS OF NINEVEH

The people of Nineveh show a practical understanding of the cult. In 3:5, they "believe" in God (ויאמינו אנשי נינוה באלהים), "declare a fast" (ויקראו צום), and "put on sackcloth" (וילבשו שקים). The king likewise dons sackcloth and sits in the dust (v. 6) and calls a general fast (v. 7). He further encourages everyone to "wear sackcloth" (ויתכסו שקים), "call fervently to God" (ויקראו אל אלהים בחזקה), and "give up their evil ways and their violence" (וישבו איש מדרכו הרעה ומן החמס אשר בכפיהם) (v. 8). At the same time, the people of Nineveh and their monarch fail to do what the sailors do; they neither offer sacrifices nor make vows.[9]

1.4. SUMMARY

All the characters, from the sailors via Jonah to the people of Nineveh, are involved in activities that can be categorized as belonging in the cultic sphere. Although the book features neither priests nor Levites, there are sacrifices and references to the temple. Furthermore, even though the book of Jonah does not mention the Sabbath or any other religious festival, there are prayers and fasts. It would be too much to state that the cult is a characteristic trait of the book of Jonah; yet cultic concerns contribute to its overall story line in a way that hitherto may not have been fully appreciated.

2. JONAH 2 IN THE BOOK OF JONAH

It is a definite possibility that the psalm in chapter 2 of the book of Jonah originated independently from the rest of the book or, alternatively, that the prayer

---

[9] See Sasson, *Jonah*, 342.

was written for its present place in the book of Jonah by a later author. Phrased differently, while its form (i.e. being a prayer) in itself does not disturb the general flow of the narrative, several aspects of its content and theology differ from what is found in the rest of the book of Jonah.[10] As hinted at above, this psalm is a key contributor to the portrayal of the character of Jonah as a man concerned with the cult. Moreover, the focus on the (Jerusalem) temple in chapter 2 sets the chapter apart from the surrounding material.

If the psalm in Jonah 2 is a later, editorial edition (either composed by the editor or an original text which the redactor added to the existing narrative), then the sudden focus on the temple in this text appears in a new light. It suggests that the interpretative tendency to make the book of Jonah concerned with the cult began already prior to reaching its final form. In other words, the redactor of the book of Jonah is the first among many interpreters who attempted to transform the book of Jonah into a text concerned with the cult.

3. JONAH AND THE CULT IN THE BOOK OF THE TWELVE

The understanding of the book of Jonah as a book dealing with the cult is enhanced by its incorporation into the Book of the Twelve.

As noted by many scholars, there is a strong connection between Jonah and Joel, exemplified by the shared use of the so-called "thirteen attributes of mercy" (Jonah 3:9; 4:2; Joel 2:13–14).[11] Wöhrle, for instance, argues that Jonah was reworked and added to the Book of the Twelve as part of a so-called *Gnaden-*

---

[10] See, e.g., the discussions in Wolff, *Obadiah and Jonah*, 78–79, and Sasson, *Jonah*, 17–18, 205. For a different view, see James Limburg, *Jonah* (OTL; London: CSM Press, 1993), 31–33, who argues that Jonah 2 plays an essential role in the development of the plot. For a unique take on the matter, see also Hugh S. Pyper, "Swallowed by a Song: Jonah and the Jonah-Psalm Through the Looking-Glass," in *Reflection and Refraction: Studies in Biblical Historiography in Honour of A. Graeme Auld* (ed. Robert Rezetko, Timothy H. Lim, and W. Brian Aucker; VTSup 113; Leiden: Brill, 2007), 337–58. He suggests that Jonah 2 is the earliest text which constituted the impetus for the composition of the surrounding narrative: chs. 1, 3–4 are the "narrative outworking of the metaphors of the psalms" (pages 345–46).

[11] See, for example, Thomas B. Dozeman, "Inner-Biblical Interpretation of Yahweh's Compassionate Character," *JBL* 108 (1989): 207–23; Thomas M. Bolin, *Freedom Beyond Forgiveness: The Book of Jonah Re-examined* (JSOTS 236 / Copenhagen International Seminar 3; Sheffield: Sheffield Academic Press, 1997), 169–71, and John Strazicich, *Joel's Use of Scripture and the Scripture's Use of Joel: Appropriation and Resignification in Second Temple Judaism and Early Christianity* (BIS 82; Leiden: Brill, 2007), 149–55.

korpus ("grace-edition"). The same editor further added material to books which were already part of the Twelve. Among these additions, Wöhrle positions Joel 2:12–14.[12] Thus, Joel 2:12–14 is contemporary with Jonah 3:9 and 4:2 as components in the Book of the Twelve.

Schart, however, challenges this view as he argues that the thematic tension that forms the basis for Wöhrle's redaction-critical discussion is not a sign of gradual composition; rather it is a characteristic of the genre of the book of Jonah (being a satire). Further, the affinity between Jonah 3:9 and Joel 2:12–13 is not a sign of redactional activity but instead of one author (Jonah) imitating an earlier author (Joel).[13] The book of Jonah, according to Schart, is thus the later book which was inserted into the Book of the Twelve where Joel, against which Jonah serves as a foil, already had a place.[14] It follows that "Jonah must be read with Joel in mind." If the reader is not familiar with Joel, then s/he will miss the puns. The quotations from Joel which appear in Jonah further serve to strengthen the irony: the character of Jonah does the very opposite of what he confesses.[15]

I am open to the possibility that the redactor responsible for including Jonah in the Book of the Twelve also added material to other books in order to make the message of Jonah cohere with the surrounding books and/or to conform already existing books to the ideals of the editors. In the present context, however, my main concern rests with the readers' experience. When reading Jonah within the wider context of the Book of the Twelve, the echoes of Joel adds a cultic dimension to Jonah. In my view, the "thirteen attributes of mercy" as the formula appears in Jonah 3:9 and 4:2 has no cultic connotations. However, when read together with the same formula in Joel 2:13–14, appearing as it does directly after a call to fast, weep, and mourn (v. 12b, ובצום ובבכי ובמספד) and referring to grain offerings and drink offerings (v. 14bβ, מנחה ונסך לה' אלהיכם), the readers are encouraged to understand also Jonah 3:9 and 4:2 as cultic proclamations.

---

[12] Jakob Wöhrle, *Der Abschluss des Zwölfprophetenbuches: Buchübergreifende Redaktionsprozesse in den späten Sammlungen* (BZAW 389; Berlin: de Gruyter, 2008), 365–399. According to Wöhrle, the redactional layer in Jonah comprises Jonah 1:5b, 6, 8aβ, 10abα, 14, 16; 2:2–10; 3:6–10; 4:1–4, 6*, 10–11. For the addition, of Joel 2:12–14, see Wöhrle, *Abschluss*, 400.

[13] Aaron Schart, "The Jonah-Narrative within the Book of the Twelve," in *Perspectives on the Formation of the Book of the Twelve: Methodological Foundations, Redactional Processes, Historical Insights* (ed. Rainer Albertz, James D. Nogalski, and Jakob Wöhrle; BZAW 433; Berlin: de Gruyter, 2012), 109–28 (123).

[14] Ibid., 115.

[15] Ibid., 112.

Affinity also exists between Jonah and Malachi, an affinity which anew causes the reader of the Book of the Twelve to "read" the cult into the book of Jonah. The reference to the sailors in Jonah 1:16 is reminiscent of the statement in Mal 1:11 about God's name being great among the nations and incense being offered in God's name (by the gentiles).[16] As Schart has argued, the sailors who sacrifice to YHWH in Jonah 1:16 constitute a good example of gentiles who offer sacrifices outside of the Jerusalem temple. Furthermore, the people of Nineveh form additional candidates for gentiles whose worship is pleasing to the God of Israel.[17] According to Schart, Mal 1:11 (as well as v. 14) is redactional in character, inserted alongside the book of Jonah at the same time into the Book of the Twelve.[18]

Disregarding whether or not we accept the redactional quality of Mal 1:11 and 14, Schart's insight vis-à-vis the affinity between Jonah and Malachi is pertinent in the present context. I accordingly suggest that when reading Jonah in the wider context of the Book of the Twelve, the reference to the cult of YHWH in Jonah 1:16 is deepened by its intertext in Mal 1:11.

To sum up, when the book of Jonah is read intertextually together with the rest of the Book of the Twelve, not only are existing references to the cult strengthened (Jonah 1:16) but new connections to the cult are being forged (Jonah 3:9; 4:2).

4. Jonah and the Cult in Rabbinical Judaism

It must be a feat to contain so comparably little in terms of cultic language and yet to obtain paramount cultic significance in later Judaism and Christianity. It is not an exaggeration to say that the book of Jonah fulfils chief cultic functions in both traditions. It is well-known that the book of Jonah constitutes the *Haftarah* reading for the *Minhah* on the Day of Atonement (b. Meg. 31a), although it is not clear how far back this tradition reaches.[19] Likewise, the book of Jonah has an important liturgical role in the various Easter celebrations, prompted by the

---

[16] For the interpretation of this verse, see Lena-Sofia Tiemeyer, *Priestly Rites and Prophetic Rage: Post-exilic Prophetic Critique of the Priesthood* (FAT 2/19; Tübingen: Mohr Siebeck, 2006), 259–63.

[17] Schart, "The Jonah-Narrative," 125–26. See also his article in the present volume.

[18] Schart, "The Jonah-Narrative," 126.

[19] See further Daniel Stökl Ben Ezra, *The Impact of Yom Kippur on Early Christianity: The Day of Atonement form Second Temple Judaism to the Fifth Century* (WUNT 163; Tübingen: Mohr Siebeck, 2003), 55.

understanding in Matt 12:39–41 of the Jonah narrative as a typology for Jesus' death and resurrection.[20]

In the remainder of this article, we shall see how the Rabbis, and to a limited extent also the Mediaeval Jewish exegetes, employed different methods in order to bring the text of Jonah closer to Jerusalem, its temple, and its cult, thus continuing the trend that we observed in the book of Jonah itself and in the Book of the Twelve.

No equivalent tendency exists among Christian Interpretation. Nearly all Church Fathers understood Jonah to be a type for Christ: both descend to the depth of Sheol and both are brought back to life on earth again. At the same time—and rather surprisingly—they do not (to my knowledge) highlight the fact that Jonah is willing to die in order to save the sailors (Jonah 1:12).[21] They also comment extensively on the fasting and repentance of the people of Nineveh and points to them as examples to emulate.[22] Thus, it is fair to say that they deepen the cultic aspects that already exist in the biblical text. At the same time, it is rare that they introduce cultic matters that are not evident in the biblical text, beyond the notion that Jonah, as a type for Christ, is the great sacrifice in Christian writing, inspired by Matt 12:39–41 and Luke 11:29–32. The commentaries by the reformers Calvin and Luther attest to a similar situation.[23]

4.1. THE SAILORS AND SACRIFICES IN THE TEMPLE IN JERUSALEM

Many rabbis read the cult into the narrative about the sailors. Jonah 1:16 tells us that the sailors make sacrifices to YHWH (ויזבחו זבח לה'). This statement, however, constituted a theological problem for the rabbis. Targum Jonathan accordingly offers a slightly different text: "and [the sailors] promised to offer a sacrifice before the Lord."[24] Radak, following Targum Jonathan, points out that the sail-

---

[20] For a succinct discussion, see Sasson, *Jonah*, 28–29.

[21] For instance, Chrysostom, *Homilies on Repentance and Almsgiving* 3.8, discusses Jonah's request to the sailors to be thrown into the sea; yet does not refer to Jonah's willingness to die as any form vicarious sacrifice. For an English translation, see *ACCS. Old Testament XIV: The Twelve Prophets*, 133.

[22] See, e.g., the collection of texts cited in *ACCS. Old Testament XIV: The Twelve Prophets*, 140–45.

[23] See further John Calvin, *Commentary to the Minor Prophets. Vol. 3: Jonah, Micah, Nahum* (trans. John Owen; Grand Rapids, MI: Eerdmans, 1950), and Martin Luther, *Jonah, Habakuk* (ed. H.C. Oswald; Luther's Work, 19; St Louis, MO: Concordia Publishing House, 1974).

[24] The English translation is taken from Kevin J. Cathcart and Robert P. Gordon, *The Targum of the Minor Prophets. Translated, with a Critical Introduction, Apparatus,*

ors cannot have made sacrifices to YHWH then and there on the ship, as Jonah 1:16 appears to say. Rather, they *promised* to make (future) sacrifices before God (in the temple in Jerusalem).[25] As to the sailors' act of "making vows," this according to Radak refers to giving charity to the poor.[26] By putting the sacrifices ahead in time and by changing their location, this translation solves the problem of having Gentiles offering sacrifices to YHWH outside the temple in Jerusalem.[27] This interpretation reads the cult into the text of Jonah insofar as it reads the official Jerusalem temple cult into it. The sacrifices are no longer random sacrifices which took place in the middle of the Mediterranean; they are proper and cultically acceptable ones carried out in the central sanctuary in Jerusalem.

A variant of this interpretation is found at the end of chapter 10 of Pirqe de-Rabbi Eliezer (henceforth PRE).[28] As the sailors saw all the miracles that God did to Jonah (i.e. his salvation by and adventure together with the fish), they abandoned their idolatry, returned to Joppa, went up to Jerusalem, and circumcised the flesh of their foreskins. This retelling is a paraphrase of Jonah 1:16. Notably, the sailors in PRE do not sacrifice (as in the biblical text) but instead allow themselves to be circumcised. As Friedlander comments, the term "sacrifice" is reinterpreted to refer to the sacrifice of the blood of the covenant which is shed during circumcision.[29] Thus, when the sailors sacrifice and make vows, what they are really doing is converting (to Judaism). PRE 10 ends with a reference to the thirteenth blessing of the 'Amida, that is, to pray for the welfare of the righteous converts.[30]

---

and Notes (Aramaic Bible 14; Edinburgh: T&T Clark, 1990), 106. See also n. 29. This reading was inspired by the extended meaning of נדר = "to vow," i.e. "to promise." See further Sasson, *Jonah*, 139. The Aramaic texts of Jonah 1:16 reads:
ודחילו גבריא דחלא רבא מן־קדם יוי ואמרו לדבחא דיבח קדם יוי ונדרו ושלימו נדרין:

[25] Radak, *Rabbinic Bible*, Jonah 1:16 (ואמרו ותרגומו פירושו אלא בספינה זבח זבחו אין). 'ה קדם דבח לדבחא). See also TJ Jonah 1:16 "and they promised to offer a sacrifice before the Lord" (ואמרו לדבחא דיבח קדם יוי ונדרו נדרים).

[26] Radak, *Rabbinic Bible*, Jonah 1:16 (שאר נדרים זולתי זבח כמו לתת צדקה לעניים).

[27] Cathcart and Gordon, *Targum of the Minor Prophets*, 106, n. 29.

[28] Leivy Smolar and Moses Aberbach, *Studies in Targum Jonathan to the Prophets* (New York: Ktav Publishing House / Baltimore, MD: Hebrew College, 1983), 123, discuss potential links between Targum Jonathan of Jonah and PRE. They suggest that the reading of TJ may form the basis for the midrash preserved in PRE.

[29] *The Chapters of Rabbi Eliezer the Great According to the Text of the Manuscript Belonging to Abraham Epstein of Vienna* (translated and annotated with Introduction and Indices by Gerald Friedlander; London: Kegan Paul, Trench, Trubner & Co, 1916), 72. See also Rachel Adelman, *The Return of the Repressed: Pirqe De-Rabi Eliezzer and the Pseudepigrapha* (SJSJ 140; Leiden: Brill, 2009), 233, including n. 57.

[30] Adelman, *Return of the Repressed*, 234, including n. 60.

4.2. Jonah and (Self-)Sacrifice

As to the character of Jonah, a few Jewish texts depict Jonah as an example of self-sacrifice on behalf of others (cf. Jonah 1:12). The Jewish-hellenistic sermon *On Jonah*, attributed to Philo, is a case in point. Jonah is approached by the sailors and asked to leave the ship and go to another ship so that the storm would leave their ship in peace. After his soliloquy where he realizes that he should not seek his own salvation but instead show himself to be a God-fearing prophet and save the human beings on the ship, Jonah "gives himself to the angry Sea."[31] Siegert, in his commentary of the text, argues that although this notion could be understood as an alternative (and competing) reference to Jesus' teaching, it is more likely to be part of a shared Hellenistic ethical-religious ideal of self-sacrifice on behalf of others.[32]

Yom Kippur was probably the *Sitz im Leben* of Pseudo-Philo's sermon *On Jonah*, possibly as preached in the synagogue in Alexandria.[33] This sermon can, in fact, be regarded as the earliest evidence for the connection between Yom Kippur and the book of Jonah and the earliest extant *Yom Kippur* sermon. What is less clear is whether the description of the fast in *On Jonah* merely seeks to elaborate on the biblical portrayal of the fast of the Ninevites in the book of Jonah or if it is influenced by actual (Alexandrian) practices during the observance of *Yom Kippur*.[34]

The idea that Jonah committed suicide on behalf of others is also alluded to in Mekilta de-Rabbi Ishmael 1.3 (7–8):

> 7.A. R. Nathan says, "Jonah went only to commit suicide in the sea
> B as it is said 'And he said to them, "Take me up and cast me forth into the sea"' (Jonah 1:12)."
> 8.A. As so you find that the patriarchs and prophets gave their lives for Israel.
> ...

---

[31] For a (German) translation of the original Armenian text, see Folker Siegert, *Drei hellenistisch-jüdische Predigten*, vol. 1 (WUNT 20; Tübingen: Mohr Siebeck, 1980), 18 (sections 14–15 [lines 59–60] of the text).

[32] Folker Siegert, *Drei hellenistisch-jüdische Predigten*, vol. 2 (WUNT 61; Tübingen: Mohr Siebeck, 1992), 134.

[33] See further Folker Siegert, "Early Jewish Interpretation in a Hellenistic Style: The Sermons *On Jonah* and *On Samson*," in *Hebrew Bible, Old Testament: The History of Its Interpretation*. vol 1.1 (ed. Magne Sæbo; Göttingen: Vandenhoeck & Ruprecht, 1996), 191–92.

[34] Stökl Ben Ezra, *Impact of Yom Kippur*, 55, 57–58.

> 8.D. Lo, in every passage you find that the patriarchs and prophets gave their lives for Israel.[35]

In parallel, other classical Jewish texts interpret Jonah's behavior in Jonah 1:12 more negatively. PRE 10, for example, depicts Jonah as a sacrifice, but he is not the one who offers up himself. Rather, in line with the biblical account, he pushes the burden of the sacrifice upon the sailors.[36]

4.3. PILGRIMAGE

Somewhat surprisingly, given the complete absence of textual support in the book of Jonah itself, several classical Jewish texts associate the book of Jonah with pilgrimage to Jerusalem. Among them, Mekilta de-Rabbi Ishmael 17.1 speaks of people who fulfil ritual requirements. Among them, Jonah's wife is mentioned as a person who goes up to the festivals to Jerusalem.

> K. The wife of Jonah used to go up for festivals to Jerusalem.[37]

Thus, a woman never mentioned in the biblical book is reported as setting out on a pilgrimage to Jerusalem.[38] This tradition is attested in other places in Rabbinic writing as well. The Jerusalem Talmud (y. Ber. 2:2–3), for example, states that Jonah's wife used to go on a pilgrimage but she was at one point sent home. From this we can learn that women (as well as slaves and children) are exempt from the obligations of reciting the *Shema'* and from wearing *tefillin*.

> They asked: Lo, Michal daughter of Kushi used to wear Tefillim. And Jonah's wife used to go up to Jerusalem on the pilgrimages, and the sages did not object.

---

[35] English translation, see Jacob Neusner, *Habakkuk, Jonah, Nahum and Obadiah in Talmud and Midrash: A Source Book* (Studies in Judaism; Lanham, MD: University Press of America, 2007), 63.

[36] Adelman, *Return of the Repressed*, p. 231.

[37] English translation, see Neusner, *Habakkuk, Jonah, Nahum and Obadiah*, 64.

[38] Cf. Louis Ginzberg, *The Legends of the Jews*. Vol. 4 *Bible Times and Characters from Joshua to Esther* (Philadelphia: The Jewish Publication Society of America, 1968), 253.

R. Hezekiah in the name of R. Abbahu, "they sent the wife of Jonah home and the sages objected to Michael the daughter of Kushi's actions."[39]

Another passage in the Jerusalem Talmud (y. Sukkah 5:1) mentions that Jonah would also go on a pilgrimage to Jerusalem. On one of these occasions, the prophetic spirit ascended upon Jonah.

> "And it was written, 'He went down to Joppa'" (Jonah 1:3).
> Was it not necessary to say, "He went down to Akko"?
> Said R. Jonah, "Jonah b. Amittai was one of those who came up for the festivals [to Jerusalem] and he came in for the rejoicing of *bet hashshoebah*, and the Holy Spirit rested upon him.
> "This serves to teach you that the Holy Spirit rests only on someone whose heart is happy.[40]

As we can see, the biblical character of Jonah, as well as that of his (non-biblical) wife, is co-opted to perform the cultic action of pilgrimage to Jerusalem. In this rather unintuitive manner, later interpreters "read" yet another cultic aspect into the book of Jonah.

4.4. FASTING

As mentioned above, the book of Jonah has a strong connection to the Day of Atonement. One key shared element is, of course, fasting. Several rabbinic texts appeal to fasting of the people of Nineveh in order to show the correct way of fasting.

Beginning with the Mishnah, Ta'anit 2:1 cites Jonah 3:10, as well as Joel 2:13, in order to clarify how one should fast. Ta'anit 2:4 continues by listing people whose prayer God has heard: Abraham on Mt. Moriah, the people of Israel at the Red Sea, Joshua at Gilgal, Samuel at Mispeh, Elijah at Mt. Carmel, Jonah in the fish, and David and Solomon in Jerusalem.[41] We can thus see that not only the Ninevites' fasting but also Jonah's prayer are being used to serve as the basis for the liturgy of the Day of Atonement.

Later in Pesiqta de-Rab Kahana 28:3, the Ninevites's repentance serves as an example of the power of repentance.

---

[39] English translation, see Neusner, *Habakkuk, Jonah, Nahum and Obadiah*, 65. See also y. Ber. 9:1 (Neusner, 67), for yet another instance of this idea. In this latter text, Michal is identified with the daughter of Saul.

[40] English translation, see Neusner, *Habakkuk, Jonah, Nahum and Obadiah*, 68.

[41] English translation of these passages, see ibid., 57–58.

> R. Huna in the name of R. Joseph said: "Also changing one's name and the doing of a different sort of deed will have the same effect
> [...]
> "We know that the doing of a different sort of deeds makes a difference from the case of the men of Nineveh, as it is said, 'And God saw their works, that they turned from their evil ways.'"⁴²

In parallel, other sources do not commend the Ninevites. On the contrary, their fasting is deemed to be insincere. In y. Taʻan. 2:1, for example, the Jerusalem Talmud states that the people of Nineveh acted cruelly towards their animals in order to force the animals to cry out (thus explaining Jonah 3:8).

> III.A. S-Y. Said R. Simeon b. Laquish, "The repentance that the men of Nineveh carried out was deceitful."
> What did they do?
> R. Hunah in the name of R. Simeon b. Halaputa: "They set up calves inside, with the mothers outside, lambs inside, with the mothers outside, and these bellowed from here, and those bellowed from there.
> "They said, 'If we are not shown mercy, we shall not have mercy on them.'
> "This is in line with that which is written: 'How the beasts groan! The herds of cattle are perplexed because there is no pasture for them; even the flocks of sheep are dismayed'" (Joel 1:18)
> Said R. Aha, "In Arabia that is how they act [toward their beasts, threating them cruelly]."
> "But let man and beast be covered with sackcloth, and let them cry mightily to God; [yes, let everyone turn from his evil way and from the violence which is in his hands]" (Jonah 3:8).⁴³

As we can see, the rabbis focused on the cultic aspects on the book of Jonah and expanded on them, both positively and negatively.

4.5. (LACK OF) IDOL WORSHIP

What or whom did the people of Nineveh worship prior to Jonah's arrival in Nineveh? The biblical text is unconcerned with this question, probably because the answer (i.e. idols) would have been self-understood. For Abraham Ibn Ezra, however, this is a pertinent question. Noting that the list of their acts of repent-

---

⁴² English translation, see ibid., 78.

⁴³ English translation, see ibid., 68–69. The same notion of the Ninevites' deceitful fasting is recorded also in Pesiqta de-Rab Kahana 24:9. See Neusner, *Habakkuk, Jonah, Nahum and Obadiah*, 77–78.

ance in Jonah 3:5 does *not* include breaking idols and destroying altars, Ibn Ezra therefore concludes that they cannot have been worshipping idols: if they had, they would have been required to destroy them in order to repent fully. Ibn Ezra supports his conclusion with another observation, namely, the use of the phrase לאלהים in Jonah 1:3. This term, so Ibn Ezra, reveals that (1) the people of Nineveh had been "fearers of God" in the past and that (2) they had only begun to do evil in the days of Jonah. This, in turn, explains why God would send a prophet to them in the first place.[44] In this way, Ibn Ezra brings the people of Nineveh closer not only to the God of Israel but also to his cult. The people of Nineveh had worshipped him in the past and were now being brought back to his cult.

On the same topic of idol worship but speaking about the sailors, the biblical text makes clear that the sailors worship their own gods up until Jonah 1:14 when they begin to call upon YHWH. Targum Jonathan understands their turning to the God of Israel to happen earlier, however, evidenced by its addition וחזו ארי לית בהון צרוך at the end of v. 5. Having prayed, each man to his idol, "they saw that they were useless."[45] In other words, the sailors abandoned their beliefs in their own deities prior to both the calming of the storm and YHWH's miraculous saving of Jonah through the fish.

These two examples show again that later interpreters are endeavouring to bring the book of Jonah closer to cultic matters. It is telling that the very *absence* of references to smashed alters and destroyed statues triggered Ibn Ezra's statement regarding the Ninevites' habits of worship.

Conclusion

As we have seen in this article, there is more cult in the book of Jonah than what is obvious at a brief glance. Moreover, when read together with the rest of the Book of the Twelve, the extant references to the cult are deepened and other references appear. This tendency continues in Rabbinic literature, with the result that in Jewish tradition the book of Jonah is a book that not only holds a key ritual function at the Day of Atonement but also contains a multitude of (more or less hidden) references to cultic matters such as fasting, praying, pilgrimage, and sacrifice.

---

[44] Ibn Ezra, *Rabbinic Bible*, commentary to Jonah 1:3 (final part):
ופירוש לאלהים כי היו יראיים השם הימים הקדמונים רק עתה בימי יונה החלו לעשות רע ולולי זה שהיו בתחילה אנשי השם לא היה שולח נביאו אליהם והנה ראינו ששב תשובה גמורה אין כמוה ולא תמצא כתוב ששברו מזבחות בעלים או גדעו פסילים מזה נלמוד שלא היו עכו"ם:
For an English translation and discussion, see Steven Bob, *Go to Nineveh: Medieval Jewish Commentaries on the Book of Jonah* (Eugene, OR: Pickwick, 2013), 22–23.

[45] For an English translation, see Cathcart and Gordon, *Targum of the Minor Prophets*, 105.

8
THE "IDOLATROUS PRIESTS" IN THE BOOK OF ZEPHANIAH

Jason Radine

The small book of Zephaniah presents particularly difficult challenges to the historical critic, as it contains scant few historical anchors or indicators of context within its mere three chapters. The task of this paper is to attempt to shed some light on whatever can be learned about the priests that are condemned in this small booklet. It will be suggested here that the priests condemned in the book of Zephaniah refer to priests at the end of the Judahite monarchy whose behavior is considered within the book as part of the general misbehavior of the people that led to Judah's destruction at the hands of Babylon. This paper will be focused on the so-called "idolatrous priests" that appear in Zeph 1:4, as this verse may contain usable information to illuminate the identity of the priests condemned by Zephaniah beyond generic attacks on priests simply as part of leadership, as in Zeph 3:4.[1]

1. כמר PRIESTS

Priests specifically appear twice in the book of Zephaniah, at 1:4–5 and 3:4. The more distinctive of the references to priests is at 1:4b where the unusual term *kĕmārîm* appears, in a clumsy phrase reading *šēm hakkĕmārîm 'im hakkōhănîm*, "the name of the *kĕmārîm* with (or among) the priests." *Kĕmārîm* is a very rare

---

[1] I would like to thank Dr. Lena-Sofia Tiemeyer for inviting me to submit an article to this volume and to present it at the Society of Biblical Literature Annual Meeting in San Diego in 2014.

term in the Hebrew Bible, appearing otherwise only in Hos 10:5 and 2 Kgs 23:5. The term in Zeph 1:4 is generally rendered as "idolatrous priests"[2] or left untranslated.[3] As Ehud Ben Zvi and Wolfgang Schütte have pointed out, "idolatrous priests" cannot be the specific meaning in biblical Hebrew, as the term *kōhēn* is used far more often for every sort of priest of various other iconic deities in the Hebrew Bible.[4]

The term appears to be predominantly Aramaic, appearing in that language and as an Akkadian cognate as *kumru(m)*. Christoph Uehlinger identified the term with Aramean-Assyrian religious practices that had spread throughout the orbit of the western Assyrian Empire, specifically engaged in astral worship such as the bowing to the hosts of heaven in Zeph 1:5.[5] A comprehensive study by Michael Pietsch has shown that *kōmer* is simply the standard Aramaic term for priest and that the Akkadian cognate is generally used to refer to priests localized west of Mesopotamia, that is, in the area of Aram.[6] Even when this term is used far from the Aramean area, it seems to refer to priests generally derived from this area.[7] Thus, the term should not be limited in meaning to astral priests specifically, or to priests specifically of the deity Baal, as again, the term *kōhănîm* is far more frequent as a term for foreign or illegitimate priests in gen-

---

[2] So NRSV, NKJV, NIV, ESV, NASB. JPS has "priestlings" with the note: "*Heb.* Kĕmārîm, *a term used only of priests of heathen gods.*"

[3] "Chemarims" in KJV, ASV, WEB. HCSB has "pagan priests."

[4] Ehud Ben Zvi, *A Historical-Critical Study of the Book of Zephaniah* (BZAW 198; Berlin: de Gruyter, 1991), 67–69, and Wolfgang Schütte, "Der Priestertitel *kmr*," *BN* 119/120 (2003): 42.

[5] Christoph Uehlinger, "Astralkultpriester und Fremdgekleidete, Kanaanvolk und Silberwäger: Zur Verknüpfung von Kult- und Sozialkritik in Zef 1," in *Der Tag wird kommen: Ein interkontextuelles Gespräch über das Buch des Propheten Zefanja* (ed. Walter Dietrich and Milton Schwantes; SBS 170; Stuttgart: Katholisches Bibelwerk, 1996), 49–83, esp. 76–77.

[6] Michael Pietsch, "'Götzenpfaffen' oder 'Astrakultpriester'? Eine sprach- und religionsgeschichtliche Studie zu den alttestamentlichen *kemarîm*," in *Israel zwischen den Mächten: Festschrift für Stefan Timm zum 65. Geburtstag* (ed. Michael Pietsch and Friedhelm Hartenstein; AOAT 364, Münster: Ugarit-Verlag, 2009), 237–46. I wish to thank Dr. Harald Samuel for providing me with a copy of his paper, "Telling Terminology: *kmr* and *khn* in Hebrew and Aramaic Texts," presented at the SBL Annual Meeting in Baltimore, Maryland, in 2013, which introduced me to some of the issues concerning the term *kĕmārîm*.

[7] Pietsch, "Götzenpfaffen," 233–37, and Hermann Spieckermann, *Juda unter Assur in der Sargonidenzeit* (FRLANT 129; Göttingen: Vandenhoeck & Ruprecht, 1982), 85–86.

eral in Biblical Hebrew.⁸ The term as used in Aramaic seems to mean, non-derogatorily, any priest within the general Aramaic orbit, serving Aramaic or sometimes also Mesopotamian deities. Since the term *kĕmārîm* seems to be specific only in that it is an Aramaic term in a Hebrew text, it is most plausible that the term refers to priests of Aramaean background or rite.

One can speculate that the *kĕmārîm* were associated with the copy of the altar in Damascus that the Judahite king Ahaz had built for use in Jerusalem in 2 Kgs 16:10–16, to be used as his royal shrine. Second Kings 16:18 states that Ahaz did this "because of the king of Assyria." Second Kings 23:12 tells us that "altars on the roof of the upper chamber of Ahaz" still existed at the time of Josiah's religious purge, and that these were destroyed by Josiah's people. It stretches our evidence too far to make a solid claim, but it is possible that the *kĕmārîm* were associated with Damascene worship practices introduced into Jerusalem by Ahaz, whether related to the single altar that he had the priest Uriah build in Jerusalem, the altars on his rooftops, or some other structures.⁹ It is possible that the elimination of these shrines, which Ahaz may have built "because of the king of Assyria," may have been an act of freeing Judah from Assyrian elements as Judah shook off Assyrian domination during the empire's decline in Josiah's reign. This is not to say that Assyria imposed its religion by force on to Judah, but it was likely prudent for Judahite kings to offer token religious obeisance to Assyria.¹⁰

As noted above, the term *kĕmārîm* appears three times in the Hebrew Bible: Zephaniah 1:4; Hosea 10:5; and 2 Kgs 23:5. Within Zeph 1:4, the *kĕmārîm* seem to be associated with the worship of Baal, rooftop astral worship, and swearing to YHWH and by "*malkām*." The word *malkām* has variously been interpreted as

---

⁸ Hubert Irsigler, *Zefanja* (HThKAT; Freiburg: Herder, 2002), 109–10, recognized the term as a general Aramaic term for priest but saw the *kĕmārîm* in Zeph 1:4 as Aramean/Assyrian astral priests who were consulted by Judahite families for oracles and swearing/conjuration rituals.

⁹ The worship practices supposedly imitated by Ahaz may have been Assyrian rather than locally Aramean, as pointed out by Jonas C. Greenfield, "Aspects of Aramean Religion," in *Ancient Israelite Religion* (ed. Patrick D. Miller, Jr. et al.; Philadelphia: Fortress, 1987), 67–78 (70).

¹⁰ Spieckermann, *Juda unter Assur*, esp. 369–72, took the position that Assyria did impose some religious obeisance onto its subject peoples, while Mordechai Cogan, "Judah under Assyrian Hegemony: A Reexamination of *Imperialism and Religion*," *JBL* 112.3 (1993): 403–11, took the position that religious influence from all sides occurred in seventh-century Judah due to the increased mixing of peoples under the Assyrian regime without necessarily being imposed, and his view was followed by Johannes Vlaardingerbroek, *Zephaniah* (HCOT; Leuven: Peeters, 1999), 70–72.

"their king" (as apparently in the MT and also in LXX), "Milcom" the Ammonite deity (Lucianic version, Peshitta, and Vulgate), and "Molekh," the deity or type of deity associated with child-burning. Adele Berlin advocated for the reading "Molech" because this deity appears elsewhere in the Hebrew Bible in proximity to some of the other practices condemned in Zeph 1:4–5, and because swearing by a human being such as a king is relatively rare.[11] However, these are not compelling reasons to reject the MT reading of "their king."

Marvin Sweeney has particularly observed that YHWH and *malkām* are introduced by different prepositions in this verse, *la* for the former and *bĕ* for the latter, thus reading "sworn to YHWH" and "sworn by their king." [12] Thus, *malkām* could well be in a different category than YHWH, and thus not a god. Sweeney suggested that the *bĕ* preposition indicates "the party that authorizes or guarantees compliance with the oath" as opposed to "the party to whom the oath is made."[13] Noting the close association of YHWH and Davidic kings in much of the Hebrew Bible, Sweeney argued that YHWH and the king could be seen together in the monarchic period, but that with the end of the monarchy, Second Temple interpretations disassociated *malkām* with the monarch and in turn associated it with a deity, thus accounting for the Lucianic, Peshitta, and Vulgate renderings. Sweeney's support of the MT reading is persuasive, particularly in view of the different prepositions employed. Thus, the understanding of *malkām* as "their king" is to be preferred to "Molech," and the passage should be translated as Sweeney does, "who are sworn to YHWH and who are sworn by their king."[14]

The *kĕmārîm* of Hos 10:5 are associated with worship of a calf icon at Bethel, and will mourn (MT "exult") for the icon when it is carried off to the king of Assyria. This passage in Hosea is immediately preceded by a diatribe

---

[11] Adele Berlin, *Zephaniah: A New Translation with Introduction and Commentary* (AB 25A; New York: Doubleday, 1994), 75–77. See also Irsigler, *Zefanja*, 114–18.

[12] Marvin Sweeney, *Zephaniah: A Commentary* (Hermeneia; Minneapolis, MN: Fortress, 2003), 70–71. Vlaardingerbroek, *Zephaniah*, 69–70, reads *malkām* as "their king" but understands it as referring to any deity other than YHWH in this case.

[13] Ibid., 71.

[14] Ibid., 55. On page 56, Sweeney notes that the *Niphal* form of the verb *šbʿ* can be passive or active, thus "those who swear/are sworn (to)." Brian Peckham, *History and Prophecy: The Development of Late Judean Literary Traditions* (ABRL; New York: Doubleday, 1993), 496 (endnote 236), suggested that "it seems that taking an oath by their kings (1:5bβ) had to do with services for the dead kings at their royal mortuary shrines," based on a similar practice in Jer 22:18–19. That passage in Jerermiah, however, indicates only mourning for the dead king Jehoiakim in general, not a formal mortuary cult.

against saying empty oaths and people crying out that no king can save them. This is notable, as Zeph 1:4–5 also features the *kĕmārîm* in close association with oaths and a king. Hubert Irsigler suggested that the *kĕmārîm* of Hos 10:5 may have been state cult priests of the Northern Kingdom of Israel.[15] At 2 Kgs 23:5 the *kĕmārîm* are priests who were appointed by the kings of Judah to make offerings at high places around Jerusalem and throughout Judah, and who are deposed by Josiah. This passage is followed immediately by one referring to people who made offerings to Baal and the astral deities. As noted above, certainly not all priests of Baal and/or astral deities are *kĕmārîm*, so such forms of worship are likely not inherent in the definition of the term. Nonetheless, 2 Kgs 23:5 does have some resemblance to Zeph 1:4 in that at both passages, *kĕmārîm* seem to be associated with Baal and the astral deities.[16]

While these three references are disparate and sparse on details, they do have in common an association with oaths and kings.[17] Second Kings 23:5 specifies that the *kĕmārîm* were appointed by the kings of Judah,[18] which as said above, might relate to Ahaz's royal altar if there is any historicity to that altar. In Hosea 10:3, Israelites say, "We have no king, for we do not fear YHWH, and the king—what can [or will] he do for us?" This statement can be interpreted in a variety of ways, as an arrogant denial of any authority, or a cry that the Israelite king is unable to help them due to their lack of respect for YHWH. The people say "empty oaths" in Hos 10:4, and the *kĕmārîm* appear in the next verse. The *kĕmārîm* are directly related to the Bethel shrine in Hos 10:5, which is called a royal shrine in Amos 7:13. If the *kĕmārîm* are royally appointed priests (in this case in the Northern Kingdom), then perhaps their oaths become empty as they realize their royal patrons are unable to save them from the coming disaster. The idol that the *kĕmārîm* maintained then goes, somewhat ironically, to the "great king" of Assyria (Hos 10:6). The case may be stronger in Zephaniah, where the *kĕmārîm* swear *to* YHWH *by* their king, in the MT reading. As mentioned earlier,

---

[15] Irsigler, *Zefanja*, 110.

[16] According to Spieckermann, *Juda unter Assur*, 211, "Baal" or "Baals" refers to non-YHWH-istic religion in general, not necessarily to the specific deity "Baal." However, Vlaardingerbroek, *Zephaniah*, 64–66, responds that since the astral deities are mentioned in Zeph 1:4, the reference to Baal in the same verse is specifically the individual deity Baal.

[17] For a comparison between the swearing in Zeph 1:5 and the Assyrian *māmītu* oaths, see Knud Jeppesen, "Zephaniah I 5B," *VT* 31.3 (1981): 372–73.

[18] Gösta W. Ahlström, *Royal Administration and National Religion in Ancient Palestine* (SHANE 1; Leiden: Brill, 1982), 68, n. 121, wrote that 2 Kgs 23:5 suggests that the cultic duties of the *kĕmārîm* "were thus part of the official Judahite religion until the time of Josiah."

there is no linguistic or even content-related reason to reject the MT and LXX reading of "their king," except to form a parallel contrast with YHWH earlier in the verse with another deity. If the *kĕmārîm* are priests associated with the general Aramean religious orbit, they may have worshipped Milcom along with or as Baal in addition to YHWH, and so the reading Milcom is a possibility. However, "their king" works as well and better fits the MT in terms of both prepositions and the MT vowel pointing.

The question of which god or gods the *kĕmārîm* venerate is related to another important question about the *kĕmārîm*: are they foreign or native to Israel/Judah and Israelite/Judahite YHWH-ism? While some have seen the *kĕmārîm* as foreign priests officiating in Judah, Ben Zvi, Sweeney, and Berlin have seen the *kĕmārîm* as YHWH-istic priests who are being disparaged in Zeph 1:4, and were part of the general YHWH-istic priesthood in monarchic Jerusalem.[19] Thus, in the latter view, the *kĕmārîm* should not be sharply distinguished from the *kōhănîm* in the same verse. While the phrase *'im hakkōhănîm* in Zeph 1:5 has often been seen as an explanatory or inclusive gloss on "*kĕmārîm*,"[20] Sweeney and Berlin read "the priests" together with the *kĕmārîm*. Sweeney suggested that the *kĕmārîm* may have been a group in addition to the *kōhănîm*, in which case the verse would read, "the *kĕmārîm* with the *kōhănîm*" and thus as "the cultic attendants with the priests" in Sweeney's rendering.[21] Alternatively, Berlin suggested that the *kĕmārîm* may have been a specified group of priests, in which case the phrase should be rendered, "the *kĕmārîm* among the *kōhănîm*" and thus, "the idolatrous priests among the priests."[22]

Looking at the balance of the evidence both in the ancient Near Eastern attestations of the *kmr* priests and the attestations of the *kĕmārîm* in the Hebrew Bible, the best answer to the foreign or native question is both-and. The presence of references to Baal or astral deities does not decide the matter one way or the other, as Baal and astral deities were always worshipped in Iron Age Palestine (although theophoric onomastica suggest mostly YHWH-istic names in mo-

---

[19] For the view that the *kĕmārîm* are foreign, cf. among others Irsigler, *Zefanja*, 110, and Spieckermann, *Juda*, 85–86. For the view that they were YHWH-istic, see Ben Zvi, *Zephaniah*, 68; Sweeney, *Zephaniah*, 68, and Berlin, *Zephaniah*, 75.

[20] Out of many examples that could be given, John Merlin Powis Smith, "A Critical and Exegetical Commentary on the Book of Zephaniah," in J.M.P. Smith, William Hayes Ward, and Julius A. Bewer, *A Critical and Exegetical Commentary on Micah, Zephaniah, Nahum, Habakkuk, Obadiah, and Joel* (ICC; Edinburgh: T&T Clark, 1912), 187–88, and Guy Langohr, *Le livre de Sophonie et la critique d'authenticité* (ALBO 5.17; Leuven: Peeters, 1976), 5–6.

[21] Sweeney, *Zephaniah*, 55, 68–69.

[22] Berlin, *Zephaniah*, 74–75.

narchic Judah).²³ The head of the pantheon in the Aramean heartland was the storm god Hadad (also known as Rammān), who was apparently equivalent to Canaanite Baal.²⁴ Thus, the *kĕmārîm* may have worshipped essentially Hadad/ Rammān as Baal, along with other, possibly astral deities in the Aramean pantheon. The biblical descriptions of condemned worship associated with the *kĕmārîm* are too vague and stereotypical to be sure of any details as to the content of their ritual practice.²⁵

The fact that the *kĕmārîm* term is Aramaic suggests that at least foreign practice is involved, if not foreign personnel. There is no indication in the three biblical attestations that the *kĕmārîm* as individual people were foreigners. The relative rarity of this term in the Hebrew Bible suggests, however, that it may have a more definite referent than just being an insult to native YHWH-istic priests,²⁶ as such an insult would be expected to be seen more often given the frequent diatribes against priests viewed as deviant by biblical writers throughout the biblical corpus. When priests are condemned again in Zeph 3:4, the term *kĕmārîm* is not used as a slur or otherwise (although this may have redactional reasons). If *'im hakkōhănîm* is not a gloss, and it does not need to be, then the *kĕmārîm* are distinguished from other priests in Judah. Second Kings 23:5, even if not historically accurate about the Josianic reform, does portray the *kĕmārîm* as a special group of religious practitioners that was royally appointed, and the term appears in conjunction or at least proximity with oaths to a king in Zephaniah 1:4 and possibly also in Hos 10:5. As mentioned above, 2 Kgs 16:10–18 states that Ahaz built an Aramean altar in Jerusalem and 1 Kgs 11:7 states that Solomon built altars of foreign deities in Jerusalem. While the former cannot be

---

²³ Ben Zvi, *Zephaniah*, 68–69, n. 114.

²⁴ Greenfield, "Aspects," 67–70. Edward Lipiński, *The Aramaeans: Their Ancient History, Culture, Religion* (OLA 100; Leuven: Peeters, 2000) wrote on page 627, "While Baal became the standing cognomen and practically the proper name of the Storm-god in the Canaanite world of the first millennium B.C., the name *Rammān*, "the Thunderer," was often used among Aramaic-speaking populations instead of Hadad." On the relationship between Hadad and Aramean kings and kingdoms (as two separate issues), see Paul E. Dion, *Les Araméens à l'âge du fer: Histoire politique et structures sociales* (EBib n.s. 34; Paris: Gabalda, 1997) 247–53. Dion pointed out there that in Aramaic usage, Hadad was more often a national god than a dynastic or personal god of the king, but could also appear in the latter role.

²⁵ There is no indication that the *kĕmārîm* were associated with specifically Assyrian forms of worship beyond the phrase "because of the king of Assyria" in regard to Ahaz's Damascene altar in 2 Kgs 16:18 (if that is even relevant to the *kĕmārîm*), although 2 Kgs 17:29–31 and Amos 5:26 suggest that specifically Assyrian deities were worshipped in monarchic-era Israel.

²⁶ Ben Zvi, *Zephaniah*, 68–69, sees the term as more slur than reality.

regarded as historically certain and the latter is almost certainly not historical, these passages may reflect a reality of kings establishing foreign worship in Jerusalem for diplomatic purposes, which makes sense on the face of it.

All in all, it is most likely that the biblical *kĕmārîm* were priests of an Aramean rite who served a specifically royal function, serving at the behest of the king. They themselves were probably not foreigners, but practiced a ritual tradition of Aramean origin. While the *kĕmārîm* seem to have been royally appointed, the deities they worshipped were probably not personal deities of the Judahite kings and their families, but more likely a part of state policy. The *kĕmārîm* may have had a partly diplomatic function, serving as a royal acknowledgement of a general Aramean cult for better relations with Assyria or any potentate approaching Israel or Judah from the northern direction. Zephaniah 1:4 may be referring to these *kĕmārîm* along with other priests, or simply as a group among the other priests. The priests referred to in general in Zeph 3:4 may or may not include the *kĕmārîm*. The *kĕmārîm* are seen in the book as part of the general corruption of powerful officials, including those who wear "foreign attire" in Zeph 1:8. Even if the *kĕmārîm* served a partly diplomatic function originally, they may have eventually become an established part of Judahite religious life in general.

2. The Priests in the Book of Zephaniah and the Reform of Josiah

If it is the case that the *kĕmārîm* served a diplomatic purpose in relation to dominant powers to Judah's north and north-east and did not become part of Judah's own religious life outside of that, the *kĕmārîm* may have become superfluous after the withdrawal of Assyria in the late seventh century BCE. The Assyrian withdrawal may have played a role in the elimination of the *kĕmārîm* in Josiah's purge. Of course, the statement in 2 Kgs 23:5 that Josiah deposed the *kĕmārîm* does not mean that the *kĕmārîm* were actually eliminated, as the veracity of such a statement depends on the totality of Josiah's reform or its historicity at all. We must turn to this issue, as it is crucial for dating the book of Zephaniah and understanding the priests who appear in it. The book's superscription (Zeph 1:1) dates the activity of Zephaniah to Josiah's reign, but does not specify any time period within that reign. Space does not permit a full study here of the historicity of the Josianic reform, but some comments can be made nonetheless.

Questions about the historicity of Josiah's reform, or purge, is complicated by the well-known differences between the order of events and their motivations in 2 Kgs 22–23 and 2 Chr 34–35. These two accounts differ on when Josiah began the purge and why, and the relationship of the "law book" to the reform. Second Kings presents the law book as a major motivator for the purge, whereas 2 Chronicles presents the law book as something encountered while the purge was already well underway.[27] Beyond these two accounts, there is very little solid historical evidence that such a religious reform or purge ever took place, and thus several scholars have rightly cast doubt on the purge's historicity.[28] For example, Reinhard Kratz has argued that the original account of Josiah's religious actions in 2 Kgs 22 and 23 contained originally only the king's removal of a few then-superfluous signs of Assyrian domination along with a temple renovation, but that this account was expanded with a massive reform project to make Josiah into an idealized Deuteronomistic king.[29]

A couple of clues about Josiah's policies can be seen from the book of Jeremiah that might be independent of the biblical historical accounts. Jeremiah 22:15–16 praises Josiah's general qualities of justice and care for the poor and needy. However, Jeremiah 3:6–10 states that during the time of Josiah, Israel's "false sister" Judah did not return to YHWH with her whole heart, but only in pretense. Jer 3:6–10 portrays some sort of insufficient return to Jeremiah's standard of YHWH-ism, but without the glowing praise that 2 Kgs 22–23 has for it. This suggests that there may in fact have been some form of religious change toward exclusivist YHWH-ism under Josiah, although almost certainly not on the scale of what is portrayed in 2 Kgs 22–23 and 2 Chr 34–35.

Scholars have generally accepted the Josianic dating for at least the original statements of the prophet Zephaniah, with some exceptions, and thus the Josianic reform has been the major anchor around which more precise dating is attempted. Within the reign of Josiah, the majority of works throughout the history of modern research have tended to see Zephaniah's activity as occurring early in Josiah's reign, before the king's reforms began and thus prior to 622/1 BCE. This is based on the fact that some of the same religious practices supposedly eradicated by Josiah are described as still occurring, especially in Zeph 1:4–6. In this view, it is often thought that Zephaniah might have inspired or prompted Josiah's reform.[30] The similarities between Zeph 1:4–6 and the purges carried

---

[27] Vlaardingerbroek, *Zephaniah*, 17–18, follows the Chronicles view of the relationship between the reform and the law book, arguing that Josiah would not have needed a book to know that reforms were necessary, and that the reform probably began as a political action to throw off waning Assyrian dominance.

[28] For some of the evidence problems, cf. J. Maxwell Miller and John H. Hayes, *A History of Ancient Israel and Judah* (2nd ed., Louisville, KY: Westminster John Knox, 2006), 439–61.

[29] Reinhard Kratz, *The Composition of the Narrative Books of the Old Testament* (trans. John Bowden; London: T&T Clark, 2005), 131.

[30] The early-Josianic dating was favored by G.G.V. Stonehouse and G.W. Wade, *The Books of the Prophets Zephaniah and Nahum and Habakkuk* (Westminster Commentaries; London: Methuen & Co., Ltd; Stonehouse was the author of the Zephaniah com-

out by Josiah in 2 Kgs 23 suggest at least a Dtr connection. Thus, Josef Scharbert suggested that while it is unknowable if Zephaniah actually did inspire or prompt Josiah's reform, the Dtr author(s) of 2 Kgs 23 may have made use of Zeph 1:4–6 in the composition of 2 Kgs 23.[31] Timo Veijola went somewhat further than most in suggesting that Josiah followed the urgings of Zephaniah by seeking out YHWH and humbling himself. Thus, "Es ist deutlich, daß Joschija nach dem Reformbericht von 2.Kön 23 als ein frommer König auftritt, der durch die Beseitigung der heidnischen Elemente aus Jerusalem und dessen Umgebung das von Zefanja angekündigte Strafgericht abzuwenden versuchte."[32]

The pre-reform Josianic dating is also often supported by the fact that priests, prophets, and officials are sharply criticized, but only "the king's sons" in 1:8 and not the king himself. Thus, the reasoning goes, Josiah was either pious already before the reform or not accountable due to his minority and so is not criticized.[33] Both arguments concerning "king's sons" are rather strange, as Josiah is too young before his reform to have any children old enough to be

---

mentary), 8–10, who both suggested that Zephaniah's preaching contributed to the Josianic Reform even if Zephaniah was not directly involved in it. Stonehouse also included a late Josianic stratum in his redaction history of the book, but included Zeph 1:4 in the original, early-Josianic stratum (Stonehouse, *Zephaniah*, 14–17). In Stonehouse's view, the early-Josianic Zephaniah was part of a prophetic movement urging against foreign alliances, and hence the diatribes against foreign worship in Zeph 1:4–5. Cf. also Maria Eszenyei Szeles, *Wrath and Mercy: A Commentary on the Books of Habakkuk and Zephaniah* (trans. George A.F. Knight; ITC; Grand Rapids, MI: Eerdmans, 1987), 61–63. Josef Scharbert, "Zefanja und die Reform des Joschija," in *Künder des Wortes: Beiträge zur Theologie der Propheten* (ed. Lothar Ruppert, Peter Weimar, and Erich Zenger; Würzburg: Echter, 1982), 237–54 (237) draws the analogy of Micah perhaps inspiring Hezekiah's reform in Jer 26:19 (attributed to Josef Schreiner), and that Jeremiah may have inspired Josiah's reform.

[31] Scharbert, "Zefanja," 248.

[32] Timo Veijola, "Zefanja und Joschija," in *Der Tag wird kommen: Ein interkontextuelles Gespräch über das Buch des Propheten Zefanja* (ed. Walter Dietrich and Milton Schwantes; SBS 170; Stuttgart: Katholisches Bibelwerk, 1996), 9–18, quotation on page 13.

[33] Smith, "Zephaniah," 168–69, supported the argument that Josiah was too young to be accountable. Arvid S. Kapelrud, *The Message of the Prophet Zephaniah: Morphology and Ideas* (Oslo: Universitetsforlaget, 1975), 17–18, suggested that Zephaniah's criticisms of the upper class were dangerous, and so his own tradents added the "on that day" language at a very early written stage to soften the attack into a prediction of a possibly remote future. Kapelrud, *Zephaniah*, 42, suggests that the "king's sons" could have been real Judean princes or simply Baalists; if Judean royalty, then Josiah would have been in his minority at the time.

morally accountable (unless the king in this verse is Manasseh or Amon).[34] He begins his reform at the age of twenty-six according to 2 Kgs 22:3, and at the age of twenty in 2 Chr 34:3. If by the "king's sons" the sons of Manasseh or Amon are meant, then this condemnation would include Josiah as well. If the author of Zeph 1:8 wanted to excuse Josiah among other princes, it should have condemned "the brothers of the king." In any case, those who argue for a pre-reform dating of Zephaniah's activities take the book to be a reflection of the religious conditions of Judah during Josiah's early reign, when perhaps Judah was run by regents, and Zephaniah himself is often seen as a forerunner of the reform itself.[35]

A minority of scholars has dated the initial composition of the book to the time during the reform, after it began, all the way to near the end of Josiah's reign, at least prior to 612 BCE when Nineveh fell. Noting Dtr language in the book of Zephaniah, O. Palmer Robertson suggested that Zephaniah the prophet drew on the Dtr language of the emerging book of Deuteronomy, and that the prophet drew on the language and ideas of Deuteronomy to help and support Josiah's continuing reform.[36] Late Josianic datings sometimes rest on the supposition that the "remnant of Baal" in Zeph 1:4 suggests a highly reduced Baalism, but as has been rightly pointed out, *šě'ār* can mean "down to the last remainder (or vestige)."[37] Further, it has been noted that if Josiah did carry out a religious purge, the criticisms of Jeremiah show that the religious practices supposedly purged by Josiah either returned or were never really eliminated.[38] Of course, dating the original stratum of the book of Zephaniah within the Josianic religious reform assumes the historicity of such a reform program. As stated earlier,

---

[34] Veijola, "Zefanja," 17–18, regarded the king's sons in Zeph 1:8 as being Josiah's sons, whose corrupt character was apparently already evident while Zephaniah was preaching during Josiah's reign. Henry Ferguson, "The Historical Testimony of the Prophet Zephaniah," *JBL* 3 (1883): 42–59 (42), dates the career of Zephaniah to the last years of Josiah's reign to accommodate Josiah's sons being old enough to be criticized.

[35] Examples of this view are discussed below.

[36] O. Palmer Robertson, *The Books of Nahum, Habbakuk, and Zephaniah* (NICOT; Grand Rapids, MI: Eerdmans, 1990), 32–34, 253–57.

[37] Among others, Smith, "Zephaniah," 169. J.J.M. Roberts, *Nahum, Habakkuk, and Zephaniah: A Commentary* (OTL; Louisville, KY: Westminster/John Knox, 1991), 171, writes that cutting off a "remnant" or "name" means to cut off descendants who carry on one's memory; thus, YHWH's cutting off the name of certain priests and the remnant of Baal refers to a future time when even their memory will be forgotten. Roberts means here that the "remnant" statement does mean that Baalism is reduced, and thus does not indicate a late-Josianic dating.

[38] For example, David W. Baker, *Nahum, Habakkuk and Zephaniah* (TOTC; Leicester: Inter-Varsity Press, 1988), 81–82.

the historicity of the reform as described in 2 Kings and 2 Chronicles is rather doubtful.

Redactionally, different parts of the book of Zephaniah can relate to the reign of Josiah in different ways. Klaus Seybold dated the initial stratum of the book's composition later than most at 615 BCE,[39] but dated Zeph 1:4–6 to the exilic period. Seybold saw this pericope as a later addition because in his view, (1) it was a prose paratactic list inserted into a poetic passage, (2) the listed wrongs do not relate to the pre-586 BCE Jerusalem temple, suggesting that it no longer exists, and (3) it seems dependent on 2 Kgs 23:4–20 in Seybold's view.[40] Seybold wrote, "Vergleicht man 1,4ff mit 2 Kön 23,4–20, dem dtr bearbeiteten Bericht von Joschijas Reformmaßnahmen, finden sich wenige Aussagen, die dort nicht vorkommen oder dort nicht anklingen," including the *kĕmārîm*.[41] Against Scharbert's suggestion that either Josiah himself or at least the Dtr narrator drew on Zephaniah's speeches, Seybold noted that a mention of Zephaniah in 2 Kings then should be expected, as prophetic fulfillment is important to Dtr (such as in 1 Kgs 13). Seybold suggested instead that the dependence is the other way around, that Zeph 1:4–6 is based on 2 Kgs 23 or some similar account.[42] He pointed out further that Zeph 1:4–6 is not calling for a reform, but announcing a catastrophe on Judah overall, and thus is looking back on 587 BCE. The guilt is too general, the punishment too total, to be a realistic reform program and must instead be about YHWH's decisive judgment in 587 BCE. As Seybold considered Zeph 1:4–6 to be the only real candidate for a Josiah connection and that this pericope postdates Josiah, then the book of Zephaniah thus has nothing to do with Josiah's reform except retrospectively.

While Seybold's view is possible, it should be remembered that with the 2 Kgs 23 narrative, Josiah does receive a prophecy of absolute certain doom from

---

[39] Klaus Seybold, *Nahum Habakuk Zephanja* (ZBK 24.2; Zürich: Theologischer Verlag, 1991), 88.

[40] Klaus Seybold, *Satirische Prophetie: Studen zum Buch Zefanja* (SBS 120; Stuttgart: Katholisches Bibelwerk, 1985), 75–81.

[41] Ibid., 77.

[42] Ibid., 77–78. Similarly, Lothar Perlitt, *Die Propheten Nahum, Habakuk, Zephanja* (ATD 25/1; Göttingen: Vandenhoeck & Ruprecht, 2004), 104–5, suggests that 2 Kgs 23 cannot be based on Zephaniah, but that the book of Zephaniah may be drawing on 2 Kgs 23 or at least on the activities of the Josianic reform movement. Also, Christoph Levin, "Zephaniah: How This Book Became Prophecy," in *Constructs of Prophecy in the Former and Latter Prophets and Other Texts* (ed. Lester L. Grabbe and Martti Nissinen; ANEM 4; Atlanta: Society of Biblical Literature, 2011), 117–39 (126–27, 138), argued that 1:4–6 is the "sin of Manasseh," drawn from both 2 Kgs 23 and from Ezekiel, in the postexilic period.

Huldah in 2 Kgs 22:15–20, and yet he still has hopes to stave off the disaster. This is not to say that Huldah's communication with Josiah is historical, just that the author of 2 Kgs 22–23 at least could envision a situation in which Josiah was told that Judah has no hope and yet the king undertakes a religious reform anyway. So, a doom message from Zephaniah, if it was transmitted to Josiah, could have prompted rather than deterred him from undertaking his religious purge.[43] In any case, the religious practices condemned by 2 Kgs 23 were probably the norm in late monarchic Judah, as attested by similar condemnations in various other parts of the Hebrew Bible.[44]

The Josianic setting can also be explored from a territorial rather than religious perspective without assuming a religious reform, particularly by focusing on the Oracles against the Nations (OAN). This approach can be seen in the work of Duane Christensen, who proposed that the Zephanic OAN were produced in 628 BCE in order to support a Josianic military conquest or reconquest of lands lost to Philistia, Ammon, and Moab over the preceding century, based partly on Josiah's supposed invasion of the former Assyrian province of Samerina.[45] There is, however, no biblical nor extra-biblical support for a

---

[43] Irsigler, *Zefanja*, 70–71, saw Zephaniah the prophet as a forerunner of the Josianic reform but not as a partisan supporter of it, because the prophet spoke of a certain doom for Judah and spoke out against the wealthy in general.

[44] Walter Dietrich, "Die Kontexte des Zefanjabuches," in *Der Tag wird kommen: Ein interkontextuelles Gespräch über das Buch des prophenten Zefanja* (ed. Walter Dietrich and Milton Schwantes; SBS 170; Stuttgart: Katholisches Bibelwerk, 1996), 19–37 wrote at page 29, n. 36, "M.E. gab es aber nicht nur in den Köpfen deuteronomistischer Theoretiker, sondern in der politisch-religiösen Praxis im Juda des 7. Jahrhunderts assyrogenen Gestirnsdienst und assyrophile 'Pfaffen'." Tchavdar S. Hadjiev, "Zephaniah and the 'Book of the Twelve' Hypothesis," in *Prophecy and Prophets in Ancient Israel: Proceedings of the Oxford Old Testament Seminar* (ed. John Day; New York: T&T Clark, 2010), 325–38, concluded on page 334 regarding the book of Zephaniah: "There is little in it that can unquestionably be regarded as Deuteronomostic." For the general question of a possible Deuteronomistic "Book of the Four" of which Zephaniah would have been a part (but without specific discussion of Zephaniah), see Jason Radine, "Deuteronomistic Redaction of the Book of the Four and the Origins of Israel's Wrongs," in *Perspectives on the Formation of the Book of the Twelve: Methodological Foundations—Redactional Processes—Historical Insights* (ed. Rainer Albertz, James D. Nogalski, and Jakob Wöhrle; BZAW 433; Berlin: de Gruyter, 2012), 287–302.

[45] Duane Christensen, "Zephaniah 2:4–15: A Theological Basis for Josiah's Program of Political Expansion," *CBQ* 46 (1984): 669–82, cautiously followed by Baker, *Zephaniah*, 82–83.

supposed Josianic invasion towards Judah's west or east, and Josiah's reported activities in Samaria do not necessarily constitute an invasion.[46]

A different territorial-Josianic proposal without positing any historical military activities was made by Anselm Hagedorn, who suggested that the original core of the book of Zephaniah consisted of the oracles against Philistia, Moab, and Ammon, and that these formed "a salvation oracle for Judah during Josiah's reign."[47] In Hagedorn's view, the author of this Josianic-era salvation oracle saw the demise of Assyria, as patron of Philistia, Moab, and Ammon, as a sign of divine wrath against those three lands. Hagedorn followed Reinhard Kratz in seeing the Josiah narrative in 2 Kings as having been expanded with a large-scale reform movement only at the hands of Dtr redactors, and Hagedorn added that the book of Zephaniah only took on the appearance of being supportive of Josiah's reform (including Zeph 1:4) when it underwent a Dtr redaction along with the expansion of the Josiah narrative. Thus, both Zephaniah and Josiah become pro-dtr-reform together, in the exilic-era *Fortschreibung*.[48] Such a late dating of most of the book of Zephaniah solves many problems and has much to commend it, and if correct, demonstrates that the entire question of early or late Josianic context may have no bearing on discerning the historical identity of the condemned priests in the book.

3. Post-Josianic Datings

While the space and focus of this paper does not permit a full redactional study of the book of Zephaniah, some comments will be made here in favor of an exilic dating for the bulk of at least the book's first two chapters, which include Zeph 1:4. The book may include actual Josiah-era materials, but these may not be discernible now from the book's exilic form. The book almost certainly underwent postexilic additions especially in the second half of its third chapter (thus, not including Zeph 3:4), but these additions lie outside the purview of this paper.

One proposal for an exilic dating of nearly the entire book of Zephaniah was made by J. Philip Hyatt.[49] First, Hyatt noted that even if a modern reader

---

[46] Cf. Miller and Hayes, *History*, 459–60.

[47] Anselm C. Hagedorn, "When Did Zephaniah Become a Supporter of Josiah's Reform?" *JTS* 62.2 (2011): 453–75 (467). I thank Dr. Hagedorn for giving me an off-print of his very interesting article.

[48] Ibid., 470–75.

[49] J. Philip Hyatt, "The Date and Background of Zephaniah," *JNES* 7.1 (1948): 25–29.

believes in the historicity and success of Josiah's reform, numerous biblical texts attest that the kind of worship condemned by Josiah in 2 Kgs 23 and 2 Chr 34 continued to be practiced on an apparently wide scale all the way to the end of monarchic Judah. Turning to the OAN, Hyatt pointed out that there is cause for specific anger against Ammon and Moab in 2 Kgs 24:2, when Nebuchadnezzar sends Moabites and Ammonites to raid Judah when Jehoiakim revolts against Babylon.[50] Hyatt further suggested that the oracle against the Cushites in Zephaniah 2:12 refers to the Egyptians by reference to the then-passed Ethiopian Twenty-Fifth dynasty, and he related this oracle to the defeat of the Egyptians at the Battle of Carchemish in 605 BCE.[51] The association of Zeph 2:12 with the battle of Carchemish was also suggested by Brian Peckham, who similarly supported an early sixth century dating for the book.[52] Additionally, Hyatt argued that the oracle against Assyria in Zeph 2:13–15 reflects Nineveh's fall in 612 and subsequent abandonment.[53] Hyatt had more difficulties in explaining the oracle against Philistia in Zeph 2:4–7, suggesting that this oracle is more sympathetic to Philistia, and may reflect a possible Philistine alliance with Judah in Judah's revolt against Babylon.[54] Hyatt's position here however cannot be agreed to, as Zeph 2:5 is not at all sympathetic to Philistia.[55] Peckham associated the oracle against Philistia with Nebuchadnezzar's campaign against Egypt and Philistia in 604–601 BCE.[56]

Following Hyatt's late dating of the book of Zephaniah, Donald Williams, perhaps too daringly, suggested identifying the prophet Zephaniah with the priest Zephaniah who is executed by the Babylonian captain of the guard in 2 Kgs 25:18 // Jer 52:24.[57] Since this priest Zephaniah was alive at the end of the Judahite monarchy he would be contemporary with the dating for the origin of the book of Zephaniah advanced by Williams and Hyatt. Zephaniah is described in 2 Kgs 25:18 as a "second priest." In the context of that passage, he appears to be second-in-command to the chief priest, Seraiah. A priest named Zephaniah

---

[50] Ibid., 28.
[51] Ibid., 28.
[52] Peckham, *History*, 14.
[53] Hyatt, "Date," 29.
[54] Ibid., 29.
[55] Eric Lee Welch, "The Roots of Anger: An Economic Perspective on Zephaniah's Oracle Against the Philistines," *VT* 63 (2013): 471–85, proposed that Zeph 2:4–7 reflects a seventh-century Judahite resentment of Ekron's dominance in the olive oil industry while exploiting formerly Judahite olive orchards, and that the Zephaniah passage expresses hope for the demise of Ekron and the rehabilitation of the orchard lands by Judah.
[56] Peckham, *History*, 14.
[57] Donald L. Williams, "The Date of Zephaniah," *JBL* 82 (1963): 77–88.

appears in Jer 21 and 29 as a friend of Jeremiah, who consults Jeremiah for oracles and protects him against the attempts of one of his enemies, Shemaiah, who wanted him arrested. This suggests that Zephaniah may have been on the side of the exclusivist YHWH-ists, like Jeremiah. Although Williams did not notice this, the term "second priest" may mean more than just second in command. Second Kings 23:4 describes "priests of the second order" as being among Josiah's officials who engage in the violent purges of non-YHWH-istic religion in Judah and southern Samaria. Perhaps this "second order" of priests was identified with an exclusivist YHWH-ist side of Judahite religion, regardless of the extent of Josiah's religious actions, and perhaps the priest Zephaniah was a member of this order. It might also go some way to explaining why he is executed by the Babylonian captain of the guard rather than being merely exiled (2 Kgs 25:21). Nonetheless, the priest named Zephaniah is most likely not to be identified with the prophet Zephaniah to whom the book of Zephaniah is attributed, and Williams's identification of the two Zephaniahs has not gained scholarly acceptance.[58] Since the book of Zephaniah is set in Josiah's time, it is unlikely that an exilic author(s) would use the name of a living, contemporary, well-known person. More likely, there was a historical prophet named Zephaniah at the time of Josiah, in whose name this book was written.

While many of Hyatt's and Williams's arguments have their problems, their overall dating may well be correct and can be better supported, as major portions of the book reveal several indications of a late monarchic or exilic dating. First, while the prediction of disastrous destruction and exile can be made at any time, the harsh and panicky tone of the Day of the Lord sayings throughout the book suggests a fearsome imminent catastrophe.[59] Whether one was pro- or anti-reform in the time of Josiah's reign, it would be hard to see a horrific disaster as imminent. Judah was understandably reasserting itself, and while it did face danger and domination from Egypt, this apparently did not involve any catastrophe for Judah beyond the killing of Josiah himself. Secondly, the oracle against Nineveh does, as Hyatt and also Peckham suggested, read like an *ex eventu* prophecy that Nineveh will be overthrown and abandoned when this event had already happened. Thirdly, in the closing years of the seventh century and beginning of the sixth, Babylonian violence did come down to Ammon, Moab, and

---

[58] E.g., Irsigler, *Zefanja*, 67.

[59] Michael H. Floyd, *Minor Prophets* (2 vols.; FOTL 22; Grand Rapids, MI: Eerdmans, 2000), 2:177–78, noted that the Babylonian exile need not have happened for exile to be imagined, and that the Northern Kingdom of Israel had already been exiled in any case. Similarly and with more examples of pre-620s BCE exiles in Palestine, see Sweeney, *Zephaniah*, 17–18, *contra* Vlaardingerbroek, *Zephaniah*, 194, who considers exilic themes to be of exilic provenance.

Philistia together in a way that had not occurred during the Assyrian period. Philistia came under violent attack from Babylon in the end of the seventh century BCE, Ammon fell under the dominance of Babylon around 582 BCE, and Moab probably around the same time if not also in the 580s, as both Ammon and Moab appear to have joined in Zedekiah's rebellion against Nebuchadnezzar according to Jer 27:3.[60] In spite of these factors, the superscription itself is not necessarily in error, but is an intentional establishment of setting for the book of Zephaniah.

Most of these arguments for an exilic dating can also apply to a slightly earlier dating, to the last years of the Judahite monarchy on the eve of the Babylonian invasion. Marco Striek proposed that a substantial pre-Deuteronomistic form of the book of Zephaniah was composed by the prophet himself around the year 604 BCE as a paraenesis urging the Judahites to change their ways in view of the Day of YHWH being fulfilled among the other nations.[61] Similarly, Tchadvar Hadjiev identified the initial composition of the book in the closing years of the Judahite monarchy, but while there was still a possibility of averting the coming disaster.[62] The oracles against Ammon and Moab discussed above, however, indicate a date after Nebuchadnezzar's campaigns in Transjordan, but the Zephanic OAN may derive from a later stratum. A greater precision for the earliest stage of the book of Zephaniah (including or excluding its OAN) beyond the last decade of the seventh and first two decades of the sixth century is likely impossible, but the most likely case is shortly after 586 BCE, unless there is a compelling reason to separate the OAN from it literary context. Thus, it is proposed here that the bulk of the book of Zephaniah was an early exilic work, written to be read as a prophecy from the time of Josiah, "predicting" and explaining the fall of Judah while at the same time urging the survivors to change their ways.

If the bulk of the book of Zephaniah is dated to the end of the Judahite monarchy, finally some sense can be made out of the criticism of "the king's sons" in Zeph 1:8. Following the Josianic setting of the book, the king would be

---

[60] For details, see Jason Radine, *The Book of Amos in Emergent Judah* (FAT 2.45; Tübingen: Mohr Siebeck, 2010), 175–78, 180–83.

[61] Marco Striek, *Das vordeuteronomistische Zephanjabuch* (BBET 29; Frankfurt am Main: Peter Lang, 1999), 217–33.

[62] Tchadvar Hadjiev, "The Theological Transformations of Zephaniah's Proclamation of Doom," *ZAW* 126.4 (2014): 506–20. This first stratum was in Hadjiev's view supplemented by an exilic stratum explaining the disaster of 587 BCE, followed again by a postexilic stratum with more eschatological overtones. Hadjiev recognized the uncertainties dating parts of the book of Zephaniah before or after 587 BCE, and expressed an openness about some of his proposed dates.

Josiah, and "the king's sons" would thus be Josiah's sons. Those sons were the Judahite kings Jehoahaz, whose mother was Hamutal (2 Kgs 23:31), and Jehoiakim, whose mother was Zebidah (2 Kgs 23:36). It is also possible that we should include Judah's last king, Zedekiah; this king, originally named Mattaniah, was also a son of Hamutal and thus probably also a son of Josiah (2 Kgs 24:18 || Jer 52:1). The only remaining Judahite king after Josiah is Jehoiachin, son of Jehoiakim (2 Kgs 24:6); as a grandson of Josiah, he might also be called one of the king's sons. So, the "king's sons" of Zephaniah 1:8 could refer to the last kings of Judah, whose behavior contributed to the fall of Judah in the perspective of the exilic book of Zephaniah.

Conclusion

The book of Zephaniah was initially composed around the time of the Babylonian conquest of Judah, probably shortly afterward, and presented as the prophecies of a man named Zephaniah who purportedly lived during the time of Josiah, predicting a terrible destruction for Judah and Jerusalem. He thus appears somewhat like a Huldah character, situated in the time of Judah's relatively "good" king (from an exclusivist Yahwist perspective), announcing Judah's disastrous fall. The Zephaniah figure blames the fall of Judah on a variety of factors, among which are a type of probably native Judahite, Aramean-rite priests, the *kĕmārîm*, who worked in specific loyalty to kings prior to Josiah and probably also afterwards. The *kĕmārîm* are thus portrayed as part of the corrupt leadership of Judah who led the country into disaster, along with the *kōhănîm* (at least in Zeph 3:4, whether or not their appearance in 1:4 is a later addition), wealthy merchants, corrupt officials, and the succession of Josiah's sons and grandsons who ruled the kingdom of Judah in its last days.

9
THE PRIESTHOOD IN THE PERSIAN PERIOD: HAGGAI, ZECHARIAH, AND MALACHI

Lester L. Grabbe

A full picture of the priesthood in the Persian period would require a careful study of all the textual and other sources (archaeology, etc.) available. I have already done that in outline.[1] The books of Haggai, Zechariah, and Malachi are often grouped together because of the general Persian dating and also certain themes. My purpose here, in accordance with the aims of the present volume, is to look specifically at what these three books—Haggai, Zechariah, Malachi— say about priests and the priesthood, and to consider these results in the context of the Minor Prophets.

---

[1] See Lester L. Grabbe, *A History of the Jews and Judaism in the Second Temple Period 1: Yehud: A History of the Persian Province of Judah* (London: T&T Clark, 2004), 224–34. There I interact with the main study on the subject, which is Joachim Schaper, *Priester und Leviten im achämenidischen Juda: Studien zur Kult- und Sozialgeschichte Israels in persischer Zeit* (FAT 31; Tübingen: Mohr Siebeck, 2000). Cf. also Risto Nurmela, *The Levites: Their Emergence as a Second-Class Priesthood* (SFSHJ 193; Atlanta: Scholars Press, 1998); also my review of Schaper: Lester L. Grabbe, "Review of Schaper, *Priester und Leviten im achämenidischen Juda*," *JQR* 93 (2002–3): 609–11.

1. THE THREE PROPHETIC BOOKS

Haggai, Zechariah, and Malachi make a natural grouping among the prophetic literature, all apparently from the Persian period. Haggai and Zech 1–8 ostensibly cover the same period of time and address similar themes, especially the "diarchy" of governor and high priest (see below) and the rebuilding of the temple. Zechariah 9–14 is made up of two oracles (9–11 and 12–14), but Malachi forms essentially a third oracle alongside these. As will be discussed, all three seem to be the product of cultic prophets or of priests. One of the interesting points is that these three seem to have some essential differences from Ezra-Nehemiah.

1.1. HAGGAI

The persona of Haggai's author is unknown, though it is possible that he was a cultic prophet.[2] The books of Haggai and Zechariah seem to be closely related and are both ostensibly associated with the Persian period. Haggai has only two short chapters, both of which are devoted to a series of prophetic exhortations to get on with rebuilding the temple, accompanied by promises of the blessings which will follow as a result. The impression is that the oracles arise out of an actual historical situation in which the community is experiencing hardships. The oracles are dated and cover only a few short weeks, from the first day of the sixth month (1:1) to the twenty-fourth day of the ninth month (2:10, 20), all in the second year of Darius (520 BCE).[3] The people are suffering misfortunes because of failure to rebuild the temple and restore proper worship. Implied in this rebuilding, though, is the restoration and renewal of the Jewish religious community.

---

[2] Cf. Lester L. Grabbe, *Priests, Prophets, Diviners, Sages: A Socio-historical Study of Religious Specialists in Ancient Israel* (Valley Forge: Trinity Press, 1995), 112–13.

[3] The dates in Haggai and Zechariah are sometimes seen as problematic. Diana Edelman, *The Origins of the "Second" Temple: Persian Imperial Policy and the Rebuilding of Jerusalem* (London: Equinox, 2005), rejects their dating entirely and redates the books to the mid-fifth century BCE. Although we cannot be certain that the dates given in Haggai and Zechariah are trustworthy, I am not willing to redate the whole lot to a century later. See Lester L. Grabbe, "'They Shall Come Rejoicing to Zion'—Or Did They? The Settlement of Yehud in the Early Persian Period," in *Exile and Restoration Revisited: Essays on the Neo-Babylonian and Persian Periods in Memory of Peter R. Ackroyd* (ed. Gary N. Knoppers and Lester L. Grabbe, with Deirdre Fulton; LSTS 73; London/New York: T&T Clark, 2009), 116–27.

The message seems to be simple and straightforward (more so than Zechariah), with the focus almost entirely on the rebuilding of the temple. Haggai especially emphasizes how the people have worried too much about their own welfare and have neglected to rebuild the temple (Hag 1:2–11). The prophet does not envisage a temple made from exotic materials imported from abroad (as does Ezra 3:7) but calls on the people to build with local materials (Hag 1:8). The important thing is to get on with the building so that the economic troubles being experienced will be reversed through divine favor (Hag 1:8–11; 2:14–19). Restoration of the Judaean community in Palestine seems to be a major theme of the book, but one it shares with Zech 1–8. The "people of the land" are evidently to be included in the community and not demonized as in Ezra and Nehemiah (cf. Hag 2:4).

In line with this anxiety about rebuilding the temple, a number of references are made to priests. Most of the concern in Haggai (and Zechariah) is about the high priesthood. Of particular importance (as also in Zechariah) is the high priest Joshua, who is the subject of a number of individual prophecies, along with Zerubbabel. Leadership of the community is invested in a sort of diarchy, with Zerubbabel as the governor of the province (evidently appointed by the Persians) and Joshua as high priest (Hag 1:12). Although there was an officially appointed governor most or all the time during the Persian period, the high priest would still have been the main religious representative of the people. Also bound up with this is the "messianic" theme that appears (in both Haggai and Zech 1–8). Haggai emphasizes the role of Zerubbabel (a member of the royal family) as God's "signet ring" (Hag 2:4–9, 20–23).

Haggai 2:11–19 seeks a ruling (*tôrāh*) from the priests with regard to a cultic matter. The purpose of this is to introduce a prophecy, but it shows the convention that priests made rulings on such matters. The implication is that Haggai already knew the answer to the two questions; otherwise, his prophecy would have made no sense. In this case, therefore, a well-established priestly practice with regard to the transmission of holiness and impurity seems to be known, but this suggests at least an inner-priestly set of regulations, if not one taught more widely to the non-priestly community.

1.2. ZECHARIAH

Like Haggai, Zechariah might have been a cultic prophet.[4] The evidence is the following: certain men ask the priests of God's house and the prophets whether to continue to mourn in the fifth month as was their custom, after which the

---

[4] Grabbe, *Priests, Prophets, Diviners, Sages*, 80.

word of YHWH comes to Zechariah to speak to the people and the priests (Zech 7). This suggests not only the existence of cultic prophets in the temple ("God's house") alongside the priests, but also that Zechariah was himself numbered among them. This would closely associate him with the temple priests, making him possibly even a priest himself.[5] It would have been possible for him to be both a priest and a prophet (like Jeremiah and Ezekiel).[6]

Once again (as in Haggai) we see a major focus on the high priest. In Zech 3, Joshua is pictured in filthy garments, as a burnt stick pulled out of the fire. Although accused by the Adversary (*haśśāṭān*), the Angel of YHWH rebukes the latter and has the filthy garments stripped from Joshua, to be replaced with a crown and proper priestly garments. Thus, the guilt of the past (caused by the sins of the people—presumably including the priests—of Jerusalem) is symbolically removed. This in turn presages the coming of "the Branch"—the Davidic ruler (who is the subject of prophecies in Zech 6:12–13 and other prophets, such as Jer 23:5–6). A second prophecy concerns two crowns (Zech 6:9–15). One is for the high priest, and the other is for the Branch. The high priest will sit on a throne and will cooperate in harmony with the messianic figure of the Branch in rebuilding the temple and in ruling the people. Several of Zechariah's visions also relate to Joshua, often in conjunction with Zerubbabel or with the messianic figure called the Branch.

It is expected that Zerubbabel will be enthroned as ruler (Zech 6). It is generally thought that Zerubbabel is "the Branch" in Zechariah, though some argue that this is a reference to a future messianic figure.[7] As in Haggai, some of the prophecies in Zechariah focus on both Joshua and Zerubbabel the governor. They relate to them as the leaders of the restoration and the ones credited with the responsibility for the rebuilding of the temple. They are the recipients of, or the central actors in, various prophecies and visions. For example, both the high priest and the governor are represented by olive trees in Zech 4 (though the focus is on Zerubbabel who will take the lead in rebuilding the temple). They both hear and heed the prophecies of Haggai about rebuilding the temple (Hag 1:12–13; 2:1–4).

As in Haggai, leadership of the community is invested in a sort of diarchy, with Zerubbabel as the governor of the province and Joshua as high priest (Zech

---

[5] Thomas Pola, *Das Priestertum bei Sacharja: Historische und traditionsgeschichtliche Untersuchung zur frühnachexilischen Herrschererwartung* (FAT 35; Tübingen: Mohr Siebeck, 2003), 45, argues that Zechariah served as a priest as well as a prophet but denies that he was a cult prophet.

[6] Cf. Grabbe, *Priests, Prophets, Diviners, Sages*, 76–77.

[7] See, e.g., Walter H. Rose, *Zemah and Zerubbabel: Messianic Expectations in the Early Postexilic Period* (JSOTS 304; Sheffield: Sheffield Academic Press, 2000).

3–4). In spite of an officially appointed governor by the Persians, the high priest was still the main representative of the people to the administration, going beyond his religious duties. Also bound up with this is the "messianic" theme that appears in both Haggai and Zech 1–8. Zechariah recognizes both Joshua and Zerubbabel as anointed (Zech 4): they are both crowned and sit on thrones.

Finally, Zech 6:9–15 describes how Zechariah is to take members of the community, make crowns, and place a crown on Joshua's head. One called the Branch would rebuild the temple and sit on a throne to rule; alongside him would also sit a priest. Joshua is obviously intended to be the priestly leader of the community, though the identity of the Branch is debated. "The Branch" might have been Joshua at one stage, though in the present context he might be Zerubbabel or, more likely, a figure to come in the future.

1.3. MALACHI

Malachi is closely bound with Zechariah in its present structural arrangement, forming a "third oracle" after the two in Zech 9–14. Also, the final section of the book seems to be a conclusion for the whole of the Book of the Twelve (Mal 3:22–24 [Eng. 4:4–6]). A number of different structural analyses of Malachi have recently been given,[8] some using the *rîv* pattern (contention or legal complaint) as the basis (though this is problematic). The book takes the form of a series of questions and answers. The terms "disputation" and "diatribe" have also been used. Like Zech 9–14, Malachi is difficult to date. A number of recent English-language commentators put it in the Persian period.[9] It has several issues in common with Ezra-Nehemiah, but this is not definitive since the dating of these books is also in question.[10]

---

[8] Andrew E. Hill, *Malachi: A New Translation with Introduction and Commentary* (AB 25D; New York: Doubleday, 1998).

[9] David L. Petersen, *Zechariah 9–14 and Malachi* (OTL; London: SCM Press, 1995); Paul L. Redditt, *Haggai, Zechariah, Malachi* (NCBC; London: Marshall Pickering, 1995); Andrew E. Hill, "Dating the Book of Malachi: A Linguistic Reexamination," in *The Word of the Lord Shall Go Forth: Essays in Honor of David Noel Freedman in Celebration of His Sixtieth Birthday* (ed. Carol L. Meyers and Michael O'Connor; ASOR Sp. Vol. Series 1; Winona Lake, IN: Eisenbrauns, 1983), 77–89, and idem, *Malachi*.

[10] Grabbe, *History of the Jews*, 72.

There are a number of themes in the book: critique of the priesthood, but the author could still be a priest[11] or Levite;[12] tithing (3:6–12); improper sacrifice (1:6–14); and husband-and-wife relations (2:13–16). The criticisms especially focus on proper cultic observance, with the priests themselves being strongly taken to task along with the people (1:6–2:9; 3:6–12). Lest it be thought that Malachi attacks the priesthood, however, it can be argued that he was himself part of the priestly establishment.[13]

Malachi 1:6–2:9 is a concerted critique of the priesthood, charging the priests with allowing defective animals to be offered on the altar, thus defiling it. Whereas YHWH's name is honored among the other nations with incense and a pure offering, YHWH's table in Jerusalem is defiled (1:1–14). God made a covenant with Levi who gave proper instructions (תורת אמת), because the lips of a priest guard knowledge (דעת), and instruction (תורה) is sought from them; he is the messenger (מלאך) of YHWH (2:6–7). Unfortunately, the Levites corrupted that covenant and disregarded God's ways (2:8–9).

As already noted above with regard to Zechariah, the author of Malachi seems to be closely associated with the temple. Malachi's identity is not given in the book; however, there is a good chance that he was himself a priest (as well as a prophet, like Jeremiah and Ezekiel). Indeed, this is suggested by the name Malachi ("my messenger") which seems to be evoked by the reference to the priest as God's messenger in 2:7. If so, this passage represents an internal critique of the priesthood by one of its own members.

A major question is Malachi's view of the organization of the priesthood. Is it a two-tier priesthood? It has been argued by O'Brien that Malachi makes no differentiation between priests and Levites.[14] Since no clear distinction is made in the few references to priests, Levites, and "sons of Levi," she may be correct; however, the book is a very short one. Since priests are also "sons of Levi," even in sources which separate the Aaronites from the rest of the Levites, the writer of Malachi may be using "Levites" and "sons of Levi" loosely.[15] None of the passages seems to be decisive. It would be unusual—and interesting—if a late text like Malachi regarded all Levites as altar priests. Schaper had also argued

---

[11] Rex A. Mason, "The Prophets of the Restoration," in *Israel's Prophetic Tradition: Essays in Honour of Peter R. Ackroyd* (ed. Richard Coggins, Anthony Philips, and Michael Knibb; Cambridge: Cambridge University Press, 1982), 137–54 (149–50).

[12] Redditt, *Haggai, Zechariah, Malachi*, 152.

[13] Mason, "The Prophets of the Restoration," 149–50.

[14] Julia O'Brien, *Priest and Levite in Malachi* (SBLDS 121; Atlanta: Scholars Press, 1990), 47–48, 111–12.

[15] Cf. Beth Glazier-McDonald, *Malachi: The Divine Messenger* (SBLDS 98; Atlanta: Scholars Press, 1987).

that Malachi knows the distinction between altar priests and Levites, though it does not suit Malachi's purpose to discuss it.[16]

2. DISCUSSION: PRIESTS IN THE MINOR PROPHETS

The information about priests in these three Persian books does not seem to overlap a lot with that of priests elsewhere in the Minor Prophets. One area with some overlap, however, lies in the political sphere. Throughout much of the period of the monarchy, there seems to have been a "chief priest" or "high priest."[17] Although this figure was always under the control of the king—who was regarded as the chief cultic figure—it is not surprising that an office of "chief priest" existed. Sometimes this individual is involved in the national politics (cf. 2 Kgs 11–12). In the books of Haggai and Zechariah, however, we find a new development. Joshua is not just the head of the priests but also takes his place alongside the provincial governor Zerubbabel (Hag 1:1, 14; 2:2). This is probably mainly because of the importance of the temple and cult to the Persian province of Judah, but it may already suggest the shouldering of some civic duties by the high priest. We probably already see the beginning of the path to national office that came to fruition in subsequent centuries.

Some other areas where the discussions in Haggai, Zechariah, and Malachi touch on those elsewhere in the Minor Prophets includes the question of cult prophets. It has been proposed, for example, that Amos and even Jeremiah were cultic prophets. Also, the division of the priests into altar priests and lower clergy (priests and Levites) seems presupposed in Ezra 2 and Neh 7. There is also the question of priestly torah: that is, priests made *ad hoc* rulings having to do with the cult and temple and the practices relating to them. It is implied that many such practices were widely known outside the priesthood, as well, suggesting that the priests taught the practices in some way.

CONCLUSION

We can now come to some conclusions about the priesthood in the Persian period. Here are some of the main points arising out of this discussion:

---

[16] Schaper, *Priester und Leviten*.

[17] Cf. Grabbe, *Priests, Prophets, Diviners, Sages*, 60–62, and idem, *Judaic Religion in the Second Temple Period: Belief and Practice from the Exile to Yavneh* (London: Routledge, 2000), 144–45.

- Priests seem to be divided into altar priests and Levites.
- Cultic prophets are still somewhat controversial, but even though they are not explicitly named or discussed in the text, there is considerable evidence for their existence. One can argue that all three prophets here—Haggai, Zechariah, Malachi—were cultic prophets. One or more may have been priests, but cultic prophets would most likely have come from the ranks of the altar priests or the Levites.
- Priests give instruction and possess a body of sacred knowledge. The *tôrāh* that Haggai seeks from the priests shows that this was their normal function (to give rulings on temple or cultic matters) but also implies that this ruling was correctly anticipated by Haggai, which might suggest a wider teaching of such matters beyond the priestly circles.
- Priests are critiqued and criticized. We find this especially true in Malachi, but criticism of the priests is also implicit in Haggai and Zechariah, since they should take the lead in getting on with building the temple.
- Importance of the high priest. The high priest Joshua was especially responsible for taking a leadership role in the task of rebuilding the temple, in both Haggai and Zechariah.

10
KING, PRIEST, AND TEMPLE IN HAGGAI-ZECHARIAH-MALACHI AND EZRA-NEHEMIAH

Paul L. Redditt

People under foreign domination, even domination less harsh than by earlier powers as Persia seems to have been in comparison with the Assyrians and Babylonians, typically want freedom to conduct at least their internal political affairs and to worship their God or gods as they see fit. This paper will trace such thinking in several postexilic texts. It will depict Haggai and Zech 1–8 as the repository of thought of prophets who foresaw a vital connection among temple, priest, and king in postexilic Yehud, but whose hopes were left unfulfilled. Zech 9–14 explained why: priests and Davidides alike had failed to be faithful to God. Malachi looked toward a temple-centered community too, but specifically from the perspective of a critic of the temple priesthood. The book Ezra-Nehemiah, by contrast, arose post 445 (assuming at least some authentic "memoirs" of Nehemiah) down to about the mid-second century BCE and staked out the perks of the returnees over against those who had never been in exile.[1]

---

[1] See briefly Paul L. Redditt, *Ezra-Nehemiah* (SHBC; Macon: Smyth & Helwys, 2014), 30–32, and the literature discussed there.

1. KING AND PRIEST IN HAGGAI

The book of Haggai bills itself as the word of God to Zerubbabel son of Shealtiel and to Joshua the high priest in Jerusalem (Hag 1:1). The sequence of names, Zerubbabel first, then Joshua, probably is significant: the political figure is named ahead of the priest. That sequence appears again in Hag 1:12, 14; 2:2, and 2:4. Otherwise Joshua is not mentioned in the book of Haggai. Haggai 2:1–10 describes an exchange between the prophet and the priests, but that passage moves in verse 15 to discuss God's turn toward the people of Yehud. Haggai 2:20–22 returns to Zerubbabel, with a prediction of his future role in Yehud as God's king-like servant, but it does not mention Joshua or other priests at all. Each of these prophetic sayings will be discussed in order.

Haggai 1:1–6 blames the prevailing economic hardships of late sixth century BCE Yehud on the people's failure to rebuild the temple.[2] One may wonder if the return of exiles—in whatever number[3]—contributed to the stark condition of the countryside he describes in 1:6, 10–11. Judah and Jerusalem had suffered extensively at the hands of Babylon, and Babylon's replacement by Persia as the chief power in Yehud probably had little positive impact on the economic fortunes of its inhabitants. The return of exiles—again, in whatever number—perhaps taxed the resources of the countryside at least as much as any wealth the returnees managed to bring benefitted it.

Continuing, Hag 1:4–6 reports one side of a dialogue between the people at large, who claimed that the time to rebuild had not yet come, and the prophet, who insisted that it had. This dialogue has an echo in Ezra 4:4–5, which states that locals stymied early efforts to rebuild the temple. Haggai's message to his contemporaries in 520 BCE addresses their situation as Haggai saw matters. The people were still experiencing hardship because the temple still lay in ruins (vv. 7–11). Similarly, Ezra 3:1–7 reports that the returnees gathered and only repaired the altar "in the seventh month" (Ezra 1:1). Scholars typically assume that the year 538, the second year of Cyrus, was intended. Ezra 4 mentions local resistance to rebuilding the temple itself, and reports that work on it stopped. Ezra 5 reports that work was resumed under the goading of Haggai and Zechari-

---

[2] Tim Meadowcroft, *Haggai* (Readings; Sheffield: Sheffield Phoenix Press, 2006), argues that Hag 1:1–2 constitutes the first "oracle" of five in Haggai. Still, vv. 3–6 constitute a response to v. 2 and the subject continues through v. 15a.

[3] The number of Returnees was set at 42,360 in both Ezra 2:64 and Neh 7:67, despite differences in the component numbers, which did not add up to that number. See Redditt, *Ezra-Nehemiah*, 81–85. Many scholars now agree that the number was impossibly too high, perhaps making more sense as a count as late as the second century BCE.

ah, presumably in the second year of King Darius, i.e., 520 BCE (see Hag 1:1; 2:1, 10, 20; and Zech 1:1, 7). Any previous work at the site was ignored by Haggai, who described the temple as lying in ruins. Haggai 1:12–14 reports that Zerubbabel and Joshua, with all the people, "obeyed the voice of YHWH and of the words of Haggai" and came to rebuild the temple.

Haggai 2:2 reports that God again directed Haggai to speak to Zerubbabel and Joshua. After a series of rhetorical questions addressing the plainness of the new temple under construction, Haggai promised that God would beautify it, indeed would make it more splendid than Solomon's temple (v. 9). In addition, Hag 2:23 also promised that God would make Zerubbabel "like a signet ring" on the hand of King YHWH.[4] The implication is clear: God also would restore the Israelite (or at least Yehudite) monarchy in the person of Zerubbabel. As readers of the Bible know, however, Zerubbabel disappeared from the pages of Haggai/Zechariah after Zech 4:10, that is, ca. 520 BCE.[5] The suggestion that the name Zerubbabel stood originally in Zech 6:11, while plausible, simply underscores the mystery concerning for whom the crown/crowns mentioned there was/were made.

Haggai 2:10–14 works with the role of priests in matters of determining cleanliness and uncleanliness. On the one hand Haggai asked the priests whether ritual cleanliness was transferable from one item—for example purified meat—to another, and he was told it was not. On the other hand Haggai asked if someone contaminated by touching a dead body touched otherwise ritually clean food, would he render it ritually unclean? The answer was affirmative. Meyers and Meyers explain the verse succinctly: "Holiness cannot be communicated indirectly, but defilement can."[6]

The superscription to Hag 2:20–23 dates that message on the twenty-fourth day of the month. God directed Haggai to address Zerubbabel, announcing that God would make him "like [God's] signet ring," the ring used to seal or "sign" documents. Zerubbabel would be God's visible "signature," God's sign that a new day was dawning. The passage predicts God's overthrow of the "throne of

---

[4] Hans Walter Wolff, *Haggai: A Commentary* (CCS; trans. Margaret Kohl; Minneapolis, MN: Augsburg, 1988), 19, notes that the designation "governor" appears in the editorial heading of the saying (v. 21), but not in the prophetic saying itself (v. 23).

[5] Scholars sometimes suggest that Zerubbabel died in Jerusalem fairly soon, and he might have, but possibly he simply pursued his own interests in Jerusalem and/or returned to Babylon. His name, after all, meant "seed of Babylon." In any case Zech 3 and 4 have in view a diarchy, i.e., local leadership consisting of a Davidide and the high priest.

[6] Carol L. Meyers and Eric M. Meyers, *Haggai, Zechariah 1–8* (AB 25B; Garden City: Doubleday, 1987), 57.

the kingdoms" (Persia), and it envisions a role for the Davidide Zerubbabel in the life and/or governance of Yehud. On that happy note, the book of Haggai closes.

Those chapters are little more than vignettes, briefly sketching Haggai's urging the people to rebuild the temple and championing Zerubbabel as God's new David. In the larger context of the Twelve, they breathe the same air as Amos 9:11: "On that day I will raise up the booth of David that is fallen, and repair its breaches, and raise up its ruins." That verse, however, was focused on the monarchy and Jerusalem, while the book of Haggai was focused on the temple. Also, the messages of Haggai provide an excellent introduction to Zech 1–8, wherein Zerubbabel and Joshua still stand front and center as God's two leaders for the postexilic community.

2. THE DISCUSSION OF PRIESTS IN ZECHARIAH 1–8

The book of Zechariah presents itself as the record of three addresses (1:1–6; 1:7–6:15; and 7:1–14:21) by Zechariah ben Berekiah ben Iddo, the sixth century contemporary of Haggai, though neither book mentions the other prophet despite the fact that superscriptions (Hag 1:1; 2:1, 10, 20; Zech 1:1, 7) make them contemporaries.[7] Zechariah 1–8, moreover, distinguishes itself from Zech 9–14 by subject matter and literary style. Zechariah 1–8 consists first of an introductory piece (1:1–6) justifying the exile. Then eight visions follow in the first six chapters, supplemented by a brief narrative (Zech 7:1–7) and by a series of prophetic speeches (Zech 7:8–8:23). The dates provided in Zech 1:1, 1:7, and 7:1 are redactional, though Zech 1:7 is the fullest date.

The vision accounts in Zech 1–6 are prefaced by a prophetic narrative (1:1–6) in which God commands God's people to repent and return to God. It contains a prohibition, gives a command, and reports a divine discourse about the disobedience of the ancestors, i.e. the inhabitants of Jerusalem and Judah before the Babylonian captivity. The longest date formula in Zechariah, however, appears in Zech 1:7. Verses 1:1 and 7:1 appear to be variations on it.

The structure of Zech 1–6 is clear. This section of the paper will be limited to those chapters:

---

[7] Al Wolters, *Zechariah* (HCOT; Leuven, Paris, Walpole, MA: Peeters, 2014), 22, says that since there are no decisive arguments otherwise he holds to the traditional view that Zechariah himself wrote all fourteen chapters. Of course, there are no decisive arguments that the text is authentic either, so his decision is not based on argument and reason but traditional ascription. In either case the discussion here concerns the text as it stands, not the history of its writing.

Exhortation: 1:1–6
First Three Visions: 1:7–17 (concerning four horses); 2:1–4 [Eng. 1:18–21] (four horns); 2:5–9 [Eng. 2:1–5] (the new Jerusalem).
Exhortation: 2:10–17 [Eng. 2:6–13]
Vision (concerning Joshua, but with no interpreting angel): 3:1–10
Central Vision about Zerubbabel (secondarily expanded): 4:1–14
Last Three Visions: 5:1–4 (a flying scroll); 5:5–11 (an ephod and a woman); 6:1–8 (four chariots)
The Narrative concerning the Branch: 6:9–15

Zechariah 1:7–6:15 includes five passages of particular interest here: two that deal with Jerusalem and the temple in Zech 1:7–17; 2:5–17 [Eng. 2:1–13], and one that concerns the temple and Zerubbabel in 4:1–14. The fourth, Zech 3:1–10, deals with the high priest Joshua. Zechariah 1:7–6:15 closes with the fifth, a discussion of the crowning of the Branch (6:9–15). All five concern the temple and will be discussed briefly, in order.

First is Zech 1:7–17, a vision. Zechariah sees a man riding a horse, but the man turns out to be an interpreting angel (v. 9). He announces God's fury at the nations for sacking Jerusalem and destroying the temple. He also announces God's repentance from divine anger against Jerusalem/Zion and God's new-found compassion, which divine repentance would result in the temple's being rebuilt, the restitution of Judah's cities, and prosperity accompanied by peace. The announcement is followed by a vision of four horns and four smiths, sent by God to punish the nations that had wrecked Judah.

Next, Zech 2:5–17 [Eng. 2:1–13] is a literary compound, opening with the account of a third vision (2:5–9 [Eng. 2:1–5]), continuing with a song (vv. 10–16 [Eng. vv. 6–12]), and concluding with a call for silence before God, such as one might hear in a worship service (v. 17 [Eng. v. 13]). The vision account addresses Jerusalem's weak status as a city without a defensive wall. God promises to be its wall of defense, a theological, not a military statement (v. 9 [Eng. v. 5]). How much of Jerusalem's preexilic wall might have been standing is impossible to estimate. Nehemiah 2:11–15 suggests extensive damage to it, presumably inflicted both by the Babylonians and time, perhaps worse in some places than in others. It is unclear whether Nehemiah attempted to rebuild the wall at its preexilic largest, or even would have needed to do so, but he perhaps was able to rebuild/repair enough of the wall in strategic places to encircle at least part of the city.[8] Whatever he did, however, took only fifty-two days to complete (Neh 6:15); he could not have constructed very much. For the vision in Zech

---

[8] It is impossible to say what Nehemiah did or did not build, since no wall standing in Jerusalem today can be ascribed to him. See briefly Redditt, *Ezra-Nehemiah*, 241–44.

2:5–9 [Eng. 2:1–5], however, the state of the physical wall was irrelevant; God would defend the city. God would be a wall of fire protecting it from future attack and glorifying God's self to God's people. (Zech 9:8 offers a similar picture of God defending the city.) For a people who had perceived the city defeated, looted, and left destitute as a symbol of God's ineptness, its renewal would show all Yehud who was God in Jerusalem. Any future hope for the city lay in the majesty and power of God.

Verses 10–16 [Eng. vv. 6–12] present a further development of or an elaboration on verses 5–9 [Eng. vv. 1–5] in the form of an address to the exiles in Babylon, explicitly calling them also to return to Jerusalem. The reference in verse 12 [Eng. v. 8] to plundering Babylon on the way out is perhaps a quiet allusion to and reuse of Exod 12:36, which says that the Israelites "plundered" the Egyptians as they left for Israel. The verses could be dated any time after 539 BCE, since exiles dwelled in Babylon from 597 and onwards. Still, in this context a date in 520—or shortly thereafter—makes perfectly good sense. Verse 17 [Eng. v. 13], moreover, bears a close resemblance to Hab 2:20. Both call upon the people to keep their silence, Hab 2:20 because God had (re)entered God's holy place, and Zech 2:17 because God had roused God's self from God's holy dwelling place. Verse 17 also rounds off the first three visions.

Third, Zech 3:1–10, emphasizes the purification of the high priest and his installation as the chief in charge of the temple. Scholars often suggest that the passage is a later addition to a collection of seven other vision narratives arranged in this pattern.[9]

    IV. (4:1–6a, 10b–11, 13–14) God at the Center
      III. (2:5–9 [Eng. 2:1–5]) Measure Jerusalem
      V. (5:1–4) Cleanse Jerusalem
        II. (2:1–4 [Eng. 1:18–21]) Destroy Babylon
        VI. (5:5–11) Send wickedness to Babylon
          I. (1:7–17) Colored horses; nations at rest
          VII. (6:1–8) Horses, wagons; God at rest[10]

---

[9] See recently Lena-Sofia Tiemeyer, *Zechariah and his Visions: An Exegetical Study of Zechariah's Vision Report* (LHBOTS 605; London: Bloomsbury T&T Clark, 2015), 54.

[10] See chart and discussion in Redditt, *Haggai, Zechariah, Malachi*, 40–42. See also, for example, Klaus Seybold, *Bilder zum Tempelbau: Die Visionen des Propheten Sacharja* (SBS 70; Stuttgart: Katholisches Bibelwerk, 1974), 16–17, and Karl Elliger, *Das Buch der zwölf kleinen Propheten* (ATD 25; Göttingen: Vandenhoeck & Ruprecht, 1982), 2.103.

Even so, Edgar W. Conrad epitomizes the function of chapters 3 and 4 in Zech 1–8 with the headings "Cleaning up the Priesthood" and "Stirring up Zerubbabel."[11]

Ina Willi-Plein suggests instead that Zech 3:1–7 was the original vision narrative around which the other seven were built.[12] While that suggestion makes sense, Zech 3 does not fit into the seven-fold pattern of the other visions. Hence, she is probably not correct. Why build a structure around a previously existing text, which structure does not fit? Many scholars, including this author, instead see chapter 3 as secondary. Either way, verse 8 does mention the coming of God's servant the Branch, whether originally or secondarily. Regardless of the time of origin of Zech 3:1–10, the role of the high priest also appears in Zech 4 too—again perhaps secondarily. His appearance in both chapters reflects the importance of his role in the events of 520 BCE and thereafter. Likewise, Ezra 3:2, 8; 4:3; 5:1–2; and 6:14 all discuss Joshua's and Zerubbabel's role, though Ezra 1:8, 11 and Ezra 5:16 refer to Sheshbazzar instead.

Zechariah 3:1–7 relates the trial and cleansing of Joshua the high priest, who was wearing filthy clothes, representing, presumably, his defilement from life in Babylon. The Accuser was prepared to accuse him before God. Instead, YHWH accused the Accuser, validated Joshua for service in the temple, and reclothed him for his office as priest. Zechariah 3:1–7 thus portrays Joshua as ritually contaminated (by his life in Babylon?) and depicts YHWH's cleansing him for service in the new temple.

The ensuing verses (3:8–10) report God's speech during or after the cleansing. In them YHWH speaks of a stone "set before Joshua," having seven facets. YHWH announces the divine intention to engrave each with an inscription, but that action is not reported. Towner suggests that the mention of engraving was an allusion to the engraved "rosette of pure gold" fastened to the front of the regalia of the high priest in Exod 28:36–38.[13] The name Zerubbabel, moreover, does not appear here or elsewhere in the book of Zechariah at all except in 4:6–10, though Zech 3:8 promises that God will bring God's servant the Branch, typically assumed to be Zerubbabel. The passage concludes (Zech 3:10) with the use of a saying that also appears in Mic 4:4. It reads literally: "You will invite,

---

[11] Edgar W. Conrad, *Zechariah* (Readings; Sheffield: Sheffield Academic press, 1999), 88, 100.

[12] Ina Willi-Plein, *Haggai, Sacharja, Maleachi* (ZBK 24.4; Zürich: Theologischer Verlag Zürich, 2007), 84.

[13] W. Sibley Towner, exegetical note on Zech 3:9, in *The HarperCollins Study Bible* (New York: HarperCollins, 1993), 1415. In Exod 28:36, the prescribed inscription reads "Holy to the Lord."

each his neighbor, under the vine and under the fig tree."[14] Petersen notes the parallel to 1 Kgs 5:5 [Eng. 4:25], which reads "During Solomon's lifetime Judah and Israel lived in safety, from Dan even to Beer-sheba, all of them under their vines and fig trees." That verse evokes peace and equanimity. Zechariah 3:10, therefore, appears to invoke that same peaceful co-existence between Joshua and the Branch, who would lead Yehud amicably side by side. What powers and what division of power (if any) the author saw for this diarchy is left unspoken.

Fourth, Zech 4:1–14 stands as the centerpiece of the seven-vision sequence that constitutes the basic structure of the visions, and it balances Zech 3 in the visions of Zech 1:7–6:8 as they stand. Chapter 4 is also complex. Verses 1–3 describe a vision. Zechariah sees a lampstand of gold with seven oil lamps, each having seven lips (each lip, presumably, holding a wick). Readers probably may assume that Zechariah was describing his version of the seven-branch candelabra used in the temple. Verses 4–7 interpret the vision, though the explanation seems forced. It is far from clear what the mountain is that will become a plain before Zerubbabel through God's spirit. Verses 8–10a, however, are straightforward: Zerubbabel is identified as the one that had founded or laid the foundation of the temple; he would be the one to finish the task. This analysis obscures an important form-critical observation made often by scholars, notably recently by Lena-Sofia Tiemeyer, namely that verses 6ab–10a stand out from their context on form critical and other grounds and they report the activity of Zerubbabel.[15] Verse 10b continues the primary narrative. Nevertheless, as the text stands, Zerubbabel is placed alongside Joshua as key figures. The name Zerubbabel disappears then, and in verse 11 the seer asks the meaning of the olive trees beside the candelabra, a question a reader might have anticipated right after vv. 2–3. The answer (v. 14) is that the trees represent "two anointed ones," who stand beside the Lord of the earth. Presumably they were Zerubbabel and Joshua, though the text does not say so.

As Zech 4 stands, moreover, verses 4–10a constitute a dialogue between the prophet and the angel. Their purpose is to highlight the role of Zerubbabel. As mentioned above, verse 9 announces that the hands of Zerubbabel had laid the foundation of (or had founded) the temple, and his hands would complete it. Verses 12–14 then tie together Zech 3 and 4 by proclaiming Joshua and Zerubbabel as "the two anointed ones who stand beside the Lord of the whole earth." The hope for the Davidide Zerubbabel as it stands in Zech 4:1–14 is a hope for

---

[14] Incidentally, it is possible that Zech 3:8 was the original text and that the eschatological verse Mic 4:4 was late enough to borrow from it.

[15] Tiemeyer, *Zechariah and his Visions*, 50.

shared leadership between Zerubbabel and Joshua, presumably under the thumb of the Persian Emperor—though that limitation is quietly ignored.

This dual leadership is sometimes termed a diarchy by scholars, though how much shared political rulership and/or temple leadership the prophet or redactor might have envisioned for each man is not clear. This much is clear: the chapter stated that the high priest Joshua and the Davidide Zerubbabel would each have his own functions *in the temple*. In any case the heart of Zech 4 is that Zerubbabel had founded the temple and that he would finish building it. All modern readers can say is that someone finished it, but no biblical or other text actually details Zerubbabel's role.

The last three visions (Zech 5:1–4; 5:5–11; and 6:1–8) resemble the first three (Zech 1:7–17; 2:1–4 [Eng. 1:18–21]; and 2:5–9 [Eng. 2:1–5]) in length and content. In order they depict the punishment of theft (the pillaging of Jerusalem?), the sending of iniquity back to Babylon, and the pronouncement that iniquity's departure comforted the interpreting angel. Together those six visions provide the frame for all the attention to Joshua and Zerubbabel in Zech 3:1–4:14. Those two chapters differ substantially in length and subject from the other six, and they show extensive redactional work. They also leave open the question of what happened to Zerubbabel.

Zechariah 6:9–15 concludes the description of Zechariah's visions. Those verses pertain directly to the issue of king, priest, and temple as well. The passage contains an unusual command: namely to make crowns (v. 11; see also v. 14) to set on the head of Joshua. Verse 11 is widely deemed corrupt, though there is nothing inherently suspect about the idea that an official would have several crowns for use at differing functions. What might seem surprising here is that Joshua was the one designated to wear the crowns. Since, however, Lev 8:9 says Aaron wore one, the designation of Joshua to wear crowns in Zech 6:11 and 14 is not as troublesome as scholars sometimes suppose. Be that as it may, Zerubbabel is not mentioned again; he simply disappears from the text after Zech 4:6 and 10 (and 14 by implication). It is fair to ask what happened to him, but in doing so one should not lose sight of the fact that Zerubbabel actually is mentioned by name only in Zech 4:6, 7, 9, and 10. It is fair to suggest then that Zechariah, or at least whoever passed on his traditions, was less concerned with Zerubbabel than was Haggai (Hag 2:20–23), and both perhaps were less interested than was the author of Ezra/Nehemiah, who mentioned the returnee Zerubbabel nine times. What is more, Zech 6:9–15 points to ongoing interaction between returnees in Jerusalem and exiles in Babylon, an interaction that Ezra 7–10 and the book of Nehemiah make clear continued, with people traveling in both directions.

In short, the books of Haggai and Zechariah taught that an acceptable life— religiously and politically—was possible under the more-or-less lenient policies of the Persian court. Religiously that life would center on the temple and its sacrificial system. Politically, *perhaps* that hope included at least a limited degree of local rule under Zerubbabel. In any case the house of David remained important religiously, apparently economically, and perhaps politically in allegiance to the Persians. No one besides the priests and Davidides looked politically viable to Haggai and Zechariah.

3. Davidides, Priests, and Prophets in Zechariah 9–14

It will be useful to begin this discussion by sketching a literary history of the rise of Zech 9–14. The place to commence is with the observation that Zech 9 is headed simply with "Oracle." It is not ascribed to Zechariah. Indeed that name does not appear again after the superscription in Zech 7:1. It is a widely-held conclusion of critical scholarship that someone else added the last six chapters, a conclusion heartily endorsed here. Still, one may still raise the question of the relationship between Zech 9 and Zech 1–8.

As just mentioned, the superscription consists of one word: "Oracle." The subject matter of Zech 9 first is the restoration of the old Davidic kingdom including part of Syria, Tyre and Sidon, and the five Philistine cities (vv. 1–7), with God defending the temple as a garrison against all who came and went (v. 8). Then verses 9–10 portray a new king, one who would be righteous and "saved," humble and riding on a donkey (not a war horse or even a mule). Finally, verses 11–17 predict that God would bring home the remaining exiles, make use of them as the weapon of the divine warrior (v. 13), and make of Yehud a bountiful land.[16] Whatever else one might say about that view, one would have to admit that it is not *Realpolitik*. Zechariah 10:1, 3b–12 articulates the reunification of Judah and Israel, but makes no mention of a Davidic king. Indeed, nei-

---

[16] Despite the contention of numerous scholars that the reference to Greece in Zech 9:13 necessitates a date after Alexander for Zech 9–14, it does nothing of the sort. David L. Petersen, *Zechariah 9–14 and Malachi* (OTL; Louisville, KY: Westminster John Knox, 1993) 3–6, for example, dates Zechariah 9–14 in its entirety to the Persian period. Paul D. Hanson, *The Dawn of Apocalyptic* (Philadelphia: Fortress, 1975), 316, notes that scholars have dated these chapters anywhere from 620 to 333 BCE and settles (p. 353) on the very end of the sixth or early fifth century. See also Byron G. Curtis, *Up the Steep and Stony Road* (AcBib 25; Atlanta: Society of Biblical Literature, 2006), 277, who dates the entirety of Zechariah 9–14 between 515 and 475 BCE. Curtis's lower date, however, probably should be lowered to ca. 400 BCE, in view of the real possibility that the reference to "the one whom they have pierced" was an allusion to the stabbing of a priest named Jesus by his brother Johannes, who was high priest from 411 to 408 BCE (Josephus, *Ant.* 11.7.1). See below.

ther does the rest of Zech 11–14, even though Zech 12:10–13:1 deals explicitly and negatively with the "house of David." Simply stated, a revival of the Davidic monarchy became a dead issue in the book of Zechariah after chapter 9. Instead, Zech 14 culminates with a vision of God becoming king over all the earth. That is a very different kind of *Politik*. Since it is only Zech 9 that pursues the restitution of the Davidic monarchy, the earlier one dates that chapter the more compelling would the dating be. By this line of reasoning, a date from shortly after 520 down to about 490 BCE seems warranted for Zech 9. Other material in Zech 10–14 probably arose later.

Though the temple assumed its role as the sole legitimate place of worship in Yehud, neither Zerubbabel nor any other Davidide became monarch. Nor did tiny Yehud restore the traditional boundaries of David's kingdom. Instead, something precluded the realization of a new Davidic Empire under a new David. Something also went wrong with the priestly side of Zechariah's predictions. Zech 10 dropped all mention of a king, with God performing all the militaristic deeds of a king. Zech 11 provided an explanation in the form of an allegory, in which the priests, symbolized by the shepherds, had sinned by collaborating with the Persians, symbolized by the merchants.[17] Zechariah 12–13 portrayed coming difficulties, including more warfare. It will be useful to examine those two chapters a little more closely.

Zechariah 12:1–9 depicts the nations in the future congregating before Jerusalem to besiege it, only to fall victim to the besieged city in the wake of God's enabling its defenders to defeat the besiegers. Zechariah 12:10–13:1 depicts the ritual cleansing of both the house of David and the house of Levi (i.e. priests and Levites), though not the restitution of the monarchy. Zechariah 13:2–6 condemns false prophecy. Whether the author of those verses thought that all prophets were false will be left unaddressed here, except to say it need not have. Zechariah 13:7–9 turns its attention to a man/shepherd, who was God's associate.

Those three verses constitute one of the most enigmatic passages in the book of Zechariah. In that passage God calls the divine sword to awake against God's shepherd, the man who was God's associate. Since hope for a monarch disappeared after Zech 9, and the house of David became part of the problem, along with the priests, it is within those two groups, who together constituted the Jerusalemite leadership, that readers should search for the identity of the "one they have pierced" mentioned in Zech 12:10. Scholars have puzzled over his

---

[17] Paul L. Redditt, "Prophecy and the Monarchy in Haggai and Zechariah," *CBQ* 76 (2014): 436–49 (445).

identity, but Otto Plöger points in the right direction for the answer.[18] The high priest from 411 to 408 BCE was Johannes. According to Josephus (*Ant.* 11.7.1) Johannes slew his brother Jesus in the temple while the two men quarreled. Josephus opined: "there never was so cruel and impious a thing done, neither by the Greeks nor Barbarians." One can imagine the city in a state of uproar, shock, and grief that such an event had occurred in the temple area. Josephus was more interested in divine than human reaction, however, so he attributed the ensuing response by the Persian army to divine retribution. Zechariah 13:7 likewise has God instruct the divine sword of punishment to strike the shepherd with the result that the sheep would be scattered. (With leaders such as theirs, how could the people succeed?) The aftermath would be a time of purging until the people called on the name of God.

Zechariah 14 then reviews the chaos that would precede the new day that it announces. Zechariah 14:1–15 repeats some of the same sentiments as Zech 12:1–5, but in other words and adding different images. Then verses 16–21 soar in their vision of God's triumph over the surrounding nations and God's reigning, not a Davidide or a priest, over a restored Israel from the city of Jerusalem, to which city exiles and foreigners could come to observe feast of Booths.

4. The Discussion of Priests in the Book of Malachi

The book of Malachi not only is an individual book, but also it concludes the postexilic trilogy of Haggai-Zechariah-Malachi, the Book of the Twelve, and the Law and the Prophets as well. It was appended to Haggai-Zech 1–14, perhaps after that complex reached more or less its full length, by means of a cobbled superscription and shared texts. The superscriptions in Zech 12:1 and Mal 1:1 share the double redactional heading "Oracle. The word of the Lord." Both sets of texts contain the motif of God's refining the people by fire (Zech 13:9 and Mal 3:3), and both articulate the kingship of God (Zech 13:9 and Mal 1:14).

Malachi begins by discussing Jacob and Esau, the latter the ancestor of the Edomites. It deals with priests and Levites. It makes reference to Moses and Elijah, the two who respectively embodied the law and the prophets. It argues with the priests about how to do their jobs. It condemns common worshippers,

---

[18] Otto Plöger, *Theocracy and Eschatology* (trans. S. Rudman; Richmond, VA: John Knox Press, 1969), 88. See Redditt, "Prophecy and the Monarchy in Haggai and Zechariah," 447. Wolters, *Zechariah*, 417–18, however, argues that God was the one pierced, despite noting that fifty or so Hebrew manuscripts read "him whom they have pierced." That reading is followed by most scholars and critical editions of the Hebrew text instead of "me whom they have pierced," which stands in the MT.

not for ethical failure, but for not tithing and for offering impure sacrifices, two priestly concerns. Malachi also envisions the purification of the Levites and condemns the laity for not tithing. Further, it commands people to obey the book of Moses. The book of Malachi, therefore, appears to be a book about the temple, its priests and Levites, sacrifice, worship and worshippers. It calls both priests and Levites to obedience in their leadership of the people. In doing so it is the worthy successor of Zech 9–14, which attacks them for their failures along with those of the Davidides and false prophets.

5. The Treatment of Davidides, Prophets, and Priests in Ezra-Nehemiah

What light does Ezra-Nehemiah throw on the topic of postexilic concern for king, priest, and cult? The most obvious answer is that in Ezra-Nehemiah, as in Malachi, local kingship was a dead issue. To be sure, eleven passages mention David by name, but only Ezra 3:10 calls him king, and only Neh 13:26 mentions another Israelite king by name: Solomon. Ezra 5:11 also refers to the latter as the great king who built the first temple without actually naming him. Apparently, the only human king of Yehud that mattered after the exile was the Persian king. Nehemiah 6:7 reports that Sanballat and Geshem had charged Nehemiah with refurbishing the wall of Jerusalem because he wanted to make himself king in Yehud. Nehemiah, however, the former cupbearer to the Persian king, serving in Jerusalem only with that king's explicit permission, adamantly denies their charge. More perplexing is Ezra's take on who led the return to Yehud reported in Ezra 1–2. On the one hand Ezra 1:8 mentions Sheshbazzar, not Zerubbabel, and Ezra 5:16 says Sheshbazzar was the governor and the one who "founded" or who "laid the foundation" of the temple. On the other hand Ezra 2:2 lists Zerubbabel as the first leader of the returnees. That list (Ezra 2:2b–67) and its parallel in Neh 7:7b–69), however, is notoriously late, setting as it does the number of returnees at a level the whole population of Yehud likely did not reach until the second century BCE.[19] Untangling this conundrum lies outside the scope of this paper and the ability of this author. The difficulty does remind readers that Ezra-Nehemiah as it stands is a literary product written beginning perhaps as late as

---

[19] Charles E. Carter, *The Emergence of Yehud in the Persian Period* (JSOTS 294; Sheffield: Sheffield Academic Press, 1999), 201, estimates the maxim population of Yehud at 13,350 during Persian Period I and 20,650 during Persian Period II.

the "Memoirs of Nehemiah" (post 445 assuming they are authentic) and continuing until the second century BCE.[20]

Ezra-Nehemiah, however, does have a perspective on the issues of king, priest, and cult in the postexilic period. In the opening scene the pagan king Cyrus of Persia acknowledged that Israel's God YHWH had made him king over "all the kingdoms of the earth." As is well known, Cyrus himself bragged in an inscription that has survived that he was "king of the world, great king, legitimate king, king of Babylon, king of Sumer and Akkad ..., whose rule Bel (god of Babylon) and Nebo (tutelary god of the ancient city of Borsippa and eldest son of the god Marduk) loved, and whom they wanted as king to please their hearts."[21] Ezra-Nehemiah did not question the fairness of the Babylonian captivity or the nature of Persian rulership, but it did remind its readers that it was YHWH that "stirred up the spirit of Cyrus" to allow the exiles to return to Jerusalem and Judah (Ezra 1:1–4). Ezra 3:10 depicted the priests and the Levites praising God. Ezra 3:12–13 and Ezra 4:1–5 introduced the desire of YHWH-ists who had remained behind in Judah during the exile to participate in the rebuilding of the temple. Their desire and Ezra's rebuff set the stage for opposition by Sanballat and Tobiah "the Ammonite" in Neh 4:1–5 and Neh 6:1–14. It is doubtful, however, that either man thought of himself as non-YHWH-ist. (The name Tobiah at any rate was a compound with the shortened form of the name YHWH: Yah is good). Presumably neither they nor their people were willing to concede Jerusalem and surrounding Yehud to the exclusive control of returnees, for which failure the book of Ezra-Nehemiah condemns the two men and their followers. Moderns might ask, however, why anyone local should have conceded control of anything in Jerusalem or elsewhere to returnees from Babylon—aside, of course, from direct Persian command.

What came to be at issue was who had rights to leadership and worship in the temple. The book of Ezra comes to its disturbing conclusion in Ezra 9–10, namely that only returnees from Babylon had the right to worship there. Also disturbing—to this reader anyway—was the insistence that returnee men divorce their local, i.e., Yehudite, wives. The insistence of the author of Ezra 9–10 on calling those wives "Canaanites, Hittites, Perizzites, Jebusites, Ammonites, Moabites, Egyptians, and Amorites" was nothing more than a case of name calling. All of those groups would have long been absorbed into the entire Hebrew population. Differently stated, the returnees were as likely as those who had

---

[20] Whether there was also a set of "Memoirs of Ezra" is less clear still. Only Ezra 8:21–9:15 is written in the first person singular, and it is a narrative of Ezra's trip from Babylonia to Yehud.

[21] "Cyrus Cylinder," in *The Ancient Near East: An Anthology of Texts and Pictures* (ed. James B. Pritchard; Princeton and Oxford: Princeton University Press, 2011), 282.

never left Yehud to have descended from such groups. Indeed, the book of Ruth ends with the short note that the Moabitess Ruth was the great grandmother of David himself. That note attacks the type of reasoning found in Ezra 9–10 on the grounds that no king of Judah would have been allowed to worship in the temple that the unworthies David and Solomon built!

The book of Nehemiah details the repair of the old walls of Jerusalem.[22] At that point the whole city and not just the temple became holy ground. Nehemiah 9:38–13:31 adds to this picture. Only "leaders of the people" were allowed to live in Jerusalem. They are numbered by their fathers' houses: 468 from Yehud, 928 from Benjamin, 822 priests, 242 assistants, 128 warriors, 284 Levites, and 172 guards, for a total of 3044 persons. Some modern archaeologists, however, calculate the entire population for Persian I Yehud as low as 12,000 or so persons. Others place the figure higher, but it was not likely very large. Likewise, estimates of the population of Jerusalem have ranged as low as 626.[23] Even if these modern estimates are far too low, modern readers would do well, probably, to accept the account in Nehemiah as a generalization that priests, Levites, and temple personnel (and perhaps few if any others) lived in Jerusalem, but to be cautious about the numbers.

More to the point of this study is that the text considered all of Jerusalem and not just the temple as "holy" space. Still, the author could not get around the presence of overarching Persian control, even if through Yehudite cooperatives. The book of Nehemiah, moreover, depicts a layman, not priests and Levites, as rightfully exercising political control of the city. Perhaps separating political and religious officials was one way of limiting Persian or other local control of the temple. Still, Nehemiah too is depicted as desiring exclusive returnee control of both the city and the temple and with condemning marriage between the descendants of returnees and all locals. In that insistence he distances himself, as Ezra had, from the vision of the nations coming to Jerusalem to observe the feast

---

[22] See David Ussishkin, "The Borders and Size of Jerusalem in the Persian Period," in *Judah and the Judeans in the Persian Period* (ed. Oded Lipschits and Manfred Oeming; Winona Lake, IN: Eisenbrauns, 2006), 147–66 (159). He argues that a wall around the entire preexilic city was in view. He may be correct, but archaeologists have found no trace of a wall that can be attributed to the fifth century. That result is perhaps not surprising. According to Neh 6:15, the reconstruction took only from August 11 until October 2, 445, suggesting minimal repairs or even makeshift construction. In any case the narrative was promoting a theological agenda, not reporting raw data. See also note 17 above.

[23] See the discussion of the whole issue by David Ussiskin, "Nehemiah's City Wall and the Size of Jerusalem," in *New Perspectives on Ezra-Nehemiah* (ed. Isaac Kalimi; Winona Lake, IN: Eisenbrauns, 2012), 101–30 (116).

of booths in Jerusalem with which the book of Zechariah closes. The book of Nehemiah also joins the book of Ezra in insisting that people like Jehoida, one of the sons of the high priest Eliashib, was unfit to serve in the temple and banned that priest (Neh 11:28–30). If, however, the concluding phrase in Zech 14:21 "there shall no longer be traders (Canaanites) in the house of the Lord" envisions the elimination of Persian control over the temple, the book of Nehemiah holds out no such expectation.

Conclusion

Evolving and even conflicting hopes for a king, for priests, and for the temple stood at the forefront of Haggai, Zechariah, Malachi, and Ezra-Nehemiah. Haggai seems to have expected Zerubbabel to rule alone, but the most people in Persian Period Yehud could have hoped for was local political leadership by a Davidide under strict accountability to Persia. Zechariah 3 and 4, however, hoped for a Davidide with a priest alongside him in control of the temple, but that limited hope for a local king turned eschatological in Zech 9 and disappeared in Zech 10. By Zech 11 the shepherds of the flock were priests, and the voice(s) behind Zech 11–14 condemned the priesthood and adopted (Zech 14:9) an eschatological, even mythical anticipation of the direct rulership of God and worship by all who desired to do so without the necessity of priests or the nuisance of Persian oversight (Zech 14:20–21). The book of Malachi calls both priests and Levites to obedience in their leadership of the people. In that sense it is the worthy successor of Zech 9–14, which attacks them for their failures—along with those of the Davidides and false prophets. Ezra-Nehemiah, by contrast, distances itself from the vision of the nations coming to Jerusalem to observe the feast of booths in Jerusalem with which the book of Zechariah closes, and it insists on restrictive access to the temple, both its offices and its services.

11
ON THE WAY TO HIEROCRACY:
SECULAR AND PRIESTLY RULE IN THE BOOKS OF HAGGAI AND ZECHARIAH

Jakob Wöhrle

The books of Haggai and Zechariah are important documents of the early postexilic time. These books give insights into the political, social, and cultic developments during the time of the rebuilding of the second temple. By this means they give insights into the reconstitution of the postexilic Judean community.

The books as they stand present the early postexilic time as a time in which the different leaders of the people and the people itself cooperatively worked together. According to the present form of the books, Zerubbabel, the governor of the Persian province Yehud, grandson of the former Judean king Jehoiachin, and Joshua, the high priest, were jointly responsible for the rebuilding of the second temple and the people obediently supported this project.

This view upon the early postexilic time is, however, the product of a later redactional reworking of the books of Haggai and Zechariah. It is the view of the secondary narrative framework of the books, by which the books as they stand present a kind of prophetic chronicle about the time of the rebuilding of the second temple.[1] In this narrative framework, Zerubbabel and Joshua indeed

---

[1] For the narrative framework of the book of Haggai (1:1, 3, 12a, 14–15; 2:1–2, הגדול*[4 . . . יהושע וחזק], 10, 20, 21a) and the book of Zechariah (1:1–7, 14aβ–17aα; 2:10–14; 4:9b; 6:15; 7:1, 7, 9–14; 8:1–5, 7–8, 14–17, 19b), which trace back to two successive redactional reworkings of the books, see the detailed analyses in Jakob Wöhrle, *Die frühen Sammlungen des Zwölfprophetenbuches: Entstehung und Komposition* (BZAW 360; Berlin: de Gruyter, 2006), 317–20, 362–64, 367–85.

appear as working hand in hand on their main project, the rebuilding of the second temple (Hag 1:1, 12a, 14; 2:2, 4*), and the members of the people appear as loyal followers of their leaders (Hag 1:12a, 14; cf. Zech 1:6).

A closer look at the books of Haggai and Zechariah and the multi-layered redactional development of these books gives a more differentiated view of the political and social developments of the early postexilic time. It gives insights into a discourse about the concrete form of the community's political (re)constitution. Especially, it reveals different opinions about who should have the leadership over the people—if like in preexilic times a Davidic king shall stand at the head of the society or if the high priest, too, shall play a leading role.

The following article will describe this political discourse as it can be reconstructed out of the redaction history of the books of Haggai and Zechariah. It will focus upon the political concepts and especially upon the political role of the secular and the priestly leader in the different redactional levels of these books.

1. THE RESTORATION OF DAVIDIC KINGSHIP IN HAGGAI 2:23

The book of Haggai preserves the oldest literary evidence of the postexilic time.[2] The literary kernel of the book consists of a collection of prophetic words, all of which stem from the time of the rebuilding of the temple.[3] These words trace back to a classical prophetic milieu. The words criticize the people's resistance against the rebuilding of the temple and they summon the people and especially the Judean governor Zerubbabel to start this project.

This early collection of prophetic words underwent several redactional reworkings. Especially, later redactors added the chronological framework of the book, by which the individual words were—partly against their original setting—combined with certain dates before and after the start of the temple building.[4] Only on this literary level, Joshua, the high priest, has been introduced as a second individual addressee besides Zerubbabel (1:1, 12; 2:2, 4). Further redactions added the word about the uncleanness of the people in Hag 2:11–14, the announcement of a universal judgment against the nations in 2:6–8, 21a, 22 and some smaller additions in 2:5aα, 17, 18bα.

---

[2] For the formation of the book of Haggai, see Wöhrle, *Sammlungen*, 288–322.
[3] Hag 1:2, 4–11, 12b, 13; 2:3, 4*(without וחזק יהושע...הגדול), 5aβb, 9, 15–16, 18abβ, 19, 23.
[4] See above note 1.

Remarkably, the primary layer of the book—the collection of prophetic words from the time of the temple building—ends in Hag 2:23 with the following word:

> ²³On that day, says YHWH Sabaoth, I will take you, Zerubbabel, son of Shealtiel, my servant [עבד], says YHWH, and make you like a signet ring [חותם]; for I have chosen you [בחר], says YHWH Sabaoth. (Hag 2:23)

Haggai 2:23 presents a promise to Zerubbabel, the governor of the Persian province Yehud and grandson of the former Judean king Jehoiachin. Remarkably, this promise given to a Davidian is significantly determined by motifs of the older royal theology.[5] Like the former Davidic kings Zerubbabel is called YHWH's servant (עבד),[6] and like the former Davidic kings Zerubbabel is said to be chosen by YHWH (בחר).[7]

Even more remarkable is the promise to Zerubbabel that he will be like a signet ring (חותם). As commonly seen, this statement alludes to Jer 22:24–25 saying to Jehoiachin, Zerubbabel's grandfather, that even if he would be a signet ring on YHWH's right hand, he would be torn off and given into the hands of Nebuchadnezzar, the king of Babylon. Jeremiah 22:24–25 thus, through the image of the signet ring, announces the rejection of king Jehoiachin and, by doing so, announces nothing less than the end of the Davidic rule.[8]

That Hag 2:23 calls Zerubbabel, Jehoiachin's grandson, not only YHWH's servant and his chosen one, but also his signet ring, shows—despite all assumptions to the contrary—that this oracle annuls the word against Jehoiachin in Jer

---

[5] For the terms used in Hag 2:23, see Janet E. Tollington, *Tradition and Innovation in Haggai and Zechariah 1–8* (JSOTS 150; Sheffield: JSOT Press, 1993), 137–44; Wolter H. Rose, *Zemah and Zerubbabel: Messianic Expectations in the Early Postexilic Period* (JSOTS 304; Sheffield: Sheffield Academic Press, 2000), 209–15; John Kessler, *The Book of Haggai: Prophecy and Society in Early Persian Yehud* (VTSup 91; Leiden: Brill, 2002), 227–38, and Martin Leuenberger, *Haggai* (HThKAT; Freiburg: Herder, 2015), 244–49.

[6] 2 Sam 3:18; 7:5, 8; 1 Kgs 3:6; 8:24, 25, 26; 11:13, 32, 34, 36, 38; 14:8; 2 Kgs 19:34; 20:6; Isa 37:35; Jer 33:21, 22, 26; Ps 89:4, 21; 132:10; 1 Chron 17:4, 7; 2 Chron 6:15, 16, 17, 42 (David); 2 Chron 32:16 (Hezekiah); cf. Ezek 34:23, 24; 37:24, 25 (a new David).

[7] 2 Sam 6:21; 1 Kgs 8:44; 11:34; Ps 78:70; 1 Chron 28:4; 2 Chron 6:6 (David); 1 Chron 28:5, 6, 10; 29:1 (Solomon).

[8] Cf., e.g., William L. Holladay, *Jeremiah* (2 vols.; Hermeneia; Philadelphia: Fortress, 1986–1989), 1:605–606; Gunther Wanke, *Jeremia* (2 vols.; ZBK 20,1–2; Zürich: Theologischer Verlag, 1995–2003), 1:201–202, and Kessler, *Haggai*, 231.

22:24–25 and announces the reestablishment of the Davidic dynasty.[9] Haggai 2:23 promises to Zerubbabel the kingship over Judah.

---

[9] See, e.g., Karl Marti, *Das Dodekapropheton* (KHAT 13; Tübingen: Mohr, 1904), 390; Georg Sauer, "Serubbabel in der Sicht Haggais und Sacharjas," in *Das ferne und das nahe Wort: Festschrift Leonhard Rost zur Vollendung seines 70. Lebensjahres am 30. November 1966 gewidmet* (ed. Fritz Maass; Berlin: Töpelmann, 1967), 199–207 (204); Karl-Martin Beyse, *Serubbabel und die Königserwartungen der Propheten Haggai und Sacharja: Eine historische und traditionsgeschichtliche Untersuchung* (AzTh 48; Stuttgart: Calwer, 1972), 56; Sara Japhet, "Sheshbazzar and Zerubbabel—Against the Background of the Historical and Religious Tendencies of Ezra-Nehemiah," *ZAW* 94 (2009): 66–98 (77–78); Henning Graf Reventlow, *Die Propheten Haggai, Sacharja und Maleachi* (ATD 25,2; Göttingen: Vandenhoeck & Ruprecht, 1993), 30–31; Tollington, *Tradition and Innovation*, 137–44; Rex Mason, "The Messiah in the Postexilic Old Testament Literature," in *King and Messiah in Israel and the Ancient Near East: Proceedings of the Oxford Old Testament Seminar* (ed. John Day; JSOTS 270; Sheffield: Sheffield Academic Press), 338–64 (342); Kessler, *Haggai*, 226–29; Redditt, "The King in Haggai-Zechariah 1–8 and the Book of the Twelve," in *Tradition in Transition: Haggai and Zechariah 1–8 in the Trajectory of Hebrew Theology* (ed. Mark J. Boda and Michael H. Floyd; LHBOTS 475; New York: T&T Clark, 2008), 56–82 (58–60); James D. Nogalski, *The Book of the Twelve* (2 vols.; SHBC; Macon: Smyth & Helwys, 2011), 2:796; Daniel F. O'Kennedy, "Haggai 2:20–23: Call to Rebellion or Eschatological Expectation?" *OTE* 27 (2014): 520–40, and Leuenberger, *Haggai*, 246. In current research, however, several scholars question the view that Hag 2:23 promises the reestablishment of the Davidic dynasty. See, e.g., Carol L. Meyers and Eric M. Meyers, *Haggai, Zechariah 1–8: A New Translation with Introduction and Commentary* (AB 25B; New Haven, CT: Yale University Press, 1987), 68–70, 83–84; Rose, *Zemah and Zerubbabel*, 208–243; Ina Willi-Plein, *Haggai, Sacharja, Maleachi* (ZBK 24,4; Zürich: Theologischer Verlag: 2007), 48–50, and Greg Goswell, "Fate and Future of Zerubbabel in the Prophecy of Haggai," *Bib* 91 (2010): 77–90. According to their view, the terms used in Hag 2:23 are not specific enough to think of such an expectation. They point to the fact that the designation "servant of YHWH" (עבד) is not only used for the Davidic kings, but also for other persons like Abraham (e.g. Gen 26:24), Jacob (Ezek 28:25; 37:25), Moses (e.g. Exod 14:31; Num 12:7), Joshua (Josh 24:29; Judg 2:8), Elijah (1 Kgs 18:36; 2 Kgs 9:36; 10:10), Jonah (2 Kgs 14:25), or Isaiah (Isa 20:3); and the same holds true for the motif "chosen by YHWH" (בחר), which is used for kings, but also for persons like Abraham (Neh 9:7), Moses (Ps 106:23), Aaron (1 Sam 2:28; Ps 105:26), or Deutero-Isaiah's servant (Isa 41:9; 42:1; 43:10; 49:7). Additionally, according to Rose, *Zemah and Zerubbabel*, 236–38, the term חותם has no specific royal overtones. Since a signet ring is an object of great value the designation of a person as such a signet ring would just describe this person as valuable. Thus, in his view, Jer 22:24 says that Jehoiachin has lost his value, while Hag 2:23 promises that Zerubbabel will be of value for YHWH. However, it has to be taken into consideration that Hag 2:23 is not addressed to anyone but to Zerubbabel, the Davidian and the grandson of king Jehoiachin. Directed to a Davidian, a promise with

Haggai 2:23 thus shows how in prophetic circles at the beginning of the postexilic time the hope for and the expectation of a complete restoration of the preexilic political conditions—the reestablishment of Davidic kingship under the Davidian Zerubbabel—emerged.[10] Due to the Persian hegemony this expectation must have been rather explosive.[11]

2. ROYAL-PRIESTLY DIARCHY IN ZECHARIAH 4:1–14* AND 6:9–14*

Like the book of Haggai, the book of Zechariah is the product of a long-term redactional development.[12] The literary kernel of the book consists of two early collections: first, the collection of originally seven night visions in Zech 1–6,[13] and second, a collection of three short narratives, the narrative about a promise to Zerubbabel in Zech 4:6–10*, the narrative about the production of crowns in Zech 6:9–14*, and the narrative about questions concerning the fasting in Zech 7–8*.

These early kernels of the book of Zechariah are to be dated a few years later than the primary layer of the book of Haggai. For example, the word to Zerubbabel in Zech 4:9 presupposes that the rebuilding of the temple has already be-

---

several terms, all of which are at least often used to designate the special relationship between YHWH and the king, can only be understood as promise of a new Davidic king; and directed to the Davidian Zerubbabel, the promise that he will be like a signet ring, which takes up a specific motive from a judgment oracle against his grandfather, can only be understood as reversal of this judgment oracle and thus as promising the reestablishment of the Davidic rule. For the critique of Rose's approach, cf. also Robert C. Kashow, "Zechariah 1–8 as a Theological Explanation for the Failure of Prophecy in Haggai 2:20–23," *JTS* 64 (2013): 385–403 (387, note 11).

[10] Martin Hallaschka, *Haggai und Sacharja 1–8: Eine redaktionsgeschichtliche Untersuchung* (BZAW 411; Berlin: de Gruyter, 2011), 108–20, however, holds the view that the promise to Zerubbabel in Hag 2:23 is a late, Hellenistic addition to the book, in which Zerubbabel has to be understood just as cipher for a new Davidic king. However, Hag 2:23 fits very well into the primary layer of the book. Cf. Wöhrle, *Sammlungen*, 313–17. Additionally, it can hardly be explained, why Zerubbabel, whose activity is restricted to a very certain time and whose significance has in further times rather been diminished than increased (see below), should have become a cipher for the expectation of a new Davidic king.

[11] Cf. Rainer Albertz, *A History of Israelite Religion in the Old Testament Period* (2 vols.; trans. John Bowden; London: SCM, 1994), 2:451–54.

[12] For the formation of the book of Zechariah, see Wöhrle, *Sammlungen*, 323–66.

[13] Zech 1:8–14aα, 17aβb; 2:1–9; 4:1–6aα, 10a*(from שבעה־אלה)b, 11, 13–14; 5:1–11; 6:1–8.

gun. Additionally, these early kernels of the book of Zechariah trace back to a different milieu. While the book of Haggai stems from prophetic circles, the book of Zechariah goes back to priestly circles.

In the course of the further formation of the book, the two early collections—the night visions and the narratives—have been combined and expanded. Of greater importance is that the vision about the accusation against the high priest Joshua in Zech 3 is a later addition.[14]

The oldest parts of the book of Zechariah include two words, which show a rather specific political concept. Remarkable is, at first, the night vision about the lampstand and the two olive trees in Zech 4:1–14*. At the end of this vision, in Zech 4:14, one finds the following explanation of the two olive trees:

> [14]Then he said: These are the two sons of oil [בני היצהר], who stand by the Lord of the whole earth. (Zech 4:14)

---

[14] Thus already Alfred Jepsen, "Kleine Beiträge zum Zwölfprophetenbuch III," *ZAW* 61 (1945/48): 95–114 (95–97). See also, e.g., Christian Jeremias, *Die Nachtgesichte des Sacharja: Untersuchungen zu ihrer Stellung im Zusammenhang der Visionsberichte im Alten Testament und zu ihrem Bildmaterial* (FRLANT 117; Göttingen: Vandenhoeck & Ruprecht, 1977), 201–203; Adam S. van der Woude, "Serubbabel und die messianischen Erwartungen des Propheten Sacharja," *ZAW* 100 Supplement (1988): 138–156 (146); Reventlow, *Propheten*, 52; Holger Delkurt, *Sacharjas Nachtgesichte: Zur Aufnahme und Abwandlung prophetischer Traditionen* (BZAW 302; Berlin: de Gruyter, 2000), 146–47; Thomas Pola, *Das Priestertum bei Sacharja: Historische und traditionsgeschichtliche Untersuchungen zur frühnachexilischen Herrschererwartung* (FAT 35; Tübingen: Mohr Siebeck, 2003), 221; Reinhard G. Kratz, *Das Judentum im Zeitalter des Zweiten Tempels* (FAT 42; Tübingen: Mohr Siebeck, 2004), 81; Nogalski, *Book of the Twelve*, 2:858. On formal grounds, the secondary nature of Zech 3 becomes obvious by the fact that this vision, different from all other night visions, does not include a conversation between the prophet and the interpreting angel, in which the meaning of the vision is explained. Yet, different from all other night visions, the prophet is not an active part of this vision at all. He just sees a scene in the heavenly assembly. Additionally, as will be shown below, this night vision is determined by a political concept, which differs from the earlier material of the book. Thus, it seems more than probable that Zech 3 is not an integral part of the book; contra Wilhelm Rudolph, *Haggai—Sacharja 1–8—Sacharja 9–14—Maleachi* (KAT 13,4; Gütersloh: Gütersloher, 1976), 93; Meyers and Meyers, *Haggai*, lvii-lviii; Tollington, *Tradition and Innovation*, 34–35; Bob Becking, "Zerubbabel, Zechariah 3–4, and Post-Exilic History," in *Israel's Prophets and Israel's Past: Essays on the Relationship of Prophetic Texts and Israelite History in Honor of John H. Hayes* (ed. Brad E. Kelle and Megan Bishop Moore; LHBOTS 446; New York: T&T Clark, 2006), 268–79 (272–79), and Lena-Sofia Tiemeyer, *Zechariah and his Visions: An Exegetical Study of Zechariah's Vision Report* (LHBOTS 605; London: Bloomsbury, 2015), 116.

Zechariah 4:14 thus interprets the two olive trees as two "sons of oil" (בני היצהר). It is a controversial point of debate, however, who is meant by the two "sons of oil." In older as well as in parts of younger research scholars assumed that the two "sons of oil" are Zerubbabel and Joshua, who through the image of the "sons of oil" are depicted as anointed ones and thus as entrusted with regal duties.[15]

Against this view, it has been argued that the term יצהר is nowhere else used for the anointing of a king. Thus, several other interpretations for the "sons of oil" have been made.[16] For example, Mark Boda thinks of Haggai and Zechariah,[17] Holger Delkurt identifies the sons of oil with the people as a whole,[18] and Wolter Rose with heavenly beings.[19]

However, it has to be considered that the olive trees interpreted in Zech 4:14 as the "sons of oil" are shown to the prophet Zechariah and thus have to be distinguished from him. This strongly speaks against the assumption that the "sons of oil" represent Haggai and Zechariah. And due to the fact that Zech 4:14 mentions exactly two "sons of oil," all interpretations on a group of persons—be it the people or heavenly beings—are rather improbable.[20]

Thus, the old assumption that the two "sons of oil" represent Zerubbabel and Joshua is still the most probable solution. Additionally, the term "sons of oil"— although using the unusual word יצהר—is still best explained as presenting

---

[15] E.g., Julius Wellhausen, *Die kleinen Propheten* (3rd ed.; Berlin: de Gruyter, 1963), 183; Marti, *Dodekapropheton*, 414; Rudolph, *Haggai*, 108; Jeremias, *Nachtgesichte*, 183–84; Rex Mason, *The Books of Haggai, Zechariah and Malachi* (CBC; Cambridge: Cambridge University Press, 1977), 48; Reventlow, *Propheten*, 59–60; Tollington, *Tradition and Innovation*, 175–78; Pola, *Priestertum*, 78–81; Michael R. Stead, *The Intertextuality of Zechariah 1–8* (LHBOTS 506; New York: T&T Clark, 2009), 184–85; Willi-Plein, *Haggai*, 96.

[16] See also the comprehensive discussion of Zech 4:14 in Tiemeyer, *Zechariah*, 159–65.

[17] Mark J. Boda, "Oil, Crowns and Thrones: Prophet, Priest and King in Zechariah 1:7–6:15," *JHS* 3,10 (2001): 3; cf. Anthony R. Petterson, *Behold your King: The Hope for the House of David in the Book of Zechariah* (LHBOTS 513; New York: T&T Clark, 2009), 81.

[18] Delkurt, *Nachtgesichte*, 213–23.

[19] Rose, *Zemah and Zerubbabel*, 202–205; cf. Tiemeyer, *Zechariah*, 163–65.

[20] More than improbable is also the new proposal by Hallaschka, *Haggai*, 235–37, according to whom the two "sons of oil" refer to Zerubbabel and Darius. Since Zech 4:14 says that the two "sons of oil" stand side by side by the Lord of the whole earth, they seem to have an equal status. This strongly speaks against an interpretation of such an unequal pair of persons like Zerubbabel and Darius.

Zerubbabel and Joshua as two anointed ones and thus as entrusted with regal duties.

This fits with the observation that the "sons of oil" according to Zech 4:14 stand "by the Lord of the whole earth." With this, Zech 4:14 attests to the "sons of oil" a kind of direct access to YHWH. In older texts of the Hebrew Bible such a direct access to YHWH is a privilege of the prophets, but also, as Ps 110:1 or Jer 30:21 show, a privilege of the king.

In Zech 4:14 the Davidian Zerubbabel and the high priest Joshua are thus—through the image of the "sons of oil"—depicted as anointed ones and—due to the portrayal that the sons of oil stand by the Lord of the earth—they are described as having direct access to YHWH. Zerubbabel and Joshua thus both get regal honors. They are both and jointly entrusted with the political leadership of the Judean community. Zechariah 4:14 shows the rather specific concept of a diarchy under a royal and a priestly ruler.[21]

Against this background, the report about the coronation of the high priest Joshua in Zech 6:9–14 is noteworthy.[22] The text as it stands reads as follows:

> [9]And the word of YHWH came to me, saying: [10]Take from the exiles, from Heldai, Tobijah, and Jedaiah, who have come from Babylon, and go the same day to the house of Josiah the son of Zephaniah. [11]Take silver and gold and make crowns [עטרות] and set (one) on the head of the high priest Joshua the son of Jehozadak, [12]and say to him: Thus says YHWH Sabaoth: Behold, a man, whose name is branch [צמח], he shall branch out of his place, and he shall build the temple of YHWH [ובנה את היכל ה']. [13]And he shall build the temple of YHWH [והוא יבנה את היכל ה'], he shall bear honor, and he shall sit upon his throne [על כסאו] and rule. And a priest shall sit upon his throne [על כסאו], and counsel of peace shall be between the two of them. [14]And the crown [העטרת] shall be for Helem, Tobijah, Jedaiah, and Hen the son of Zephaniah, as a memorial in the temple of YHWH. (Zech 6:9–14)

The text of Zech 6:9–14 is bound up with some problems.[23] In particular, it is astonishing that Zech 6:11 mentions עטרות "crowns" in plural—i.e. at least two

---

[21] E.g., Tollington, *Tradition and Innovation*, 176; Albertz, *History*, 2:453; Mason, "Messiah," 348, and Pola, *Priestertum*, 78–81.

[22] The final verse of the chapter, Zech 6:15, is a late addition to the text, which can be left aside for our considerations; cf. Karl Elliger, *Das Buch der zwölf kleinen Propheten: Die Propheten Nahum, Habakuk, Zephanja, Haggai, Sacharja, Maleachi* (6th ed.; ATD 25.2; Göttingen: Vandenhoeck & Ruprecht, 1967), 131–32; David L. Petersen, *Haggai and Zechariah 1–8* (OTL; London: SCM, 1985), 279; Tollington, *Tradition and Innovation*, 46–47, and Hallaschka, *Haggai*, 263.

crowns—which the prophet shall make. But the rest of the text presents the coronation of only one person, the high priest Joshua.

In older approaches it has frequently been assumed that Zech 6:9–14 originally mentioned not only the coronation of Joshua, but also the coronation of Zerubbabel. However, when Zerubbabel—for whatever reason—disappeared, all passages mentioning Zerubbabel would have been erased from the text.[24]

In more recent times, this proposal is rarely supported. Now, it is often assumed that the text of Zech 6:9–14 from the beginning mentioned only one crown. Due to the fact that the consonantal text of Zech 6:14 documents just one crown, the plural עטרות "crowns" in Zech 6:11 is seen as a scribal error, a misreading of an original singular form. Zechariah 6:9–14 thus had always mentioned the coronation of just one person, the high priest Joshua.[25]

Admittedly, the findings in Zech 6:9–14 are very complicated and every explanation of the text is a bit speculative.[26] The starting point of any analysis should be, however, the mere fact that the text as it stands documents in Zech 6:11 the plural form עטרות "crowns" and that this reading is also supported by the versions of the text.[27]

Against this background, it is noteworthy that Zech 6:11–13 mentions two persons: the high priest Joshua and a person called צמח "branch."[28] About these two persons Zech 6:13 says that each one sits on his own—individual—throne

---

[23] Cf. the research reviews of Rose, *Zemah and Zerubbabel*, 163–71; Pola, *Priestertum*, 234–41, or Hallaschka, *Haggai*, 263–64.

[24] See, e.g., Johann Gottfried Eichhorn, *Die hebräischen Propheten* (3 vols.; Göttingen: Vandenhoek & Ruprecht, 1816–19), 3:353–55; Heinrich Ewald, "Versuche über schwierige Stellen des A. T.," *ThStKr* 1 (1828): 338–60 (358–59); Ulrich Kellermann, *Messias und Gesetz: Grundlinien einer alttestamentlichen Heilserwartung: Eine traditionsgeschichtliche Einführung* (BibS(N) 61; Neukirchen-Vluyn: Neukirchener, 1971), 59–60; Beyse, *Serubbabel*, 77–84, 91; Jeremias, *Nachtgesichte*, 218; Albertz, *History*, 2:453; Nogalski, *Book of the Twelve*, 2:880.

[25] Cf. with differences regarding the details Reventlow, *Propheten*, 71; Tollington, *Tradition and Innovation*, 121; Robert Hanhart, *Sacharja 1–8* (BKAT 14.7.1; Neukirchen-Vluyn: Neukirchener, 1998), 407–408; Rose, *Zemah and Zerubbabel*, 46–48; Pola, *Priestertum*, 242–47; Kratz, *Judentum*, 82; Marko Jauhiainen, "Turban and Crown Lost and Regained: Ezekiel 21:29–32 and Zechariah's Zemah," *JBL* 127 (2008): 501–11 (508 with note 35); Petterson, *Behold your King*, 104–107, and Hallaschka, *Haggai*, 260–61.

[26] Not without reason, Mason, "Messiah," 346, states about Zech 6:9–14: "It would be a brave exegete who would claim to know the one, true meaning of it."

[27] LXX: στεφάνους; VUL: coronas.

[28] That Joshua and the "branch" mentioned in Zech 6:9–14 are to be understood as two different persons, is convincingly shown by Boda, "Oil," 4.3.1.

(על כסאו),²⁹ and that the counsel of peace shall be between the two of them (עצת שלום תהיה בין שניהם). The mentioning of two persons sitting side by side on a throne as office holders of equal status could thus be taken as a first hint that an older version of the text documented not only the coronation of Joshua but also the coronation of a further person.

Additionally, it is remarkable that Zech 6:12–13 documents twice and directly after each other the statement "he will build the temple of YHWH" (בנה את היכל יהוה). This could be seen as a mere repetition.³⁰ However, since no reason for such a repetition can be found, it could also be taken as further evidence that a previous version of the text spoke about two different persons, who were seen as jointly responsible for the rebuilding of the temple.

Finally, Zech 6:14 is noteworthy. The consonantal text of this verse says that "the crown" (העטרת) shall be in the temple as a memorial for the donators. This verse is surely a secondary addition to the narrative,³¹ which becomes obvious by the fact that Zech 6:14, different from 6:10, mentions the names Helem and Hen instead of Heldai and Josiah.³² Remarkably, the storage of a crown in the temple described in this verse can hardly refer to the aforementioned crown of

---

²⁹ However, several scholars question the view that Zech 6:13 presents the high priest Joshua sitting on his own throne. For example, Wellhausen, *Propheten*, 185; Marti, *Dodekapropheton*, 421; Elliger, *Buch*, 128, and Mason, *Haggai*, 61, amend the text according to LXX (ἐκ δεξιῶν αὐτοῦ) and read מימינו so that the high priest would just be "on the side" of the "branch." Others like Jepsen, "Beiträge III," 108; Rudolph, *Haggai*, 128; Petersen, *Haggai*, 273; Rose, *Zemah and Zerubbabel*, 64, and Pola, *Priestertum*, 226, maintain the MT, but understand the phrase על כסאו in the sense of "he is besides his [the branch's] throne." However, the reading of the LXX is surely a simplification of the more difficult MT version. And since Zech 6:13 uses the identical phrase על כסאו both for the "branch" and for the priest, it seems to be very unlikely that this phrase should have a different meaning at these two instances. Thus, the most probable solution is that according to Zech 6:13 both the "branch" and the high priest sit upon their individual throne; cf. Meyers and Meyers, *Haggai*, 361; Reventlow, *Propheten*, 72, and Hallaschka, *Haggai*, 262.

³⁰ Rudolph, *Haggai*, 131; Petersen, *Haggai*, 276; Meyers and Meyers, *Haggai*, 358; Reventlow, *Propheten*, 72, and Pola, *Priestertum*, 246.

³¹ Marti, *Dodekapropheton*, 421; Elliger, *Buch*, 130–31, and Hallaschka, *Haggai*, 266.

³² The different names documented in Zech 6:10 and Zech 6:14, are often understood as mere variants. See, e.g., Petersen, *Haggai*, 273; Meyers and Meyers, *Haggai*, 364, and Reventlow, *Propheten*, 71. The question remains, however, why Zech 6:14 uses such variants. This seems best explained by the assumption that a later hand is responsible for this verse.

Joshua.³³ The text gives no indication that the crown should have been removed from Joshua,³⁴ and it lacks any information why the high priest should have lost his crown. Therefore, it seems to be much more probable that Zech 6:14 refers to another crown. It describes nothing less than the storage of the second crown, whose production is noted in Zech 6:10. The secondary verse Zech 6:14 thus explains what happened to this second crown.

That such an addition had been necessary is again best explained by the assumption that the narrative underwent a secondary reworking by which an older version mentioning the coronation of two persons was altered into a new version in which all hints to the coronation of the second person have been deleted. By adding Zech 6:14 the redactors responsible for this new version wanted to explain the whereabouts of the second crown mentioned in 6:10, which according to the text as it stands has not been used to coronate a person.³⁵

The mentioning of crowns in the plural, the juxtaposition of two persons, the branch and the priest, who sit on their own throne, the double statement "he will build the temple of YHWH" and the secondary addition Zech 6:14 explaining the whereabouts of the second crown—all this speaks for the old thesis that Zech 6:9–14 originally described the coronation of two persons. The second person mentioned in this original version of Zech 6:9–14, of course, can have been no one else than Zerubbabel.³⁶ This assumption is already based on the reference to the rebuilding of the temple. And this assumption is further based on the term צמח "branch." This term surely alludes to Jer 23:5; 33:15 promising a new Davidic ruler called צמח "branch."³⁷ Thus, it is more than probable that the original version of Zech 6:9–14 mentioned the Davidian Zerubbabel alongside Joshua, the high priest.

All in all, everything speaks for the assumption that once an original version of Zech 6:9–14 existed, in which the prophet was told to make two crowns and to set them on the heads of the Davidian Zerubbabel and the high priest Joshua.

---

³³ Thus also Meyers and Meyers, *Haggai*, 362–63.

³⁴ *Contra* Hallaschka, *Haggai*, 272, who states "Vers 14 schließlich nimmt dem Hohepriester die Krone vom Kopf." Nothing in the text supports this assumption.

³⁵ Cf. Rainer Albertz, "The Thwarted Restoration," in *Yahwism after the Exile: Perspectives on Israelite Religion in the Persian Era* (ed. Rainer Albertz and Bob Becking; Studies in Theology and Religion 5; Assen: Van Gorcum, 2003), 1–17 (8–9 with note 31).

³⁶ Eichhorn, *Propheten*, 3:354 with n. 1; Ewald, "Versuche," 359; Kellermann, *Messias*, 59–60; Beyse, *Serubbabel*, 77–84; Jeremias, *Nachtgesichte*, 218; Albertz, *Religionsgeschichte*, 2:482, and Nogalski, *Book of the Twelve*, 2:880.

³⁷ E.g., Rudolph, *Haggai*, 99–100; Meyers and Meyers, *Haggai*, 202; Petersen, *Haggai*, 276, and Reventlow, *Propheten*, 55.

The text continued with the expectation that these two will build the temple, that they will sit each one on his own individual throne, and that the counsel of peace will be between the two of them.

This original version of Zech 6:9–14 thus again describes Zerubbabel and Joshua as jointly entrusted with regal honors. They both get a crown and they both sit on a throne. Thus, they receive the same symbols of kingship.[38] The notice that the counsel of peace shall be between the two of them further stresses their equal status. After Zech 4:1–14* the original version of Zech 6:9–14 again pursues the political concept of a diarchy under a royal and a priestly leader.[39]

Different from the circles behind the book of Haggai, stemming from a prophetic milieu, the priestly circles behind the oldest layers of the book of Zechariah thus did not vote for a complete restoration of the preexilic conditions. In the course of the new constitution of the Judean community after the time of the exile, they rather wanted to strengthen the influence of the priesthood on this community. Hence, they voted for a common leadership of a royal Davidic and a priestly ruler.

3. Hierocracy in Zechariah 3:1–7 and 6:9–14

Besides the aforementioned concept of a diarchy under a royal and a priestly ruler, the book of Zechariah, in its later layers, shows another political concept. Remarkable is, at first, that Zech 6:9–14, as shown before, underwent a secondary reworking.

In the text of Zech 6:9–14 as it stands—presumably in a rather mechanical way—all hints to Zerubbabel and his coronation were deleted. Additionally, a small note on the whereabouts of the second crown has been added in 6:14.

---

[38] Several scholars question the view that Zech 6:9–14 indeed mentions specific royal symbols; cf. Meyers and Meyers, *Haggai*, 361; Rose, *Zemah and Zerubbabel*, 51–54, 63–64, and Willi-Plein, *Haggai*, 117–19; see also Boda, "Oil," 4.3.3.2–3. They point to the fact that the term עטרה is also used to signify a profane headdress (e.g. Isa 28:1, 3, 5; Ezek 16:12; 23:42; Job 19:9; Prov 4:9; 12:4; 14:24; 16:31; 17:6) and that the term כסא is also used for the seat of lower officials or for a chair in general (e.g. 1 Sam 1:9; 2 Kgs 4:10; Neh 3:7). It has to be taken into account, however, that both terms are mainly used as technical terms for the (royal) crown and throne (for עטרה, see, e.g. 2 Sam 12:30//1 Chron 20:2; Jer 13:18; Ezek 21:31; Ps 21:4; and for כסא, see, e.g., Exod 11:5; 1 Kgs 1:13; 16:11; 22:10; Jer 1:15; Esth 1:2). Thus, in a context which speaks about a priestly leader (and in its original form also about a political leader of Davidic descent), עטרה and כסא should be understood as nothing less than the royal crown and thrown and thus as symbols of kingship.

[39] See especially Albertz, *History*, 2:453.

The text as it stands mentions only the coronation of the high priest Joshua. He is the only concrete person, which is entrusted with regal honors. He alone gets a crown. And he alone is introduced as an identifiable ruler. The branch, who sits beside the priest on his throne and who lives in peace with this priest, is not identified as a concrete person. His significance remains obscure.[40]

The redactors of Zech 6:9–14 thus transformed the diarchic concept of the original version of this text. They altered it to the new concept of a hierocracy, in which the high priest alone holds the leadership over the community.

Against this background, one further text is noteworthy: the vision about the accusation against the high priest Joshua in Zech 3.[41] This vision report describes how Joshua stands in the heavenly assembly, where he is accused by Satan. YHWH, however, objurgates Satan. The high priest's dirty clothes are then being removed. In this context, in Zech 3:5–7, one finds the following words:

> [5]And I (the messenger of YHWH) said: Let them put a clean turban [צָנִיף] on his head. So they put a clean turban on his head and clothed him with garments. And the messenger of YHWH was standing by. [6]And the messenger of YHWH assured Joshua and said: [7]Thus says YHWH Sabaoth: If you walk in my ways [הלך בדרך], if you keep my ordinances [שמר משמרת], and judge my house, and keep my courts, then I will give you access among those who are standing here. (Zech 3:5–7)

Zechariah 3:5–7 thus describes how Joshua gets a clean turban as well as new clothes. Additionally, it gives a conditional promise, according to which Joshua—if he fulfils certain duties—gets access to the ones standing around him.

Especially in more recent research, it is often assumed that according to Zech 3 Joshua receives priestly honors.[42] The turban on his head is then understood as part of the priestly regalia and the duties mentioned in 3:7 are seen as genuine priestly tasks.

Remarkable, however, is the fact that the term צָנִיף used for the turban in Zech 3:5 is never used for the headdress of the high priest. צָנִיף sometimes des-

---

[40] Cf. Nogalski, *Book of the Twelve*, 2:880: "it is all the more noteworthy that the high priest is crowned, while the mysterious 'branch' is only credited with reconstructing the temple in the final form of the text."

[41] For the secondary nature of Zech 3, see above n. 14.

[42] Boda, "Oil," 2.3–4; Michael Segal, "The Responsibilities and Rewards of Joshua the High Priest according to Zechariah 3:7," *JBL* 126 (2007): 717–34; Petterson, *Behold your King*, 46–62; Stead, *Intertextuality*, 159; Willi-Plein, *Haggai*, 86–87, and Daniel F. O'Kennedy, "Purification of Priest, Prophet and People: A Comparative Study of Zechariah 3 and 13," *OTE* 27 (2014): 231–46 (235–36).

ignates a profane piece of clothing;[43] in other passages, however, it designates the headdress of the king.[44] Yet, Isa 62:3 mentions a צניף מלוכה "a royal turban" and, remarkably enough, it mentions in parallel to this the term עטרה "crown," which is also documented in Zech 6:11, 14.

Also noteworthy is that already at the beginning of the vision, in Zech 3:1, Joshua is called the "high priest." Thus, the procedures mentioned in 3:4–5—the change of his clothes and the setting up of a turban—cannot be understood as Joshua's investiture for the office of the high priest. Especially the turban, which Joshua gets as a new piece of clothing, has to be taken as evidence that he receives a new function beyond his priestly office.

All this speaks for the assumption that Zech 3:5 describes nothing else than the coronation of Joshua. It shows Joshua's appointment as the political leader of the community. Joshua thus steps into the function of the former Davidic kings.[45]

This assumption can be corroborated by the conditional promise in Zech 3:7. The duties of the high priest mentioned in this verse are, as often seen, duties which in preexilic times applied to the Davidic king. Walking in the ways of YHWH, keeping his ordinances, judging, and even the keeping of the courts, i.e. the temple, were in preexilic times principal tasks of the king.[46] Moreover, the two duties "walking in the way" (הלך בדרך) and "keeping the ordinances" (שמר משמרת) are mentioned together only once more in the Hebrew Bible, in 1 Kgs 2:3—directed to King Solomon.

At last, the promise of Zech 3:7, according to which the high priest shall earn access to the ones standing around him, is remarkable. Since the scene of Zech 3 takes place in the heavenly assembly, this promise can only be understood in a way that it gives Joshua access to this heavenly assembly. Like mentioned be-

---

[43] Isa 3:23; Job 29:14.

[44] Isa 62:3; Sir 11:5; 40:4; 47:6; cf. Jeremias, *Nachtgesichte*, 210; Petersen, *Haggai*, 198–99, and Reventlow, *Propheten*, 53.

[45] Cf. also Wellhausen, *Propheten*, 181; Rudolph, *Haggai*, 97; Jeremias, *Nachtgesichte*, 216; Meyers and Meyers, *Haggai*, 195; James C. VanderKam, "Joshua the High Priest and the Interpretation of Zechariah 3," in *From Revelation to Canon: Studies in the Hebrew Bible and Second Temple Literature* (idem; JSJSup 62; Leiden: Brill, 2000), 157–76 (162–67); Delkurt, *Nachtgesichte*, 178, and Pola, *Priestertum*, 198–203.

[46] Cf. for the phrase "walking in the ways of YHWH" (הלך בדרך) 1 Kgs 2:3; 3:14; 11:33, 38; 2 Kgs 21:22, for "keeping the ordinances" (שמר משמרת) 1 Kgs 2:3, for the judiciary function of the king (דין) Jer 21:12; 22:16; Ps 72:2, and for the king's responsibility for the temple 1 Kgs 8:5.

fore with regard to Zech 4:14, such as access to heavenly spheres was in older texts the privilege of prophets and kings.[47]

Thus, according to Zech 3, the high priest gets honors and duties which in preexilic times were held by the king.[48] Zechariah 3 describes the investiture of Joshua as the—only—ruler over the Judean community. It describes nothing less than the establishment of a hierocracy.

With the reworking of Zech 6:9–14 and the addition in Zech 3:1–7, the circles behind the book of Zechariah thus transformed the political concept of the older layers of the book. They altered the concept of a diarchy under a royal and a priestly ruler to the new concept of the sole leadership of the high priest.

The background of this new transformation of the political concept supported in priestly circles seems to be that the Davidian Zerubbabel, who—as visible in the oldest layers of the books of Haggai and Zechariah—provoked the expectation that the Davidic kingdom would be restored, probably disappeared from the political stage. Although these incidents to a large extent lie in the dark, it is not improbable to assume that the Persians, who appointed Zerubbabel as governor over the province of Judah, due to the attempts to restore the Davidic kingdom, removed or even killed him.[49]

The priestly circles behind the book of Zechariah then probably took the disappearance of Zerubbabel as a chance to get the leadership of the Judean community on their side. For this reason, they erased Zerubbabel out of the report about the coronation in Zech 6:9–14, and they added the vision about Joshua's investiture as the only ruler over the Judean community in Zech 3.

Thus, due to the incidents around the person of Zerubbabel, the priestly circles behind the book of Zechariah gave up their older diarchic concept. They distanced themselves from any restoration of the Davidic kingdom and promoted the sole leadership of the high priest. This led to the earliest formulation of a hierocratic concept in Israel.

---

[47] See above, p. 188.

[48] Cf. VanderKam, "Joshua," 164, who states that Zech 3 "is crediting the high priest with greater responsibilities in a domain that was formerly dominated by the king."

[49] Cf., e.g., Ephraim Stern, *Archaeology of the Land of the Bible: The Assyrian, Babylonian, and Persian Periods (732–332 B.C.E.)* (New York: Doubleday, 2001), 355; Albertz, "Thwarted Restoration," 8, and J. Maxwell Miller and John H. Hayes, *A History of Ancient Israel and Judah* (2nd ed.; London: SCM, 2006), 522.

4. Priestly Interregnum according to Zechariah 3:8

After the before mentioned redactional processes in the book of Zechariah, one further, now rather short text has been added to the book of Zechariah, which again corrected the book's political concept. In Zech 3:8 one finds the following word for the high priest Joshua:

> ⁸Now listen, Joshua, high priest, you and your colleagues who sit before you! For they are men of the sign [אנשי מופת]; for, behold, I will bring my servant the branch (צמח). (Zech 3:8)

Zechariah 3:8 is, as often proposed, a later addition to the chapter.⁵⁰ This is evident in the fact that this verse compared to the foregoing text presents a different setting of the scene. While Zech 3:1–7 presupposes that Joshua stands in the heavenly assembly and there between heavenly beings, Zech 3:8 mentions the colleagues of the high priest—presumably the priests of the Jerusalem temple⁵¹—who sit before him.

Remarkably, the addition in Zech 3:8 promises that YHWH will bring his servant the branch. As explicated before, the term צמח "branch" goes back to Jer 23:5; 33:15 with its expectation of a new Davidic ruler called צמח "branch."⁵² Thus, Zech 3:8 expects the coming of such a new Davidic ruler.⁵³

Against this background, the phrase "men of the sign" (אנשי מופת) in Zech 3:8 is noteworthy. This can only be understood in a way that the priests are a sign of the coming of the branch and thus of the restoration of a new Davidic kingdom.⁵⁴

That means, however, that Zech 3:8 alters the political concept of the foregoing older parts of the vision in 3:1–7. The high priest, to whom 3:1–7 ascribes the leadership over the Judean community, appears in 3:8—together with his colleagues—just as a sign of the coming leadership of a new Davidian.

---

⁵⁰ Petersen, *Haggai*, 202; Reventlow, *Propheten*, 54; Tollington, *Tradition and Innovation*, 42–43; Delkurt, *Nachtgesichte*, 145–46, n. 1, and Hallaschka, *Haggai*, 198; *contra* Wöhrle, *Sammlungen*, 336.

⁵¹ E.g., Marti, *Dodekapropheton*, 410; Rudolph, *Haggai*, 99; Meyers and Meyers, *Haggai*, 198; Reventlow, *Propheten*, 55, and Willi-Plein, *Haggai*, 88.

⁵² See above, p. 192 with fn. 37.

⁵³ It is important to note that the branch mentioned in 3:8, different from 6:12, is a future figure. Thus, in this verse, the branch cannot be identified with Zerubbabel as, e.g., Petersen, *Haggai*, 210–11, or Willi-Plein, *Haggai*, 88, maintain.

⁵⁴ Wellhausen, *Propheten*, 181; Rudolph, *Haggai*, 100; Reventlow, *Propheten*, 55, and Hallaschka, *Haggai*, 198.

Due to the addition in Zech 3:8 the leadership of the high priest, the hierocracy promoted in Zech 3:1–7, becomes an interregnum. According to Zech 3:8, the leadership over the people is not given the high priest forever, but just until the appearance of a new Davidic king.

After the addition of Zech 3:8, the book of Zechariah still promotes a kind of hierocracy. But it restricts the leading role of the high priest to the time without a Davidic ruler. Thus, for unknown reasons, on this late redactional stage of the book of Zechariah the political role of the high priest is diminished. The expectation of a restored Davidic kingship, already promoted in the primary layer of the book of Haggai, becomes dominant again.

Conclusion

The redaction history of the books of Haggai and Zechariah gives important insights into the early postexilic discourse about the leadership over the people under the new circumstances of this time. Especially, it gives insights into changing attitudes towards the political role of the high priest.

While the prophetic circles behind the primary layer of the book of Haggai opted for the complete restoration of the preexilic conditions, a Davidic kingdom under Zerubbabel as a new king, the priestly circles behind the book of Zechariah advocated a stronger political influence of the high priest. At first, on the level of the oldest strata of the book of Zechariah, they voted for a diarchy under a royal Davidic and a priestly ruler. Then—probably after the disappearance of Zerubbabel—they even opted for the sole leadership of the high priest. This led to the earliest formulation of a hierocratic concept in Israel.

However, this hierocratic concept, as can also be seen in the book of Zechariah, was soon revised. Later redactors restricted the priest's leadership—as a kind of interregnum—to the time without a Davidic ruler.

The redaction history of the books of Haggai and Zechariah thus shows how in early postexilic times different circles put forward and promoted their individual concepts about the leadership of the people. And it shows how in this time the priests competed for greater, even for dominant influence on the political leadership—an aim which they could not achieve in this time, but which may surely have strengthened their self-consciousness for their later history.

12

HOW DOES MALACHI'S "BOOK OF REMEMBRANCE" FUNCTION FOR THE CULTIC ELITE?

James Nogalski

1. CONTEXTUALIZING THE BOOK OF REMEMBRANCE IN MALACHI 3:16–18

The "book of remembrance" in Mal 3:16 has long been misinterpreted by Christian expositors as a book containing the names of the faithful who will survive the coming day of YHWH. Both the syntax of Mal 3:16–18 and parallel expressions elsewhere in the Old Testament argue against this interpretation. Consider first the syntax of Mal 3:16–18.

Narration of creation of the book of remembrance:	[16]Then those fearing YHWH spoke among themselves, each one to his neighbor, and YHWH took note and listened. And a book of remembrance was written before him for those fearing YHWH and those respecting his name,
Result of YHWH's observation of the YHWH fearers:	[17](and they shall belong to me as a possession, says YHWH Sebaoth, for the day I am making. And I will spare them just as one spares one's own child who serves him),
Purpose of the book of remembrance:	[18]so that you will again discern[1] between the righteous and the wicked, between the one serving God and the one not serving him.

---

[1] Literally, the phrase translates: "And you will return and you will discern between the righteous and the wicked." The initial *waw* connects to the creation of the book of

The syntax of 3:16 does not fit well with the idea of equating the "book of remembrance" with "a book of life" containing the names of the faithful. The narrative response to the disputations of Mal 1:2–3:15 describes a sequence of events: first, those fearing YHWH speak among themselves; second, YHWH takes note; and third, a book of remembrance was written before YHWH *for* those who feared YHWH. In other words, the "book of remembrance" is presented to "those fearing YHWH" and not kept by YHWH as a list of names to recall.

The result of the transaction appears in the theological affirmation of Mal 3:17: YHWH will spare those who fear him on the coming day of punishment. The verse concerns the fate of those fearing YHWH, not the contents of the book. The subject "they" refers back to the YHWH fearers.

The purpose of the book is stated in 3:18: "so that you (plural) will again discern between the righteous and the wicked." The statement presumes that the "book of remembrance" will help "those fearing YHWH" to make this distinction. Restated, the book has a didactic function, one that provides insight into the intellectual training processes for cultic personnel as well as the development of scribal prophecy. The book given to the YHWH fearers will provide them the means to distinguish between two types of people: the righteous and the wicked.

In addition to the syntax of the passage, discussions of the verse have not adequately considered conceptual parallels when interpreting the expression "the book of remembrance" in Mal 3:16–18. These parallels also suggest that the "book of remembrance" represents a source to be consulted by the YHWH fearers. As we will ultimately show, this book of remembrance is best conceived as a scroll to be studied in the scribal and Levitical curriculum of the Jerusalem temple. As noted above, this "book" refers to a scroll given to the YHWH fearers intended to teach them how to discern the righteous from the wicked. In addition to Mal 3:16, the concept of "a remembrance" written in a book appears in two other Hebrew texts (Exod 17:14 and Esth 6:1) and in the Aramaic section of Ezra (4:15, 2xs). It refers to recollections of various types: the result of a battle, the royal journal of a Persian king, and a historical archive to which scribes of the Persian king Darius had access.

In Exod 17:14, YHWH commands Moses: "Write this as a remembrance in the book and put it in the ears of Joshua: 'I will utterly blot out the recollection of Amalek from under heaven.'" This statement appears after the narrative of Joshua's defeat of the Amalekites while Moses (with the help of Aaron and Hur)

---

remembrance in 3:16 and demonstrates purpose. The *waw* connects to the verb שׁוב, which frequently functions as a modular verb that means "to do again" when used in conjunction with another verb (as here with the verb בין). The action of the clause ("again discern") does not flow from being spared in 3:17, but from having received the book in 3:16.

held his hands aloft, and YHWH's statement confirms the defeat for posterity. The quote basically functions as confirmation of the permanence of the defeat of the Amalekites (17:8–13). Yet, this record is both placed in "the book" and recounted to Joshua orally (literally, "placed in the ears of Joshua"). It should be noted that the record of the event credits YHWH, not Joshua, for the victory. Thus, in Exod 17:14, the "remembrance" refers to the consequence of YHWH's actions, not human activities, and it functions as a reminder for humans, not YHWH.

In Esth 6:1, the "book of remembrances" (plural: "records") appears in apposition to "the words of the days" ("journal"). The king cannot sleep and has the book of remembrances read to him, at which point he recalls that Mordecai helped thwart the king's assassination, but that the king did not reward Mordecai's action at that time. In this text, the "book of remembrances" records actions of individuals who could be rewarded (or presumably punished) for their dealings with the king. In this sense, Esth 6:1 might offer a kind of parallel to the book of life idea often used to interpret the phrase "book of remembrance" in Mal 3:16, except that it records actions, not merely names. The Aramaic section of Ezra shows, however, that the idea of a "book of remembrance" also referred to official actions on a broader scale to document relationships between countries and people groups.

In Ezra 4, the returning Judeans attempt to rebuild the temple under Zerubbabel shortly after 538. The enemies of Judah and Benjamin thwart this attempt by writing to the new Persian king to complain about the Judeans (4:7). They tell the king to search "the book of remembrances" (in Aramaic, ספר־דכרניא). This phrase is the same as the phrase in Mal 3:16 with three exceptions: 1) the word remembrance reflects the Aramaic spelling, employing a *dalet* as the first letter rather than a *zayin*; 2) the phrase in Ezra 4:15 (like Esth 6:1) has the definite article; and 3) the noun "remembrance" in Mal 3:16 is singular while in Ezra 4:15 (and Esth 6:1) the noun is plural. None of these differences change the meaning of the term. Consequently, the Aramaic phrase in Ezra 4:15 bears directly upon the question of the nature and function of the book of remembrance in Mal 3:16. Ezra 4:15 uses the phrase "the book of remembrances" twice and is often translated "annals"—a term that fits the function of this book. The text is part of the speech of Zerubbabel's opponents to the new Persian king Artaxerxes designed to thwart the building of the temple:

> [14]Now because we share the salt of the palace and it is not fitting for us to witness the king's dishonor, therefore we send and inform the king, [15]so that a search may be made *in the annals* of your ancestors. You will discover *in the annals* that this is a rebellious city, hurtful to kings and provinces, and that sedition was stirred up in it from long ago. On that account this city was laid waste." (Ezra 4:14–15 NRSV)

The dating problems of this chapter are hopelessly problematic, but they do not change what can be said regarding the meaning of the phrase the book of remembrance.[2] The context of Ezra 4:15 makes clear that this book of remembrance refers to an official document containing historical material used to inform the actions of the king of Persia. The first reference in 4:15 even refers to it as the book of remembrance of your ancestors. Consider what this phrase implies: the Persian king's ancestors transmitted a book that purportedly included the fate of Jerusalem. These annals helped guide the actions of the Persian king as a legal document. One can hardly imagine that these annals contained only the history of Jerusalem. Undoubtedly, in the logic of Ezra 4, the annals were presumed to be far reaching and authoritative. The opponents of Zerubbabel refer to these annals with the assumption that the king (or his scribes) can consult them and verify the truth of their claims about Jerusalem. These annals would have been the state records, and would have recorded the military exploits of the Persian kings, tribute required of other countries, and the like. At the same time, however, the logic of Ezra 4 assumes that these annals would have contained records of how other nations behaved during the periods of Babylonian and Assyrian domination. Only in this case could the opponents expect the Persians to find evidence to help their claim. No evidence exists that Jerusalem ever had hostile relationships with the Persians during the Achaemenid period, but Jerusalem could be accused of having demonstrated continued resistance to Assyria and Babylon at various times. In this sense, Ezra 4 assumes that the "book of remembrance" constituted a broad ranging set of annals, as well as an apparatus that would allow these annals to be searched. Presumably, this apparatus would have been controlled by royal scribes with knowledge of and access to these archives.

Closely related to the question of the content is the question of who consults the book. Who remembers what for whom? Unlike the "book of remembrances" referenced in Esth 6:1, the book in Malachi does not remain in the possession of the king, but in the possession of the YHWH-fearers. Such is the meaning of Mal

---

[2] The letter is sent to Artaxerxes (465–424 BCE) according to Ezra 4:11, but he reigns after Darius (522–486 BCE) where one would expect a reference to Cambyses (530–522 BCE) as the king who followed Cyrus (576–530 BCE). Cyrus was the king of Persia who defeated Babylon. Ezra 4:6 also refers to Ahasuerus, a name that appears in four different Hebrew books, but who cannot be identified from any known Persian king. Theories associate Ahasuerus with Cambyses, Xerxes, Artaxerxes I, and others. The name Ahasuerus probably refers to different people in these books. For a fuller description of the dating problems, see Joseph Blenkinsopp, *Ezra-Nehemiah: A Commentary* (OTL; Philadelphia, PA: Westminster, 1988), 42–43, 110–15; H. G. M. Williamson, *Ezra, Nehemiah* (WBC 16; Waco, TX: Word Books, 1985), xxxiii–xxxv, 56–60.

3:16: "A book of remembrance was written *before* him *for* those fearing YHWH and *for* those considering his name."

This book was written "before him" (i.e., YHWH), a phrase that suggests divine authorization of the book. This first idiom involves the verb "write" plus the preposition "before" or "in front of" (לפני), and it refers to something written "in the presence of" someone, as can readily be seen in Josh 8:32: "And there, Joshua wrote on the stones a copy of the law of Moses, which he wrote in the presence of (לפני) the Israelites." The term "before YHWH," however, gives the scene a sacral connotation.[3]

By contrast, the idiom involving "write" plus the inseparable preposition ל indicates two different meanings: the purpose and/or the recipient of the writing. The use of the idiom to denote purpose is less common, but it appears clearly in Exod 24:12: "The LORD said to Moses, Come up to me on the mountain, and wait there; and I will give you the tablets of stone, with the law and the commandment, which I have written *for their instruction*" (להורתם; NRSV). This text portrays YHWH as the one writing on the stone tablets, tablets which YHWH intends to give to Moses for the purpose of instructing the people. More commonly, this idiom denotes the recipient of the writing. The stipulation concerning divorce in Deut 24:1 offers a clear example: "Suppose a man enters into marriage with a woman, but she does not please him because he finds something objectionable about her, and so he writes *for her* (לה) a certificate of divorce, puts it in her hand, and sends her out of his house" (see also Deut 24:3). In this case, the certificate is given *to* the wife as proof of divorce. Similarly, this idiom also appears reflexively, as in YHWH's command to Moses to make his own copy of YHWH's words in Exod 34:27: "The LORD said to Moses: Write *for yourself* (לך) these words; in accordance with these words I have made a covenant with you and with Israel." The command to write also implies that Moses will receive the copy of that which he writes. The Deuteronomic command that the king write "for himself" a copy of the law appears in Deut 17:18: "Now it shall come about when he sits on the throne of his kingdom, he shall write *for himself* a copy of this law on a scroll *in the presence* (מלפני) of the Levitical priests" (NAS). Note that in this verse, the law is copied on a scroll in the presence of the Levitical priests, a scenario not dissimilar to Mal 3:16 in which the "book of remembrance" is written in the presence of YHWH *for* those fearing YHWH.

When the three texts (Exod 17:14; Esth 6:1; and Ezra 4:15) mentioning remembrances recorded in a book are combined with the specific idioms for writ-

---

[3] See the discussion below, in the concluding section labeled "Implications for Mal 3:16–18."

ing, the implications are significant for understanding the nature of the "book of remembrance" in Mal 3:16. Exodus 17:14 and Ezra 4:15 offer better parallels for making sense of the phrase in the context of Malachi. Like Exod 17:14, the book of remembrance in Mal 3:16 contains the remembrance of YHWH's actions, not the names of those fearing YHWH. Like Ezra 4:15, the book of remembrance given to the YHWH fearers in Mal 3:16 should be conceptualized as the annals of YHWH's actions that will allow those fearing YHWH to consult and learn from them "so that you will again discern between the righteous and the wicked" (Mal 3:18). This image of the book of remembrance fits the syntax, the purpose, and the phrasing of Mal 3:16–18.

What then is the "book of remembrance" in Mal 3:16? The book of remembrance should be conceptualized as the annals of YHWH's actions to be consulted by those fearing YHWH *and* those considering his name in order to distinguish between the righteous and the wicked. In this sense, the book of remembrance was an actual scroll that had an authoritative force and a didactic function for those who considered themselves to be part of this group who responded positively to the message of Malachi. The authoritative force derives from the claim that the book was written *before* YHWH, which imparts divine sanction to the book of remembrance itself.[4] The didactic function of the book of remembrance derives from the purpose statement of 3:18 which indicates that the book of remembrance will allow those consulting it to distinguish again between the righteous and the wicked.

Could the book of remembrance include the book of Malachi? Yes. Malachi 3:16 presumes knowledge of the preceding disputations, so one could interpret the book of remembrance as a narrative of the recording of Malachi as a book to be consulted to help distinguish the righteous from the wicked. The relationship of Mal 3:16–18 to its immediate context becomes particularly clear at the end of Mal 3:18, which defines the righteous and the wicked in terms of their service to God: "Then once more you shall see the difference between the righteous and the wicked, *between one who serves God and one who does not serve him*" (NRSV). This phrase regarding the service to God also offers a denouement to the final disputation which is also concerned with the purpose of service to God. Malachi 3:14–15 presents itself as the speech of those turning away from service to YHWH because they see no reward for this service. They reject YHWH and he rejects them. By contrast, Mal 3:16 narrates the response of a different group, those fearing YHWH, and 3:17 implies that YHWH will spare those serving God on the impending day of judgment. The book of remembrance is officially pub-

---

[4] Note that the phrase "before YHWH" also appears in Num 17:21–22 (MT; Eng.17:6–7) and assumes a similar sacral location and process.

lished for them (3:16) and will guide them in their understanding and discerning between the righteous and the wicked (3:18).

Should the book of remembrance be limited to the book of Malachi? No. For at least two reasons, Malachi alone does not fit the characterization of a book of remembrance. First, by itself, Malachi does not have the character of a book of records that would make it suitable for providing a thorough source of remembering the acts of YHWH. It is a book that exhorts the faithful of the current generation. Second, Mal 3:18 refers to an earlier time when the distinction between the righteous and the wicked would have been possible. The verse states that the book of remembrance will make it possible to "discern *again* between the righteous and the wicked." Malachi, by itself, does not narrate a time when YHWH's people demonstrated this capacity. Rather, Malachi, with its disputational character, presumes a broken relationship from the very beginning of the collection. These two characteristics make it difficult to conceptualize Malachi alone as a book of remembrance to be consulted by those wishing to live as YHWH would have them live.

Could the book of remembrance be a reference to the Book of the Twelve? Yes. For two reasons, one could and should consider the book of remembrance mentioned in Mal 3:16–18 as some form of the Book of the Twelve. First, the Book of the Twelve has the multi-generational and didactic character that the term "book of remembrance" implies. The Book of the Twelve has a chronological structure that runs from the eighth century to the Persian period. The twelve prophetic collections that comprise the book have a clear didactic function of documenting the word of YHWH to generations of YHWH's people. The cumulative impact of reading these collections has been augmented in a number of places and in a number of ways to evoke the impression that these writings were intended by some redactors to be read as a collection and not merely as independent encounters. A number of passages demonstrate a sense of chronology on both the macro and micro levels.[5]

---

[5] Several texts in the Book of the Twelve suggest awareness of this chronological framework across the boundaries of the individual writings. Consider, for example, the repentance narrative of Zech 1:2–6 that presumes knowledge of the "former prophets" and the response of the people to Zechariah's message recounted in Zech 1:6. The term "former prophets" in 1:4 does not mean the same as the canonical designation of the "Former Prophets" but simply means "earlier prophets." See discussions of how the people's response fits into the flow of Haggai and Zechariah, and presumes that the reader knows the identity of these "former prophets" (Zech 1:4), perhaps as allusions to Hosea, Joel, and Amos, in James D. Nogalski, *The Book of the Twelve: Micah-Malachi* (SHBC; Macon: Smyth & Helwys, 2011), 824–25. See also the discussion of the "former Prophets" in the Persian period by Julia M. O'Brien, "Nahum-Habakkuk-Zephaniah: Reading

Second, Malachi itself evidences a broader literary horizon that includes the Twelve in Mal 1:2–5 (Obadiah) and 3:6–12 (Joel). Malachi 1:2–5 provides resolution to the judgment of Edom motif in the Book of the Twelve, especially when one recognizes the allusions to Obadiah these verses contain.[6] Simultaneously, the prominence of "love" in Mal 1:2–5 also picks up on the message of Hosea with which the Book of the Twelve began.[7] Closer to the end of Malachi, 3:6–12 draws upon motifs and imagery that has strong affinities with Joel.[8] Malachi's use of earlier traditions is, of course, not limited to those in the Book of the Twelve. In fact, Malachi has been at the center of discussions of the phenomenon of scribal prophecy in recent years as a number of scholars have noted how its formulations show an extensive knowledge of other texts, including those in the Pentateuch.[9]

2. CULTIC SCRIBES AND CANON DEVELOPMENT— A CHANGED AND CHANGING CONTEXT

2.1. FROM "ROYAL SCRIBES" TO "TEMPLE SCRIBES"

Scholarly discussions about the nature of the scribal culture have begun to shed light on the social setting of scribes and the literature produced and transmitted in the Persian period. Several of these discussions have provided insights into the developing scribal culture important both for Malachi and the Book of the Twelve. A significant change in the Persian period altered the characteristics of major scribal activity as it adjusted to temple patronage rather than royal patronage.

---

the 'Former Prophets' in the Persian Period," *Int* 61 (2007): 168–83. Note also the citation of Mic 4:6–7 in Zeph 3:18–19 with its message of hope for the lame and the outcast that changes from the distant future in Micah to the imminent future in Zephaniah. See the discussion in James D. Nogalski, *Micah-Malachi*, 750. Also, see the assignation of Assyria as one of Joel's locusts in Nah 3:15–16 as discussed in Nogalski, *Micah-Malachi*, 632–35.

[6] See Nogalski, *Micah-Malachi*, 1000–1001, 1012–13.

[7] See John D. W. Watts, "A Frame for the Book of the Twelve: Hosea 1—3 and Malachi," in *Reading and Hearing the Book of the Twelve* (ed. James D. Nogalski and Marvin A. Sweeney; SymS 15; Atlanta: Society of Biblical Literature, 2000), 209–13.

[8] See Nogalski, *Micah-Malachi*, 1001.

[9] Helmut Utzschneider, *Künder oder Schreiber? Eine These zum Problem der Schriftprophetie auf Grund von Maleachi 1,6–2:9* (BEATAJ 19; Frankfurt am Main: Peter Lang, 1989).

Michael Fox contrasts the social setting of the oldest portion of Proverbs with the changed setting of Ben Sirah in the Hellenistic context of the second century BCE. He avers that the middle section of Proverbs (chapters 10–29) represents neither a textbook used in a school nor a simple transcription of folk literature recorded as the wisdom from village life, as some have claimed.[10] He argues the social setting can be determined by carefully analyzing to whom and for whom the individual proverbs speak. Evidence for a school setting is lacking. He does not consider the royal family to be the target audience because they do not play a major role in the content of individual sayings. He notes that the genre of wisdom instructions in Egypt presumes a father speaking to his son, not a teacher to his student. He further notes that while some of these named authors of wisdom instructions could be fictitious, the majority come from scribes addressing their own children, or one child, and it is doubtful that scribes would have had the cache for later writers to use them fictitiously. He thus sees most of the superscriptions as genuine.[11] Fox thinks the evidence suggests that the setting of the proverbs fits best within the context of familial training of royal scribes. Even those proverbs that speak about the king typically address their message to those who work within the royal court, not to members of the king's family.[12] He concludes that these early collections have a major thematic interest in how scribes should behave among the elite, and this component ultimately serves the interests of the royal court.

Fox thus understands Prov 10–29 as a collection of collections from various ancient scholars (a term he prefers over scribes). These smaller collections within Proverbs have their own characteristics, an observation which accounts for the stylistic variety as well as some of the repetition and the same stylistic devices appearing in some parts of chapters 10–29. The incorporation of these collections, both on the smaller and the larger level, thus involves a process with a purpose.

> Such a process accounts for the great diversity and the even greater unity in Proverbs. The diversity comes from the varied sources, the unity from the redactors' own creative activity. The redactors' intervention was radical and determinative, going far beyond 'later addition' to existing proverbs. They did

---

[10] Michael V. Fox, "Social Location of the Book of Proverbs," in *Texts, Temples, and Traditions: A Tribute to Menahem Haran* (ed. Michael V. Fox; Winona Lake, IN: Eisenbrauns, 1996), 229–35.

[11] Fox, "Social Location," 230–32.

[12] Fox offers Prov 25:6–7 as a particularly illuminating example: "Do not put on airs before the king; do not stand in the place of the mighty. It is better that he say to you, come up here, etc." (translation from ibid., 235).

add, but, most important, they *selected*. They chose what to include and what to ignore, and what they chose, they reshaped. In such a process, the very notions of original and additional, of authorial and redactional, intertwine inextricably.[13]

At this point, Fox describes the process of distilling wise sayings performed by individuals who have heard such proverbs, but he overstates the inextricable nature of some of the literary sources because he has also already noted how these smaller collections can have their own observable characteristics. Fox correctly identifies the role of editorial selection and the use of existing sources to create a literary entity that is bigger than the sum of its parts.

As further illustration of insights into changes in scribal social settings, Fox also describes Ben Sirah's life as a scribe and a scholar who speaks about the rich and the poor but does not consider himself to be part of either group: Ben Sirah

> is an example of the kind of person who could write Wisdom Instructions. He was a scholar with the leisure to study and write. He speaks about the rich and the poor in a way that suggests he saw himself as neither, but his suspicion of the rich and powerful suggests he knew them, uncomfortably, firsthand. This critical stance does not make him one of the 'simple folk'. It is likely that Ben Sirah himself served before rulers (39:4) and travelled in their service (34:10–11). (There is no evidence that he was a schoolmaster; his *bet midraš*, mentioned in the much misunderstood 51:23, is the book itself.) He was a *sofer*, which should be translated 'scholar' or better 'clerk' in the medieval sense, rather than 'scribe', for being a *sofer* was not in itself a profession, but a qualification for various professional opportunities.[14]

Ben Sirah's scribal setting reflects the influence of Hellenistic emphases of educating broader segments of society, but scribes remained part of a privileged class. In this conceptualization, Ben Sirah works for patrons among the wealthy, but is not wealthy himself. Neither, however, did he work exclusively within the temple or a palace. He would, however, likely have owned a library that included most of the canonical writings that became known as the Old Testament, as well as other non–canonical writings. We will return to the topic of libraries below. First, one must consider the work of Philip Davies, which points to the significance of a major change from the monarchic to the postmonarchic periods.

---

[13] Ibid., 237.
[14] Ibid., 236.

Philip R. Davies evaluates the role of scribes in the canonizing process, and he begins with a larger social survey that includes Mesopotamia, Egypt, and the Greeks.[15] In his evaluation of scribal activity, Davies makes several important points about those who sponsored the work of scribes and the nature of scribal activities themselves.[16] He reiterates that scribes across the ancient Near East worked at the behest of either the palace or the temple. This statement has significant implications that need to be considered carefully to distinguish the work of scribes in the ancient Near East from modern presuppositions about scribes that reflect Western assumptions about the way that scribes functioned as copyists in the medieval period. Davies goes on to describe the tasks of scribes and the role they played in the power structure of ancient societies. Nevertheless, his analysis focuses more on the role played by scribes when they worked at the behest of the state apparatus than those who would have primarily served in the temple hierarchy. For Judah in the Persian period, this exclusively political focus gives short shrift to the very extensive role played by temple personnel in collecting, composing, and updating the writings that would become the canonical works we now possess.

Davies identifies several stages of development of the scribal class across the ancient Near East based upon the tasks for which writing became a functional skill. These tasks began with the recording of economic transactions, and this skill became an important part of the social structure so that taxes, conscriptions, and other public collections could be documented. The skill to record transactions led inevitably to the need for archival systems so that records could be searched and explained. Such archives were attached to the palace or the temple. Such systems also sustained the need for persons who could record business transactions and navigate records over extended periods of time and through more complex systems of bureaucracy.[17] The training (or education) required for

---

[15] Philip R. Davies, *Scribes and Schools* (Library of Ancient Israel; Louisville, KY: Westminster John Knox, 1998).

[16] Ibid., 17–19.

[17] For example, excavation of the temple at Nuzi has produced 60 clay tablets found in an archive in the temple. Though the majority of these texts concern private contracts, libraries are also found in temples, such as the small library in close proximity to the temple in the Elamite site of Kabnak dated to the fourteenth and thirteenth centuries BCE. This library consists of school texts and "a number of omen texts" that were likely part of the same collection. One of the largest temple libraries to date in the ancient Near East would be the temple library and archive at Aššur with over 300 clay tablets, approximately sixty of which are literary texts. The temple texts come from the ninth to seventh centuries BCE. See Olof Pedersén, *Archives and Libraries in the Ancient Near East 1500–300 B.C.* (Bethesda, MD: CDL Press, 1998), 20 (Nuzi), 120–22 (Kabnak), 132–34.

working in such environments involved more than the ability to read and write. The ability to master these systems created opportunities for political counselors, advisors to the ruler of the state who maintained these archives. The tasks of diplomacy and the composition of texts became important because rulers and priests may or may not have had the training to read and write in early periods, let alone compose documents such as treaties and other formal correspondence. For such scribes, their work was performed in administrative centers, and the larger the bureaucracy of a given kingdom, the more administrative centers would have existed to carry out the functions of the state and cult.

This filtering of wisdom through the lens of those working with and for the political elite played a major role in the monarchic era for developing a scribal network. Training had to take place, probably in the homes of prominent scribes as a number of recent studies have postulated, especially since so many archives and libraries in the ancient Near East have been found in private residences.[18] The training likely included, but was not necessarily limited to family members of the householder. It likely included extended family, especially if the Shaphan family can be taken as illustrative. That family was at the center of developments of the royal court from the end of Manasseh's reign in the mid seventh century until at least the early exilic period and likely beyond.[19] With the fall of the monarchy, then the eventual construction of the second temple, and finally the slow but definitive growth of the cultic bureaucracy, the nature of the sponsorship of scribal endeavors changed. This change altered both the filters and the products by which official scribal literature developed. Rather than the "king's men" (described by Fox) the official scribal culture developed into the "temple's men." This term does not mean there were no scribes trained outside of temple sponsored workshops, but it does mean that as the temple complex grew it probably included rooms or side buildings where study was undertaken and where writings were produced, reproduced, studied, and appropriated.

One such room associated with the temple complex can be inferred from Neh 13. This chapter recounts how once Nehemiah left Jerusalem after his first term as governor, the room he had given the Levites was taken over by the priest Eliashib and given to Tobiah as an apartment. Upon his return, Nehemiah threw out the belongings of Tobiah and cleansed the room for the Levites (13:8–9). He also reinstituted the offerings stored in the room (13:5, 11–12). This room is not

---

[18] See the table of contents for a list of known libraries in the ancient Near East in Pedersén, *Archives and Libraries*, iii–ix.

[19] See James M. Kennedy, "Shaphan," *ABD* 5:1159. See also the discussion of the exilic period, including Gedaliah and other relatives of Shaphan, in Rainer Albertz, *Die Exilzeit: 6. Jahrhundert v. Chr* (Biblische Enzyklopädie 7; Stuttgart: Kohlhammer, 2001), 81–85.

described as a library, to be sure, but the evidence for a library is strong, as noted by van der Toorn below.[20]

2.2. EDUCATION FROM "THE CANON" OR EDUCATION THAT LEADS TO CANONS?

Another branch of the discussion on the role of scribes in the postmonarchic era concerns the issue of the gradual stabilizing of the canon. The works of Karel van der Toorn and David Carr are particularly relevant to this issue. In a salient discussion of canonization models, van der Toorn explains why previous discussions of canon have relied upon two faulty, anachronistic models that lack close parallels in ancient settings (the classic three-stage theory and an organic process).[21] He then assesses two newer models (library catalog and scribal curriculum) that hold more potential, though he believes that the scribal curriculum model best accounts for the process.

The classic three-stage theory had a relatively prominent history from the last quarter of the nineteenth century.[22] In various forms, the theory argues that over a five hundred year span the Torah gained canonical status first (fifth century BCE), was followed by the Nebiim in a second stage (by 200 BCE), and then finally concluded when the council of Jamnia authorized the Ketubim by the end of the first century CE. Even though scholars now either doubt the so-called council of Jamnia ever took place or at least remain dubious that it ever made an authoritative declaration, the basic contours of this theory have not entirely disappeared from scholarly discussions of the development of the canon.

Consequently, a significant body of scholarship continued to see a three-stage development of the canon, but it sought to explain the development as an organic process rather than some kind of official proclamation.[23] This organic process arose because these writings were believed to come from great persons of the past who wrote books that the community came to recognize as divinely inspired, even though no definitive body can be established who actually made this decision. For van der Toorn, this theory of canon suffers from a set of

---

[20] Karel van der Toorn, *Scribal Culture and the Making of the Hebrew Bible* (Cambridge, MA: Harvard University Press, 2007), 237–39.

[21] Ibid., 233–64.

[22] Ibid., 234–35.

[23] See ibid., 235–36, and especially the bibliography on Jamnia on pages 352–53 (fn. 8). For an example of how this three-stage theory continued to be presupposed, but modified as a more fluid process, late into the twentieth century, see also Odil Hannes Steck, *Der Abschluss der Prophetie im Alten Testament* (BThSt 17; Neukirchen-Vluyn: Neukirchener, 1991), 11–24.

anachronistic assumptions that lead to the Protestant Christian canon as well as the idea of a "self-authenticating Word" that conveys a sense of individualism that also mirrors Protestant theology more than ancient settings would suggest. As a result of the problems with these two models of canon development, van der Toorn explores the potential of two more recent models.

Van der Toorn takes seriously the question of whether the canon developed from the library catalog.[24] Van der Toorn notes that Jerome refers to the Bible as both a sacred library ("*sacra bibliotheca*" in *Epistula* 5) and a divine library ("*bibliotheca divina*" in *De viribus illustribus*, 75). For this and other reasons, van der Toorn considers the analogy of a library catalog as the source for the idea of a biblical canon, based largely upon three assumptions, which van der Toorn evaluates: (1) the second temple contained a library, (2) the library contained only holy books, and (3) the specific holy writings of the temple at the point of canonization became the canon. The first assumption, that the temple at Jerusalem contained a library, has considerable support, albeit indirect.[25] The second assumption, that the temple library contained only those documents considered holy, becomes more problematic.[26] Van der Toorn counters that the relative value of written documents in an oral culture would have made any such book intrinsically valuable and that, consequently, one can hardly infer that holiness would be the only criterion involved in determining which books would have been stored at the temple. In addition to van der Toorn's objection, one should also consider the likelihood that temple scrolls could just have easily been stored in rooms within and around the temple space itself without necessarily having to be kept in the sanctuary proper. The diverse nature, for example, of the sources cited in Chronicles and Kings indicates that scribes who compiled and composed these documents knew an array of texts. Especially with Chronicles, it would be more probable that these sources were known because they existed in the temple library than because they would have been known to the owner of a personal collection of books. The writer assumes that the reader has access to them.

---

[24] Van der Toorn, *Scribal Culture*, 236–44.

[25] The temple library is mentioned in 2 Macc 2:13–15, a text likely written between the second half of the second century and the first half of the first century BCE. It credits the founding of the library to Nehemiah. Van der Toorn also sees the reference to the Book of the Law found by Hilkiah (2 Kgs 22) and Samuel's depositing of a scroll in the sanctuary (1 Sam 10:25) as evidence that suggests books were kept at the temple.

[26] Some, such as Beckwith, argue that the storing of scrolls in the temple would have only been done for sacred books which would not defile the temple: Roger Beckwith, *The Old Testament Canon of the New Testament Church and Its Background* (Grand Rapids, MI: Eerdmans, 1985), see particularly 278–91, 311–17.

The third assumption takes the second a step further by assuming that, at the point of canonization, only those writings of the canon would have constituted the library catalog in Jerusalem. Such an assumption seems even more problematic than the second given what we know about the breadth of libraries at communities like Qumran and the likelihood that the temple would have had interests in training, researching, and referencing a wider range of documents than just the ones that came to be seen as canonical. Note that, at least in the first century CE, 2 Esdras 14:45–46 divides the ninety-four books dictated to Ezra into two categories: twenty-four scrolls "for the worthy and the unworthy" to read and seventy other scrolls used only for the advanced ("for the wise among your people"). This distinction would imply that certain groups were studying books that were not disseminated for public readings. At this point, van der Toorn also distinguishes between reference libraries and comprehensive libraries.[27] The former contains only books necessary to perform certain tasks, while the latter seeks to collect and preserve all known writings, at least within certain parameters.[28] Van der Toorn also argues that the Jerusalem temple probably fell somewhere in between. He distinguishes between library catalogs and lists of holdings that have been found in libraries based upon the fact that these lists illustrate four different functions: (1) curricular lists, (2) works of a particular genre, (3) recent library acquisitions, and (4) inventories.[29] Only the last type comes close to a library catalog, but these inventories differ from library catalogs because they are not designed to help people access the books, only to record the contents of the library.

Van der Toorn is likely correct about the character of the Jerusalem library as at least a semi-comprehensive library. This characterization may be inferred from socio-political as well as religious factors, and from the fact that these concerns influenced the Second Temple library over an extended period of time. The lack of an indigenous king, for example, made the temple the logical place for the political center of Yehud. The temple bureaucracy increased over time as the collection of tithes (including taxes for the Persians) became increasingly centered at the Jerusalem temple. With this increase in bureaucratic functions

---

[27] Van der Toorn, *Scribal Culture*, 240.

[28] Temple libraries in Egypt and Mesopotamia usually fall under the category of reference libraries. Only between 6–8 percent of the libraries and archives have collections over 1,000, but those can go as high as 30,000 (see Pedersén, *Archives and Libraries*, see his summary on pages 244–47). Those temple libraries uncovered through excavation can be relatively small collections of texts related to priestly duties that would have only required a small room to house, but at least one ancient temple contained about 800 tablets (ibid., 245).

[29] Van der Toorn, *Scribal Culture*, 242–43.

came the need for an expansion of the temple personnel and the resources they needed to conduct their business. The Elephantine papyri illustrate that correspondence was conducted with the temple personnel by the late fifth to early fourth century BCE.[30] One may infer from these discussions that scribal work would have been involved in the responses to such correspondence, in addition to the need to record and preserve such correspondence (even though the letter expresses frustration that the bureaucracy in Jerusalem has not responded). Similarly, the picture of the formal correspondence between Ezra, his opponents, and the Persian authorities indicates the need for scribal activity was ongoing. Finally, the fact that Ezra himself is named as a scribe indicates the strong likelihood that the bureaucracy Ezra designed would have taken on scribal tasks.[31] Still, assuming that the suggestion has some merit that Malachi's book of remembrance concerns the authorization of a scroll as part of the training process expected of Levites sometime in the first half of the fourth century, this book of remembrance would almost certainly have been kept at the Jerusalem temple as part of a developing Levitical reference library. More will be said about this prospect below after some discussion of the presumed role of a scribal curriculum.

Perhaps the most significant aspect of van der Toorn's work concerns his treatment of the canon as, in part, derived from a scribal curriculum. Van der Toorn notes that the suggestion that the canon grew from the scribal curriculum has an advantage over the library catalog model in that it can account for both the additions to and the selectivity of the works ultimately included. A curriculum must have some level of selectivity even if the library contains more works than those scribes were required to study. Van der Toorn notes that "unlike a place in a library, inclusion in a curriculum asserts the superiority of a written text over other texts."[32] Decisions about which texts to include would have come

---

[30] In this context, letters from the Jewish community at Elephantine asking for support to rebuild its temple reference correspondence with "Johann, the high priest and his colleagues, the priests who are in Jerusalem," in a letter dated to 408 BCE. See Arthur E. Cowley, ed. *Aramaic Paryri of the Fifth Century B.C. Ancient Texts and Translations* (Eugene, OR: Wipf & Stock, 2005), 114 (letter #30, line18).

[31] See the discussion in John W. Miller, *How the Bible Came to Be: Exploring the Narrative and Message* (New York: Paulist Press, 2004), 29–30. Miller makes the point that Ezra had the authority of a potentate (Ezra 7:25–26), but deliberately set up a different kind of political constellation that accentuates the task of teaching the people rather than making sure that the king had a copy of the law. The same holds true in Nehemiah and in Chronicles according to Miller because of texts like Neh 8–10 (especially Neh 8:3, 8, 13). Note also the role of the Levites as teachers in 2 Chr 35:3.

[32] Van der Toorn, *Scribal Culture*, 245.

from the imposition of an authority; in this case, the approval of temple authorities. Van der Toorn suggests there could even have been a core and an elective curriculum. In this way, van der Toorn imagines that a library for studying the prophets would have been larger than what was actually required by a curriculum. A number of lists in Assyria actually represent a curriculum.[33]

The work of David Carr expands the work of van der Toorn at this point. Carr brings another issue into the discussion, namely the development of what he terms as "writing-supported education" that increasingly focused upon training the priests through oral instruction that was based upon written texts.[34] Carr marshals evidence that while the literacy of the administrative sector of Judah increased dramatically in the eighth through the seventh centuries BCE, the evidence for writing-supported education largely begins with the end of the seventh century during the reign of Josiah.[35] Concurrently, the educating of priests with written texts increases dramatically at this point through the elevation of the Mosaic Torah, with the finding of the book of the covenant (i.e., Deuteronomy) in the temple that portrays Moses as the prophet par excellence. For Carr, the sixth century changed the scribal and educational situation dramatically following the deportations of 597, 587, and 582 BCE.

> The temple and virtually all major structures in the land itself were destroyed. Though it is probable that some of Jehoiachin's retinue were masters of the tradition and we now have inscriptional evidence that scribes were active elsewhere in the Jewish diaspora, it is unclear how such groups would have access to written versions of the tradition, especially after the destruction of the Jerusalem palace-temple structure and the capture of its elite. Whatever sorts of correspondence characterized interchange between exiles and people in the homeland in the years 597–587 BCE, it still seems unlikely that Jews could have carried trunkloads of holy scrolls from the ruins of the temple to Babylonian exile.[36]

It seems quite probable though, as Albertz and others have concluded that scribes—aided by memory and written sources, and driven by the need to speak to changed situations—put these traditions back together. This work probably took place in Mizpah and in Babylon over the course of some decades.[37] The former included a non-priestly Mosaic Torah that highlighted Moses' prophetic

---

[33] Ibid., 246.

[34] David M. Carr, *Writing on the Tablet of the Heart: Origins of Scripture and Literature* (Oxford: Oxford University Press, 2005).

[35] Ibid., 162–73.

[36] Ibid., 168.

[37] Rainer Albertz, *Die Exilzeit*, 81–85.

role as well as versions of the history of Israel and Judah in which prophets played a crucial role. Several prophetic collections were also gathered and reshaped under the influence of this history. The Babylonian reconstruction of traditions focused more on instructional needs of Aaronide priests.

In the aftermath of the exile, education of Aaronide priests and Levites ultimately supplanted the need to educate royal descendants. Increasingly, priestly instruction focused upon the Mosaic Torah, while Levitic scribes continued to enhance the collection of the prophets (as well as the Psalter).[38] Once the temple was rebuilt, it replaced the palace as the economic center of Judah. Under the leadership of Ezra, an official Torah of Moses was published that blended the priestly and non-priestly versions of these traditions in the middle of the fifth century. The Aaronide priests retained the primary role as the priests who offered the sacrifices while the Levites were charged with secondary clerical tasks for the temple (e.g. cleaning the altars, guarding the temple gates, collecting the tithes, and producing the music). To be sure, over time both groups benefitted from the increased economic advantages of a centralized cultic system, but ten-

---

[38] Carr effectively makes this point for text-enhanced education of priests, but does not fully incorporate the Levites into his educational scenarios in the Persian period. See Carr, *Writing on the Tablet of the Heart*, 172–73, 202. The portrait of the Levites that develops in Nehemiah (whether idealized or not) highlights the teaching function of the Levites that shows knowledge of textual traditions that go beyond the Torah and include the Former Prophets and a framework for the Latter Prophets. See especially the prayer of Ezra in Neh 8–9 that summarizes the entire history of YHWH's people and includes recognizable allusions to the Torah and Joshua through Kings. This summary culminates in a statement that underscores the role of the prophets in this history corresponding to the Former Prophets: "Many years you were patient with them and warned them by your spirit through your prophets; yet they would not listen" (Neh 9:30). Further, Ezra petitions for release from the punishment in a manner that alludes to the time frame of the Latter Prophets: "Now therefore, our God, ... Do not treat lightly all the hardship that has come upon us, upon our kings, our officials, our priests, our prophets, our ancestors, and all your people, since the time of the kings of Assyria until today" (9:32). This last phrase referring to the period that began with the kings of Assyria reflects the message of the Latter Prophets whose earliest material traces to prophetic figures of the eighth century BCE. (Isaiah, Hosea, Amos, and Micah), but which also includes material that extends well into the Persian period (the explicit mention of Cyrus in Isaiah 44–45; the chronological notes in Haggai and Zechariah dating to the time of the Persian King Darius; and Malachi who references the civil leadership using the Persian word for governor). Thus, text enhanced instruction, at least for those recording the traditions of the Nebiim, was probably affiliated with the Levites by this point and already demonstrates instructional knowledge that derives from the Torah and the Prophets (even though the Latter Prophets continued to be edited until the late Persian period and the early Hellenistic period.

sions also arose periodically between these groups. The disputations of Malachi, in all likelihood, reflect one such period of disagreement.[39]

2.3. HOW WOULD THIS CURRICULUM HAVE FUNCTIONED?

Most discussions of the scribal curriculum tend to assume only one type of curriculum—that of a school setting. Certainly temple scribes would have received such training, but another model of training can also be inferred from the duties of the Levites. The Levites of the Persian period constituted a complex group of temple clerics whose duties included a wide array of tasks related to temple functions. Three such duties aid in piecing together how the Levitical curriculum was developing in the Persian period. These include: scribal composers and editors who worked in service of the temple, recurring periods of service that likely included text enhanced instruction, and the Levitic (and priestly) roles as teachers of the people.

First, as several have argued, a number of clues suggest that Levitical scribes played a significant role in the development of the canon in the Persian period.[40] Some of this evidence is more direct than others, but the cumulative picture helps to understand how the curriculum and the library were intertwined as they developed. Scribal activity in Persian period Yehud was centered in the temple, and not the royal palace. This fact would have affected the kind of training temple scribes received. Rather than working for the king, they worked for the priests and the temple. Some of these scribes would have been tasked with the composition of texts, everything from the composition of individual psalms to the collections of psalms that came to be the Psalter. These scribes would have recorded and expanded the compositions which kept the traditions of the

---

[39] For example, see the work of Julia M. O'Brien, *Priest and Levite in Malachi* (SBLDS 121; Atlanta: Scholars Press, 1988), esp. pages 143–48. She demonstrates that these disputations reflect an inner priestly debate about how the cult functions.

[40] Carr, *Writing on the Tablet of the Heart*, 201–206, 206–12. Carr demonstrates how, by the Hellenistic period, a number of pseudepigraphic works display explicit concerns with Levitic priestly interests (201–206), whereas Ben Sirah deals with many of the same motifs but in a very different way that reflects the concerns of the Aaronide priesthood more clearly. See also James D. Nogalski, "One Book and Twelve Books: The Nature of the Redactional Work and the Implication of Cultic Source Material in the Book of the Twelve," in *Two Sides of a Coin: Juxtaposing Views on Interpreting the Book of the Twelve/the Twelve Prophetic Books* (ed. Ehud Ben Zvi, James D. Nogalski, and Thomas Römer; Piscataway, NJ: Gorgias, 2009), 11–46. I postulate a close connection between the cultic interests and the cultic source blocks that play a prominent role in the Book of the Twelve as evidence of the involvement of Levitic circles.

past, including copies of the Torah (during and after the time of Ezra) and likely the scribes would have returned the scrolls of the Deuteronomistic History to the temple as well.[41] Additionally, copies of the scrolls of the prophets would have been collected there as well. According to Nehemiah, rooms for various groups appeared in the temple.[42]

Second, a number of texts, especially from the Persian period, portray the obligation of the Levites to spend designated periods of time at the temple for service.[43] The assumption in these middle to late Persian period texts appears to be that Levites would rotate times of service at the temple.

Third, one must consider the role of the Levites as teachers of the people. Concomitant with the expectation that Levites will periodically serve at the temple, the portrait of Ezra and Nehemiah highlights the role of the Levites as teachers in the Persian period (see Neh 8:3). Whereas a number of texts in the Deuteronomistic History portray the Levites in terms that are both cultic and militaristic (e.g. guarding the Ark of the Covenant) or depict them as working closely with the king in military contexts, such is not the case in these books where their cultic responsibilities take center stage.[44] The teaching role of the Levites appears to be deliberately accentuated in Ezra/Nehemiah and Chronicles.[45] Along with other cultic personnel, Ezra portrays the Levites as exempt

---

[41] These scrolls were likely kept and edited in Mizpah until some point after the reconstruction of the temple; so also, the implications of Albertz, *Die Exilzeit*, 82–83.

[42] In addition to the storehouse for the Levites that was given to Tobiah in Neh 13:4–9 before Nehemiah returned and removed his belongings, Neh 10:39 also refers to other storerooms and places where one can find the "priests that minister, and the gatekeepers, and the singers."

[43] For example, see Neh 10:34; 1 Chr 23:26–32. Also, the Chronicler's comment that Jeroboam prevented the Levites from going to Jerusalem assumes that periodic travel to the temple by the Levites was part of the Chronicler's assumptions about how David intended temple service to function. The tradition of Levite service at the temple is already woven into the narrative of the tabernacle: Num 1:47–54; 4:2–4; 8:18–26; 18:21–26; 31:30; 31:47.

[44] For example, see 1 Sam 6:15; 2 Sam 15:24; and 1 Kgs 8:4 where the Levites guard the ark. In the latter two instances, the ark also seems to accompany the king. In Ezra, the Persian period equivalent of this function is to protect the temple treasury (see 8:29–30, 33).

[45] While the role of Levites is not entirely lacking in the Torah, it appears more prominently in Ezra-Nehemiah and Chronicles. See especially 2 Chr 17:8–9 (part of a larger episode—2 Chr 17:1–19—added to the story of Jehoshaphat in the Chronicler's account) where the Levites have the Book of the Law with them as they travel throughout Judah teaching, along with officials from Jehoshaphat's court. Levitical priests instruct the people in statutes that will keep them healthy in Deut 24:8, but the teaching responsi-

from Persian taxes (7:24). When it comes to teaching, however, once the city wall has been restored, Neh 8 portrays a kind of new beginning of the cult. As idealized as this account may be, the expanded role of the Levites likely reflects changes in their involvement within the Jerusalem cult that presupposes increased responsibilities in comparison to earlier texts (even while the Levites appear to have accepted a second tier role in the clerical hierarchy in both Ezra-Nehemiah and Chronicles).[46]

3. IMPLICATIONS FOR MALACHI 3:16–18

The brief narrative report of the creation of a book of remembrance for the purpose of instructing Levites and others in how to distinguish between the righteous and the wicked that appears in Mal 3:16–18 offers a snapshot into the world of how the scribal curriculum came to include more than the Mosaic Torah. It offers a glimpse into the authorizing process of a book (likely the Book of the Twelve) whose official publication has both a sacral and an instructional component. That this book of remembrance was written "before the LORD" provides this book with a sacred authority since it has been sanctioned by YHWH himself. That this book was given to those fearing YHWH to study so that they might discern the things of God implies that the content of this book would help the group to remember the acts of YHWH in the past so as to keep the community grounded on the proper path for the future. Malachi 3:16–18 thus records the official publication of this book to be used for instruction and housed in the temple library. In all likelihood, the initial publication of this book of remembrance dates to the first half of the fourth century BCE and reflects an expanding curriculum for the temple elite to aid their instruction of the people. This publi-

---

bilities have expanded in Ezra and Nehemiah. In Ezra, Levites serve as ministers of the temple (8:15–20) and they help to fund the temple (2:69–70) and aid the priests in weighing the gold and silver (8:30, 33). They are also given oversight over the building of the temple (3:8) and performed as singers when the temple foundations were laid (3:10). The fact that these last duties are described as in accordance with the directions of king David (see also Ezra 8:20) indicates that the passage has a very different understanding of the role of the Levites than is presented in the Kings' account of the temple construction, which ascribes the temple building to Solomon without indicating a prominence for the Levites like one finds in Chronicles.

[46] Merely the distribution of references to Levites shows a significant increase in frequency. In Samuel and Kings, Levites are only mentioned four times combined (1 Sam 6:15; 2 Sam 15:24; 1 Kgs 8:4; 12:31) whereas the Levites as a group are mentioned more than seventy times in Chronicles, more than twenty times in Ezra, and more than forty times in Nehemiah.

cation does not, however, mark the closing of the canon, merely a step along the way. Since most of the redactional models of Malachi recognize Mal 3:22–24 as a later addition to Malachi, and also recognize the allusions to the beginning of Joshua, and the mention of Moses and Elijah within 3:22–24 as a means of joining the Torah with the Nebiim, it seems probable to suppose that the publication of this book of remembrance preceded the closing of the prophetic canon.[47] Nevertheless, the authorization of this book represents a significant moment in that process.

---

[47] See, for example, Christophe Nihan, "The 'Prophets' as Scriptural Collection and Prophecy during the Second Temple Period," in *Writing the Bible: Scribes, Scribalism and Script* (ed. Philip R. Davies and Thomas Römer; Durham: Acumen, 2013), 67–85 (77–78); and Thomas Römer, "From Prophet to Scribe: Jeremiah, Huldah and the Invention of the Book," in ibid., 86–96 (94–95).

13
CULT AND PRIESTS IN MALACHI 1:6–2:9

Aaron Schart

Within the Book of the Twelve, the writing of Malachi contains the longest unit dealing with cultic matters and the priests: Mal 1:6–2:9. Malachi represents the last writing of the Twelve and as such a reader expects at this place of the composition of the whole book the final and decisive word on a topic that has been dealt with several times by different prophets before. The end of a composition is a fitting place, where an author can emphasize or clarify things, before the author comes to an end and must leave it to the decision of the reader to draw the intended conclusions. Judging on the basis of the importance of the topic of the cult, and the priests specifically, in the eleven writings before, it is not surprising that especially the priests and the way in which they perform their duties seem to be so important that already the second disputation speech deals with this topic extensively. The reader gets the impression that the behavior of the priests, who are addressed explicitly (Mal 1:6; 2:1), is crucial for the question whether God's love and honor is revered adequately in Israel. This paper tries to explore the redaction history that led to the final text.

1. FORM-CRITICAL ANALYSIS

A sound foundation from which to start the form-critical analysis is the consensus that the writing of Malachi comprises six disputation speeches that share the same structure: a speaker who represents the divine voice refutes arguments of a specific group against God. In order to convince the opponents that their arguments are not only invalid but represent an attack on God's faithful character, the speaker formulates a logical basis which is undisputed between the parties.

In the second step the author quotes the opinion of the opponents. The quotation, however, does not give an accurate representation of what the opponents have actually said, but rather formulates what the speaker perceives as the intention of what the opponents actually do. In the third step the prophet tries to refute the arguments of the opponents. A prominent feature of this part consists of rhetorical questions that appeal to the ability of the audience to recognize and appreciate good arguments.[1]

The second disputation speech (Mal 1:6–2:9) is the lengthiest and most complicated one. It basically follows the structure of the *Gattung* but also displays some significant deviations. One has to distinguish between three speech acts which at the same time make use of different genres: the first one is a disputation speech (Mal 1:6–14), the second, starting with the phrase ועתה אליכם, is a threat (2:1–4a, 9), and a third part is embedded in this threat: a historical retrospective (2:4b–8) that starts with the phrase להיות, "in order that there will be."

2. Source-critical Analysis

Many of the studies that deal with the priests in Malachi take this passage to be a coherent unit written by one author.[2] However, there are many tensions, some of which can best be interpreted as a result of redactional activity.[3]

---

[1] For an explanation of the *Gattung* "disputation speech," see Aaron Schart, "Disputationswort," *Das Wissenschaftliche Bibellexikon im Internet* (www.wibilex.de), 2010.

[2] Beth Glazier-McDonald, *Malachi: The Divine Messenger* (SBLDS 98; Atlanta: Scholars Press, 1987), 42–80; Julia M. O'Brien: *Priest and Levite in Malachi* (SBLDS 121; Atlanta: Scholars Press, 1990), 81–82, and Lena-Sofia Tiemeyer, *Priestly Rites and Prophetic Rage: Post-exilic Prophetic Critique of the Priesthood* (FAT 2/19; Tübingen: Mohr Siebeck, 2006), 18. Joachim L. Schaper, "The Priests in the Book of Malachi and their Opponents," in *The Priests in the Prophets: The Portrayal of Priests, Prophets and Other Religious Specialists in the Latter Prophets* (ed. Lester L. Grabbe and Alice O. Bellis; JSOTS 408; London/New York: T&T Clark, 2004), 177–88 (179), admits that the text is a redactional unit, but discusses only the final text, not its earlier layers.

[3] Arndt Meinhold, *Dodekapropheton 8: Maleachi* (BKAT 14.8; Neukirchen-Vluyn: Neukirchener, 2006), 77, so far presents the most radical source-critical theory. According to him, the oldest layer only comprises Mal 1:6–8a; 2:1, 9a, which was expanded by a very complicated redactional process.

2.1. THE FORMULA אמר יהוה צבאות

I would like to start with the formula אמר יהוה צבאות, "the Lord of Hosts has said," which is attested eleven times within the passage Mal 1:6–2:9.[4] The formula often appears to be overly emphatic, superfluous, or disruptive to the flow of the poetic line and its rhythm.

Especially telling is the case of Mal 1:13 where the formula is completely displaced and even inserted into the midst of a verbatim quotation of the opponents! In this case it is obvious that the formula was inserted at the wrong place secondarily, but in many other cases the formula was probably inserted by a redactor or a scribe.[5] Only in Mal 1:6bα the formula is essential for the context and cannot be deleted, because the speaker's voice is identified with that of YHWH and the opposition between YHWH and the addressees is introduced, which is fundamental for the whole passage.

Scholars who wish to find a consistent pattern as to how this formula purposefully separates God's own words from those of the prophet finally must surrender. Rather, the formula seems to stress the fact that every word of the speech is exactly identical with the word of God.[6]

Why this formula was considered by someone or by several scribes as being so significant that it was spread across the writing in an irregular and arbitrary way is difficult to assess.[7] My assessment is that the opponents, against whom the disputation speeches are directed, did not give up their view. Rather, they questioned whether the author of the speeches was inspired by God. Those scribes who transmitted the writing of Malachi, in turn, insisted on their position and gave it greater authority by adding the formulas. Likewise, I would surmise that the opponents not only held their opinions, thereby insisting that they were fully in line with God's will, but also felt that the prophet did not represent their intentions in an accurate way. Many modern scholars would agree, because it is highly unlikely that the priests, for example, would deliberately and explicitly despise the name of YHWH (Mal 1:7, 12). In order to counter the resistance on the side of the opponents, the redactors who collected and published the disputation speeches added these formulas in order to underline that the prophet repre-

---

[4] The formula is attested in Mal 1:6bα, 8b, 9b, 10b, 11b, 13aα, 13b (without צבאות which is a scribal error), 14b; 2:2aα, 4b, 8b.

[5] E.g., Karl Marti, *Das Dodekapropheton* (KHC 13; Tübingen: Mohr, 1904), 463.

[6] Rainer Kessler, *Maleachi* (HThKAT; Freiburg im Breisgau: Herder, 2011), 131–32.

[7] Helmut Utzschneider, *Künder oder Schreiber Eine These zum Problem der "Schriftprophetie" auf Grund von Maleachi 1,6–2,9* (BEATAJ 19; Frankfurt am Main: Lang, 1989), 38.

sented the thoughts of the opponents in a way that truly reflects God's perspective.

2.2. MALACHI 1:6–7

Jakob Wöhrle has developed source-critical analysis of the second speech significantly.[8] Especially relevant is his idea that the basic layer in Mal 1 was not directed against the priests but against some group of lay people instead.[9] This hypothesis can satisfactorily explain why we have in the passage which is explicitly directed against the priests (Mal 1:6; 2:1) several statements that are clearly aimed at lay people. That this is the case was universally acknowledged, but was not seen as a signficant tension. The explanation usually was that the priests are responsible even for the misconduct of the lay people. This explanation certainly has some appeal, as it is indeed the task of the priests to control the temple cult: especially, they had the last word when it came to decide whether an animal could be sacrificed. If they made the wrong decision, the lay people who depended on the cultic system were misled and unintentionally offered sacrifices, which were not acceptable from the perspective of God. However, it would not have been appropriate for the prophet to attack the innocent lay people. Therefore, it was more satisfying to find a solution in which the lay-

---

[8] Jakob Wöhrle, *Der Abschluss des Zwölfprophetenbuches: Buchübergreifende Redaktionsprozesse in den späten Sammlungen* (BZAW 389; Berlin: de Gruyter, 2008), 222–33. Kessler, *Maleachi*, 234, has criticized Wöhrle's hypothesis, because his criteria for reconstructing an older layer were unwarranted. Kessler's critique, however, is much too radical and therefore not helpful. Kessler's ideas that an ancient author could arbitrarily shape a text against all standards of the *Gattung* better match postmodern literature than the world of old Israelite scribes. His example of the letter of Mesad Hashavyahu (TUAT 1, 249–50), where the author begins with speaking of himself in the third person and then changes unnecessarily to first person speech and back to third person, is not a convincing example against source criticism. First of all, one has to differentiate between an archival text and a literary text, as both follow different standards. Secondly, it is very probable that the text stems from two authors: the primary author is the worker, who appeared before the scribe, who actually wrote the letter, and who described his matter of concern orally, presumably in a state of anger. Then the professional scribe created the text according to the standards of the *Gattung* and used the oral report of the worker as a source for his text. In this way the tensions in the final text can easily be explained as a result of redactional activity. In the end, one has to evaluate every argument of Wöhrle's hypothesis and appraise its merits.

[9] Wöhrle, *Abschluss*, 225.

people were accused of what they did and the priests were accused of those things for which they were truly responsible.

Wöhrle has reconstructed a basic layer that is exclusively interested in the lay people and does not mention the priests. This layer comprises the following verses: Mal 1:6 (without הכהנים), 7b, 8a, 9b, 10b, 11b, 12*(without מגאל הוא), 13–14.[10] This layer was reworked by a redactor who added the following verses: Mal 1:6*(הכהנים), 7a, 10a, 12*(מגאל הוא); 2:1–9.[11] This redactor redirected the speech towards the priests (in Mal 1:6 the word הכהנים was inserted into the older material; in Mal 2:1 it was used in a passage formulated by the redactor him- or herself).

Wöhrle's source-critical analysis of Mal 1:6–7 is convincing, but needs to be further refined. The earlier layer which was aimed at a certain group of lay people will be referred to as, for the sake of convenience, the "lay people-layer." This layer can be distinguished from the second layer which will be referred to as the "priests-layer" because of its use of the vocative "priests" and by its distinct terminology:

- The lay people-layer uses the word שלחן, "table" (Mal 1:7b), the other layer the term מזבח, "altar" (Mal 1:7aα), to denote the place where the offerings are brought to God. The term שלחן, "table" is primarily used to refer to the place where food offerings are laid down, whereas מזבח, "altar," refers to the place for animal sacrifice.
- The lay people-layer accuses the opponents of despising (root בזה, Mal 1:6b) YHWH's name (שם, Mal 1:6b), whereas the priests-layer accuses the opponents of defiling the "bread" (לחם) or, even more dramatically, God directly (root גאל, Mal 1:7a).[12]
- Turning to the offerings, the lay people-layer speaks of people who bring מנחה, "an offering." to God (Mal 1:10b, 13), the offerings are also called לחם, "food," in Mal 1:12b. This terminology is used to refer to food offerings.[13] In contrast, the priests-layer presupposes animal sacrifice and is con-

---

[10] Ibid., 259.

[11] Ibid., 259. According to him, Mal 1:8b, 9a, 11a are even later insertions.

[12] In Mal 1:7a it is disputed whether the statement that God is defiled directly is original or an error by a later scribe. I would follow those who retain the 2m.sg. suffix גאלנוך as the *lectio difficilior*, e.g., Wilhelm Rudolph, *Haggai, Sacharja 1–8, Sacharja 9–14, Maleachi* (KAT 13.4; Gütersloh: Gütersloher, 1976), 257, against Wöhrle, *Abschluss*, 223, n. 16.

[13] The term מנחה "offering" never unambiguously refers to animal sacrifices; as a technical term it solely refers to food offerings. Likewise, it is only in Lev 22:25 and in Num 28:2, both verses belonging to very late additions to the Pentateuch, where it is

cerned with the quality of the animals (Mal 1:8: no blind, crippled or diseased animal should be sacrificed to YHWH).[14]

2.3. MALACHI 1:8

The status of Mal 1:8 is complicated. Malachi 1:8a and 8b are clearly two separate units. The use of the verb נגש and the root זבח in Mal 1:8a pick up terminology from Mal 1:7a. In addition, Mal 1:8a smoothly connects to Mal 1:7a and represents a fitting answer to the question of the opponents, who wanted to know how they specifically defiled YHWH. As a consequence, Mal 1:8a should belong to the priests-layer.[15]

Malachi 1:8b suddenly brings in a new theme. The opponents are asked ironically whether the Persian governor would accept the offerings which they bring to YHWH. One is supposed to conclude that the governor would of course not be pleased, and even more so YHWH.[16] At the same time, the first word of the verse presents several problems: (1) the root that denotes the bringing of the offerings changes from נגש to קרב, (2) the priests are now addressed in the singular (it is possible that the speaker singles out a specific opponent and asks him), and (3) the suffix הו is singular but should be in the plural if referring to the sacrifices mentioned in the sentences before. These are difficulties that allow one to suspect that Mal 1:8b is secondarily inserted. On the other hand, this break may also be explained by the vivid style of this disputation speech.[17] As a consequence, both halves of Mal 1:8 should belong to the priests-layer.

---

unambiguously clear that לחם "food" refers to animal sacrifices. In the other cases, which Wöhrle, *Abschluss*, 224, enumerates, it is ambiguous at best whether לחם refers to animals.

[14] Wöhrle, *Abschluss*, 224.

[15] Ibid., 226, tries to argue that Mal 1:8 is directed against lay people. However, Schaper, "Priests," 181, has shown that the usage of the verb נגש in this context denotes the priestly service. In addition, the final decision, whether an animal is allowed to be sacrificed, belongs to the priests. As a consequence, they are responsible if blemished animals are sacrificed.

[16] Kessler, *Maleachi*, 144.

[17] Wöhrle, *Abschluss*, 231, is convinced that Mal 1:8b is "sicherlich sekundär" (certainly secondary), however Kessler, *Maleachi*, 142–43, has good arguments to explain why the tensions are completely in line with the context.

2.4. MALACHI 1:9A

Malachi 1:9a is rather isolated within its context. It is neither the regular office of the priests to appease (root חלה) God's face nor is it the goal of the sacrifices to achieve this.[18] The request represents an interjection in which the speaker unites himself with the people around him ("mercy on us," first person plural). In addition, God is referred to as אֵל, not as YHWH.[19] The vocabulary alludes to the famous *Gnadenformel*, as attested for example in Exod 34:6.[20] Within the flow of the argument, it would be most fitting if the sentence had an ironical meaning, because the speaker knows in advance that the priests will not be able to heed this imperative.[21]

2.5. MALACHI 1:9B–10

Malachi 1:9b, without the superfluous formula אמר יהוה צבאות, seems to belong to the lay-people layer. It uses the expression מידכם, "from your hands" (Mal 1:9b, 10b, 13), which, as Wöhrle has rightly observed, in the context of sacrifice refers to the hands of lay people.[22] In contrast, Mal 1:10a seems again to be an interjection without cohesion within its context comparable to Mal 1:9a. Since it uses the word מזבח, it should belong to the priests-layer.

Malachi 1:10b, without the displaced formula אמר יהוה צבאות, belongs to the basic layer, because it uses the word מנחה and refers to the hands of the opponents. The declaration whether a sacrifice pleases YHWH (root רצה in Mal 1:10b, 13) is the genuine task of the priest, yet the addressees of the declaration are the lay-people who brought the sacrifice to YHWH.

2.6. MALACHI 1:11

Again, all of a sudden, the general statement in Mal 1:11 interrupts the series of sentences in direct address and a new topic is introduced: the cult of the nations. In addition, the framing sentence גדול שמי בגוים, "great is my name among the nations," singles out this verse. Also, the acceptance of non-Israelite cultic offer-

---

[18] Kessler, *Maleachi*, 146.
[19] Wöhrle, *Abschluss*, 231.
[20] Kessler, *Maleachi*, 146, and Meinhold, *Maleachi*, 120.
[21] The vast majority of commentators see irony at work here. Wöhrle, *Abschluss*, 231, and Kessler, *Maleachi*, 146, deny an ironical meaning.
[22] Wöhrle, *Abschluss*, 227.

ings that were celebrated at distant, presumably unclean places does not integrate smoothly with the mindset of the other disputation speeches.²³ As the verse Mal 1:11 belongs to neither the lay people-layer nor the priests-layer, one has to postulate a third layer. Because of the importance of the nations, it may be designated as "nations-layer."

2.7. MALACHI 1:12–13

Malachi 1:12a is closely tied to Mal 1:11b because אותו refers back to YHWH's name in Mal 1:11. At the same time, the sentence serves as a transition to the following statement in Mal 1:12b. Mal 1:12b represents an unmotivated repetition of Mal 1:7b. It seems reasonable to conclude that the whole verse Mal 1:12 was inserted by the same redactor who inserted Mal 1:11 in order to build a smooth transition to Mal 1:13.²⁴

Further, in Mal 1:12 the words מגאל הוא are secondary.²⁵ The same is true for the phrase ואת־הפסח ואת־החולה in Mal 1:13.²⁶ Both additions disturb the syntax of the sentences and were likely inserted by the redactor of the priests-layer in order to adjust the meaning of the older layer to that of the priests-layer. In Mal 1:12, the redactor picks up the word מְגֹאָל from Mal 1:7aα and thereby makes clear that the accusation of the older layer, namely to despise (root בזה) YHWH's name, and that of the priests-layer, namely to offer defiled sacrifices on the altar, are two sides of the same coin. Likewise, the phrase ואת־הפסח ואת־החולה repeats words from Mal 1:8aβ in order to explain to the reader what the metaphorically used גזול should mean: namely, nothing more than what was stated in Mal 1:8a. Thus the redactor wants the reader to identify the "robbed things" with the blemished animals. The simplest hypothesis would be to attribute these later additions to the same redactor who added the priests-layer.²⁷

---

²³ Wöhrle, *Abschluss*, 232.

²⁴ Curt Kuhl, "Die 'Wiederaufnahme'—ein literarkritisches Prinzip?" *ZAW* 64 (1952): 1–11 (2), has found that redactors, who insert a text passage into a given text, sometimes repeat words, phrases or sentences at the end of their interpolations that stem from the place, where they started to insert their own interpolation, in order to resume the flow of the original text ("Wiederaufnahme").

²⁵ Wöhrle, *Abschluss*, 231. The word וניבו probably is a scribal error and should be deleted.

²⁶ The sentence is clearly overloaded, but which words came in later? Most commentators consider גזול to be secondary (e.g., Meinhold, *Maleachi*, 70), but it is much easier to explain why someone inserted the citation from Mal 1:8aβ than the word גזול.

²⁷ Wöhrle, *Abschluss*, 230.

As Wöhrle has shown, there are significant hints that Mal 1:13 was originally directed against lay people: the word תלאה, "burden" (Mal 1:13a), much more likely refers to the difficult economic situation of the lay-people than to something from which specifically the priests have to suffer.[28] Likewise, the accusation that the addressees bring "robbed things" to the altar (גזול, Mal 1:13) most naturally refers to lay people, because priests would have difficulties to detect this moral fault by examining the animal for possible blemishes.[29]

2.8. MALACHI 1:14

The verse Mal 1:14 comprises two propositions, which are difficult to relate to one another. The first half (Mal 1:14a) lays a curse on a person who is cheating YHWH by withholding a good male animal, which was promised with a vow, and offering a bad animal instead. The curse brings in a new *Gattung* into the context that creates a tension. Yet, the tension may not be significant enough to postulate a source-critical break. Since the curse is clearly aimed at lay people it should belong to the lay-people layer, although clear terminological overlap cannot be shown.[30]

With Mal 1:14b the topic of the nations resumes. In addition, the sentence "my name is revered among the nations" is found twice in almost identical form within Mal 1:11. As a consequence, it is highly probable that Mal 1:14b belongs to the same redactor who inserted Mal 1:11b–12a.[31]

2.9. MALACHI 2:1–8

According to Wöhrle, all of Mal 2:1–9 belongs to the second so-called priests-layer.[32] However, within Mal 2:1–9 verses 4b–8 clearly stand out as a retrospective historical passage.[33] The phrase להיות that connects this passage with the

---

[28] Ibid., 228.
[29] Ibid., 229. Rudolph, *Haggai*, 264, admits this difficulty, and concludes that גזול must refer to animals "die von wilden Tieren angefallen und verletzt worden sind." Cf. also Pamela J. Scalise, "Malachi," in *Minor Prophets II* (John Goldingay and Pamela J. Scalise; NIBCOT 18; Peabody, MA: Hendrickson Publishers; Milton Keynes, UK: Paternoster, 2009), 317–69 (335) ("torn by predators"). However, this inference is unwarranted. See Utzschneider, *Künder*, 27, and Meinhold, *Maleachi*, 135.
[30] Wöhrle, *Abschluss*, 229.
[31] As in other cases, the formula אמר יהוה צבאות was inserted later.
[32] Wöhrle, *Abschluss*, 232.
[33] Meinhold, *Maleachi*, 85–86.

preceding context is used awkwardly. Normally it introduces the goal of the action, but in this case it introduces a retrospective perspective. In addition, the verses bring in a new concept, namely "the covenant with Levi" (Mal 2:4), also termed "the covenant with the Levite" (Mal 2:8b), even though the flow of the argument would require a covenant with the "priests" instead. It is clear that the final text identifies the priests and "the Levite," but the terminological difference is better explained, if the passage stems from a different hand. Together with "Levi," a new task comes into play: the teaching of torah. How this task is related to the offerings, which are in the focus of Mal 1:6–14, is left unexplained. Finally, the passage is framed by two almost identical lines (Mal 2:4b//8b).

The verse Mal 2:7 seems to be secondary within its context. The verse represents a tricolon within a series of bicola. Also, the verse interrupts the series of tempus *qatal* verbs which look back in the past, and makes a general statement instead (tempus *yiqtol* two times, followed by a nominal sentence). Especially verse 8 is designed as a sharp contrast to verse 6, which is softened by Mal 2:7. In addition, Mal 2:7 speaks of YHWH in the third person in the midst of a speech by YHWH. Finally, the ideal office of "a priest" (the singular form in Mal 2:7 stands in contrast to the plural used in the rest of the text) is described as providing דעת, "knowledge," and תורה, "torah," an unmotivated doublet to Mal 2:6a.[34]

The interpolation wants, on the one hand, to make clear that the task of the Levite to interpret and apply the torah (Mal 2:6a) belongs to the priest. On the other hand, the competence of the priest exceeds that of the Levite, because the priest is the "messenger of YHWH" which is a unique title for a priest.

2.10. MALACHI 2:9

Malachi 2:9 comprises two elements that need to be treated separately. In the first half, it is envisioned how YHWH will respond to those who despise YHWH's name. Ironically, YHWH will despise those people just as they despised YHWH, (the root בזה is picked up from Mal 1:6b, 7b, 12b).[35] This would be a fitting end to the whole section. As a consequence, the second half (Mal 2:9b), which unexpectedly returns to the speech act of accusation, appears superfluous; however, it follows yet another accusation. This time, the terminology, the phonology, the grammatical structure, and the metaphors are reminiscent of Mal 2:8a (דרך,

---

[34] Rolland Emerson Wolfe, "The Editing of the Book of the Twelve: A Study of Secondary Material in the Minor Prophets" (Ph.D. diss., Harvard University, 1933), 235; Marti, *Dodekapropheton*, 467–68, and Meinhold, *Maleachi*, 86–87.

[35] Meinhold, *Maleachi*, 75.

בתורה), and the phrase נשא פנים is used in Mal 1:8b, 9b.[36] Whereas the first half seamlessly fits into the basic lay people-layer, the intention of the second half transcends the cultic realm and reminds the reader that the whole torah, not only the cultic laws, needs to be fulfilled.[37] Therefore, it may stem from an even later hand than the one responsible for the priests-layer.

2.11. SUMMARY

Although the source-critical analysis is difficult, because the indicators for source-critical breaks are not always strong and some may be better explained by oral development or as stylistic variations, the combined evidence makes it plausible that there was a layer directed against lay people. To this basic layer a second layer was added which expanded the basic layer in such a way that the resulting speech strives to convince the priests, despite their opinion to the contrary, that they neglected their duties. This second layer may therefore be called the "priests-layer." A third layer contrasts the present activities of the priests, which offend YHWH's name and honor, with the ideal phase in history when God made a covenant with Levi and when Levi acted faithfully according to this covenant. A fourth layer with a significant profile included the statements which deal with YHWH's relation to the nations. Later, some isolated interpolations were inserted, which do not readily fit with any of these four layers. Summing up, the following hypothesis seems probable:

- the lay people-layer: Mal 1:6*, 7b, 9b, 10b, 13*, (14a); 2:9a
- the priests-layer: Mal 1:6 (only הכהנים "priests"), 7a, 8, 10a; 2:1–4a
- the Levi-layer: Mal 2:4b–6, 8
- the nations-layer: Mal 1:11, 12*, 14b
- further interpolations: Mal 1:9a; 2:7, 9b.

Each layer contains its own view on the cult of the criticized people.

---

[36] The word פנים in Mal 1:9b does not fit well into its context. On the one hand, the sense of the sentence "they lift up a face with the help of the torah" is difficult to determine. If it does mean "to show partiality" here (cf. 2 Chr 19:7; Deut 16:19), it would bring in a completely new aspect, which is unlikely at the closing of the section (Marti, Dodekapropheton, 468). Therefore, a simpler solution may be to assume a scribal error, e.g., one could restore פנים to פני, "my (= YHWH's) face," and let אינכם govern the second half, thus yielding a sense like "you do not care about me, when you apply the torah" (Marti, Dodekapropheton, 468).

[37] Meinhold, Maleachi, 75.

3. The Critique of the Lay People-layer: Bringing "Robbed Things" to Yhwh

The basic layer represents a vivid disputation speech, which seems to be coherent, at least in a broad sense.[38]

1:6a	בן יכבד אב	ועבד אדניו
6bα1	ואם־אב אני	איה כבודי
6bα2	ואם־אדונים אני	איה מוראי
6bα3	אמר יהוה צבאות	בוזי שמי [...] לכם
6bβ	ואמרתם	במה בזינו את־שמך
7b	באמרכם	שלחן יהוה נבזה הוא
9b	מידכם היתה זאת	הישא מכם פנים [...]
10b	אין־לי חפץ בכם [...]	ומנחה לא־ארצה מידכם
13aα	ואמרתם הנה מתלאה	והפחתם { אותי } [...]
13aβ	והבאתם גזול [...]	והבאתם את־המנחה
13b	הארצה אותה מידכם [...]	
(14a)	וארור נוכל ויש בעדרו זכר	ונדר וזבח משחת לאדני
2:9a	וגם־אני נתתי אתכם נבזים	ושפלים לכל־העם

The speech is aimed at a specific group who is addressed directly by the speaker of the disputation speech. The main fault of this group seems to be that it brings מנחה, "food offerings," to the table of the Lord in a way which the prophet perceives as despising Yhwh's name. This, of course, is a grave insult against

---

[38] The status of Mal 1:14a was already discussed. The transition from one line to the other is not always smooth. For example, it is difficult to ascertain to what זאת in Mal 1:9b specifically refers, but this is difficult on the basis of the final text, too. In Mal 1:13aβ a scribal error needs to be corrected (אותי instead of אותו).

God's person. The personal, inner-family relation to the father is the model against which the cultic service is measured. And, as a consequence, the prophet announces in the name of God that the offerings of this group will not be accepted by YHWH. The decisive point seems to be that the opponents offer גזול, "robbed things," to God (v.13). The underlying accusation that the opponents are robbers probably is meant metaphorically: as in Mic 2:2, the accused persons commit no crimes against formal law, but use legal stipulations in order to violate the intention of these. They increase their own riches by taking advantage of the weakness of their neighbours, who lose the material basis of their life.[39]

4. THE PRIESTS-LAYER: ACCEPTING BLEMISHED ANIMALS

The priests-layer changes the opponents of the disputation speech: the כהנים, "priests," are brought in as the officials, who are primarily responsible for the cult. The decisive accusation seems to be that they accept animals for sacrifice that are not acceptable for this purpose. As Lena-Sofia Tiemeyer has phrased it: "the prophetic criticism in Mal 1:8, 13aβ–14a targets anew the priests' negligence, this time accusing them of insufficient care for God's cult to ensure that the sacrificial animals fitted the prescribed regulations."[40] The final judgment, whether the quality of an animal matches the obligatory rules, was indeed the genuine task of the priests. As a consequence, the priests are rightly being held responsible.

A reason why blemished animals should be excluded is not given. One has the impression that the speaker does not need to give a reason, because this norm is a stipulation included in the torah and therefore needs no further explanation or motivation. And indeed, two passages are usually identified to which the prophet seems to allude: Deut 15:19–23 and Lev 22:17–25.[41] Because Lev 22:22 enumerates more criteria than Deut 15, it is quite obvious that it presupposes Deut 15 and expands its shorter list. Malachi 1:8 also expands the list with the word חלה, "weak, ill." In addition, as Malachi does need a stipulation upon which to build its argument, it must at least presuppose Deut 15.[42] Since Lev

---

[39] See, for example, Rainer Kessler, *Sozialgeschichte des alten Israel: Eine Einführung* (Darmstadt: Wissenschaftliche Buchgesellschaft, 2006), 114–26.

[40] Tiemeyer, *Priestly Rites,* 214.

[41] For example Scalise, "Malachi," 332; Karl William Weyde, *Prophecy and Teaching: Prophetic Authority, Form Problems, and the Use of Traditions in the Book of Malachi* (BZAW 288; Berlin: de Gruyter, 2000), 131.

[42] As Utzschneider, *Künder,* 49, points out, Mal 1:8 could also rely on a textual variant of Deut 15:21, be it an oral or written version.

22:22 and Mal 1:8a have nothing in common, besides what is also found in Deut 15:21, both probably drew independently from Deut 15:21.[43] In any case, the priests-layer threatens the priests by announcing that God will curse their blessings and will throw the excrement of the slaughtered animals in their faces, thereby making them unclean for any office in the sanctuary (Mal 2:2–3a).

5. The Levi-Layer: Failing to Teach Torah

The Levi-layer brings a different function of the priests into the foreground: their office of teaching the torah. The word תורה can be understood in a very narrow sense, as if the torah only consists of making decisions in cultic matters, for example, whether an animal can be accepted or whether a sacrifice pleases God. This narrow sense is suggested because the accusations in the context concentrate on cultic matters.[44] However, reading Mal 2:4b–6, 8 isolated from its context, a wider understanding of torah that includes moral norms becomes more appropriate.[45]

The Levi-layer appeals to an ideal state of the priesthood in the foundational time of Israel, including a covenant with Levi. Although we do not know for sure to what the phrase "covenant with Levi" refers, it nevertheless can be inferred that teaching of torah also includes remembering God's glorious acts in the past. The descendants of Levi fail to be faithful to their history with God.

6. The Nations-Layer: God's Name is Revered all over the World

Through the addition of Mal 1:11–12, 14, the topic of "the nations" enters the discourse. The cultic critique that was directed against the priests in Jerusalem is contrasted by the redactor with the ideal model of the cult of the nations. Their cultic acts serve as a norm against which Israel's conduct is measured. The questions of where exactly, what precisely, when actually, and especially who "among the nations" can bring offerings to YHWH, are left open.[46] But it is clear that the people among the nations who bring offerings do so, without coming to the temple in Jerusalem and without any guidance or teaching of *torah* by the

---

[43] Weyde, *Prophecy,* 133, proposes that Mal 1:8 drew on Deut 15:21 and also on Lev 22:22.

[44] Meinhold, *Maleachi,* 153.

[45] Henning Graf Reventlow, *Die Propheten Haggai, Sacharja, und Maleachi* (ATD / Neues Göttinger Bibelwerk 25.2; Göttingen: Vandenhoeck & Ruprecht, 1993), 144.

[46] Meinhold, *Maleachi,* 128.

priests there.⁴⁷ It seems to be enough that they acknowledge YHWH as "mighty king," which presumably implies more than only bringing offerings.⁴⁸ Offerings would not be pure and acceptable if the nations would not live up to the norms of God's reign.

7. THE HISTORICAL SETTING

The source-critical analysis is important for the reconstruction of the groups that stand behind the text. It is no longer necessary to find a coherent view on the priests that includes every line. One has to imagine that different groups rewrote the text in different times. Because they held different views on the cult and the priests, the final text is not coherent in these matters.

Since the lay people-layer does not even mention priests, the redactor of this layer presumably saw no need to attack them explicitly. From the perspective of the author, the priests probably had their share of responsibility, but those who were really responsible were the lay people.

The priests-layer redirected the critique against the priests. In this layer the priests are those who are responsible for misconduct in cultic matters. This could mean that in the meantime the situation had shifted and the priests indeed played a much more active role in promoting cultic life that was considered to be wrong by the author of the layer. Alternatively, the shift in emphasis could be explained by the assumption that this author, in contrast to the author of the lay people-layer, applied new norms and held different views on how the cult should work.

The priests-layer mentions only priests and no Levites. This could imply that the author of this layer did not know of Levites at the temple. This is unlikely, however, because Levites were already active at the temple in preexilic times and continued to be part of the temple cult in postexilic times. It seems to be more probable that the Levites do not appear in the text because the author of this layer concentrated the critique on the animal sacrifices of which the Levites were not in charge. Likewise, the blessing of Israel with the text from Num 6:24–27, to which this layer alludes, is also an exclusive task of the priests.⁴⁹

---

[47] Utzschneider, *Künder*, 57.

[48] Ina Willi-Plein, *Haggai, Sacharja, Maleachi* (ZBK 24.4; Zürich: Theologischer Verlag Zürich, 2007), 243.

[49] Especially Michael Fishbane, *Biblical Interpretation in Ancient Israel* (Oxford: Clarendon Press, 1985), has shown how many concepts from the priestly blessing are used in Mal 1:6–2:9, mostly in an ironical mode. The priests fail to achieve the goal of their office: to bless Israel, and will therefore be cursed.

The next layer, the Levi-layer, brought in "Levi" and the "Levite." In addition, a new task is mentioned, namely to teach torah (Mal 2:6). Although the *terminus technicus* "Levites" is not used in the text, it is reasonable to assume that the reader identified the descendants of Levi with the Levites who served as a *clerus minor* at the temple. Although it is not stated explicitly that the Levites belong to a lower level of the hierarchy of the temple staff, nothing in the text contradicts such an understanding. In any case, the redactor who inserted the Levi-passage (Mal 2:4b–6, 8) into the priests-layer must have held the opinion that the priests belong to the descendants of Levi, otherwise the insertion would make no sense within the flow of the argument. The same is true for the redactor who inserted Mal 2:7, who uses the term כהן within a context that deals with the covenant with Levi and declares that the "priest"—like the Levite—has the function to teach torah.

The nations-layer again does not mention any priests. It is only implicit that the priests in Jerusalem should respect and accept the offerings of people from other nations and should, by implication, try to integrate god-fearers from all over the world into the cultic service in Jerusalem.

Whoever inserted Mal 1:9a presupposed that it was the priest's task to appease YHWH, if the people have sinned against YHWH in the first place. Interestingly, the verse does not mention explicitly the expiation that can be done with sacrifices according to the Priestly source nor the feast of Yom Kippur. Instead, like Moses at Sinai (Exod 32:11), the priests must talk to God directly in order to urge him to be merciful.

8. The Context of the Book of the Twelve

8.1. Methodological Considerations

How and when the writing of Malachi became a part, presumably the last part, of a corpus that comprised several prophetic writings is difficult to tell. One has to evaluate different sets of arguments.[50]

The first set of arguments concerns the form of the involved writings. If different writings display significant similarities beyond those that are characteristic of the shared *Gattung*, these similarities could derive from an author intend-

---

[50] For methodological thoughts on how it can be determined that a writing belongs in the context of a larger corpus, see Aaron Schart, *Die Entstehung des Zwölfprophetenbuchs: Neubearbeitungen von Amos im Rahmen schriftenübergreifender Redaktionsprozesse* (BZAW 260; Berlin: de Gruyter, 1998), 133–40.

ing to include them within one collection. Verbal, together with grammatical and syntactical, repetitions are common indicators in this respect.

The second set of arguments concerns the content of the involved writings. If one writing cannot be understood by the reader without him/her having read a different writing beforehand, it is likely that this writing was included in a corpus and was positioned before the other.

The third set of arguments concerns redactional activities across the involved writings. A famous example is the stitching technique that some words or phrases, or even sentences, from the end of one piece of writing were inserted deliberately at the beginning of the following one.[51] To this set also belong compositional strategies to build structures that stretch over different writings. A famous example are the superscriptions of the D-corpus (Hos 1:1; Amos 1:1; Mic 1:1; Zeph 1:1) that construe a chain of prophets, in which Hosea was for a certain period accompanied by Amos and later by Micah.[52]

8.2. THE LAY PEOPLE-LAYER

If one examines the earliest written source, the lay people-layer, it is obvious that it alludes to different passages within the Book of the Twelve. One example is the use of the root גזל, "to rip off, rob" (Mal 1:13aβ), which alludes to Mic 2:1–2. The use of the root גזל, "to rip off, rob," is telling for the reader of the Book of the Twelve. This root was used by Micah to describe the sins of the people of Jerusalem:

> [1]Woe to those who devise wickedness ...
> [2]They covet fields and seize them (root גזל), // and houses, and take them away;
> they oppress a man and his house, // a man and his inheritance. (Mic 2:1–2)

The same root is used in Mic 3:2:

> [1]Hear, you heads of Jacob // and rulers of the house of Israel!
> Is it not for you to know justice?
> [2]you who hate the good and love the evil,
> who tear the skin from off my people (root גזל)
> and their flesh from off their bones. (Mic 3:1–2)

---

[51] James Nogalski, *Literary Precursors to the Book of the Twelve* (BZAW 217; Berlin: de Gruyter, 1993), 21–57, has studied this technique extensively.

[52] Schart, *Entstehung*, 39–46.

The transgressions that Micah brought to light resulted in the prediction that the first temple on Mount Zion would be destroyed (Mic 3:12). The reader of the Book of the Twelve can thus conclude that, when the crimes resume, the second temple will be in danger of being destroyed again. The rebuilding of the temple seems not to have changed the relation of the people to God fundamentally.

Another example is the statement מנחה לא־ארצה in Mal 1:10b, which alludes to Amos 5:22. Amos rejected the cult of his contemporaries using priestly terminology ironically. Again, it is a very sad experience of the reader of the Book of the Twelve that a significant group of the people—even after having heard cultic critique by several prophets, after the exile, and even after God granted a new temple—still does not communicate with God in an adequate way. At the end of the chain of prophets, this experience comes as a climactic insight: there will always be people who do use the name of God and perform rites on God's behalf but do not revere God rightly or show due respect.

Allusions like this suggest that the author of the lay people-layer wanted to display continuity to famous passages of his great forerunners, but they are not sufficient to postulate that this layer already was part of a multi-prophets corpus.

8.3. THE PRIESTS-LAYER

The priests-layer includes some more significant indicators. Ruth Scoralick has collected some observations which may suggest that the critique of priests in Hosea (Hos 4) and that in Mal 1:6–2:9 form a frame around the Book of the Twelve.[53] These observations are:

- Hos 4 follows chapters 1–3, which deal with the love of God. Likewise, the first disputation speech deals with the love of God to Israel.
- The passage Hos 1:2–9 culminates in the removal of YHWH's name "I am not 'I will be' for you!" (Hos 1:9). Likewise, YHWH's name is of central importance for Mal 1:6–2:9. Because YHWH's name is despised, the cult is not effective and the blessing of the people is interrupted.

---

[53] Ruth Scoralick, "Priester als 'Boten' Gottes (Mal 2,7)? Zum Priester- und Prophetenbild des Zwölfprophetenbuches," in *Die unwiderstehliche Wahrheit: Studien zur alttestamentlichen Prophetie. Festschrift für Arndt Meinhold*, (ed. Rüdiger Lux and Ernst-Joachim Waschke; ABGe 23; Leipzig: Evangelische Verlagsanstalt, 2006), 415–30, 427–28.

- The priests are responsible for the knowledge of God in Hos 4:1, 6 and in Mal 2:7. The combination of the terms דעת and תורה is only attested in Hos 4:6 and Mal 2:7 within the Twelve.[54]
- Of less importance is that the offspring of the priests is included in the punishment of the priests (Mal 2:3, however, the text is uncertain) and that the root כשל (Hos 4:5; Mal 2:8) and the word עון (Hos 4:8; Mal 2:6) are used in both passages.

These observations are of different weight. With the exception of Mal 2:7, they are not specific enough to conclude securely that a compositional frame was intended from the outset. They are certainly meaningful for the reader if it can be established on other grounds (e.g., the sequence on one scroll) that Hos 4 and Mal 1:6–2:9 form such a frame. Malachi 2:7, however, makes perfect sense if a redactor wanted to refer back to the first passage within the Twelve, where priests had been criticized. By doing so, the redactor may have sought to demonstrate that YHWH, even after the long history of apostasy, had not neglected the initial covenant with the priests. Malachi 2:7, however, represents a later interpolation. As a result, it cannot be postulated that the priests-layer was part of a multi prophets-corpus.

8.4. THE LEVI-LAYER

The Levi-layer displays no signs that allow us to conclude that it is part of a larger composition. The root כשל, "stumble" (Mal 2:8a), may allude to Hos 4:5 where it is proclaimed that an unnamed priest and a prophet will "stumble." However, in Malachi the *Hiphil* is used and a deliberate framing is not detectable. More interesting is the "covenant of Levi" (Mal 2:4b, 8b). The concept of a covenant with God can be found within the Twelve prominently in Hosea (Hos 2:20; 6:7; 8:1) and one time in Zechariah (Zech 11:10). Although it is remarkable that the concept of a covenant with God is with one exception attested only in Hosea and Malachi, i.e. what constitutes a frame around the Book of the Twelve, the differences within this concept are so significant that one cannot postulate a multi prophets-corpus on this basis.

---

[54] Meinhold, *Maleachi*, 159.

8.5. THE NATIONS-LAYER

The nations-layer, however, shows several indicators that suggest that this layer conceived Malachi as part of a multi prophets-corpus.

The first argument is that the nations-layer cannot be understood adequately without Jonah. If the reader had not read Jonah before, Mal 1:11 is unintelligible. Nowhere else in the Old Testament is it stated as a given fact that foreign nations, who do not even know the name of YHWH, bring food offerings to the God of Israel from the distant places where they live. That the portrayal of the nations as faithful admirers of YHWH is indeed in effect and is not only a hope for the end of history is demonstrated by the sailors in the Jonah-narrative (Jonah 1). They and especially the king of Nineveh are presented exactly as the type of persons among the nations who fear God. The sailors learn the name of YHWH and pray to him (Jonah 1:14) and even offer a sacrifice to him (Jonah 1:16). Because Jonah did not mention the name YHWH in his message to the city, the king does not use the name YHWH, but האלהים, "the god," instead. Nevertheless he perceives God's character as compassionate in the same way as it was revealed to Moses at Mount Sinai: the king alludes to Moses plea in Exod 32:12 and Jonah himself confirms that the king instinctively appealed to YHWH's compassionate character (Jonah 3:10, cf. Exod 34:6).

The second argument is the redactional technique of stitching together writings which follow after the other. The statement that "YHWH's name is great among the nations" and the title "king" (Mal 1:11, 14b) allude to Zech 14:9, 16. The collection of Malachi serves to illustrate that the eschatological picture of Zech 14 is already operative in the present time.[55] If Israel understands fully what will happen at the end of history, it should not wait for the time to come, but instead act accordingly in the present time.

To my mind, these arguments confirm the hypothesis that it was the redactor of the nations-layer who attached the formerly independent writing of Malachi to a preexistent multi-prophets book.[56]

---

[55] See also Aaron Schart, "Putting the Eschatological Visions of Zechariah in their Place: Malachi as a Hermeneutical Guide for the Last Section of the Book of the Twelve," in *Bringing out the Treasure: Inner Biblical Allusion in Zechariah 9–14* (ed. Mark J. Boda and Michael H. Floyd; JSOTS 370; London: Sheffield Academic Press, 2003), 333–43.

[56] In my model, Malachi was attached to the Joel-Obadiah-corpus which comprised ten writings. See Schart, *Entstehung*, 291–303.

8.6. THE LATER INTERPOLATIONS

The later interpolations Mal 2:7 and Mal 1:9a confirm this judgment. Concerning Mal 2:7 it was already mentioned that the interpolation alludes to Hos 4:6. In addition, the title מלאך יהוה can also be found in Hag 1:13 and may stem from the same redactor, although it is left unclear how the status of Haggai relates to that of a priest who is otherwise routinely called a נביא "prophet" (Hag 1:1, 3, 12; 2:1, 10).[57]

The short interpolation Mal 1:9a alludes to the self-disclosure of YHWH at Mount Sinai (Exod 34:6). The allusion to Exod 34:6 belongs to a network of similar allusions and citations at several places within the Twelve (Joel 2:13; Jonah 3:10; 4:2; Mic 7:18–20; Nah 1:2b–3a). Taken together, they describe God's essence as a just and compassionate God who will of course punish apostasy and wickedness, but ultimately is determined to forgive, despite the fact that Israel and the nations (see Jonah) have provoked God's anger.[58] In Mal 1:9a, this serves as a reminder to the reader that at the inner heart of the cult lays the necessity to reconcile God with God's people—and God will respond.

CONCLUSION

The disputation speech Mal 1:6–2:9 functions as a conclusion to the different passages that contain cultic critique in the Book of the Twelve. The importance of the cult as the field where Israel has to prove its reverence for God is definitely highlighted. There is no idea that Israel could exist without temple or without priests. On the contrary, the redaction history of the passage shows that the importance of the priests increased over time. On the level of the final text, the

---

[57] Marti, *Dodekapropheton*, 468.
[58] The network was discovered by Raymond C. van Leeuwen, "Scribal Wisdom and Theodicy," in *In Search of Wisdom* (ed. Leo G. Perdue, Bernard B. Scott and William J. Wiseman; Louisville, KY: Westminster John Knox: 1993), 31–49, and studied intensively by Ruth Scoralick, *Gottes Güte und Gottes Zorn: Die Gottesprädikationen in Exodus 34,6f und ihre intertextuellen Beziehungen zum Zwölfprophetenbuch* (HBS 33; Freiburg im Breisgau: Herder, 2002). Wöhrle, *Abschluss*, 363–419, postulates a redactional layer, the "Gnadenkorpus" to which all the allusions and citations belong. This hypothesis needs further evaluation. For a first step, see Aaron Schart, "The Jonah-Narrative within the Book of the Twelve," in *Perspectives on the Formation of the Book of the Twelve: Methodological Foundations, Redactional Processes, Historical Insights* (ed. Rainer Albertz, James D. Nogalski, and Jakob Wöhrle; BZAW 433; Berlin: de Gruyter, 2012), 109–28.

cult, the office of the priest, and the obedience of the torah are intertwined (Mal 2:7, 9b). Even if misconduct and defilement lead to the shutting down of the temple in the present time, in the future the incriminated cult and the priesthood will be cleansed (Mal 3:3–4) but not abolished.

The second disputation speech is not a literary unity but comprises at least four different layers. The basic layer contained statements directed against one specific group of lay people. The basic norm that is violated is that the people who bring offerings to God have to be in a status of moral integrity. They cannot, for example, offer robbed things to God. This critique is more or less in line with the critique of cultic acts contained in the former prophets in the Book of the Twelve.

Within the second so-called priests-layer, stipulations from the torah that deal with the quality of sacrificial animals are not only cited, but also taken to be the authoritative basis for the accusations of the prophet. As a consequence, the prophet appears as a person who applies the norms of the torah to the behavior of his or her contemporaries.

The Levi-layer highlights the teaching function of the priests. It is presupposed by the redactor that all priests belong to the offspring of Levi.

The inclusion of Malachi within the Book of the Twelve, whenever this was done exactly, brought along the concept that it is appropriate for the cultic service of God that the cult of the nations is perceived as a positive example and, by implication, as enriching the cult in Jerusalem.

In Mal 2:7 the priest, being a teacher of torah, is understood to be the "messenger of YHWH" and, by implication, to have equal status with a prophet whose most important function is to act as a messenger of YHWH. Nevertheless, the harsh critique of the priests contained in the disputation speech makes it clear that the task of the Levitical priests to serve as a communicator between YHWH and the people needs to be controlled by a prophet. In the end, only priests that accept prophetical control are eligible to serve as God's representatives.

AUTHOR INDEX

Aberbach, M., 124 n.28
Adelman, R., 124 n.29–30
Ahlström, G.W., 66, 67 n.11, 69, 85 n.11, 88 n.20, 135 n.18
Albertz, R., 34 n.9–10, 177 n.11, 180 n.21, 181 n.24, 183 n.35, 183 n.36, 184 n.39, 187 n.49, 202 n.19, 207, 210 n.41
Allen, L.C., 66–67, 69, 85 n.9
Anderson, F.I., 37 n.20
Assis, E., 51 n.1–2, 53 n.5, 54 n.6 and n.8–9, 55 n.11, 56 n.12, 56 n.15–17, 57 n.17, 58 n.19, 61 n.30, 70, 71 n.27, 72 n.30, 75, 79, 82 n.2
Baker, D.W., 141 n.38, 143 n.45
Barker, J., 51 n.1, 54 n.7 and n.9, 55 n.10 and 11, 55 n.12, 58 n.18
Barstad, H.M., 12 n.11, 25 n.43, 106
Barton, J., 51 n.1, 54 n.9, 62 n.33, 62 n.35, 66, 69 n.18, 70, 74, 74 n.38, 77, 83 n.4, 84 n.7, 85 n.10, 87 n.16, 87 n. 17, 88 n.18, 88 n.20, 102
Becker, U., 110 n.62, 113 n.68
Becking, B., 178 n.14
Beckwith, R., 204 n.26
Begrich, J., 56 n.13
Ben Zvi, E., 10 n.5, 31 n.1, 72 n.30, 132, 136, 137 n.23, 137 n.26
Bentzen, A., 103
Bergler, S., 113 n.68
Berlin, A., 134, 136
Beyse, K.-M., 176 n.9, 181 n.24, 183 n.36

Bič, M., 103 n.22
Blenkinsopp, J., 45 n.43, 194 n.2
Bob, S., 129 n.44
Boccaccinni, G., 44 n.39
Boda, M.J., 52 n.4, 55 n.11, 55 n.12, 56 n.15, 59 n.20 and n. 22–23, 59 n. 24, 60 n.28, 61 n.30–31, 62 n.32–33, 62 n.34, 76 n.44, 179, 181 n.28, 184 n. 38, 185 n.42
Bolin, T.M., 120 n.11
Bos, J.M., 10 n. 2, 11 n. 10
Brongers, H.A., 85 n.10
Butterworth, M., 59 n.25
Carr, D.M., 44 n.39, 47, 203, 207, 208 n.38, 209 n.40
Carroll, R.P.,67
Carter, C.E., 169 n.19
Cathcart, K.J., 43 n.35, 123 n.24, 124 n. 27,129 n.45
Chalmers, R.S., 43 n.35
Christensen, D., 143
Cogan, M., 133 n.10
Coggins, R., 67, 75 n.39
Collins, J.J., 34 n.9
Conrad, E.W., 163
Cook, S.L., 33 n.6, 35 n. 15, 58 n.18, 67, 78
Cooper, A., 76 n.45
Cowley, A.E., 206 n.30
Craigie, P.C., 103 n.22
Crenshaw, J.L., 70, 84 n.6, 84 n.7, 87 n.15, 88 n.18
Cripps, R.S., 100
Cross, F.M., 34 n.10, 39 n.26
Curtis, B.G., 166 n.16

Davies, P.R., 201
Day, J., 38 n.22, 41 n.33
Dearman, J.A., 10 n.5, 27 n.46
Delkurt, H., 178 n. 14, 179, 186 n.45, 188 n.50
Dell, K., 47 n.51
Dietrich, W., 143 n.44
Dijkstra, M., 111 n.64
Dillard, R.B., 67, 82 n.2, 88 n.20
Dion, P.E., 137 n.24
Dozeman, T.B., 120 n.11
Edelman, D., 150 n.3
Eichhorn, J.G., 181 n.24, 183 n.36
Eidevall, G., 109 n.53 and n.57
Elliger, K., 90 n.22, 162 n.10, 180 n.22, 182 n.29, 182 n.31
Engnell, I., 67
Ernst, A.B., 101 n.9
Ewald, H., 181 n.24, 183 n.36
Ferguson, H., 140 n.34
Fishbane, M., 227 n.49
Floyd, M.H., 146 n.59
Foresti, F., 107 n.43
Fox, M., 199–200, 203
Freedman, D.N., 37 n.20, 106 n.40, 109 n.54
Friedlander, G., 124
Garrett, D.A., 51 n.1, 67, 69 n.17
Geoghegan, J.C., 32 n.5
Ginzberg, L., 126 n.38
Glazier-McDonald, B., 90 n.22, 93 n.32, 94 n.34, 96 n.39, 154 n.15, 214 n.2
Gordon, R.P., 123 n.24, 124 n.27, 129 n.45
Goswell, G., 176 n.9
Grabbe, L.L., 149 n.1, 151 n.4, 152 n.6, 150 n.2–3, 153 n.10, 155 n.17
Greenfield, J.C., 133 n.9, 137 n.24
Greer, J., 110 n.59

Gunkel, H., 55
Gunneweg, A., 104
Hadjiev, T.S., 143 n.44, 147
Hagedorn, A.C., 144
Haldar, A., 103
Hallaschka, M., 177 n.10, 179 n.20, 180 n. 22, 181 n.23, 181 n.25, 182 n.29, 182 n.31, 183 n.34, 188 n.50 and n. 54
Halpern, B., 34 n.10, 35 n.14, 38, 38 n.24 and n.25
Hanhart, R., 181 n.25
Hanson, P.D., 166 n.16
Harper, W.R., 100
Hartenstein, F., 26 n.44
Hayes, J.H., 139 n.28, 144 n.46, 187 n.49
Hayes, K., 70
Healy, J.F., 19 n.27
Hendel, R.S., 101 n.12
Hiebert, T., 67 n.12, 69 n.18
Hilber, J., 102 n.18
Hill, A.E., 90 n.22, 97 n.41, 153 n.8 and n.9
Hoffman, Y., 33
Holladay, W.L., 70 n.23, 175 n.8
Horst, F., 107 n. 44 and n. 46
House, P.R., 57 n.15
Hutton, J.M., 34 n.10
Hyatt, J.P., 144–45
Irsigler, H., 133 n.8, 134 n.11, 135, 136 n.19, 143 n.43, 146 n.58
Japhet, S., 176 n.9
Jaruzelska, I., 10 n.3
Jauhiainen, M., 181 n.25
Jeppesen, K., 135 n.17
Jepsen, A., 178 n.14, 182 n.29
Jeremias, C., 178 n.14, 179 n.15, 181 n.24, 183 n.36, 186 n.44, 186 n.45

Jeremias, J., 11 n.9, 15 n.19, 21 n.31, 22 n.32, 23 n.34, 24 n.39, 27 n.46, 57 n.15, 64, 72 n.30, 106 n.39, 107 n.43, 107 n.46, 108 n.51, 112 n.65, 113 n.69
Kaiser, O., 101 n.9
Kapelrud, A.S., 66, 67 n.11, 103, 140 n.33
Kashow, R.C., 177 n.9
Keel, O., 24 n.37
Kellermann, U., 181 n.24, 183 n.36
Kelly, J.R., 76 n.45
Kennedy, J.M., 202 n.19
Kessler, J., 43 n.36, 175 n.5 and n.8, 176 n.9
Kessler, R., 215 n.6, 216 n.8, 218 n.16, 218 n.17, 219 n.18 and n.20–21, 225 n.39
Kim, H.C.P., 76 n.45
Klawans, J., 100 n.1 and n.3
Koch, K., 49 n.57, 107 n.43, 107 n.45–46
Köhlmoos, M., 21 n.30
Kratz, R.G., 139, 144, 178 n.14, 181 n.25
Krüger, T., 38 n.23, 102 n.12
Küchler, M., 24 n.37
Kuhl, C., 220 n.24
Landy, F., 10 n.4, 23 n.33
Langohr, G., 136 n.20
LeCureux, J.T., 51 n.3, 57 n.15, 62 n.32, 63 n.36, 63 n.39, 64 n.42, 70 n.23, 71 n.25, 71 n.29, 73 n.33–34, 76 n.46
Leeuwen, R.C. van, 233 n.58
Leuchter, M., 32 n.2–5, 34 n.10, 35 n.12–13, 36 n.16, 39 n.26, 44 n.38, 46 n.44, 49 n.56
Leuenberger, M., 175 n.5, 176 n.9

Levin, A., 36 n.17, 41 n.33, 42 n.34
Levin, C., 142 n.42
Levinson, B., 45 n.43
Lewis, T., 37
Limburg, J., 120 n.10
Lindblom, J., 116 n.1
Linville, J.R., 70, 71 n.25, 71, 78–79, 112 n.65
Lipiński, E., 137 n.24
Lundbom, J.R., 32 n.5
Lust, J., 108 n.47
Lyons, T., 51 n.1, 57 n.16, 62 n.33
Marsman, H.J., 14 n.18, 20 n.29
Marti, K., 100 n.5, 176 n.9, 179 n.15, 182 n.29, 182 n.31, 188 n.51, 215 n.5, 222 n.34, 223 n.36, 233 n.57
Martin-Achard, R., 106 n.41
Marx, A., 86 n.13, 91–93
Mason, R.A., 154 n.11 and n.13, 176 n.9, 179 n.15, 180 n.21, 181 n.26, 182 n.29
Mays, J.L., 101 n.8, 106 n.41
McComiskey, T., 107 n.43, 107 n.44
McConville, G., 69 n.17
McKenzie, S.L., 36 n.15, 93 n.32
McLaughlin, J., 110 n.60
Meadowcroft, T., 158 n.2
Meinhold, A., 214 n.3, 219 n.20, 220 n.26, 221 n.29, 221 n.33, 222 n.34, 222 n.35, 223 n.37, 226 n.44, 226 n.46, 231 n.54
Meyers, C.L., 159, 176 n.9, 178 n.14, 182 n.29–30, 182 n.32, 183 n.33, 183 n.37, 184 n.38, 186 n.45, 188 n.51
Meyers, E.M., 159, 176 n.9, 178 n.14, 182 n.29–30, 182 n.32, 183

n.33, 1983 n.37, 184 n.38, 186
   n.45, 188 n.51
Miller, J.M., 139 n.28, 144 n.46,
   187 n.49, 206 n.31
Miller, P.D., 111 n.64
Mitchell, C., 48 n.55
Möller, K., 106 n.41
Mowinckel, S., 47, 102, 110 n.62
Müller, R., 108 n.48
Murtonen, A., 103 n.22
Neusner, J., 126 n.35, 126 n.37 and
   39, 127 n.40–41, 128 n.42, 128
   n.43
Nihan, C., 45 n.43, 212 n.47
Nissinen, M., 33 n.6, 38 n.21, 39
   n.27, 40 n.31, 102 n.16
Nogalski, J.D., 31 n.1, 32, 48 n.53,
   51 n.1, 57 n.15, 63–64, 71 n.26,
   72 n.30, 72, 73 n.35, 108, 176
   n.9, 178 n.14, 181 n.24, 183 n.36,
   185 n.40, 198 n.8, 197 n.5, 198
   n.6, 209 n.40, 229 n.51
Norin, S., 108 n.49
Nurmela, R., 149 n.1
Nyberg, K., 14 n.18, 20 n.29
O'Brien, J., 82 n.1, 89 n.21, 94
   n.33, 94 n.34, 95 n. 37, 96 n.39,
   154, 197 n.5, 209 n.39
O'Kennedy, D.F., 176 n.9, 185
   n.42
Oblath, M., 34 n.9
Ogden, G.S., 66, 67 n.11, 69 n.19,
   70, 83 n.4
Pakkala, J., 34 n.10
Paul, S., 101, 107 n.41, 110 n.56,
   112 n.65–67
Peckham, B., 134 n.14, 145
Pedersén, O., 201 n.17, 202 n.18
Perlitt, L., 142 n.42
Petersen, D.L., 48, 90 n.22, 94
   n.33, 96 n.40, 153 n.9, 164, 166
   n.16, 180 n.22, 182 n.29, 182
   n.30, 182 n.32, 183 n.37, 186
   n.44, 188 n.50 and n.53
Petterson, A.R., 179 n.17, 181 n.25,
   185 n.42
Pfeifer, G., 107 n.44
Pietsch, M., 21 n.30, 132
Plöger, O., 168
Pola, T., 152 n.5, 178 n.14, 179
   n.15, 180 n.21, 181 n.23, 181
   n.25, 182 n.29–30, 186 n.45
Polley, M., 102
Pritchard, J.B., 170 n.21
Pyper, H.S., 120 n.10
Radine, J., 143 n.44, 147 n.60
Redditt, P.L., 53 n.5, 63 n.40, 70,
   90 n.22, 153 n.9, 154 n.12, 157
   n.1, 158 n.3, 161 n.8, 162 n.10,
   167 n.17, 168 n.18, 176 n.9
Reventlow, H.G., 104, 176 n.9, 178
   n.14, 179 n.15, 181 n.25, 182
   n.29–30, 182 n.32, 183 n.37, 186
   n.44, 188 n.50–51 and n.54, 226
   n.45
Roberts, J.J.M., 141 n.37
Robertson, O.P., 141
Römer, T., 212 n.47
Rose, W.H., 152 n.7, 175 n.5, 176–
   77 n.9, 179, 181 n.23 and n.25,
   182 n.29, 184 n.38
Rudnig-Zelt, S., 9 n.2
Rudolph, W., 101 n.10, 109 n.55,
   178 n.14, 179 n.15, 182 n.29–30,
   183 n.37, 186 n.45, 188 n.51, 188
   n.54, 217 n.12, 221 n.29
Rüterswörden, U., 19 n.27
Samuel, H., 132 n.6
Sasson, J.M., 76 n.44, 116–17, 118
   n.7–8, 119 n.9, 120 n.10, 123
   n.20, 124 n.24
Scalise, P.J., 221 n.29, 226 n.41

Author Index

Schaper, J.L., 149 n.1, 154, 214 n.2, 218 n.15
Scharbert, J., 140, 142
Schipper, J., 34 n.10
Schütte, W., 132
Scoralick, R., 230, 233 n.58
Segal, M., 185 n.42
Seifert, B., 10 n.5
Seitz, C.R., 71 n.26
Sellin, E., 100 n.4
Seow, C.L., 43 n.37, C.L., 44, 102 n.16
Seybold, K., 142, 162 n.10
Siegert, F., 125
Simkins, R.A., 56 n.15, 70
Smith, J.M.P., 136 n.20
Smith, M.A., 37 n.19, 41 n.32, 46 n.47–48
Smolar, L., 124 n.28
Soggin, A., 101 n.10, 109 n.55
Spieckermann, H., 132 n.7, 133 n.10, 135 n.16, 136 n.19
Stager, L.E., 35 n.11
Stark, C., 14 n.18
Stavrakopoulou, F., 34 n.10
Stead, M.R., 179 n.15, 185 n.42
Steck, O.H., 203 n.23
Steins, G., 110 n.61
Stern, E., 187 n.49
Stökl Ben Ezra, D., 122 n.19, 125 n.34
Stonehouse, G.G.V., 139 n.30
Strazicich, J., 76 n.45, 120 n.11
Striek, M., 147
Stuart, D., 70, 71 n.25, 94 n.34
Sweeney, M.A., 33 n.6, 51 n.1, 53 n.5, 58 n.18, 59, 64, 67, 69 n.17, 70, 71 n.27, 72, 74 n.36, 74, 84,

87 n.14 and n.16, 134, 136, 146 n.59
Szeles, M.E., 140 n.30
Thiessen, M., 36 n.16
Tiemeyer, L.-S., 16 n.22, 24 n.38, 45 n.42, 47 n.50, 60 n.26, 60 n.29, 113, 122 n.16, 162 n.9, 164, 178 n.14, 179 n.16, 179 n.19, 214 n.2, 225
Tollington, J.E., 175 n.5, 176 n.9, 178 n.14, 179 n.15, 180 n.21, 180 n.22, 181 n.25, 188 n.50
Toorn, K. van der, 40 n.31, 33–34, 40, 44 n.37, 46 n.45, 48 n.54, 203–207
Towner, W.S., 163
Tucker, G.M., 111 n.63
Uehlinger, C., 24 n.37, 132
Ussishkin, D., 171 n.22
Utzschneider, H., 198 n.9, 215 n.7, 221 n.29, 226 n.42, 227 n.47
VanderKam, J.C., 186 n.45, 187 n.48
Veijola, T., 140–41
Verhoef, P.A., 90 n.22
Vielhauer, R., 9 n.2, 33 n.6, 44 n.37
Vlaardingerbroek, J., 133 n.10, 134 n.12, 135 n.16, 139 n.27, 146 n.59
Volz, P., 100
Vuilleumier, R., 95 n.36, 104
Wade, G.W., 139 n.30
Wallace, H.N., 93 n.32
Wanke, G., 175 n.8
Waschke, E.-J., 112 n.66, 113 n.68
Watson, D., 70
Watts, J.D.W., 107 n.44, 198 n.7
Watts, J.W., 44 n.39
Welch, E.L., 145 n.55

Wellhausen, J., 99–100, 179 n.15, 182 n.29, 186 n.45, 188 n.54
Werlitz, J., 105 n.37
Weyde, K.W., 225 n.41, 226 n.43
Whitt, W.D., 36 n.15
Williams, D., 145–46
Williamson, H.G.M., 194 n.2
Willi-Plein, I., 163, 176 n.9, 179 n.15, 184 n.38, 185 n.42, 188 n.51 and n.53, 227 n.48
Wöhrle, J., 59 n.25, 63, 121, 173 n.1, 174 n.2, 177 n.10 and n.12, 216–17, 218 n.13–15, 219, 220 n.23 and n.25, 221, 233 n.58
Wolfe, R.E., 222 n.34
Wolff, H.W., 51 n.1, 66–67, 69 n.17, 69–71, 84 n.5, 84 n.7, 86 n.12, 87 n.16, 87 n.17, 88 n.19, 101 n.9, 106 n.41, 117 n.4, 120 n.10, 159 n.4
Wolters, A., 160 n.7, 168 n.18
Woude, A.S. van der, 178 n.14
Würthwein, E., 103–104
Zevit, Z., 100 n.3

SCRIPTURE INDEX

HEBREW BIBLE

GENESIS
Genesis, book of, 36 n.15
26:24, 176 n.9
38:21, 14 n.17
38:22, 14 n.17

EXODUS
Exodus, book of, 33
12:36, 162
15:3–12, 42
15:13–17, 42
15:13, 36 n.16
15:17, 42
17:8–13, 193
17:14, 192–93, 195–96
20:18, 56 n.14
24:12, 195
27:3, 110 n.58
28:36–38, 163
28:36, 163 n.13
29:38–42, 54 n.9
32:7, 39
32:11–14, 110
32:11, 228
32:12, 232
34:6–7, 76
34:6, 219, 232–33
34:27, 195
38:3, 110 n.58

LEVITICUS
1:3–4, 109, n.52
chs. 4–5, 91 n.24
7:12, 117

8:9, 165
16:8–10, 116
22:17–25, 225
22:22, 108 n.52, 225, 226 n.43
22:25, 217 n.13
23:13, 38 n.25, 54 n.9
23:18, 54 n.9
25:9, 56 n.14

NUMBERS
1:47–54, 210 n.43
3:6–13, 94 n.34
4:2–4, 210 n.43
4:14, 110 n.58
6:15 54 n.9
6:24–27, 227
ch. 7, 113 n.58
8:5–22, 94 n.34
8:18–26, 210 n.43
10:9, 56 n.14
10:1–10, 56 n.14
12:7, 176 n.9
15:24, 54 n. 9
17:21–22, 196 n.4
18:8–32, 84 n.8
18:21–26, 210 n.43
ch. 25, 94 n.33 and n.34
28:2, 217 n.13
28:3–9, 54 n.9
29:11, 54 n.9
29:16–39, 54 n.9
31:30, 210 n.43
31:47, 210 n.43

DEUTERONOMY
Deuteronomy, book of, 32, 38, 45,
  94 n.34, 141
1:1–5, 32
ch. 12, 107, 112
12:5, 108
15:19–23, 225
15:21, 226
16:19, 223 n.36
17:18, 195
18:1–5, 84 n.8
18:15–22, 45 n.43
18:15–18, 45, 46
23:18, 14 n.17
24:1, 195
24:3, 195
24:8, 210 n.45
ch. 28, 88 n.20, 93 n.32
29:24–26, 58
ch. 32, 36
32:10, 42
32:13, 42
32:16, 40
32:17, 39, 38 n.25, 39
ch. 33, 95 n.34
33:8–10, 94 n.34
33:29, 42
ch. 34, 32
34:10–12, 46

JOSHUA
Joshua, book of, 208 n.38, 212
6:4–20, 56 n.14
6:5, 56 n.14
6:10, 56 n.14
6:16, 56 n.14
6:20, 56 n.14
7:14–18, 116
8:32, 195
24:29, 176 n.9

JUDGES
2:8, 176 n.9
3:27, 56 n.14
6:34, 56 n.14
7:18, 56 n.14
7:20, 56 n.14
7:21, 56 n.14
11:30, 117
15:14, 56 n.14
20:9, 116
20:26, 86

1 SAMUEL
Samuel, book of, 210 n.45 and n.46
1:9, 184 n.38
1:11, 117
1:21–22, 117
2:28, 176 n.9
4:5, 56 n.14
6:15, 210 n.44, 211
10:24, 56 n.14
10:25, 204 n.25
14:35–42, 116
17:52, 56 n.14

2 SAMUEL
1:12, 86
3:18, 175 n.6
6:21, 175 n.7
7:5, 175 n.6
7:8, 175 n.6
12:30, 184 n.38
15:24, 210 n.44

1 KINGS
Kings, the book, 4, 204, 208 n.38
  210 n.45 and n.46, 211 n.46
1:13, 184 n.38
1:50–53, 106
2:3, 186
2:28–29, 106

3:6, 179 n.64
3:14, 186 n.46
5:5, 164
7:40, 110 n.58
7:45, 110 n.58
7:50, 110 n.58
8:4, 210 n.44, 210 n.46, 211
8:5, 186 n.46
8:24, 175 n.6
8:25, 175 n.6
8:44, 175 n.7
9:6–9, 58
11:7, 137
11:13, 175 n.6
11:32, 175 n.6
11:33, 186 n.46
11:34, 175 n.6–7
11:36, 175 n.6
11:38, 175 n.6, 186 n.46
12:25, 34
12:26–30, 107
12:28, 34
12:31, 34
12:26–30, 107
12:28, 34
12:31, 34
13, 142
13:33–34, 107
14:8, 175 n.6
14:24, 14 n.17
15:15, 14 n.17
15:30, 107
16:11, 184 n.38
16:31, 107
18:36, 176 n.9
22:10, 184 n.38
22:47, 14 n.17

2 KINGS
2 Kings, book of, 138–39, 142–43, 144
4:10, 184 n.38
9:36, 176 n.9
10:10, 176 n.9
11–12, 155
14:25, 119, 176 n.9
16:10–18, 137
16:10–16, 133
16:18, 133
17:29–31, 137
19:34, 175 n.6
20:6, 175 n.6
21:22, 186 n.46
chs. 22–23, 138–39, 143
ch. 22, 139, 204 n.25
22:3, 141
22:15–20, 143
ch. 23, 38, 140, 142–43, 145
23:4–20, 142
23:4, 146
23:5, 4, 14 n.16, 15, 132, 133, 135, 137–38
23:7, 14 n.17
23:12, 133
23:15, 107
23:15–16, 106 n.39
23:31, 146, 148
23:36, 148
24:2, 145
24:6, 148
24:18, 148
25:15, 110 n.58
25:18, 145
25:21, 146

ISAIAH
Isaiah, book of, 59 n.23, 99, 208 n.38
1:1–20, 59 n.23
3:23, 186 n.43
ch. 6, 112
10:1–11, 70 n.24
20:3, 176 n.9
28:1, 184 n.38
28:3, 184 n.38
37:35, 175 n.6
41:9, 176 n.9
42:1, 176 n.9
42:13, 56 n.14
43:10, 176 n.9
chs. 44–45, 208 n.38
49:7, 176 n.9
62:3, 186

JEREMIAH
Jeremiah, book of, 32, 38, 38 n. 25, 94 n.34, 99–100, 111, 113, 139, 152, 154
1:1, 32
1:13–16, 70 n.24
1:15, 184 n.38
2:11, 38 n.25
3:6–10, 139
5:7, 38 n.25
6:1, 56 n.14
6:22–23, 70 n.24
7:9, 38 n.25
11:12–13, 38 n.25
11:17, 38 n.25
12:16, 38 n.25
13:18, 184 n.38
14:1–15:4, 55 n.11
14:11–12, 111
14:12, 108 n.52
20:1–6, 111
ch. 21, 146

21:12, 186 n.46
22:8–9, 58
22:15–16, 139
22:16, 186 n.46
22:18–19, 134 n.14
22:24–25, 175
22:24, 175, 176 n.9
23:5–6, 152
23:5, 183, 188
23:13, 38 n.25
26:19, 140 n.30
27:3, 147
ch. 29, 146
29:24–32, 111
30:21, 180
ch. 33, 95 n.34
33:15, 183, 188
33:18–22, 94 n.34
33:21, 175 n.6
33:22, 175 n.6
33:26, 175 n.6
41:5, 54 n.9, 75, 75
51:64b, 32
52:1, 148
52:24, 145

EZEKIEL
Ezekiel, book of, 95 n.34, 142, 152, 154
16:12, 184 n.38
20:40–41, 108 n.52
21:31, 184 n.38
23:2–4, 95 n.34
23:42, 184 n.38
28:25, 176 n.9
34:23, 175 n.6
34:24, 175 n.6
37:24, 175 n.6
37:25, 176 n.9
41:22, 91 n.23
44:16, 91 n.23

44:15–16, 94 n.34
44:23–24, 94 n.34

HOSEA
Hosea, book of, 199, 208 n.38
chs. 1–3, 28, 230
1:1, 74 n.35, 229
1:2–9, 230
1:9, 11, 230
ch. 2, 37
2:1–2, 37, 39, 41
2:9, 13
2:15–19, 39
2:15, 13
2:16–17, 37, 95 n.34
2:20, 231
ch. 3, 28
3:4, 13, 28
3:5, 13
chs. 4–11, 11, 13, 19, 28
ch. 4, 6, 230, 231
4:1, 231
4:4–10, 81
4:4, 15
4:5, 16, 231
4:6–9, 73
4:6, 95 n.35, 231, 233
4:7–8, 24
4:7, 15
4:8, 15, 19, 231
4:9, 16, 19
4:11, 19, 21
4:12, 12 n.14, 19, 20, 28
4:13, 14, 16, 18, 20, 24
4:14, 14–16, 18, 20
4:15, 18 n.26
5:1–6:6, 23
ch. 5, 21, 23
5:1, 10, 16, 22–23

5:2, 22
5:3, 22–23
5:4, 18, 22–23
5:5, 22
5:6, 17–18, 21–23
5:7, 22
5:8, 56 n.14, 22–23
5:9, 22
5:10, 22
5:12, 23
5:15, 18
ch. 6, 21, 23
6:1–3, 11, 21, 23, 27
6:1, 22
6:2, 22
6:3, 23 n.35, 27
6:4–6, 22
6:5, 16, 23
6:6, 21, 23, 28, 74
6:7, 231
6:9, 16, 23, 81
7:13–16, 26, 27
7:13, 16, 26
7:14, 26–27
7:16, 27
8:1, 17, 231
8:2, 11, 27
8:5, 18, 24
8:6–8, 24
8:6, 18, 24
8:10, 70 n.24
8:11–12, 73
8:11, 18–19, 24
8:13, 17, 24
ch. 9, 19
9:1–5, 25
9:1–2, 25
9:1, 24
9:3–6, 17

9:3–5, 24
9:3–4, 24
9:4, 17
9:5, 25
9:6, 17
9:7, 11, 16–17, 27
9:8, 16–17, 45
9:15, 17
9:15, 24 n.36
ch. 10, 25
10:1, 18–19, 25–26
10:2, 19, 25–26
10:3, 11, 26
10:4, 26
10:5–8, 25, 135
10:5, 4, 14 n.16, 15, 25, 132–35, 137
10:6, 25, 135
10:7, 26
10:8, 15, 19, 26
11:1–4, 38–40
11:1, 39
11:5, 39 n.27
chs. 12–14, 39
ch. 12, 39
12:5–6, 39 n.27
12:5, 39 n.27, 42 n.35
12:10–15, 28
12:14, 39, 45
12:13–14, 39
ch. 13, 28
13:1, 28
13:2, 18 n.25, 28, 117
13:4–6, 40
13:4–11, 40
13:5, 40
13:9–11, 40
13:14–14:1, 41–42
ch. 14, 41, 62 n.32, 72, 73, 79
14:1–3, 56 n.15
14:2–9, 42

14:2–5, 73 n.33
14:2–4, 42
14:2–3, 70 n.23
14:3–4, 42
14:3, 73
14:5–9, 41
14:5, 70 n.23
14:9, 28
14:10, 43–44, 48
14:14, 73

JOEL
Joel, book of, 232 n.56
chs. 1–2, 2, 52, 53, 61, 65, 69, 75
ch. 1, 87 n.16
1:2–2:27, 51, 53–54, 57–58
1:2–3, 53
1:2, 55, 57, 68, 73 n.33
1:3, 68
1:4, 83
1:5, 53–54, 68, 73, 89 n.20
1:8–17, 59
1:8–10, 58
1:8–9, 54–56
1:8, 53–54, 57, 68, 81
1:9, 68–69, 84
1:10, 57
1:11, 53–54, 84
1:12–13, 56
1:12, 57, 83
1:13–2:17, 54–55
1:13–20, 57
1:13–14, 53, 55, 57, 68, 71, 85, 87
1:13, 53–54, 68–69, 73
1:14, 55 n.10, 68, 85
1:15–20, 56–57
1:15, 55
1:16, 87, 90
1:17–20, 83
1:18, 57, 84, 128
1:19–20, 57

1:19, 83
1:20, 84
ch. 2, 56, 69, 71
2:1–11, 87 n.16
2:1, 53
2:2, 55, 71
2:3, 83
2:4–9, 55
2:4, 87 n.16
2:5, 87 n.16
2:7, 87 n.16
2:9, 71
2:10, 55
2:11, 53, 76
2:12–14, 2, 62 n.32, 65, 68–69, 73–74, 78, 79, 121
2:12–13, 56 n.15, 79, 121
2:12, 53, 69, 70 n.23, 71, 73, 86
2:13–14, 76, 120–21
2:13, 53, 56, 71, 127, 233
2:14, 53, 56–57, 69, 71, 76, 86
2:15–17, 53, 55, 68
2:15–16, 57
2:15, 53, 68
2:16, 53, 68
2:17, 53, 68, 75, 78, 87–88, 90
2:18–27, 57, 76, 87, 89
2:18–19, 62 n.33
2:18, 53, 88
2:19, 53, 88
2:20, 70 n.24
2:21–23, 57
2:21, 53–54
2:22, 53
2:23, 53
2:28–32, 58, 66 n.2
3:1–4:21, 51, 78, 82 n.3
3:1–21, 66 n.2
3:1–5, 58, 66

3:5, 58
ch. 4, 58
4:16, 78
4:17, 78
4:21, 78

AMOS
Amos, book of, 2–3, 32–33, 43, 71–74, 77, 81, 82, 99–114, 197 n.5, 208 n.38, 230
chs. 1–2, 103
1:1, 74 n.35, 103, 105, 229
1:3–2:3, 103
1:2, 107, 114
1:3–2:16, 104
2:4–5, 73
2:6–8, 105
2:8, 34 n.10, 68, 73, 105
2:12, 73
3:14, 68, 73, 105–6, 109, 111, 114
chs. 4, 57 n.15
4:4–5, 73, 100–103, 106, 107, 109, 114
4:9, 71
4:6–11, 104
4:13, 104, 107, 113
5:4–5, 69, 100, 103, 106–7, 109, 111–12, 114
5:4, 18 n.26, 106, 114
5:5, 18 n.26, 106
5:8, 104, 107, 108
5:16–17, 111
5:18–20, 70, 103, 108
5:21–26, 69, 73
5:21–24, 82, 100–103, 108–109, 114
5:21–22, 108–109
5:22, 6, 230
5:25, 100, 109

5:26, 137 n.25
6:1–7, 110
6:4–7, 110
6:4–6, 110
6:6, 111
6:7, 111
6:14, 70 n.24
7:1–6, 103, 106, 110
7:1–2, 71
7:7–8, 103
7:9, 111
7:10–17, 73, 105, 111
7:10–11, 111
7:10, 81
7:13, 111
7:13, 135
7:14–15, 104
7:14, 104, 106
7:15, 104
7:17, 111
8:1–2, 103
8:3, 73, 111
8:10, 111
8:13–14, 112
8:14, 112, 114
9:1–4, 113
9:1, 112–14
9:5–6, 104, 107, 113
9:11, 160
9:11–15, 114

OBADIAH
Obadiah, book of, 63 n. 37, 63
  n.38, 74 n.36, 198, 232 n.56

JONAH
Jonah, book of, 2, 4, 6, 61, 62 n.33,
  67, 76 n.45, 77, 232–33
ch. 1, 118–19, 232
1:3, 118, 127, 129
1:5, 115, 117, 121 n.12, 129

1:6, 116, 121 n.12
1:7, 116
1:8, 121 n.12
1:10, 121 n.12
1:12, 118, 123, 125–26
1:14, 116, 129, 232
1:15, 116
1:16, 117, 119, 122–25, 232
ch.2, 118–21
2:2–10, 121 n.12
2:3, 118
2:5, 118
2:8, 118
2:9, 119
2:10, 119
chs. 3–4, 119
ch. 3, 79
3:4, 76
3:5, 119, 129
3:6–10, 121 n.12
3:6, 119
3:7, 76, 119
3:8, 119, 128
3:9, 76, 120–21
3:10, 77, 127, 232–33
ch. 4, 77, 118–19
4:1–4, 121 n.12
4:2, 121–22, 233
4:6, 121 n.12
4:10–11, 121 n.12

MICAH
Micah, book of, 32, 43, 63, 72, 77,
  81, 82, 140 n.30, 197 n.5, 208
  n.38, 229, 230
1:1, 73 n.35, 229
1:2, 118
1:5–7, 73
2:1–2, 6, 229
2:2, 225, 229
3:1–2, 229

3:2, 229
3:5, 19
3:11, 15, 81
3:12–4:5, 72, 74
3:12, 230
4:1–5, 78
4:4, 163
4:6–7, 298 n.5
6:6–8, 73, 82
7:18–20, 69, 233

NAHUM
Nahum, book of, 32, 63 n.37, 63
  n.38, 69 n.20, 81
1:2–3, 233
3:15–16, 198 n.5

HABAKKUK
Habakkuk, book of, 63 n.37, 63
  n.38, 81
1:1–11, 70 n.24
1:1–5, 69 n.20
2:20, 118, 162

ZEPHANIAH
Zephaniah, book of, 4, 52 n.4, 63,
  81, 131, 140 n.30, 198 n.5
ch. 1, 70
1:1, 138, 229
1:4–6, 4, 139–40, 142
1:4–5, 131, 134–35
1:4, 14 n.16, 15, 81, 131, 133 n.8,
  135–38, 140 n.30, 141, 144, 148
1:5, 132, 135 n.17, 136
1:8, 138, 141, 147
2:4–7, 145
2:5, 145
2:12, 145

2:13–15, 145
3:4, 81, 131, 137–38, 144, 148
3:18–19, 198 n.5

HAGGAI
Haggai, book of, 2, 4, 5, 52, 62, 81,
  97, 114, 149–50, 173, 173–77,
  189, 297 n.5, 208 n.38, 233
ch. 1, 29
1:1–6, 158
1:1–2, 158 n.2
1:1, 150, 155, 158–60, 173 n.1,
  174, 233
1:2–11, 151
1:3, 173 n.1, 233
1:4–6, 158
1:5–11, 97
1:6, 158
1:8–11, 151
1:8, 151
1:10–11, 158
1:12–15, 62 n.33
1:12–13, 152
1:12, 151, 158, 173 n.1, 174, 233
1:13, 233
1:14–15, 173 n.1
1:14, 155, 158, 174
2:1–10, 158
2:1–4, 152
2:1–2, 173 n.1
2:1, 159–60, 233
2:2, 155, 158, 159, 174
2:4, 151, 158, 173 n.1, 174
2:5, 174
2:6–8, 174
2:9, 159
2:10–14, 159
2:10, 150, 159–60, 173 n.1, 233
2:11–19, 151

2:11–14, 174
2:14–19, 151
2:15–19, 97
2:17, 174
2:18, 174
2:20, 150, 159–60, 173 n.1
2:21, 173 n.1, 174
2:22, 174
2:23, 159, 175–77

ZECHARIAH
Zechariah, book of, 2, 4, 5, 48 n.55, 52, 59, 61–62, 81, 114, 149–46, 159, 163, 173
chs. 1–8, 160–66
chs. 1–6, 177
1:1–7, 173 n.1
1:1–6, 59–60, 62 n.33, 160–61
1:1, 160–61
1:2–6, 197 n.5
1:4, 197 n.5
1:6, 60, 174, 197 n.5
1:7–6:15, 58–60, 160–61
1:7–6:8, 164
1:7–17, 161, 162, 165
1:7, 166–67
1:8–17, 59
1:8–14, 177 n.13
1:14–17, 173 n.1
1:17, 177 n.13
2:1–9, 177 n.13
2:1–4, 161–62, 165
2:5–17, 161
2:5–9, 161–62, 165
2:9, 161
2:10–17, 161
2:10–16, 161–62
2:10–14, 173 n.1
2:17, 161–62
chs. 3–4, 163–64, 172
3:1–10, 161, 162, 172, 178, 184–87

3:1–7, 5, 158, 163, 184, 187–89
3:1, 186
3:4–5, 186
3:5–7, 185
3:5, 186
3:7, 185–86
3:8–10, 163
3:8, 6, 163, 188–89
3:10, 163
4:1–14, 152–53, 161, 163–64, 177–78, 184
4:1–6, 162, 177 n.13
4:2–3, 164
4:4–10, 164
4:4–7, 164
4:6–10, 163–64, 177
4:6, 165
4:7, 165
4:9, 165, 173 n.1, 177
4:10–11, 162
4:10, 159, 165, 177 n.13
4:11, 164, 177 n.13
4:12–14, 164
4:13–14, 177 n.13
4:14, 5, 162, 164, 178–80, 187
5:1–11, 60, 177 n.13
5:1–4, 162, 165, 167, 165
5:5–11, 161–62, 163–65
6:1–15, 152
6:1–8, 60 n.26, 161, 162, 165, 177 n.13
6:9–15, 60, 152–53, 161, 165
6:9–14, 5, 171, 177, 180–81, 183–85, 187
6:10, 183
6:11–13, 181
6:11, 159, 165, 180–81, 186
6:12–13, 182
6:13, 181
6:14, 163, 165, 181–84, 186–87
6:15–8:23, 60

6:15, 60, 173 n.1, 180 n.22
7:1–14:21, 160
chs. 7–8, 2, 52, 59–62, 177
7:1–7, 160
7:1, 59, 160–61, 166, 173 n.1
7:5–6, 61
7:5, 60
7:7, 173 n.1
7:8–8:23, 160
7:9–14, 173 n.1
8:1–5, 173 n.1
8:7–8, 173 n.1
8:14–17, 173 n.1
8:16–19, 61
8:18, 59
8:19, 173 n.1
chs. 9–14, 3, 58–59, 63 n.38, 150, 153, 157, 160, 166, 169, 172
chs. 9–11, 150
chs. 9–10, 52 n,4, 58
ch. 9, 166–67, 172
9:1–7, 166
9:8, 162, 166
9:9–10, 166
9:11–17, 166
9:13, 166
chs. 10–14, 5, 167
ch. 10, 167, 172
10:1, 166
10:3–12, 166
chs. 11–14, 167, 172
ch. 11, 58, 167, 172
11:10, 231
chs. 12–13, 167
12:1–9, 167
12:1–5, 168
12:1, 168
12:10–13:1, 167
12:10, 66 n.3, 167

ch. 13, 29
13:2–6, 167
13:7–9, 167
13:7, 168
13:9, 168
ch. 14, 167–68, 232
14:1–15, 168
14:9, 7, 172, 232
14:16–21, 168
14:16, 6, 232
14:20–21, 172
14:21, 59, 172

MALACHI
Malachi, book of, 2–7, 32, 48, 62–64, 81–83, 86 n.13, 89–98, 149–50, 153–55, 157, 172
chs. 1–2, 52
1:1–14, 154
1:1, 168
1:2–3–15, 192
1:2–5, 81, 89 n.21, 198
1:6–2:9, 74, 89–90, 154, 213–25, 230–31, 233
1:6–14, 154, 214, 222
1:6–8, 214 n.3
1:6–7, 216–18
1:6, 213, 215–17, 222–24
1:7–8, 90
1:7, 90–91, 93, 215–18, 220, 222–24
1:8, 81, 94, 215 n.4, 217–18, 220, 225–226
1:9–10, 219
1:9, 93, 97 n.41, 215 n.4, 217, 219, 223–24, 228, 233
1:10, 90, 215 n.4, 217–19, 223–24, 230
1:11–12, 221, 226

1:11, 219–21, 223, 232
1:12–14, 94
1:12–13, 90, 220–21
1:12, 91, 215–17, 220, 222–23
1:13–14, 217, 225
1:13, 215, 217, 219–21, 225
1:14, 168, 215 n.4, 221, 223–24, 226, 232
1:16, 90
2:1–9, 217, 221
2:1–8, 221
2:1–4, 214, 223
2:1, 213, 214 n.3, 216–17
2:2–3, 94 n.33, 226
2:2, 93, 215 n.4
2:3, 231
2:4–9, 94
2:4–8, 214, 221
2:4–6, 223, 226, 228
2:4, 222, 231
2:6–7, 154
2:6, 222, 228, 231
2:7, 154, 222, 223, 228, 231–34
2:7–9, 90
2:8–9, 154
2:8, 215 n.4, 222–24, 226, 228, 231
2:9, 214, 222–24, 234
2:10–16, 82, 89
2:13–16, 154
2:17–3:5, 89, 95
2:17, 90, 95
ch. 3, 89 n.21
3:1–6, 52
3:1–5, 95
3:3–5, 96
3:3–4, 89 n.21, 96, 234
3:3, 90, 95, 168
3:4, 96
3:5, 96
3:6–12, 89, 154, 198
3:7–15, 52

3:7–12, 96
3:8–10, 82
3:10–11, 97
3:13–21, 89 n.21
3:13–16, 154
3:14–15, 196
3:16–24, 52
3:16–18, 191–197
3:16, 47, 48, 52, 191–93, 195–97
3:17, 192, 197
3:18, 192, 196–97
3:22–24, 48, 153, 212

PSALMS
11:4, 118
21:4, 184 n.38
34:5, 108
34:11, 108
50:14, 117
61:5, 117
66:13, 117
72:2, 184 n.46
78:70, 183 n.7
79, 58
79:1, 118
81:4, 56 n.14
89:4, 175 n.6
89:21, 175 n.6
105:26, 176 n.9
106:23, 176 n.9
107:22, 117
110:1, 180
111:10, 48
116:17–18, 117
132:10, 175 n.6

PROVERBS
Proverbs, book of, 48, 199–200
1:7, 48
4:9, 184 n.38
9:10, 48

chs. 10–29, 199
12:4, 184 n.38
14:24, 184 n.38
16:31, 184 n.38
17:6, 184 n.38
25:6–7, 199 n.12

JOB
Job, book of, 78
19:9, 184 n.38
29:14, 186 n.43
36:14, 14 n.17

EZRA
Ezra, book of, 2, 4–5, 46, 49, 82, 94
 n.33, 150, 153, 157, 165, 169–72,
 210 n.44, 210
chs. 1–2, 169
1:1–4, 170
1:1, 158
1:8, 163, 169
1:11, 163
ch. 2, 155
2:2–67, 169
2:2, 169
2:64, 158 n.3
2:69–70, 211 n.45
3:1–7, 158
3:2, 163
3:7, 151
3:8, 163, 211 n.45
3:10, 169–70, 211 n.45
3:11, 56 n.14
3:12–13, 170
3:13, 56 n.14
ch. 4, 158, 193–94
4:1–5, 170
4:3, 163
4:4–5, 158

4:6, 194 n.2
4:7–11, 158
4:11, 194 n.2
4:14–15, 193
4:15, 193–196
ch. 5, 158
5:1–2, 163
5:11, 169
5:16, 163, 169
6:14, 163
chs. 7–10, 165
7:24, 211
7:25–26, 206 n.31
8:15–20, 211 n.45
8:15–19, 46
8:20, 211 n.45
8:21–9:15, 170 n.20
8:29–30, 210 n.44
8:30, 211 n.45
8:33, 210 n.44, 211 n.45
chs. 9–10, 170–71

NEHEMIAH
Nehemiah, book of, 2, 4–5, 46, 49,
 82, 94 n.33, 150–51, 153, 157,
 165, 169–72, 206 n.31, 208 n.38,
 210–11
2:11–15, 161
3:1–7, 158
3:7, 184 n.38
4:1–5, 170
4:12, 56 n.14
6:1–14, 170
6:7, 169
6:15, 161, 171 n.22
ch. 7, 155
7:7–69, 169
7:67, 158 n.3
7:67, 158 n.3

chs. 8–10, 206 n.31
chs. 8–9, 208 n.38
ch. 8, 46, 211
8:3, 206 n.31, 210
8:8, 206 n.31
8:13, 206 n.31
9:7, 176 n.9
9:30, 208 n.38
9:32, 208 n.38
9:38–13:31, 171
10:34, 210 n.43
10:35–40, 96 n.40
10:39, 210 n.42
11:1, 116
11:28–30, 172
13:26, 169
ch. 13, 202
13:4–9, 210 n.42
13:5, 202
13:8–9, 202
13:11–12, 202
13:26, 169

ESTHER
1:2, 184 n.38
4:3, 86
6:1, 192–95

1 CHRONICLES
1–2 Chronicles, book of, 46, 139 n.27, 204, 206 n.31, 210
17:4, 175 n.6
17:7, 175 n.6
20:2, 184 n.38
28:4, 175 n.7
28:5, 175 n.7
28:6, 175 n.7
28:10, 175 n.7
28:17, 110 n.58
29:1, 175 n.7

2 CHRONICLES
2 Chronicles, book of, 138, 142
4:8, 110 n.58
4:11, 110 n.58
4:22, 110 n.58
6:6, 175 n.7
6:15, 175 n.6
6:16, 175 n.6
6:17, 175 n.6
6:42, 175 n.6
15:3, 46
17:1–19, 210 n.45
17:7–9, 46
17:8–9, 210 n.45
32:16, 175 n.6
chs. 34–35, 138–39, 145
34:3, 141
35:3, 46, 206 n.31

BEN SIRAH
11:5, 186, n.44
34:10–11, 200
39:4, 200
40:4, 186 n.44
47:6, 186 n.44
51:23, 200

NEW TESTAMENT
MATTHEW
12:39–41, 123

LUKE
11:29–32, 123

APOCRYPHA
2 ESDRAS
14:45–56, 205

2 MACCABEES
2:13–15, 204

TEXTS FROM THE CLASSICAL WORLD
JOSEPHUS
Antiquities
11.7.1, 168

ON JONAH
125

RABBINIC TEXTS
MISHNAH
Taanit 2:1, 127
Taanit 2:4, 127

BABYLONIAN TALMUD
b.Meg. 31a, 122

JERUSALEM TALMUD
y. Ber. 2:2–3, 126
y. Sukkah 5:1, 127
y. Ta'an. 2:1 128

MEKILTA DE-RABBI ISHMAEL
1:3 (7–8), 125
17:1, 126

PESIQTA DE-RAB KAHANA
28:3, 127

PIRQE DE-RABBI ELIEZER
ch. 10, 124–26

CONTRIBUTORS

Mark J. Boda is Professor in Old Testament at McMaster Divinity College; Professor, Faculty of Theology, McMaster University, Hamilton, Ontario, Canada.

Göran Eidevall is Professor in Old Testament-Hebrew Bible at Uppsala Universitet, Uppsala, Sweden.

Lester L. Grabbe is Professor Emeritus at University of Hull, Hull, England, United Kingdom.

Jutta Krispenz is Professor in Old Testament at Universität Marburg, Marburg, Germany.

Jason T. LeCureux is Lecturer in Old Testament at Charles Stuart University, Brisbane, Queensland, Australia.

Mark Leuchter is Associate Professor in Hebrew Bible at Temple University, Philadelphia, Pennsylvania, USA.

James Nogalski is Professor in Old Testament at Baylor University, Waco, Texas, USA.

Jason Radine is Associate Professor of Religion at Moravian College, Bethlehem, Pennsylvania, USA.

Paul L. Redditt is Professor Emeritus in Old Testament at Georgetown College, Georgetown, Kentucky, USA.

Deborah W. Rooke is Research Fellow at the Oxford Centre for Christianity and Culture, Regent's Park College, University of Oxford, Oxford, England, United Kingdom.

Aaron Schart is Professor in Old and New Testament at the Universität Duisburg-Essen, Essen, Germany.

Lena-Sofia Tiemeyer is Reader in Hebrew Bible/Old Testament at the University of Aberdeen, Aberdeen, Scotland, United Kingdom.

Jakob Wöhrle is Professor in Old Testament at Carl von Ossietzky Universität Oldenburg, Oldenburg, Germany.

www.ingramcontent.com/pod-product-compliance
Lightning Source LLC
Chambersburg PA
CBHW020645300426
44112CB00007B/244